Everyday Life

Everyday Life

A Poetics of Vernacular Practices

Roger D. Abrahams

PENN

University of Pennsylvania Press
Philadelphia

10   9   8   7   6   5   4   3   2   1

Published by
University of Pennsylvania Press
Philadelphia, Pennsylvania 19104-4011

Library of Congress Cataloging-in-Publication Data

Abrahams, Roger D.
Everyday life : a poetics of vernacular practices / Roger D. Abrahams.
p.   cm.
ISBN 0-8122-3841-9 (cloth : alk. paper)
Includes bibliographical references and index.
1. Culture—Semiotic models.   2. Manners and customs.   3. Anthropological linguistics.   I. Title.
GN357 .A27   2005
306'.01—dc22
                                                 2004061152

This book is for Archie Green, a mensch for the ages, the poet of vernacular practices, and a masterful if unknowing marriage-broker. This is not the Big Book we dreamed about, but a testimony to the breadth and depth of an ancient friendship.

Contents

Introduction

A poetics of everyday life? Perhaps I mean a poeticizing of everyday practices, looking at vernacular culture as animated by our making and doing things with style. Our lives are replete with artifacts growing from our propensity to form groups through the creation of ways of speaking which give form to shared concerns and ideals. As Kenneth Burke has it, "There are no forms of art which are not forms of experience outside of art" (Burke 1931). But how do we sense, in common, when art is present, and use this state of being as a way of understanding our own cultural practices? The line between those practices which ask simply for our conscious attention and those which call for aesthetic or, at least, stylistic judgment can easily be confounded.

Richard Rorty describes this attempt to find whatever poetics there are in the vernacular and gives voice to its implicit assumptions.

A poeticized culture would be one which would not insist that we find the real wall behind the painted one, the real touchstones of truth as opposed to touchstones which are merely cultural artifacts. It would be a culture which, precisely by appreciating that all touchstones are artifacts, would take as its goal the creation of ever more various and multicolored artifacts. (Rorty 1989: 53–54)

We look for meanings, not behind our vernacular artifacts and interactions, but *in* them.

Edward Sapir, a poet as well as pioneer linguist, asserted that language itself constituted "the most significant and colossal work that the human spirit has evolved—nothing short of a finished form of expression for all communicable experience." Extolling its capacity to constantly reshape itself, he continues: "Language is the most massive and inclusive art we know, a mountainous and anonymous work of unconscious generations" (Sapir 1921: 220). Yet, as any writer will attest, language yields up its artful power only grudgingly. For there are other selves with whom we hold constant conversations, selves who speak in tongues not entirely under anyone's personal control except the phantoms of these "unconscious generations." Studying other cultures from the perspective of our Western, Anglophonic tongue, we seek to familiarize ourselves with their keywords for life and art. Our own vernacular speech will bear up under such scrutiny as well.

This address to vernacular culture may appear as an abomination to those not enamored of "the near, the low, the common," as Ralph Waldo Emerson put it in "The American Scholar": "the meal in the firkin, the milk in the pan; the ballad in the street; the news of the boat; the glance of the eye; the form and the gait of the body." Emerson, like many speakers in the early American republic, saw New World vigor in the juxtaposition of the highest and the most common registers of the vernacular. The poetics of the vernacular begins with the ability of speakers to command the widest variety of ways of speaking, soaring high and digging deep with an understanding of the dynamic contrasts this code-switching animates. If freedom lies in the ability to make choices, dealing with vernacular life allows the whole ideal to be expressed within a single sentence, or represented in a representative object.

Keeping Company

This book considers the ways in which ordinary Americans keep company with one another, in casual and serious talk, at play, and in performance and celebration. It explores the entire range of social gatherings, from chance encounters and casual conversations to the heavily rehearsed shows found at theaters and stadiums, or in the more open venues of parades and festivals. It focuses not just on the ways we pull off our interactions, stylized or otherwise, but also on the vernacular terms we have developed in common to discuss and judge performances.

Central to this understanding is the presumption of goodwill that we make about how others will treat us. We presume that our gregariousness reveals a useful excess of feeling and that having a good talk is a palliative for any misunderstandings that arise. We have learned from experience that this friendliness is not necessarily shared; unfounded assumptions about our cultural commonalities can lead to social and political complications, especially in times of declared animosity. But the social compact is constituted by our talking with one another. With strangers and acquaintances alike, we act on the useful fiction that "talking it out" will lead to mutual understanding and the possibility of shared enjoyment. So this book explores not just our comfortable interactions with family and friends and the assumptions that underlie intimate acquaintance but also our naïveté and the high premium we pay for presuming the palliative powers of having a good talk, even an argument we can then talk through.

Although friendly conversation seems natural, it is, in fact, deeply cultural, providing a moral center for everyday communication. Certain terms of judgment underlie our discussions of the everyday. The appropriateness of what we say and do is often debated; an action may be judged playful by some and offensive by others. How studied should one be, and how do we judge going through the formalities? The degree of self-conscious agreement that we feel impelled to uphold is itself revealing of the tensions that swarm beneath the surface of our interactions. Equally important for the purposes of this book, conversation conducted under the sign of friendliness provides a baseline against which other ways of speaking may be judged. Consider the implications of the ubiquitous idea that when people sit down and talk together, our common human concerns can be relied upon to encourage agreement. Even if disagreement enters this terrain, it can fuel the sense of achievement when, at last, consensus is reached.

This analysis of expressive interaction starts with the commonsense view that we are our own best interpreters and addresses the entire range of communicative acts through the terms we use to describe them ourselves. The rich resources of our everyday vernacular speech enable us to use words and gestures from the past as models for social interaction in the present. As a folklorist, I have catalogued the conversational repertoire we have inherited from our elders and forebears that we presume ties us together morally and serves to repair relationships. In the simple forms of vernacular expression, the proverbs we invoke and the jokes we tell, we see the elementary tactics of using the past to resolve problems in the present. These memorable, fixed phrases come to mind habitually, but they are far from simple when we attend to how they are deployed in daily interaction.

To the extent that we repeat one another's lines and go on to tell our life stories when encouraged by others, we purvey such fictions as our interpretation of what "really" happened at some point of passage in our lives. As we attempt to craft and recraft our identities, the stories we tell on ourselves stake out our place whenever we choose to be sociable. To call this "self-fashioning" sounds a bit theatrical, but having so many choices and making them for ourselves calls for a good deal of anxious self-examination. Ironically, in engaging in the presentation of self, we make our choices more self-consciously. We transform our experiences into retellable and interpretable tales and turn our interactions with others into performances. Reducing the flow of life to story and performance carries a myriad of discontents. We attain a generic sense of order and common understanding, but we amplify the subjunctive while subduing the declarative side of life. We become conscious of how crafted our lives have become, and objectifying ourselves makes our lives seem awfully predicable. Freeze-framing social interaction helps us to interpret its possible meanings, but we lose the freedom and unselfconsciousness of the spontaneous play we enjoyed when we were children. Here the machinery of nostalgia kicks in.

In searching for ourselves amid the shifting scenes of daily life, and especially as we seek to alleviate the anxiety and depression that arise from facing personal losses or foreclosed possibilities, the everyday becomes a constant search for what goes by the term *identity*. How can one achieve identity in a world that promises an infinity of choices and then takes them away? In the worse case, we alienate ourselves from our own lives. So we live for those moments in which we lose ourselves, giving over to the flow of the occasion and experiencing the delights of letting go. We seek to merge our all-too-limited selves with some larger group of celebrants and to escape the constraints of our daily existence by plunging into in the seemingly unbounded possibilities offered by theater, rituals, and festivals.

I am continually amazed by the creativity and diversity of people's disposition to play, sing, and dance to one another as they introduce festivity into their lives. Such celebrations are not as separate from the social relations of common life as they may seem, despite their being set off in special times and places. Rituals and festivals constitute and renew social groups. Power is asserted, parodied, overturned, and ritually reconfirmed through such customary practices. In the past, social relations were enacted, even embodied in rough and popular or royal and spectacular enactments: parades and processions, court proceedings, mock hangings, and ritualized shamings. The depth of historical memory conveyed in such high-energy performances as Carnival and Mardi Gras enters into the present as different cultural groups assert and renegotiate their places on a transnational stage.

The seasonal celebrations once observed by custom have now become spectacular programmed events. Communal rituals that historically were embedded in common work and that satirized, subverted, and reinscribed social relations have become large-scale, more tightly scheduled and framed, even commodified events. The pleasures of good work have been ceded to good times, the focused intensity of play and the periodic high times of festive occasions. In the more public forms of communal celebration, the threat that those on the bottom of the social hierarchy or on the margins of the dominant culture might overturn or invade and transform the prevailing order has been deliberately contained. And yet, as close examination of patterns of global circulation reveals, the possibility of transformation is constantly renewed. Situating performances within unstable relations of power yields new insights into contemporary circumstances. As previous national boundaries are eroded, we have become ever more concerned with the flow of power that accompanies "development" and more aware of the moral and political questions arising from the uneven and unstable distribution of agency and responsibility.

The Poetics and Politics of Common Culture

This approach to traditional forms of expressive culture begins with rhetorical analysis of the smallest, most gnomic of folklore forms. Drawing on Kenneth Burke's ideas and the literary techniques of text analysis, this project pursues folklore texts across contexts and parses the ways in which they are constructed, either through borrowing from past usage or by adhering to the pattern of expectations defined by a genre. These simple forms (*einfache formen*) are organized according to their constituent elements and the situations in which they are employed.

Folklore materials are treated here not only in terms of their traditional origin and dissemination but with special address to their everyday usage in living contexts. Once the body of traditional expression is organized in such a way that the relationships among the simple forms can be sketched in, the ambiguity and intensity of play and other framed enactments invite attention. The simple forms employed in conversation pale in contrast to deeply focused games and the extended festival activities through which community is put into practice. So this study moves from more private interactions to ever more public modes of display and interrogates shared understandings of communal festivities. Situational and frame analysis are employed to account for this wider range of traditional presentations and representations.

Rendering folklore in written texts renders it stable enough for formal analysis, but takes away the sense of enthusiasm and enjoyment, even ecstasy observed in play and performance. Structuralist and sociolinguistic approaches to interpretation encompass other dimensions of these events as they unfold. Structuralism asks us to understand the meanings attributed to a performance from the perspective of the performers themselves, and ethnomethodological approaches enable us to bring observation closer to experience. In order to discover the terms by which both performers and audiences understand, explain, and evaluate what is taking place, this work scrutinizes our vernacular expressive system, treating common terms for play and celebration as worthy of exploration.

Viewing this project in relation to the development of the field clarifies not only the approach to folklore demonstrated here but also the contributions that folklore makes to the broader study of expressive culture. Ironically, just when text-oriented folkloristics began to lose its vigor, symbolic anthropology began applying the text as a metaphoric explanation for cultural enactments. Clifford Geertz, Victor Turner, Erving Goffman, and many others began taking literary text production very seriously, often using such New Critical terms as *metaphor*, *ambiguity*, and *authorial* to define their own projects (Geertz 1983: 4–9). Then all of the ethnographic disciplines entered into the postmodern project of examining the cultural filters provided us by texts and situational analyses of "Others." We were reminded of the unintended political uses to which our labors had been put and the ways in which official intervention and financing might have affected our perspectives. In the discipline of folklore, this self-examination emerged from the pressures placed by contemporary social and intellectual changes on the very idea of culture, community, and indigenous creativity implicit—and, sometimes, explicit—in the invention of "the folk" and the projection of the exotic "Other."

This self-consciousness, too, can productively be scrutinized if it is first anchored in our vernacular practices. Distinctions between real and fake, authentic and invented, natural and artificial abound in contemporary American culture, as in the discipline of folklore. These false dichotomies reveal that, despite what we experience as the fragmentation of our world, we continue to search for the sense of wholeness and connection that is inherent in any coherent worldview. The struggle to discover the *real*, the *authentic*, and the *natural* is often confused with the idea of folklore itself. Indeed, it has a long history in the discipline of folklore, as in other fields of the humanities and interpretive social sciences (Ben-Amos and Goldstein 1975; Ben-Amos 1984; Bendix 1997; Stewart 1991).

The *folk* was an invention by negation, in contrast to society dominated by the *modern*—that is, made up of urban, bourgeois, and bureaucratic statebuilders. The folk, under these conditions, was imagined as living in the condition of whole-being which had vanished from the center but was still to be found at the peripheries of the nation-state, people who carry on the old ways and resist the incursions of metropolitan authorities. Conceived as social, cultural, and technological isolates, they were reassuring in the seemingly organic quality of their communities. The folk not only served as a convenient fiction by which hegemony over certain territories might be claimed but also offered a refuge for discontented urbanites. Cultural rebels seeking to escape the city and its contaminations counted their neighbors as the *folk*. Since these people were commonly unlettered, they were regarded as a living repository of the oral resources of the entire people before the advent of print and other technological devices mediating communication. This imagined way of life did not have to be observed up close; rather, it served as a resource that urban prominenti might draw on to recharge their depleted cultural energies. In such a realm, the real and the authentic were maintained as a measure of both progress and decadence.

Folklorists became the translators and gatekeepers between worlds. Folklorists assumed that folk communities, if they could be found, would reveal earlier forms of expressive interaction, performance, and celebration of life-passage in their customs. The backwardness and poverty of those living in these enclaves were regarded as evidence of their integrity. The lack of city-bred contaminations was an important feature of this imagined community, for isolation had insulated the folk from modernity. Even if the lore was affected by oral transmission from the putative past, even if it produced variant versions of songs and stories, the oldest and most authentic forms could be reconstructed by using the techniques of comparative analysis previously developed for analyzing classic texts and holy writ.

I explore these moral dilemmas and political quandaries by scrutinizing the keywords introduced into the vernacular that sidestepped the insular implications of *folk, traditional community, indigenous peoples*, and other terms which described bounded communities as if they were not subject to the globalization of expressive exchange. As cultural activities previously confined to ethnic groups are increasingly performed in public for audiences of outsiders, the meanings of *identity* become subject to intergroup negotiation. Craft products circulate as commodities in cosmopolitan marketplaces, consumed in ways that not only alienate them from the circumstances of their production but also transform the conditions of expressive labor. Terms such as *hybrid* and *creole*, which gave a name to the transformation of cultural forms that occur as people encounter one another in borderlands and develop new styles of speech and performance under the destabilizing conditions of cultural contact, are now extended from people on the move to the transmutations that attend transnational communication. In the process, these terms for *diaspora* get shorn of their memories of trauma and longings for redemption. Despite all these terminological corrections, nostalgia remains implicit in our own frames of reference and affects how we describe other peoples' ways.

The poetics and politics of folklore's analytic practices have undergone profound alterations of perspective: text-centered approaches broadened into performance-oriented ones; and then all were subjected to the deconstructive postmodern stance of the late twentieth century, which involved an ironic return to some of the textual assumptions of mid-century. For folklorists, the dawning recognition of the limitations of studying expressive culture as if it existed apart from social, economic, and political contexts illuminated the compromises made by those involved in developing public presentations of traditional performers. The reflexive moment in ethnography made us conscious of our cooptation by the very systems of power we thought that we were reacting against. We turned to the history of our own disciplines to understand the ways in which the academic study of culture emerged within the newly global mercantile, colonial, and industrial worlds. The bicentennial celebration in 1976 with a summer-long festival of American Folklife at the Smithsonian Institution in the nation's capital and the centenary celebration of the American Folklore Society in 1987–1988 dramatized the importance of historicizing our disciplinary practices. This self-consciousness informed our discussion of the morality of how we collected folklore and presented the results of our fieldwork. It seemed more important than ever to involve the tradition-bearers we had encountered in the field in the publication of their cultural treasures.

The trajectory of this book traces the development of the field and reflects critically upon our habitual assumptions. But what is true of folklore and ethnography is equally, albeit differently, true of our common culture. Since we embody our deepest values in those terms and proclivities which usually remain below the level of conscious examination and verbal expression, reflecting upon our assumptions and examining our ways of recognizing others as we go about our ordinary lives and pursue extraordinary experiences are integral to this project. Elucidating the poetics and politics of everyday life is a challenging yet common human endeavor. The entire range of expressive culture, from simple conversations through games and theater to festivals and rituals, represents the most profound human cultural accomplishments. *Homo Sapiens* meets *Homo Ludens*, the playful among us, and *Homo Narrans*, the natural storyteller.

From a Rhetoric of Simple Forms to Enactments of Community

This book is organized in four parts. The first, "The Many Forms of Goodwill," focuses on the forms of social practice most susceptible to being textualized and studied in terms of their constituent elements. As these simple forms enter into conversation, they rest on and reinforce the goodwill principle fundamental to everyday interaction in informal settings. The second part, "Goodwill Tested," turns to occasions when more scripted performances arise in the midst of playful engagements and celebratory acts. In these more complex interpersonal communicative forms, rules link multiple players with spectators and expectations are shared by performers and audiences. Here agonistic motives are expressed and contained by the aesthetic ordering of games and performances. The last two parts examine how vernacular ideas of order animate the more innovative uses to which traditional practices are put. Part three, "Social Imaginaries," explores the places in which groups and their representatives interact across boundaries of cultural difference and the rules that develop in such borderlands. It proceeds by mapping the ways in which we imagine ourselves and others and the zones in which intergroup conflict is both enacted and contained, revealing not only the dynamics of cross-cultural interaction but also the trajectory of social and cultural change. "Terms for Finding Ourselves," the fourth and final part, scrutinizes the vocabulary and syntax of the keywords through which we attempt to understand the new cultural formations that are emerging amid processes of globalization. The perspective taken here is more self-critical than celebratory. In hijacking terms from past understandings of group identity and cultural change, popular culture and its postmodern analysts have tended to strip these terms of their historical resonances and flatten out our awareness of inequalities of power and memories of displacement, suffering, and loss.

This book scrutinizes the lenses through which we perceive and interpret—or, to put it in the terms used here, we *name* and *frame*—communicative practices in commonplace culture. If we become attuned to listening to ourselves, acknowledging that we presume to be operating within a system of manners, good and bad, we discover a rich vocabulary of talk about talk, performance, play, and celebration. These rules of thumb operate not just on the formal level but through developing a shared set of expectations with others in our expressive community. Being good company means that each of us knows how to act and to react in particular social situations. Most of the time we know, in common, what it takes to get by in conversation. Sometimes these mutual understandings remain tacit and unregistered, because to examine them explicitly reveals too much raw wool in the knit of our cultural bedcover. It seems useful, nonetheless, to spell out these commonplaces in order to reveal whatever system exists among and between them.

This study not only draws on shared experiences but addresses folk explanations of how customary behavior is learned, prepared for, and entered into fully. The group is most itself at such times, when individuals in the collectivity reach back and draw on previous experiences to animate the present. Past experiences of being a part of a community of understandings have taught us the healing powers of talking with each other, laughing and crying, eating and drinking together. Such moments are not rare; they are possible any day, every day, and serve as the common currency of collective experience.

The analytical approach suggested here requires us to develop habits of listening closely to one another and put whatever insights we gain to work for the common good. I do not argue that this system is the way the world is structured, but that this is the way we like to talk about events, eventualities, and experiences. I turn the ethnographer's view back on ourselves, constructing what Clifford Geertz called a "thick description." Within our vernacular set of names and practices, we can draw on our experience of social interactions and performances, using the terms of the everyday to describe what's right and what's not about any interaction. Our own expressive cultural practices are worthy of as much analysis as any other community of performers. These vernacular terms and habits have persisted because they have become second nature, and perhaps even (by some convenient fiction) remind us of our better nature. We can trust our internal voices, which sustain the social contracts through which we meet and interact.

If anything like community still exists beyond a reflexive nostalgia, it emerges through the agreement to celebrate itself in ceremony or festival. Meeting and moving together, a group articulates its sense of community by sharing an intense physical and emotional moment which generates feelings of togetherness. Social cohesion is inspired not only by joining up or joining in, but by recognizing our double selves: the sense that we can be deeply involved in a conversation or a performance and still make some judgment regarding what is taking place. As people stand together at a little distance to examine social conflicts, social bonds are strengthened. By this move we hope to put Marx's *alienation* or Durkheim's *anomie* out of our imaginings, along with any other term for that blend of boredom and anxiety which impinges on our lives.

Part one begins with what might well be called a rhetoric of simple forms, an analytical approach to folklore that draws deeply on the work of Kenneth Burke. It takes up those forms of expression which have an aura of age, the words or gestures that we regard as as old as the hills, the answers to the rhetorical question, "You know what they say?" When someone asks, "What is folklore?" I reply: "All those things *they* say, *they* sang, *they* played." Like grandma's recipes and nostrums, they have always been in the family. The categories folklorists use to organize this mass of material move from the smallest forms, such as proverbs and riddles, to the longer, but still single-voiced forms, such as songs and tales. I analyze these commonplace forms of folklore alongside other expressive forms not so commonly parsed: slanging matches, taunts and teases, prayers and curses, all fixed-phrase forms that demand attention in an expressive exchange. In this lifeworld, imitation is one way of announcing and demonstrating membership in a familiar performance community.

These chapters offer a plain vanilla poetics of folkish forms, vernacular keywords and phrases of conversation, argument, deep discussion, and just schmoozing. Not only are we are talkers, but we even like to talk about the way we talk—to each other, to strangers, and to combatants across the fine line of defense. Now, with so many mediated messages launched into public space, we might expect that people would become more flexible in the amount of time and energy given over to monitoring talk, or that our vigilance in testing one another's veracity would have diminished. Far from it. It is so easy to find information about one another through web searches and so convenient to keep up the flow of messages through portable electronic devices that we are in the midst of a wholesale reevaluation of such basic matters as family and friendship. But these practical techniques of recording, archiving, and analyzing everyday behavior seldom inform theoretical discussions of mediated communications, especially popular culture. The duality inherent in this approach often leads to an unfortunate opposition between tradition and authenticity on the one hand and improvisation and individual creativity on the other. Here I demonstrate the flexible and varied uses of customary forms in lived situations and interactions.

Between these small banalities and the more elevated forms of celebration lie a number of other common activities that appear tried and true and remain available in our cultural reservoirs. In our rush for the new and different, they float in the eddies, backwaters, and quiet pools, waiting for those moments when invention fails us. Even if we do not voice them, they spring to mind as ways in which our ancestors handled the ordinary trials and tribulations of daily life. The formation of group identities and the reinforcement of group boundaries are among the most salient social processes that take place in this domain.

The ways in which children and adolescents acquire performance competence in the process of growing up reveal a great deal about the shared understandings that underlie seemingly spontaneous play and group games. With children, as with outsiders who may not have internalized this set of practices, we extend the goodwill principle, assuming that they want to learn so they too can become good company. In a two-stage learning process, individuals learn how to become good listeners and observers and then attempt to produce appropriate actions. To put it in more formal terms, we judge each other in terms of both receptive and productive competences. If mistakes are made, we have ways within the vernacular system of calling attention to the gaffe and repairing any social disjunction, as we tell children how to avoid hurting others' feelings by breaking a rule in the conversational flow.

Players themselves will readily talk about the framing that goes on in play and games: how they get in and out of play, who plays well and who doesn't. The experiences that go into play—the release of energy, focus in common, a willingness to take chances or get dizzy or turn ourselves into someone else, to practice competitive moves and then employ them enthusiastically, to complicate the game in order to keep it interesting—could all be found in other high-intensity activities, such as ceremony, ritual, and theater.

The second part of this book addresses these multivocal traditions, from children's games and sports through public display events to communally organized celebrations. These traditional forms operate with special rules within the boundaries set by play and performance. Such ebullient modes of interaction are separated from the everyday precisely because of their abundance of focused energies. Participants move and feel together in a world itself in flux. Physical energies are released, and consumption in excess overwhelms the senses. Strangers jostle one another and operate by the norms of friendly talk, but here there is mutual wariness rather than a presumption of goodwill. Praise, scandal, invective, spielmaking—all overflow the bounds of ordinary life. Everything orderly is put to the test. In festivals, it seems, the boundary police have deserted their posts. When diverse groups meet in literal or metaphorical borderlands, cultural forms are on the move, exported and imported without customs duties, or even baggage inspection.

In many situations, the very extremity of these celebratory forms generates a powerful reaffirmation of a more inclusive community. Their metamorphic power cannot be entirely discounted. As we move from part two to parts three and four, we shift from interactions taking place within social groups to encounters between those who define themselves in terms of their differences. On this contested terrain, interaction is shaped less by shared understandings and more by competition and conflict. Cultural difference and social distance may be ritualized and conflict contained, but the expressive forms that emerge in these zones are qualitatively new, developing through a dynamic process of observation and exchange, imitation and parody, appropriation and theft. What was one people's vernacular becomes another's second language; new dialects, pidgins, and lingua franca are constructed amid these intense cross-cultural encounters. As groups negotiate such unstable territory, they also renegotiate the terms by which they define themselves and through which they interact with others. The very terms by which people understand their world are called into question, enriched, and transformed. So, too, exploring the expressive cultures that develop in these border zones requires us to interrogate the words we use to think with.

Keywords and Social Imaginaries

Like all the terms scrutinized in this book, the term *vernacular* itself bears examination. In recent ethnographic studies of expressive culture, *vernacularity* refers to the process by which the lowest and the highest memorable voicings and revoicings are drawn upon, residing just below the surface of consciousness, containing the most recent slang and the most ancient and archaic turns of phrase that draw attention to themselves (Kapchan 1996: 63–64). Used in this sense, vernacularity is capacious enough to encompass the traditional and the innovative, the highbrow and the popular, and to enable us to trace the movements between these registers that occur in various social interactions.

Yet *vernacular* carries its own problems into cultural discussions, for like *vulgar, popular,* and *common,* the word carries class connotations. It can describe the way the old folk talked before they learned better. Sometimes, as with Latin, Sanskrit, or Hebrew, a vernacular is elevated to the realm of official or holy writ, no longer used by the populace who had regarded it as a mother tongue. Whole strips of speech are learned verbatim by others who do not control the language but have high regard for its sacred power. Bits of the past are preserved by their sound and metric organization as much as for their meaning. Religious and secular leaders employ this language to establish gravity on the occasion of its use. To find holy words and transforming messages embodied in vulgar and archaic formulations should not surprise us. The high priests in a number of religions of the book maintain old talk for purposes of moral instruction and to pass on stories of the world as it was in the beginning. Ancient holy languages are maintained even in our contemporary secular vernacular, particularly in the form of stories and songs committed to memory. I have been especially interested in the free-floating vocabulary used to describe and judge the behavior of others, which reveals the half-buried understandings of our ancestors.

These studies in the poetics of vernacular speech encourage us to explore the system underlying the ways we converse. I focus, not on a narrative theory of beginnings, middles, and endings, but rather on the vocabulary that allows us to compare and contrast experiences and makes even disruptive happenings discussable. These terms suggest that there is a commonsense system operating beneath the surface of everyday conviviality, revealing our own rules of engagement and disengagement.

I stress friendly talk, successful performance, and celebration because I feel a need to retreat from the language of violence in which we seem submerged: the vocabulary of distrust, of paranoia, and of entitlement to victim status, which may be amplified by the echoes of violent conflicts elsewhere in our world. I have not withdrawn entirely from such subjects; the last four chapters of this book take up questions of ethnicity, cultural mixing, and diaspora. Rudeness and even more bellicose behaviors are certainly all around us, and they draw upon the same chartering power of the vernacular as the more pacific forms of talk featured here. No doubt, there is a system of manners that registers and even regulates war and genocide. Such subjects do not make their way into everyday talk except as they provide topics for lamentation, for negotiation across boundaries, and for ceremonies commemorating victimization.

Our access to our better nature is shared by everyone in hearing distance. Such sharing promises to lead to everyday words for experiences, ordinary and extraordinary, as they are employed in our conversations and our exegetical arguments. Acts and activities which have come to the surface of our talk suggest that we have a system. These are *keywords*, then, in our ongoing discussion of how to make common sense out of the flow of experience. I do not launch these arguments with the idea that, because we have generic terms for the experience of both art and life, we also have understandings in common with the others around us. In a liberal democracy, every moment is a test of our will to subjugate our individual vanities to make sure we're among friends. In the too-often contentious world, the composite of vernacular terms seems to make a bid for our moral attention.

This range of questions can be posed through Charles Taylor's formulation of the concept of social imaginaries. Taylor defines social imaginaries as "that largely unstructured and inarticulate understanding of our whole situation, within which particular features of our world show up for us in the sense they have." Social imaginaries encourage discussion of ways of speaking, acting, and making moral judgment through the terms by which we organize social existence in daily life—that is, how we "fit together with others, how things go on between them and their fellows, the expectations which are normally met, and the deeper normative notions and images which underlie these expectations . . . the social imaginary is that common understanding which makes possible common practices, and a widely shared sense of legitimacy" (Taylor 2004: 23–24).

On the surface, the ways we discuss life and its meanings give an impression of optimism about the human condition. I continue to think that friendly discussion provides the basic model of how we feel other expressive interactions should be carried out. We are surprised and even embarrassed when we encounter less friendly and comfortable behavior, but even then we have finely honed techniques for repairing the breach and restoring the flow of goodwill. License for anyone present to speak characterizes most friendly encounters, but that license is not so easily garnered when the going gets intense and the work and play of the gods are liturgically invoked. This social compact often seems to be a gauge of civility. If I deal with mutual excitements, I do not allude to historical flashpoints, those tremors which provide historical anchor points for everyone. No earthquakes here, and no disasters, no events earth-shaking enough to be registered on the Richter scale.

As the social compact is worked out and license is given to play a role in a scene or a position in a game, we enter into those zones of interaction which call for an understanding of what's going on and how things ought to go that is highly conventional and circumscribed. Roles, parts, assumed identities—all of these and more are involved as we pursue our everyday activities. All draw upon the principle of goodwill. Friendly discussions presume agreement, or at least the consensus that comfort is as important as passing on knowledge in such circumstances. We can presume we will be understood when an offer to talk accepted. How else could we understand each other's sentences, even to the point that we can anticipate what is going to be said? We can finish our relatives' and friends' sentences for them most of the time, although they may be unhappy if we do so out loud. Thus, a second codicil to the goodwill agree-ment: each person in a discussion has equal access to the floor, so to speak, and that once a sentence is begun listeners will allow it to be finished. Of course, the rules do permit interruptions, especially to express enthusiastic agreement or an agreement to disagree between friends. But equality and turn-taking are fundamental principles. Every player or performer has the same right to get up and make a fool of themselves, sometimes under cover of a drug- or alcohol-induced high or shared laughter. Commonsense rule: we will not take other people's words out of their mouths without some kind of per-mission, nor will we shout someone off stage or off the field until they have proven that they can't manage or won't conform to the rules of playing. These unwritten rules go unchallenged in most social circumstances, even when open opponents meet.

I look at the key terms of authoritative rhetoric—*tradition, custom,* even *institution*—as part of an effort to name forces that assist us in celebrating the project of self-possession, self-fashioning, self-expression, a project that sees all life as a constant achievement and all agreed-upon practices as techniques for simultaneously amplifying and questioning what it is we have agreed to in our own little groups. As William James put the matter:

Experience is a process that continually gives us new material to digest. We handle this intellectually by the mass of beliefs of which we find ourselves already possessed, assimilating, rejecting, or rearranging in different degrees. Some . . . are recent acquisi-tions of our own; but most of them are common-sense traditions of the race. (James 1970 [1903]: 61–62)

Thus experience and its associated vocabulary were, and continue to be, ele-vated to the realm of holy words. In this social dispensation, individuals may find redemption, or at least validation, in the world of the here and now, even if it is no longer attached to a divinely sanctioned plan.

Culture now achieves a new meaning, focusing on actual and repeated patterns in our daily interactions and practices. This agreement is reinforced by each act of sociability. When they are writ large in cultural displays and performances, such practices gain power through the coordination of the energies of the group involved in the celebration, which becomes, not just as assemblage of individuals, but a collectivity.

The problem facing the humanist is not so much replacing the gods but finding a language to replace the Word with new sacred words that will allow us to celebrate the survival of the human spirit. For many years, *civilization*, *progress*, and *culture* bore this burden, gracefully submitting themselves to elevation. Of these, only the last has retained its halo, through the efforts of those who recognize in this word's capacities the possibility of linking together the way the peoples live throughout the world.

Can any such "god term," to use Denis Donoghue's designation (Donoghue 1976: 23), remain holy in the relentlessly self-examining environment in which we live? Members of the academic clerisy continue to search through our everyday speech for these god terms, knowing that they are not going to come from on high. As first Matthew Arnold and later Lionel Trilling, Erving Goffman, Raymond Williams, and Victor Turner did, we try to recover new ones from the passing talk of the streets. We have seen such things happen often enough to have some confidence that it will happen again—and yet again.

Keywords, or root metaphors, must possess such integrity and value that they can be employed, defended in their use, and redeemed for the spirit that resides within them. If we have such a god term, it would be *experience*, a word I employ throughout this book. But let us keep in mind Donoghue's warning: "There is always a temptation to assume that because a god term is holy to its celebrant(s) it must be holy to everyone; a writer may make the mistake of thinking that he does not need to establish the sanctity of the word, that he has only to invoke it" (Donoghue 1976: 23). Many chapters in this book seek to discover where these god terms reside in the communicative lives of diverse groups in North America and the Caribbean. As I was searching for a common denominator for getting at the art of life, I found that, the more everyday the term, the better it suited my task. The vernacular seldom lets us down. It became something of a game for me to find the vernacular equivalents for terms of art newly minted from classical stem words, such as one finds among academic cultural theorists. *Intertextuality*, *reflexivity*, *discursive* and *metadiscursive*, *ventriloquation*, *monologic*, and *dialogic* have all been important in developing an understanding of the complexity of communication on the ground level. Yet each of them carried specially accrued technical meanings which made me feel that the very act of communicating ideas was betrayed.

Some of my disquiet with these terms emerges from the simple fact that I have been carrying on this conversation with ordinary people as well as academic colleagues over many years. But, more fundamentally, such matters of conceptualization and communication become increasingly problematic as cultural productions are performed in ever-enlarging public spaces. For the student of customary practices enacted by those claiming authenticity within particular locales, the problems of imitation and ownership of public properties are multiplied as audiences grow. Establishing rights not only to a certain composition but also to the reproduction of a style of acting, dressing, and talking raises doubts that threaten to subvert the entire enterprise. As cultural theorists sought to grasp the issues emerging in this domain, they tended to import terms from popularized social science, from above rather than below. Although these words no longer live within the realm of observational discovery, each of them—*identity, ethnicity, creolization,* and *diaspora*—confronts very real conditions which we are all facing. Each carries a complex set of meanings that allows for a high-level discussion to be held more productively among a community of scholars who use these terms as shorthand. But I found that, every time I tried to use this set of terms, I was limiting my potential audience. The ideas which I was discovering through close attention to the vernacular would, I came to feel, be better served by finding their vernacular equivalents. Ironically, in the last decade or two I see a dynamic at work in constructing public talk that goes against this bottom-up approach. Social scientists have had such a success, at least in the realm of popular reportage, that some terms developed as terms of art in one or another of these disciplines have been adopted by the vernacular, finding their way to god-term status that goes far beyond the academy. The last part of this book is devoted to a consideration of some of these keywords.

The ordering of styles used to range from high to low, with regard to the social status of the persons producing them and the places they inhabited. But the closer we came to the development of various vernacular forms, despite the seeming dominance of those exercising hegemonic control over the polity, the more cases we discovered in which the process was reversed. Just as I had first found that, in American youth culture, African American forms of expression provided the model for how young men should talk, so I discovered many other instances in which the language of the dominated superceded the official culture of the dominant group.

As our plural culture brings about negotiations among different speaking and performing communities, imitations and transgressions across the boundaries occur regularly. Even the most despised language finds its way into everyday talk: first it is used with quotation marks, and then, gathering power, it is used by journalists, comedians, and mimics of all kinds. Vernacular vigor can be located and more fully understood in the amazing variety of ways of speaking that are part of our past and continue to enrich today's talk. We hop around as we draw up new vernacular agendas and mix our messages on purpose, especially by accessing the vernacular forms of others with whom we come into significant contact. Artists and ethnographers continue to try to capture the letter and spirit of these new gestures of goodwill.

PART I

The Many Forms of Goodwill

Chapter 1
Figures of Speech

Between habit and custom lies the domain of vernacular nuggets of wisdom: proverbs, sayings, aphorisms, maxims, adages, old saws, all figures of speech that seem to thrive in thin air. Often unvoiced because they are so obviously clichéd, nevertheless they live on as guides to what should be done under certain conditions of social stress. These gnomic phrases, usually attributed to someone else's abiding wisdom, can productively be contrasted with other forms of "old talk" and archaic codes. All these floating bits of traditional currency still circulate in the vernacular, often in an anachronistic register of language. Most of them have been compiled into dictionaries by scholars more patient than I and arranged by date of first historical record. So we know that they are "real" in the positivist sense. But I am concerned here with who is empowered to invoke proverbial wisdom and under what conditions doing so is deemed advisable. These rhetorical devices draw attention to the speaker and address a moral or social question that has emerged within the lifeworld of those drawing on the vernacular. This chapter examines situations of their usage, teasing out the vernacular theory by which tradition is invoked. I ask: how does a proverb work in conversational settings? "Small pointed nothings," these short but memorable components of talk switch voices and frames of interpretation in the midst of a conversation. Supposedly impersonal and objectively delivered, they are personal all the same.

These traditional phrases came to my attention when I first encountered the differences of style and temperament between anthropologists and literary historians which were played out in the study of folklore. In the early 1960s, the American Folklore Society (AFS) met with the American Anthropological Association one year and with the Modern Language Association the next; AFS members were thought to be evenly divided between the two groups. Yet folklorists did not feel at ease in either conference. It seemed useful, then, to ascertain what differences of approach were dramatized by this split-personality test.

Toward a Rhetoric of the Vernacular

The gulf between literary and anthropological folklorists was nowhere more clearly visible than in the ways in which the two viewed the form and performance of traditional expressive culture. The literary folklorist, trained in the analysis of formal stylistics and geographical distribution, looked at the construction of a traditional item in order to analyze its constituent elements and the variations that occur as the item is transmitted over time and space. The anthropologist, generally lacking this aesthetic predilection, looked instead at the ways in which the traditional performance fits into the day-to-day life of a specific group and the cultural content of the various items of performance.

Anthropologically inclined folklorists focused particularly on when and how the group draws on traditional kernels of quoted speech. Proverbial sayings are not only gauges of the power and resources of the group but also distillations of how that group agrees the world is put together, spelling out systems of belief about such fundamental yet practical matters as political governance, economics, religion, and kinship. Literarily inclined folklorists, by emphasizing construction and dissemination, ignored how the expression of group values is allocated. They took for granted that these nuggets of wisdom or displays of word power were effective and often neglected to record, much less analyze, who deployed them under what conditions and with what consequences. Questions of practical function gave way to morphological and stylistic concerns. On the other hand, anthropologists, neglecting the stylistic component of traditional expression, failed to relate cultural values to aesthetic style within the groups they observed.

The separation of form and content, text and context that resulted from this disciplinary schizophrenia did not serve folklorists well. In response to an emerging interest in cultural meanings, folklorists came to an agreement in principle on how the two disciplines might develop common perspectives: by relating form and content, and by situating texts in social context. With the growing power of symbolic anthropology and the swing toward interpretive studies of culture, ethnographers of all sorts became more aware of the ways in which performances may be textualized so that they can be analyzed and interpreted in terms of a common vocabulary.

The limitations of these two divergent points of view are more easily discernible when they are situated within the full range of aesthetic approaches used in the past. There are four basic ways in which a work of art, traditional or otherwise, has been approached. The first underlines the importance of the shaping hand of the artist, seeing the work of art and its effect upon the audience as byproducts of the manipulative energies of the creator, performer, or interpreter. We know this approach best through Romantic criticism, but most Freudian commentators adopt it as well. The second approach centers upon the work of art as an object, divorcing the artist and the audience and dismissing both them from consideration, at least for the critical moment. This approach sees all artistic creations as self-sufficient entities; it implies that once a work is made it is capable of speaking for itself. The art object is analyzed in terms of its internal characteristics and the interrelationships among its parts.

Practitioners of the New Criticism adopted this approach, although it was used long before that movement began—for instance, by Aristotle in his concept of the dramatic unities. The third approach is primarily concerned with the way in which the performance affects the audience. In Aristotelian terms, the meaning of a work centers on its cathartic effect. The fourth approach focuses on the way in which the audience affects the performance. It analyzes how public values and conventions arise and are encouraged, and how the performer is affected by the presence of the audience and by public tastes. The last two approaches, which can be seen as reciprocal, underscore the public dimensions of artistic representations, in contrast to the more solitary concerns of the first two. Those who adopted this interactive point of view have gravitated toward the analysis of the popular arts or the popular aspects of *belles lettres*.

In terms of these four alternatives, anthropologically inclined folklorists are most interested in audience values in their forays into the field of traditional expressive culture. Especially notable are the works of symbolic anthropologists on moments of religious and secular celebration. Structuralist analysts, too, place audience at the center of their concerns with ritual and other formalized enactments. More recently, ethnographers of performance and communication have directly addressed the visible connections between expressive acts and audience reception. For folklorists in particular, studies of tourism, museums, and public commemorations make a vital contribution to this inquiry, exploring the public nature of symbolic action and representation within specific groups and elucidating the public values and practices depicted and reenacted in these cultural forms.

Literary folklorists, on the other hand, remain more directly concerned with the text and its variants, even when recording a performance in the field. This impulse emerges from the nineteenth-century hermeneutic approach to the Bible, which took the text as a source of meaning unto itself, as holy writ, rather than as the product of individual genius or the manipulation of literary formulae. Folklorists of the "Sources and Analogues" or "Geographical-Historical" schools are not concerned with the aesthetic effect of the object so much as with the distribution of its component parts in time and space. Eastern European formalist criticism, which developed out of language philosophy, has also percolated throughout this critical community. The postmodern, post-structuralist enterprise emerged in dramatic contrast to these formalistic, typological, and distributional concerns.

In America, the New Criticism was the dominant incarnation of formalism. Formal analysis of any sort begins by addressing a text in terms of the relationships of its constituent parts to its total representation. By comparing the conventions of dramatic or linguistic movement by genre or within a specific type of artistic production, formal critics elucidate the patterns of expectation brought in common by artist and audience to the moment of contemplation. In dealing with folklore items, then, formalists provide both an analytic and a predictive tool for discussing traditional materials.

These approaches to the analysis of traditional expression are neither exhaustive nor mutually exclusive. Indeed, a method which considers all aspects of the aesthetic performance—context, item, and audience—promises to yield the greatest fruits, marrying the insights provided by structuralist and symbolic anthropologists, who see folklore in its contextual frame, to the formalistic perceptions of literary critics, who see how it works. This approach to literature and other expressive manifestations of society has been articulated by critics who revived the concept of rhetoric as the art of persuasion and realized that the essence of persuasion resides in both effective form and compelling performance.

Sigmund Freud's monograph on jokes and aggression is highly suggestive to those seeking to understand the underlying messages contained within formal unities. His *Jokes and Their Relation to the Unconscious* (1905) argues that jokes function as a way of revealing buried aggressive motives through an indirect mode of voicing that allows these feelings to be uttered. Through this liberating redirection, the jokester is capable of duping others, as well as himself, about these unconscious aggravations. In the wake of this work, we see these social leaks as contributing to ego gains while avoiding the problems generated by open hostility. Freud emphasizes that this could not occur if the joking were not already a ticketed activity in which a great many social compacts are abrogated. The mechanism of sidestepping good manners helps us understand how such licensing is achieved conventionally within the dynamic of everyday talk. I think of it as the power of "justness"—as in "just kidding" or "just pulling your leg"—which embodies a bid for exemption from the rules of friendly conversation. Individual joke-tellers are not only allowed but even encouraged to deliver messages that may or may not be widely shared and understood, but which in a more direct form would be regarded as hostile, too destructive of the delicate tissue by which everyday interactions are held together. Discomforting social messages often lie just below the surface of many formulaic routines. Conventional formulas serve to induce acceptance of aggression even among the best of friends. The trick may be as simple as using familiar routines to induce the complicity of the others in the encounter, culminating in the release of energies engineered by laughing together. Potentially explosive social motives often emerge in playful circumstances.

The most nuanced and fruitful approaches for understanding this kind of social dynamic in art as in everyday life come from the work of Kenneth Burke. He argues that the forcefulness of performed words arises from the use of artistic devices as part of the machinery for living carried in the vernacular. Burke locates power in performances which strategize interpersonal exchanges, including those embodied in literature. Performances may be regarded in terms of the ways in which speaking rights are asserted and maintained. How is agreement to enter a talk engineered, or how does the artist achieve a place in the flow of events that encourages productivity? Burke argues that all language involves a process of *naming* that lulls the parties to the interaction into a comfort zone which readily accedes to would-be controlling motives. To be able to evoke the name of a social situation is to achieve magical control over the proceedings. This hegemony may then be employed to influence others through invoking names. Using the naming potential in one's voice serves the speaker in directing the way the interaction develops. Personal power attends the successful rhetorician who knows the names and numbers, not only of all the players, but of all the plays (Burke 1941).

This insight into vernacular expression appears self-evident because it has developed within vernacular social encounters and is learned as one learns to talk. The more stylistic control is exercised, the greater the degree and effectiveness of the *rhetor*. Or, to put it in terms more in tune with the subject, the greater the control of a medium of representation, the more word-magic is invoked and the more readily the message is agreed to. This angle of argument causes us to look simultaneously at the performer, the strip of talk which he or she chooses to perform, and the effects this ensemble has on the audience. Burke distinguishes between "situations" and "strategies": "We think of poetry [or any stylized form] as the adopting of various conventional strategies for the encompassing of typical situations. These strategies size up the situations, name their structure and outstanding ingredients, and name them in a way that contains an attitude toward them" (Burke 1941: 3).

Expressive folklore is made up of items of vernacular performances which call attention to themselves for their difference from other kinds of expression. From a Burkean perspective, I argue that, because of its artifice, each item of folk expression demonstrates some control over the medium. As with any work of art, materials are manipulated so that they appear coherent and vital. Both the form and performance of these items underscore the artificial character of the expression.

The full analysis of a tradition or genre thus calls for study of the organizational elements of both items and performances. The use of formalist or structuralist modes of representation led a number of ethnographers to decontextualize performances, separating texts from their contexts. High-level oppositional elements were derived from chosen texts and used to represent the way in which other such inventions are produced. Myths and tales were treated as if they were serendipitously encountered artifacts or relics to be decoded in analytic isolation from their actual voicings. These analyses have directed attention to linguistic and dramatic principles of construction without much attempt to get at the artistic quality of the organization or the context in which any item achieves its effect.

The folklorist Alan Dundes argues that the performance dimension is similarly capable of being analyzed in terms of its traditional organization;

given his analytic and interpretive bias, he calls this "the structure of context" (Dundes 1964; for exemplary analyses of traditions within specific cultures, see Dégh 1957, 1969; Crowley 1966; Finnegan 1967). Examination of "the structure of context" calls for an analysis of the relations among the participants in an aesthetic transaction—actors and observers—as they are affected by temporal, spatial, and situational factors. Each item of lore can be discussed meaningfully in terms of its linguistic and dramatic organization and the relationship between the performer and the rest of the group. In fact, understanding an item and, by extension, the tradition in which it exists begins by interrelating all these stylistic matters (Ben-Amos 1971). It is not enough to perceive how ideas and attitudes are embodied in forms that produce pleasure, beauty, and edification. Function and the relations between form and usage are equally critical.

Kenneth Burke pursues a contextualist viewpoint in urging his rhetoric of motives—that is, he analyzes the position from which each speaker voices his or her perspective and how those positions and perspectives intersect to shape the dialogue. Each item of expressive culture is best regarded as a strategy for achieving speech rights and a device for putting forth an argument. The rhetorical approach deals with all levels of formal and representational stylization simultaneously in order to show how they reinforce one another. Each argument must have a method of attack, or "strategy," and each level of item-performance contributes to the implementation of the strategy. An utterance asks for some kind of sympathetic response from the hearer, a reaction induced by the manipulation of materials (words, gestures, dramatic movement) in combination with the technique by which the speaker relates to the audience—his or her ability to animate the presentation. The rhetorical approach centers upon the aesthetic means by which sympathy is evoked, but places equal emphasis on affect. By analyzing strategy, it relates the performer and audience to the item being performed (Burke 1941).

Once this frame of reference is established, it is not difficult to recognize the many ways that strategies are embodied and used to convince others of a saying's wisdom, humor, rectitude, and depth of meaning. The problem is how to relate the levels of structure effectively. The rhetorical approach assumes that both an *item* and an *affect* exist in the performance situation and asks how the social process works with such formulaic devices. Addressing techniques of argumentation presumes that all utterances are implicated in efforts to influence others' attitudes or practices. The analyst aims to reveal the design elements being drawn upon within the performance.

Folklore, as a traditional activity, argues traditionally; it uses arguments and persuasive techniques developed in the past to cope with recurrent social or existential problem situations. In fact, the traditional nature of the expression is one of the most important techniques of persuasion in a tradition-oriented group. From this perspective, folklore provides important tactics used to maintain the stability of culture. It is employed to inculcate customs and ethical standards in the young; to reward adults with praise when they conform; to punish them with ridicule or criticism when they deviate; to provide rationalizations when institutions and conventions are questioned or challenged; to suggest that people be content with things as they are; and to provide them with compensation for or an escape from the "hardships, the inequalities, the injustices" of everyday life (Bascom 1954: 349). In rhetorical terms, by using persuasive techniques developed in the past, folklore argues for adherence to courses of action already tested by long usage. These persuasions work by educating, legislating, justifying, applying social pressure, and providing socially approved outlets for antisocial motives.

Text/Context

Considering both rhetorical intent and contextual structure allows recognition of the dynamic qualities of folklore in performance. Discussions of linguistic or dramatic structure do not generally explain these qualities in dynamic terms. Structural analysis does include description of a *progression* of sounds, motives, or ideas, but progression is less dynamic than *movement*. Movement is, in fact, the most important characteristic of any item of folklore. A sympathetic or empathic reaction is inherent in the aesthetic construction of the piece, but it takes effect only as the item is performed. Consequently, our dearest insight into affect is achieved by studying the relation between performer and audience. For the strategy of a piece to succeed in arousing the sympathy of the audience, the performer and the item must come together congruently.

It is precisely because we have both an item and a performer that our understanding of the nature of the sympathetic experience is clouded. On the one hand, the performer aims to achieve some kind of status within the group, however temporary that may be. The performance is an active part of the social drama, registering in a small way the presence of competition and conflict in everyday life. On the other hand, the item has an existence of its own, since it can be reenacted by any of a number of performers. As such, it artificially enunciates a conflict of its own. Agonism—a struggle between opposing characters and principles—is at the core of dramatic structure.

The perceived connections between the conflictual elements of social existence and the artificially agonistic components of a work of art are central to this line of analysis. This congruence in antagonism is made clear in forms like fables or proverbs, which are invoked as an aphoristic answer to a social question. Many traditional expressions stage artificial interplay in terms of observable social conflict. Hence the analysis of folklore in terms of the dynamics of daily life discovered within the performance community.

The essence of sympathy between performer and audience resides in the paradox of culture: that social cohesion is most fully sensed in terms of the antagonisms felt within the group. Community is achieved through a balance of dissociative and associative forces. Membership is announced and preserved not only through unity and adherence to law but also by culturally approved expressions of egotism and hostility and, on occasion, through the expulsion of dissident elements as means of defining consensus. Sympathy, in life as well as art, is essentially a mediating force, a recognition of the universality of strife through the ability to imagine oneself in the shoes of another. As a sympathetic activity, folklore functions as an imaginative projection, creating and mediating a world of conflict which is simultaneously a negation and an affirmation of community. Each item of traditional expression articulates conflict in some way and provides some manner of temporary resolution. Its very traditional nature promotes community. It can accomplish this mediation because it takes the form of play, projecting conflict into an impersonal and harmless milieu.

The performer does more than remember and re-present a traditional item. It is rather more fruitful to regard the performer as standing in a confrontational relationship with whoever is watching and reacting in sympathy. The performer is then privileged to insert something of herself or himself into the sheltering environment. This might be regarded as an aggressive, if not hostile, act. But inasmuch as it calls upon the sympathy of those to whom it is directed, it appears to reaffirm community attitudes. Further, its traditional character diverts attention from the egotistical essence of the performance. Performance is only one of many acceptable egocentric activities. But the more this personal aggressiveness becomes evident in the content of the performance, the more it must be controlled in some way: by rules and boundaries or by the distance created between the play world and the "real" world.

In emphasizing the aggressive egotism of the performer, we risk losing sight of the fact that he or she is permitted this position because the attitudes and plans of action which he or she transmits are condoned by the community. Expressive folklore embodies and expresses recurrent social conflicts, giving them a *name* and thus a representative and recognizable symbolic form. To handle the materials of this representation is to reveal the problem situation in a controlled context. This atmosphere of control is the primary tool of the rhetoric of a performance. When the performance operates sympathetically, this control is magically transferred from the item to the recurrent problem. Because the performer projects and resolves the conflict, the illusion is created that it can be solved in real life; with the addition of sympathy, of "acting with," the audience derives not only pleasure but also knowledge from the activity.

The controlling power of folklore, the carrying out of its rhetorical intent, resides in the ability of the item and the performer to establish a sense of identity between a "real" situation and its artificial embodiment. A psychic distance is created which allows the audience to relax at the same time it identifies with the projected situation. The audience is removed far enough from the situation so people feel there is no real risk of becoming actively involved. Presented with an anxiety-provoking situation but relieved from the actual anxiety, listeners gain control and, with it, relief. This relief becomes pleasure when the performance exercises control by the use of wit, by the imposition of rules and boundaries, by the creation of an imaginary world, or by some other limiting device which proclaims artifice. Such controls make the problem seem more impersonal and universal and less immediate and threatening. This is the essence of play: objectifying and impersonalizing anxiety situations, allowing the free expenditure of energies without fear of social consequences. This removal serves rhetoric by clearing the way for the production of pleasure and the sympathetic response. Rhetoric in its turn serves society by promoting accepted attitudes and modes of action.

Expressive folklore not only provides pleasure and catharsis but also attempts to offer guidance by allying sympathy and strategy with movement. Folklore proposes potential solutions to anxiety-provoking situations and attempts to produce action in accordance with its proposals. This didactic intent is especially evident in overtly normative forms of folklore, such as proverbs, hero tales, and fables. In the case of forms which embody antisocial motives, folklore projects these into patently ridiculous or fantastic worlds and allows for their expression in a harmless milieu, guiding action through formulas of avoidance. We see this diversion in forms as diverse as trickster tales, riddles, and festival maskings. Thus, in both normative and antisocial forms, sympathy arises in an atmosphere of control, which emerges from the fruitful coming together of an effective performer and a meaningful traditional expression.

The rhetorical approach asks the observer to witness how the control of the aesthetic object and the context combine in creating pleasure and proposing action. It demands recognition of an intimate sympathetic relation between a proposed solution to a recurrent societal problem and the movement involved in the artistic projection of the problem. And it suggests that the most feasible way of seeing this relationship is to understand what the strategy of the piece is: of what it wants to convince the hearers and how it goes about convincing them. It does this, not at the expense of the play element of culture, but rather by insisting on the essential utility of its playing-out on an apparently impersonal level.

Proverb/Riddle

The rhetorical approach is not like the scientific method, a set of procedures to be used in attacking any test situation. It is rather a point of view that proposes areas in which insights might be gained by using comparative or relational methodology. To illustrate the uses of this approach, I will compare two genres, proverbs and riddles, in terms of organizational and persuasive techniques. Similar in their linguistic organization but differing in their context of performance, the two forms are most readily contrasted through their variance in strategy.

Proverbs and riddles are short forms; both use the sentence as their linguistic frame. Both use the devices of poetry as the stylistic basis of their linguistic organization: rhythm, balanced phrasing, rhyme, metaphor, and assonance. Both are descriptions whose referents must be inferred through the aptness of their elements. They differ only in that a riddle must supply its referent and a proverb need not, as the referent is clear from the context of its usage.

Proverbs are traditional answers to recurrent ethical problems; they make an argument for a course of action which conforms to community values (Dundes 1975). Arising in the midst of a conversation, they are used by speakers to give a *name* to the ethical problem confronting them and to suggest ways in which it has been solved in the past (although the suggestion is not necessarily directed to the persons confronted by the problem). The proverb invokes an aura of moral rightness as the comfort of past community practice is made available to the present and future. Proverbs may be used directly to teach or to remind those who already know. The proverb says at one and the same time "this is the way things are and have been" and "this is the proper way of responding to such a situation." The strategy of the proverb is to direct by appearing only to clarify, by simplifying the problem and resorting to traditional solutions.

Riddles do not ordinarily arise in everyday speech, but are staged in the stylized performance of a riddle session. The riddle is a device used to entertain by formulaically creating confusion. Where the proverb persuades by providing answers, the riddle confuses by posing enigmas. To promote confusion seems to be to court chaos, but the riddle eventually provides an answer to its question. Riddles are fundamentally aggressive in design and purpose. They seem to be extensions of antisocial motives, as opposed to the apparently normative proverbs which propose and support group amity.

This antagonism is the reason riddles occur only in riddling sessions, with all the boundaries on aggressive conduct that accompany such a performance. Proverbs need no such rules or limits. To countenance aggressive behavior, groups insist that it be enacted in a harmless milieu or directed against outsiders. Riddles are one of many traditional forms of licensed aggression that, though antisocial in tendency, are not antinormative. They channel energies that are potentially destructive of the community and its values into harmless, indeed positively helpful, avenues of creative expression.

Significantly, many of the techniques by which license for hostile in-group behavior is obtained are the same as those used by normative expressions to guide action. This connection can also be seen through the comparison of proverbs and riddles. A proverb works primarily by cloaking a recommended course of action in the garb of artful expression; it gives the impression that much thought has at some time been given to the problem to which the proverb is presently addressed. Wit serves wisdom as a device of control. In riddles, wit promotes perplexity in the service of aggressive motives. The formal unity provided by wit in riddles serves as one way of restricting aggression; under the guise of wit, all sorts of subjects and motives can be exercised, or even exorcized, which are otherwise forbidden.

One of the principal distinctions between the proverb and the riddle is in the context of their use. A riddle reported by one of my students from East Texas goes: "The people of Holland make what the children of England break." The answer is "toys." In the context of a riddle session, this description is indeed enigmatic—especially, one would imagine, to a Texan! But it is easy to see how this little rhyme was formerly used as a moral comment on privileged and careless English children; in context, the referent would be understood immediately. Proverbs exist in a conversational context in which there must be a clear relation between description and referent; otherwise the strategy of the proverb fails. Riddles, on the other hand, are found in the permissive atmosphere of the riddle session in which the relation between the traits described and referent intended must be blurred to carry out the intent of the riddler.

The very construction of the riddle or the proverb, in conjunction with its context and its voicing, embodies strategy. There is something intrinsically clarifying and edifying in the construction of proverbs; and there is a confusing quality inherent in riddles. Both are economical and witty descriptions, but they differ in the way they cohere. Both have two or more elements or traits in their descriptions, but their elements stand in different relationships to one another.

In a proverb the elements of the description have an inevitable and organic relationship; they make sense together and cohere in an active way. The combination of elements sets up an image or idea in an immediately meaningful and dynamic *gestalt*. The clarity of this pattern, in combination with the felicity of phrasing, provides a tone of appropriateness and moral weight. Technical organization of materials extends beyond sound and rhythm to sense and provides the needed feeling of order, which in turn promotes sympathy and encourages future action in accord with the proverb's dictates. But sympathy and action are also induced by the dynamic relation between the elements of the description. Repeatedly, proverbs tie together the elements of their descriptions through active verbs, relating them causally or as equivalents, and it is this activity which promotes the sympathetic response. For instance, the rolling stone gains force from "gathering" even when it gathers nothing.

The riddle, on the other hand, brings together its elements in such a way that *gestalt* is impaired before the referent is voiced. The relationship of the descriptive elements is necessarily confused, causing one of four *gestalt* impairments to occur. First, a contradiction or opposition may be set up between the traits. Examples include: "What has eyes but cannot see? A potato." "What goes up the chimney down but cannot go down the chimney up? An umbrella." Second, the description may fail to give enough information to provide a complete *gestalt* and allow the recognition of the referent. For example: "What is white, then green, then red? A berry growing." Third, too much inconsequential or misleading evidence may be provided, causing a scrambling effect. A classic example that turns on the amazing capacity of the English language for homonyms is: "As I was crossing London Bridge I met a man who tipped his hat and drew his cane, and now I gave you his name. What is it? Andrew S. Cane." Finally, a false *gestalt* may be created; the traits seem to combine meaningfully with the description given, but the apparent referent is not the same as the true referent. This usually leads to a catch situation in which the respondent voices the obvious but obviously wrong answer, which is often obscene. The effect is very like that of the trick picture that can be read in two ways. For example: "What goes in hard and smooth and comes out soft and gooey? A piece of chewing gum."

When successful, the riddle is a description whose referent cannot be guessed; a proverb is one whose referent can be inferred by everyone involved. In the riddle, the answer must be supplied to bring about *gestalt*, and it is in the triumph of the parts coming together in a meaningful pattern that the strategy of the riddle is most clearly seen. The proverb enunciates a recurrent conflict or social problem and proposes a common or shared resolution. The riddle works more artificially; it establishes a little internal conflict of its own in its combination of descriptive elements, and then provides its own solution when its referent is voiced.

These similarities and differences between proverbs and riddles register social forces achieving expressive form. The normative and consensual nature of the proverb and the aggressive and licentious character of the riddle are the dominant attributes of these forms. But they are not their only rhetorical attributes. For purposes of clarity it must be noted that proverbs may also be aggressive in purpose; the speaker is, after all, attempting to impose his or her definition of the situation and his or her ideas for resolving it upon the audience. Conversely, a riddle has a kind of clarifying effect when the riddle and its referent-answer are considered as a unit.

In certain situations, these secondary or recessive characteristics may take precedence, and proverbs may be used, like riddles, for aggressive purposes. Significantly, when proverbs are so used they become part of a proverb-telling session or contest with appropriate rules. For example, John Messenger reported that among the Anang of West Africa, proverbs serve as a device of argument in the judicial system, much as precedents are employed in courts of common law; their use and misuse can profoundly affect a legal case (Messenger 1959). An even more extreme example of such proceedings is reported among the Mataco Chaco of Argentina, who devote their entire adjudication process to an exchange of proverbs between the opposing parties. Such proceedings emphasize the paradoxical, enigmatic nature of the contested occurrence; the parties seek to gain the upper hand by dazing each other with traditional expressions they contend are applicable to the case (Fock 1965).

Similarly, riddles can be used for normative purposes. A riddle known to all in the audience is still proposed in riddle sessions, not because anyone will he confused, but precisely because everyone knows the answer and all can demonstrate their knowledge together. The pleasure in the performance arises out of the mimesis of conflict, not out of any real agonistic interplay. Its recitation is a demonstration of group knowledge and cohesion. When riddles are regarded as part of traditional knowledge to be learned by initiates, the recital of the riddle with its answer is a demonstration of group solidarity. In such a situation, riddles function as catechism and exist primarily to clarify and edify, a rhetorical intent not very different from that of proverbs. However, such usages are exceptional; in most groups the dominant strategy of proverbs is to clarify and instruct, and that of riddles is to confuse and entertain.

Playing with the Power of Riddles

This distinction between the genres of proverb and riddle can cast light on the function of these forms in specific cultural situations. We can say with assurance that in most cases when riddles are invoked in a group, those who use them are trying to assert power by inducing confusion. And when people employ proverbs, they are attempting to control by appearing to clarify a problem and propose a solution. Both forms are used in interpersonal situations as a means of establishing status through the exercise of wit. There are important conventional differences from one culture to the next in the uses of both genres. By considering all levels of structure simultaneously and interrelating them through rhetorical strategy, we can gain important insight into the habits of organization and expression of specific groups, while more fully understanding the range of uses to which these genres can be put. Three distinct groups exemplify three different uses of riddles: urban American subcultures, the Bantu Venda, and communities in the British West Indies.

Descriptive riddles (such as "true riddles") are seldom found in the repertory of urban whites in the United States. When riddling descriptions do occur, confusion commonly turns on a pun or other ambiguous word usage.

Joking technique prevails over other expressions of wit. In the most common forms of enigmatic questions in such groups, the conundrum, the question serves simply as a set-up for the punch-line answer. Elephant, grape, and Polack joke-riddles rely on puns or word-play. So do the formulaic questions popular among children: "What is the difference between . . ." or "What did the ———— say to the ————?" The most widespread joke cycles resort to joke-riddle form, starting with the moron jokes of the pre-World War II era. In this cultural milieu, riddles function not only in the riddling session but in the equally restricted joke-telling session. The fact that riddles here are functional equivalents of jokes is significant, for it reveals the emphasis on brevity, word play, and contests of wit in these oral entertainments in white urban America.

This joking activity is peripheral to our major cultural concerns. Although riddling among children does train the young for adult joking, the entire activity is regarded as unimportant even by the performers themselves. This aggressive verbal activity exists in a culture in which words tend to be mistrusted or discounted. Hence such proverbs as "One picture is worth a thousand words" and "Judge a man by his actions, not his words." The devaluation of words may be the primary reason for the reliance on shorter forms of expression, of which the riddling joke-cycle is only one representative.

This peripheral position of riddle-telling may be compared to the practice in cultures which place higher value on words and verbal expression. Riddling is closer to the central concerns of such groups and more often encountered as part of important social occasions. Among the Venda of the Northern Transvaal in South Africa, John Blacking reported:

Venda riddles are used in the course of a competitive game for young people. They are educational chiefly because they may be an asset to fuller participation in Venda social life; they are not important as exercises of intellectual skill, and their contents do not appear to instruct or stimulate the imaginations of those who know them. Both riddle and answer were learned as a linguistic whole, and it is more important to know the riddle than to be able to puzzle out the answer or understand their content. Amongst the Venda, knowledge of formal language is in a sense equivalent to magical power: the individual increases his status by joining social groups, the membership of which is assured by his knowledge of certain word-formulae. The form of riddles resembles that of *milayo* formulae, which must be known by anyone who claims that he has been to certain initiation schools. Knowledge of riddles helps a Venda child to establish his identity as an individual and as a member of a junior social group, when he distinguishes himself during a riddle-contest. (Blacking 1961: 1)

Blacking emphasizes the importance of words: riddles help the child learn the exercise of wit to achieve status and prepare him or her for adult activity. He underscores the use of this verbal aggressive behavior in terms of ego growth and the achievement of identity in a group in which the range of individual expression is narrow.

In terms of rhetorical analysis, Blacking emphasizes a special use of the confusion-creating strategy in its contextual structure. He does not specify the context by reporting an individual riddling session; he only reports types of contests. There are two ways in which riddling may proceed. In one, "A asks B riddles, which B answers successfully. Eventually B is stumped, but A does not give him the answer . . . B must then ask A riddles until A too is stumped. A then reveals the answer to the original." In the other, "A asks B a riddle. B does not answer it; instead he 'buys' A's answer by posing another riddle. A answers his own first riddle and then 'buys' answer to B's riddle by posing another . . . B then answers his own first and 'buys' . . . and so on" (Blacking 1961: 3). Blacking discusses the relative importance of the two games, not just in terms of their frequency but also in terms of ways in which they reveal the values of the community.

In both games, the honors go to those who pose the problem rather than to those who solve it. Many prefer the second game as it is "easier to play" and "lasts longer"; a team can maintain its supply of riddles longer, instead of having it decimated in one blow by opponents who either know all the answers or ask the best riddles first. Moreover, in the second game a player can escape the penalties of not being able to answer a riddle by "buying" the answer with a riddle that he knows; this again stresses the importance of knowing the riddle as a linguistic whole rather than being able to puzzle it out by intellectual reasoning. In the second game a player avoids loss of face and has the satisfaction of compensating for his deficiency by striking a bargain; this might be called a more typically Venda pattern of behavior than the fiercer, ruthless competition between two individuals, whilst the others sit back and listen. The second game also reflects the Venda love of elaborating social activity with rituals that both lengthen the proceeding, and hence the enjoyment of the occasion, and also endure a balance of power and orderly behavior between parties that are in opposition. (Blacking 1961: 3)

By considering the riddle as an expressive and functional object in a dynamic context, Blacking tells us much about the Venda, not only about their riddling and other verbal behavior but also about their larger patterns of interaction and social institutions.

A similar attitude toward words as a source of power exists in many peasant communities. Riddling is a common activity in the British West Indies, which is itself an important fact about this culture (Abrahams 1967). But the place, manner, and patterns of performance are very different from those among the Venda.

The man-of-words plays a central role in West Indian life, not only in traditional entertainments but also in such institutions as government and the economy (Abrahams 1983). In contrast to the urban United States, more value is placed on working of the voice than of the hands. Traditional symbolic gestures are seldom seen in the West Indies, while equivalent verbal forms are abundant. Riddles, being available to nearly everyone in these peasant communities, serve as a basic way of developing virtuosity and demonstrating

power with words. Furthermore, the man-of-words functions most effectively—in fact, nearly exclusively—in contest situations, and riddling serves as
the model for such activity.

Although riddling may occur at any social event, especially spontaneous
activities on moonlit nights, here I examine riddling during nine-night wakes
for the dead in order to suggest some paths the rhetorical approach might take
the investigator which he might not travel otherwise. I briefly describe some
characteristics of the texture and content of West Indian riddles and then suggest ways in which they are related to the structure of context through an elaboration of the strategy of confusion.

The most noticeable textural characteristic of West Indian riddles is their
outlandish originality; although they are in English, they seem entirely foreign
to any other riddling tradition in that tongue. The local tradition is made up
primarily of true riddles, but the subjects of the descriptions are quite different
from those in mainstream English riddling. The techniques of description also
show a different emphasis. West Indian riddles tend to dramatize and personalize, to tell vignettes in first-person or familial terms.

I went to town, my face turn to town;
I came from town, my face turn to town.
—climbing a coconut tree.

Such observations extend to other traditional expressions, for West Indians
commonly find it important to become dramatically involved in all events in
their lives—that is, to break down the distinction between life and art. They
dramatize and personalize the otherwise mundane, quotidian, and indifferent
aspects of daily existence. This element of the riddle is further emphasized in
the telling, for each riddle becomes an extension of the ego of the riddler, and
in order to insist upon this identification he will dramatize its presentation as
much as possible. Some riddlers leave the house during the session not only
to think up new enigmas but also to time their entrance so they can deliver
their invention from the darkness of the door, eliciting a laugh as attention is
gained. A really clever riddle well delivered draws applause and appreciative
murmuring that can last for several minutes.

So why does riddling occur during wakes? How does it enact and reinforce group values? Every activity after the death of an individual is calculated
to involve as many people as possible, to pull the group together in the face of
death. For example, fifty or sixty men often dig the grave to pay respect to the
dead. Riddling, along with storytelling, singing, dancing, and game-playing,
the West Indian activities that involve the whole group as performers or
observers, all occur at some time during the memorial celebration. These traditional activities generate a pause in the passage of time and invoke a spirit
of license, bringing the group through a time of crisis. And there is crisis, for

death is imagined as a malevolent force which can strike anyone at any moment. This feeling is generally rationalized in Christian terms, but the attitude toward the dead is in essence a retention of African ancestor worship. This license permits performances that demonstrate the life-principle in the most primal ways, perhaps most notably in the erotic motives which are enacted in the midst of these gatherings. Songs, games, and stories focus on sex organs and sex acts which are seldom discussed on other occasions. This eroticism is observable in riddling as well. For instance, one of the most common West Indian riddles is

Poppy take longy-longy, push it in a mommy' hairy-hairy.
—making a broom.

One subject that arises in many riddling sessions is even more significant in the wake context: the living emerging from the dead, or the living carrying over the dead. There is, for instance, a notable riddle describing the living pall-bearers carrying the dead in the coffin to the graveyard and then coming back to the village. This theme was made all the more dramatic when a woman died while we were collecting folklore in Tobago. She requested that the Bongo (wake) be held in a certain way, even though she died during Lent, so that she could be there celebrating with everyone; she had so enjoyed Bongos in life that this would make dying a little easier.

This incident is a vivid, even melodramatic example of the possible conjunctions between text and context. But there is a further dimension which needs to be examined, in light of the period of license and the practice of stopping time for performance: the role of such riddles in carrying over the living in the wake of death. How can such an aggressive phenomenon as riddling contribute to the establishment of a sense of well-being and continuity in the troubled group? Part of an answer lies in the nature of riddling as a group observance in which time is stopped and troubling phenomena are depersonalized and acted out in the removed play-world of riddling. Moreover, riddling atomizes the death problem as a life riddle; by providing solutions which emphasize the triumph of life, riddling uses devices of confusion to create an atmosphere of clarification. Perhaps in this wake situation, riddles with their solutions suggest sympathetically that the larger riddle of life and death also has a solution.

This partial analysis of riddles and riddling demonstrates what can be said about the culture and aesthetic patterns of a community by considering structure and rhetoric. In all three groups, riddles are formulaic, competitive, confusing, and witty, but they fit into the life of the group and disclose its values and expressive habits in widely varying ways. Stylistic analysis placed in a rhetorical framework permits insights into culture that could not otherwise be realized. Investigators such as Blacking groped toward this intuitively. But, without a theoretical framework, they were unable to articulate the full potential of cultural insights inherent in the analysis of traditional performance.

In order to relate folklore to the dynamics of culture, we must develop a methodology that focuses on the movement of traditional items as they are used by both performers and hearers in a living situation. One way of going about the task is to attempt as best we can to document how items connected to the putative past are actually used.

The discipline of folklore, like any other, has little justification except as it enables us to understand ourselves and others. Collecting traditional material because it is "quaint" condemns ourselves to irrelevance and consigns living cultures to oblivion. Objectifying the texts of expressive culture for the purpose of analysis without putting the pieces back together in situated performance is also unsatisfying, lacking in explanatory power and comparative reach. Vernacular cultural practices can provide insight into the ways others, and we ourselves, operate on a daily basis and amid the most profound disruptions of social life. Vernacular forms and practices should be approached through actual examples of use at a specific time and place, taking into account the audience's expectations and the conventions of performance.

Chapter 2
Forms in Opposition

The shorter forms of traditional expression—not only proverbs and jokes, but also boasts and taunts, blessings and curses—were slow to attract folklorists' attention. These materials are easy to collect, even among so-called nontraditional groups; an abundance of texts has been compiled and catalogued (Jolles 1929). But their brevity and simplicity made these sayings seem less interesting than the longer and more complex forms. Their genres remained undefined in either formal or functional terms. We knew little about how, by whom, and why even the two most widely observed short forms, proverbs and superstitions, are used in everyday interactions. This serious oversight was remedied by E. Ojo Arewa and Alan Dundes in regard to proverbs and by Linda Dégh with superstitions (Arewa and Dundes 1964; Dégh 1956). Arewa and Dundes have shown that the life of the proverb lies, not only in what it apparently means and how it can influence listeners, but also in who uses the saying with whom and what range of uses are possible. They argue effectively that we cannot really know what a proverb means until we consider the context.

Such contextual information is essential to our own understanding of proverbs in conversational settings. Let us examine a proverb that has retained its vitality in our culture, which regards most traditional sayings as clichés: "Little pitchers have big ears." This metaphorical description might be unintelligible to members of other material cultures because it compares the pitcher handle, which is large enough to enable a good grip even on a small container, to a child's ear. The surface meaning of the saying is something like "children have good memories but little sense of discretion, so don't say anything in front of them that doesn't bear repeating." But this explication does not tell us much about how its voicing is part of a system of social behavior. The most common use of the proverb is by one adult speaking to another, while a child is nearby, to restrict the subjects of conversation. Less commonly, the proverb is directed at a child by an adult (who must know the child well) to inform the child that whatever he or she has heard should not be repeated. It is hardly conceivable that the proverb be directed by a child to an adult, or used by one child in conversation with another. This belongs to a class of proverbs in English used to establish a hierarchy based on age distinction, usually between child and adult. When described effectively; it can yield important insights into the workings of this important facet of our social institutions.

Because proverbs are often employed as a response to recurrent social problems, contextual information is absolutely central to an understanding both of the expressive style of specific groups and of the ways in which proverbs and other genres of traditional expression are related to the value structure of the community and the daily workings-out of institutional life.

Superstitions, by contrast, are expressed in contexts in which the problems confronted are not social but rather natural or supernatural, so there is less need to distinguish who uses superstitions with whom; in such use situations, the group tends to cohere rather than stratify. Yet context remains important to understanding the uses of superstitions. Linda Dégh has shown that superstitions are seldom encountered in the form of the "if—then" formula given in published collections. Folklorists who are concerned with gathering the greatest number of such beliefs in the shortest possible time often elicit that form or rephrase the saying in that way. Dégh argues that superstitions are commonly expressed and transmitted through memorate legends, a term developed by European folklorists in an attempt to name these stories using artificially confected terms of art (Dégh 1956). Dégh's work proved useful, but limited, precisely because of its attempts to propose a form found anyplace and everyplace. The work of Charles Briggs demonstrated that a more useful taxonomy of forms could be discovered within particular vernaculars, in his case, the kind of Spanish spoken in northern New Mexico (Briggs 1988). These stories fill in important information about who follows the superstition, in what way, and under what circumstances.

This point was brought home to me when I was collecting life-history information from the Arkansas ballad singer, Almeda Riddle. While speaking of old-time practices, she half jokingly told me the following story.

Now I am not superstitious, but here is a tale about someone who feels just about it as I. There was an old lady in the country. They came around and asked her about all these superstitions—she didn't believe in any of them. She didn't believe in hants; she didn't believe in anything but God and Jesus Christ. . . . But she said, "Brother, I'll tell you one thing. If you'll give me a good sassafras stick, and ashes made from hickory wood with a sassafras stick to stir it with, and the light of the moon to make it, I'll make as good a lye-soap as the next one." And she said, "I'll tell you another thing. If you plant your potatoes in the light of the moon you'll get not nary potatoes. You better put 'em in there in the dark of the moon." So she didn't believe in superstitions.

Now I couldn't tell you about the potatoes, but as a matter of fact that business about the soap is right, because I've made soap myself that way many times. . . . So that's right about lye soap, with the hickory and the sassafras. . . . Now I said I'm not superstitious, but even *I* don't start jobs on Friday. I don't mind starting a long trip, or something like that, but to put a quilt into the frame or to quilt it, or to begin a new top to piece it, I'd sit up until midnight Thursday night, but I wouldn't begin it on a Friday. Otherwise, I'd leave it to Saturday or Monday to start it.

The superstitions Mrs. Riddle mentions here are of less interest than the way in which they expose her attitudes and their relation to those of other members of her community. In telling this story, Mrs. Riddle establishes a value-laden point of view which is intended both as an explanation and as a model for possible emulation.

Studying these smaller genres of folklore requires a frame of reference that allows analysis of both their formal characteristics and their recurrent uses. This section compares the forms and functions of proverbs and superstitions, highlighting the ways in which functional differences parallel formal ones. I then discuss other small genres in light of the generic distinction between proverb and superstition. Finally, I argue that the study of the smaller genres is important to students of expressive culture, for it is through such traditional forms that the basic institutions of society are often put into practice.

Proverbs/Superstitions

Both proverbs and superstitions confront and attempt to control recurrent anxiety situations by giving them a *name*. Humans, as cultural beings, have a "rage for order." Anxiety arises with the intuition of chaos, of disruption of the orderly procession of life, and of dissolution of the group. Proverbs name situations in which social stability is repeatedly threatened by disruptive forces coming from within the group. Superstitions give a name to occasions in which order is in danger of being disrupted, and sometimes susceptible to being reinforced, by forces outside the group.

These traditional genres handle problems in various ways, depending upon whether the question is being faced immediately or whether the crisis has already passed but left a residual feeling of disorientation. A proverb can recommend a future course of action. Immediately, it can function as a realignment procedure. The proverb or superstition takes the edge off the shock of the disorienting experience and reimposes a sense of order by aligning this experience with others of its class through giving it its traditional name. For instance, a proverb like "haste makes waste" may be used in two quite different ways, which might be designated active and passive. In its active use, the proverb may arise in a discussion in which one person has to decide whether to rush a job or not. In its passive use, a person may hurry a job and make a costly mistake as a result; the proverb places the mistake in an understandable—and therefore controllable—category of happenings which can be avoided in the future through following its dictates.

So, too, superstitions exhibit flexibility in the range of situations in which they are employed. For instance, the widely reported superstition, "if a black cat crosses your path, you'll have bad luck," can help someone handle the experience of having an ebony feline pass in front of him. The repetition of the superstition, even if only in the mind, prepares the person for a future calamity, eliminating the shock potential. It might also cause a change in his or her future actions, whether simply through adopting a guarded attitude or by enacting a counteracting practice to avert the bad luck, such as spitting and turning around three times. These are active usages of the belief. On the other hand, if something disastrous befalls someone, the person may remember a black cat had crossed his or her path recently. The proverb gives a name to and assigns a cause for the happening, enabling the person to cope with the situation psychologically. This situation illustrates the more passive use.

Proverbs and superstitions share a great deal. Not only are they both control devices which arise in recurrent problem situations, but they use similar cause-and-effect arguments for proposing their solutions. Both are concise and sententious statements which appear to embody the wisdom accrued through the past practice of the group. But they differ not only in the areas of life in which they occur but also in the devices and formulae which they employ.

Proverbs are suggested when a member of the group collides with others, or at least threatens to do so. The occurrences of proverbs in context serve as an index to the places where the social structure of the community is weak and vulnerable and needs reinforcement and control. The study of proverbs in such situations requires that we examine not just the repertoire of sayings available to a group but also which items crop up most frequently.

Looked upon in this way, proverbs can be seen to regulate people's relations with others by setting forth solutions to the problems that repeatedly arise between them, phrasing them in a way that is at one and the same time concise, witty, memorable, forceful, and illustrative of past usage. Most important for the implementation of their rhetorical strategy, they are phrased impersonally, so that the very personal problem at hand becomes universalized. The argument of the proverb achieves its influence by being couched in objective, third-person terms. The appearance of objectivity is further heightened when the proverb employs analogic or metaphoric techniques of argument.

Superstitions, too, are impersonal in their approach and concise in their phrasing, but they do not generally employ poetic techniques. Superstitions do not call attention to themselves as meaningful statements to the same degree that proverbs do; perhaps that is why they are so often accompanied by exemplary legends. While superstitions are as concise as proverbs, they operate in a different sector of human experience. The two genres have differing themes and strategies. Proverbs attack problems of social behavior, while superstitions attempt to handle people's confrontation with extrapersonal natural or supernatural forces that threaten to disrupt the continued existence of individuals and, by extension, the group. Most superstitions attack potentially malevolent forces. Some, however, recognize the existence of benevolent forces and try to convert them to the advantage of the individual or group. All superstitions present a technique for handling change when it is brought on by forces regarded as external to the group, whether the force is invoked by a member of the group, as in magic, or emerges autonomously from a totally uncontrolled source, such as a spirit. Superstitions handle these forces in different ways, depending upon whether they have had their effect already or simply have been predicted to have an effect.

Superstitions work, first, by predicting startling events and thereby eliminating their shock potential, which is really what people cannot handle psychologically. This function is most clearly seen in those superstitions called *omens* or *portents*, such as "if you dream of marriage, a close friend is soon to die," or "if your right palm itches, you are going to get some money, but if your left palm itches, you are going to lose money." Superstitions may also provide a *counteractant* for these forces once they have had effect, as in counterspells or cures, such as "if you get measles, rub goose grease on the bumps." The remedial and predictive functions are often combined, as in "if a dog howls at night, a neighbor will die, unless you go to the crossroads, spit at the center, turn around three times, and make the sign of the cross." Finally, superstitions may set up a situation in which benevolent forces, such as good luck, prevent the onslaught of malevolent forces; for example, "if you put up a horseshoe with its face up over your door, that will give you luck and keep away bad luck."

Both proverbs and superstitions, then, present a course of future action when a person or group is confronted with a problem which threatens to disrupt the smooth course of life. Both argue impersonally, bringing to bear the manner in which the problem has been handled before. Their major difference is in the sectors of life in which they work and the language they use to suggest action. Superstitions are not phrased in as arresting and artificial a manner as proverbs because they are commonly part of legends, and the narrative gives superstition the force of authority which is built into most proverbs through their phrasing. However, the differences in technique seem more readily explicable through the demands arising out of contextual differences in usage. Since the proverb-sayer, or protagonist, is treating a social problem which may have multiple proverbial solutions, she is in the position of asserting one approach over others equally sanctioned. The poetic, often metaphorical language of the proverb can be seen as a consequence of the protagonist's recognition that the assertion may not find common agreement. To avoid possible conflict over the content of the assertion and to remove the protagonist as personally involved arguer from her argument, her recommendation is couched in indirect and impersonal rhetoric. The proverb-sayer is strategically recognizing the complexity of action in the social sphere and formulating a recommendation in such a way as to deemphasize possible interpersonal conflict and assure the greatest stability for the continuing conversation. For a statement dealing with social interaction to become a part of traditional expression, it has to afford the proverb-sayer the kind of protection from conflict that poetic language provides.

In contrast, the superstition-sayer commenting on the effects of natural or supernatural forces gives voice to a belief shared by himself and those to whom he is speaking as a response to a common problem. Since the protagonist can expect his assertion to be met with agreement, the speaker need not fear conflict as a result of self-assertion or divergent ideas for resolving the problem. Thus he can formulate the statement in much more direct language.

Certain kinds of superstitions, such as weather superstitions, are consistently found in poetic form, and therefore are commonly called "weather proverbs." The persistent conflict they involve is not between speaker and spoken-to but humans and nature. A sailor must be able to remember how to predict storms. The poetic form of "Red sky in morning, sailor take warning; red sky at night, sailor's delight" makes the knowledge more readily available. All mnemonic devices enable us to recall information under stressful conditions. The mnemonic devices in small forms of traditional expression require the least amount of interpersonal involvement, and also carry the least threat of manipulation for personal reasons, of any folklore genre.

Personal and Impersonal Viewpoints, Interpersonal and External Forces

Other types of traditional expressions, such as taunts, teases, boasts, charms, spells, curses, and prayers, are considerably more effective in promoting ego-gain than proverbs and superstitions. Traditional utterances that commonly arise in the course of everyday interpersonal communication may be grouped under the rubric of *conversational genres*. All employ a pattern of back-and-forth movement of converse and can be voiced by individuals without any special license. In other words, these conversational genres share a similar structure of context—in the face-to-face situations in which they arise—and a similar dramatic structure as well—in the way in which they set up a protagonist-antagonist relationship between the speaker and spoken-to and suggest a possible resolution to the conflict. However, because these genres typically arise in different situations, they utilize different techniques from divergent points of view and deploy varying strategies of argument.

Before examining these rhetorical strategies, it seems important to isolate their technical and contextual variables. Boasts and taunts, like proverbs, confront social problems and attempt to adjust social positioning, but they confront the problem from the first-person point of view. Superstitions are related to charms, spells, and prayers in their attempt to control extrapersonal forces, but like boasts and taunts they use the vantage of the direct personal approach.

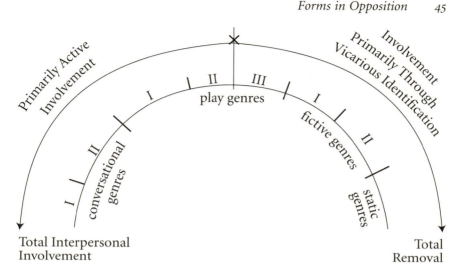

Figure 1. Range of levels of interaction between performer and audience.

The two variables in operation create four possible classes of conversational genres. These differences are paralleled by differences in the rhetorical strategies used by these related genres. Boasts and taunts are used to establish direct interpersonal power and domination. Charms, spells, and prayers attempt to control extrapersonal forces for individual gain by personifying these forces as deities and then by addressing them in the rhetoric of direct appeal. Boasts and taunts function by assuming a position of superior status operating through the power of sheer invective; prayers and charms work through the strategy of taking an inferior position to the larger inexorable forces.

These variables and the genres yielded by their interaction can be represented visually as in Figure 1.

Curses/Blessings

The major distinction established here in the personal conversational genres is between those which, like boasts, seek to persuade and to control the situation through the simple power of words, and others which, like prayers, attempt to invoke supernatural power for assistance in attaining personal control. This distinction becomes evident through the different uses of the *curse* and its close relative, the *blessing*.

Looked upon from the rhetorical point of view, the curse seems to operate completely in the social realm. And many curses do, in fact, work like taunts, consigning the spoken-to cursed-at to an inferior social position. Such curses as "You're a son-of-a-bitch" or "You're a bastard" obviously arose in a cultural milieu in which legitimate parentage meant a great deal more than it seems to today. These utterances intentionally consigned the cursed-at to a despised social realm, and they preserve some of this force in present usage.

However, most curses do not work in such a direct way. Rather, they invoke the aid of an extrapersonal force to place the cursed-at in the inferior position. The *Standard Dictionary of Folklore, Mythology and Legend* defines *curse* as "A malediction; the wishing of evil upon a person; . . . A curse invokes a power—divine, demonic, or magical—against which the person cursed has no defense, unless he in some manner propitiates the power or brings to bear against it a stronger power" (Leach 1949, 1: 271). The invocation of supernatural power is still found in modern parlance, in such exclamations as "God damn you!" and "Go to hell!" These expressions lost some of their rhetorical force through the celebrated demise of God, or more likely because of their overuse. Consequently, there are curses which fit into both categories of the personal conversational genres. The same is true of blessings.

Even those curses which call upon supernatural forces do so to adjust social alignment. The other genres in this area of the grid—spells, charms, and prayers—enlist the aid of a supernatural power to ensure the well-being of the speaker. Prayers use a different approach than charms and spells; they address the deity as a person and attempt to gin favor through the rhetoric of supplication. *Prayers* are defined as "an address to a higher power (a deity) requesting some boon or guidance" (Leach 1949, 2: 884). This is often simply an appeal for protection, as in the common rhymed couplet:

Now I lay me down to sleep
I pray the Lord my soul to keep;
And if I die before I wake,
I pray the Lord my soul to take.

The *charm* is defined in much the same terms: "An object, rhyme or chant used to perform magic by enlisting the aid of helpful spirits or by discouraging malevolent ones" (Clarke and Clarke 1965: 8). However, the strategy of the charm is different from the supplicatory techniques of the prayer. The charm or *spell* (the two terms can be used interchangeably) speaks directly to the personified force, often in demanding tones:

Rain, rain, go away,
Come again another day.

Or (Fife 1964):

Bees, stop [here]!
Wax go to Sainte-Vierge,
Honey come to me!
Come down, beauties, beauties, beauties.

On the other hand, charms often speak in the name of some deity in order to influence the spirit to whom they are directed. The reference to the deity compounds the magic rather than being the object of the appeal. Here, for instance, is a Manx charm for a toothache (Moore 1891: 98):

Saint Peter was ordained a saint
Standing on a marble stone,
Jesus came to him alone,
And saith unto him, "Peter what makes thee Shake?"
Peter replied, "My Lord and Master it is the toothache."
Jesus said, "Rise up and be healed, and keep these words for my sake,
And thou shalt never more be troubled with toothache."

The idea is that through verbal reenactment the original miracle will be replayed.

Certain charms assume a rhetorical approach very close to that of the prayer. For instance, the Manx charm against the fairies (Moore 1891: 99) is

Peace of God and peace of man,
Peace of God on Columb-Killey,
On each window and each door,
On every hole admitting moonlight,
On the four corners of the house,
And on the place of my rest,
And peace of God on myself.

Their connection with ritualized practices raises the question whether charms or spells are conversational forms of folklore, but they are included here because they involve the same mode of personal address for the same kind of persuasive purpose as proverbs and other members of this group.

Taunts and *boasts* arise in many groups primarily as items in the performance of the verbal contest that in Scottish is called "flyting"—a verse performed between two bards excoriating each other and the clan chiefs with whom they are identified—and is called "scolding" in Scandinavia and "Picong" in much of the West Indies. Nevertheless, both boasts and taunts can be observed in heightened forms of conversation. There is little difference between a boast and a taunt. The *boast* is a series of exaggerations about the powerful capacities of the speaker, intended to place his (or, less often, her) hearers in a subordinate position, usually in terms of strength and endurance. The symbols involved are closely tied to animal masculinity:

I was born in the backwoods, suckled by a bear;
I've got three sets of jawbone teeth and an extra layer of hair.
When I was three I sat in a barrel of knives.
Then a rattlesnake bit me, crawled off and died.
So when I come in here, I'm no stranger,
'Cause when I leave my ass-hole print leaves "danger."

The *taunt*, on the other hand, is directed against the others, impugning the virility of individual onlookers in such phrases as "You lily-livered, yellow-bellied sapsucker."

Taunts are, in a very concrete way, the proverbs of children: traditional devices by which members of this tradition-oriented subgroup take care of their recurrent interpersonal problems by announcing their values and their approved ways of acting. Taunts, like proverbs, point out a problem and propose an avoidance formula by making fun of the errant one. But they do so much more directly than the proverbs of adults, presumably because children cannot be expected to have sufficient control over words to know how to use proverbs in establishing canons of conduct and social relationship. Children obtain license to legislate such matters by talking directly about the problem. For instance, tattlers are placed in temporary social isolation by chanting:

Tattle-tale tit,
Your tongue shall be split,
And all the dogs in town
Shall have a little bit.

A child who bawls excessively is greeted with:

Cry, baby, cry
Stick your finger in your eye
And tell your Ma it wasn't I.

Exclusion/Inclusion

In viewing taunts as regulators of social behavior, especially among children, and as means of establishing a social hierarchy, temporary though it may be, we have been emphasizing traditional techniques for controlling through *exclusion*. Proverbs, curses, taunts, and boasts all attempt to induce future action through the establishment of the speaker as arbiter of values and modes of action. These are the traditional ways of aggressively assuming the mantle of power, although proverbs conceal the aggression involved because of the impersonal language they use. There are also traditional ways of social ordering by principles of *inclusion*: pledges, greetings and partings and other conversational punctuation marks, traditional repartee, jargon, slang, argot, and other special code languages.

These are the traditional ways in which a member of a group proclaims membership and, through this proclamation, demonstrates the group's solidarity. The group may be so exclusive that a plethora of esoteric expression is connected with membership, or it may simply require a demonstration of friendship. Consequently, the forms included here range from the password, which must be repeated at the beginning and ending of each meeting of two or more members, to the simple salutations which are common to everyday parlance.

Traditional greetings range from the formal ("How do you do?" or "Pleased to meet you") to the familiar ("Hi," "What's up?" or "How're you cuttin' it?"). The same is true of partings, ranging from "It's been a pleasure making your acquaintance" to "Later, gator." Each of these is designed to establish a social relationship that will affect future interaction between the speakers. They work through a principle of acceptance by establishing verbal contact. The more intimate the relationship and the greater the community of interest, the less formal these exchanges become. In informal interactions, special in-group expressions emerge. There is a direct relationship between the number of in-group traditions invented and the amount of emotionally charged time spent together, the values and special activities shared, and the felt need to exclude others who do not share these attitudes and activities (Jansen 1959). Consequently, although these forms are primarily used as means of denominating principles of inclusion and community, they may simultaneously operate to exclude if a nonmember is present. Nothing can be more disorienting and frustrating than an expressive demonstration of group solidarity to a nonmember.

There is a direct proportion between these esoteric factors (time, intensity, special activity, out-group exclusion) and the amount of traditional expression observable in the in-group. The development of code languages or special vocabularies makes this relationship especially clear. Occupational groups involved in dangerous work or whose members spend a lot of time together on the job develop an abundance of jargon, most relating to their work activity. Special interest groups like spelunkers, hot-rodders, or science-fiction fans do the same. Groups formed primarily for social purposes develop a body of slang terms related to their social activities; they may compose mottoes, pledges, and proverbs which are brought into the discourse of their meetings. In extreme forms, special vocabularies and languages, such as "Pig Latin," involve such esoteric coding that only those who know the rules governing verbal transformation can understand them.

The esoteric demonstration of community observable in such languages is a dimension of most of the larger, more complex genres of folklore. For instance, the performance of a tale or a ballad, by calling together a group and asking the audience to identify with and approve of the enactment, asks for a ratification of community and shared values. In a more limited way, a proverb such as "Never mind the weather as long as we're together" functions as a demonstration of solidarity in the face of external threat. This motive animates the voicing of many superstitions: they evoke community-approved responses to a threatening external force.

Conversational forms that emphasize community often do so in the face of external threats. While functioning as a normative and integrating influence in the social workings of the in-group, they work aggressively from the point of view of "the others." The taunt, the boast, and even the proverb function in this manner in specific situations. Indeed, only those genres which, like prayer, assume a passive pose do not function aggressively. Some, like the proverb, generally direct the aggressive impulse at other members of the group while casting their advice in impersonal and normative terms. Others, like the taunt, often channel the onslaught onto members of another group and therefore can speak in more personal terms. The axiom at work here seems to be: the more you know someone personally, the more impersonal or stylized your approach must be in arguing traditionally. Finally, such genres as slogans and code languages function aggressively and normatively at the same time but in regard to two different groups of hearers.

A Rhetoric of Conversational Genres

These gnomic and often fixed-phrase genres introduce flexibility into vernacular life. Offering a bit of traditional knowledge certainly involves a bid for attention and the suggestion of a way of handling a potentially disruptive, even dangerous experience. Such items of folklore are employed in many different scenes of daily life. In most cases they are directed at a specific person or a shared difficulty. Through the active employment of these devices, social relationships are maintained without much argument. In cases of high-risk experiences, spirited negotiations ensue. These sayings provide a way of attacking problem situations or seeking spiritual advice. Out of these mundane strips of activity, the sense of the group emerges if and when it is needed. The more time is spent together in what are perceived as high-risk situations, the more such shorthand techniques are employed for sharing the results of past experiences and encouraging an attitude toward and potential resolution of the problem. Of course, the more such in-group terms are employed as part of the learning experience, the more deeply membership in a group is given voice. These devices encourage the formation and maintenance of social and occupational group displays. Studying these genres points out the places at which the members of the group habitually come into conflict and the techniques by which these conflicting factors can be regulated. Such displays establish the code of membership in the group, even while they suggest ways these encounters have been handled in the past. It seems all very natural, almost commonsensical, once sociable motives animate the shared activities of whatever group enjoys a common vernacular vocabulary of responses.

This view of folklore builds upon sociologist Georg Simmel's premise that community is established through a combination of associative and dissociative phenomena. Although conflict does not necessarily further the ideal aims of the group, it is nevertheless an essential element of what he called *sociation* and we term social interaction. "If every interaction among men is a sociation, conflict—after all one of the most vivid interactions, which, furthermore cannot possibly be carried on by one individual alone—must certainly be considered as association. . . . Conflict is . . . designed to resolve divergent dualisms; it is a way of achieving some kind of unity, even if it be through the annihilation of one of the conflicting parties" (Simmel 1955: 13). Folklore represents the traditional means by which all kinds of associations are manifested and manipulated, those founded upon ego-based conflict and those arising out of sympathy.

In this overview of the small genres, the most pervasive of the traditional forms, we have examined the traditional elements of the rhetoric of everyday discourse. This topic deserves a great deal more observation and analysis from folklorists. Studies by sociologists and sociolinguists have shown that there is a traditional structure to conversations, or at least such a strict limitation of vocabulary and syntax that items of conversation are highly predictable. This predictability has been identified as an element of esoteric group identification: "the [restricted and traditional] code will develop wherever the form of the social relation is based upon some extensive set of closely shared identifications, self-consciously held by the members" (Bernstein 1964: 61).

We have not investigated the occurrence or the invention of these in-group expressive phenomena. We know little about the functioning of special languages in specific groups. It is clear from casual observation, however, that in-groups such as gangs, clubs, secret societies, and occupational units under severe stress, folklore develops as an esoteric statement of group solidarity and reflects the common aims and practices of the group and its shared ideals. The amount of apartness felt by the group and the amount of anxiety under which it exists is reflected in the amount of traditional expressions developed and the intensity of the life of such items. Even our concept of the family may ultimately have to be described in terms of the shared expressions which arise out of family stories, sayings, recipes, nicknames, and the things that are greeted with the greatest laughter when recounted.

Chapter 3
Genres

The eminent literary critic Northrop Frye provides a comfortable definition of *genre*, employing it in pursuing a generic criticism: "The purpose of criticism by genres is not so much to classify as to clarify . . . traditions and affinities, thereby bringing out a large number of literary relationships that would not be noticed as long as there were no context established for them." Frye points to the operational basis of this critical approach when he notes that "generic criticism . . . is rhetorical, in the sense that the genre is determined by the conditions established between the poet and his public" (Frye 1957: 247–48). Genre labeling assists the reader in relating different texts which might not, in the old New Critical regime, appear to be of the same type. By drawing on definitions of words as providing a force-field to organize possible meanings, genres give *names* to traditional attitudes and strategies, as they provide *frames* by which the interpretive process is begun.

Framing is achieved by setting up boundaries within which performances, celebrations, rituals, and ceremonies take place. Frames, like quotation marks, call attention to themselves and are thus, in the fashion of the times and in line with the work of Gregory Bateson, seen to operate as metacommentary on the activity taking place within the frame (Bateson 1958). Indeed, the activity continually refers to its frame—a condition of reinforcement more readily understood, perhaps, when a threat to break the frame arises. This argument may seem tightly circular, but concrete descriptions of framing appeal to such common experiences that the players themselves seem to refer to common-sense understandings. The concept of framing suggests a space and a time apart from the everyday. Within these felt boundaries, the licensed activity itself provides constant reminders of the conventions which commonly operate within the frame—formulas of behavior and agreed-upon rules to encourage staying within these bounds. In actual usage, the entrance into the framed world is cued through commonplace gestures, but there is no felt necessity to call attention to where, temporally or spatially, the framing ends.

Form, the most frequently used word in the textual explications offered by the New Criticism, focused on the ways in which poems, plays, novels, or epics achieved a sense of complex coherence. Classic texts speak directly to the reader through technical control and imaginative accessibility. By contrast, *genre* suggests that the experience of literature and other artistic media arises from the set of associations which can be drawn upon both by writers, as they compose, and by readers, as they read in an anticipatory fashion—that is, with a recognition of where this kind of fiction generally takes us.

As the concept of *genre* came into more common critical usage in the early 1970s, the contextual features of the reading experience began to be formally drawn upon within critical description and assessment. Biographical details and historical settings were reincorporated in the analysis of the production of texts. The exegete turned cultural critic explored the effects of enslavement, colonial status, and political and economic disfranchisement on textual production. New terms describing these positionings grew organically from the changing orientation toward texts, especially in the face of racial-ethnic and gay pride movements. The very idea of a national literature came under attack, as did the formal terms of artistic training. Critiques of the canon led not only to the inclusion of works presenting the voices and viewpoints of people from submerged and excluded groups but also to the expansion of its genres, with the addition of a wider variety of artifacts and reproductions, eroding distinctions between literature and other mediated publication forms.

Genre came to refer not only to the pattern of formal expectations brought in common by writer and reader but also to a set of social and psychological predispositions performers utilize in order to communicate with and affect the audience. Generic labeling by both productive and receptive members of a performance community fills in the contextual features that allow a nuanced social reading of many kinds of cultural production. Genre, then, suggests patterns of expectation which both artist and audience carry into the social and political, as well as aesthetic, transaction. In some accounts, the artist found him- or herself painted into the corner of a system of exploitations that did little for the reputation of, say, poets or poetry. Questions that follow from the old query "Cui bono?" were raised, not always without anger.

The emphasis on conventions and cues that allow the observer to recognize the forms being used is the very characteristic of genre criticism to which the literary critic often reacts negatively. To stress the conventions of a genre in *belles lettres* is to devalue, to some degree, the originality of the art object which the critic is analyzing in terms of its uniqueness. Consequently, there has been little informed commentary concerning the generative literary understandings the author brings to the creative experience and the means by which he or she elicits the same series of expectations on the part of the reading audience.

Ethnographers of communication and folklorists more readily recognized the conventional dimensions of the face-to-face performance (Ben-Amos 1976). If a tale, riddle, proverb, debate, or sermon does not provide adequate cues to this conventionality, the traditional performer will be misunderstood by the audience. Just as the singer of tales must present an item that conforms to a recognizable and accepted type, so he or she must enact it in a manner such that every part of the performance is consonant with the range of expectations for that genre. Training and close listening have made the generic markers evident for everyone involved in the transaction. They name and frame the performance with conventional devices that remind everyone of the genre being put into play.

Students of expressive culture have found their way to generic criticism by a variety of routes. The path usually taken by ethnographic reporters is to investigate what generic typological distinctions are made by the members of a specifiable community in action. Ethnographers working in Africa did exemplary studies along these lines (Herskovits and Herskovits 1958; Arnett 1957; Blacking 1961). Such analysis provides insights into the ways in which members of the group organize themselves for social and rhetorical purposes and how the social and aesthetic organizations reinforce each other, treating generic classifications as used by the group as one aspect of its culture.

This approach is of limited use to the investigator who wishes to compare cultures, whether traditional performances or those produced for reading, listening, or viewing. Comparativists trained in the philological and hermeneutic method were primarily concerned with the analysis of items which appear in the repertoire of different groups. For generic criticism to be useful, it became necessary to survey expressive types found in a great many groups in which the same items recur. Here the scholar's inability to get to the center of the discourse system of those creating in other languages led to the imposition of a generic typology that does not necessarily map very nicely onto the cultural artifacts and practices of others. Without appropriate ethnographic analysis, the reader of texts is affected by the cultural apparatus carried by the critic, not that of the group whose expressive system is the ostensible subject of analysis.

Genre criticism expands the analysis of the conventional elements of form, content, and use, whether within one community or across cultures, by providing a common frame of reference through which such conventions may be compared. It also permits one genre or group of genres to cast light on others, within one group or cross-culturally.

If terms for folklore types are to be useful, each genre must be described as a member of a class of related items and yet distinguished from the other members of the class in specific and discernible ways. In other words, one should be able not only to point to a class of expressions like proverbs and riddles but also to demonstrate how they differ from each other: for example, how games differ from rituals and myths from *Märchen* (fairy tales). We can establish a meaningful basis of comparison between the genres by making each genre a member of a class of objects or practices.

Experience collecting in the field and sharing findings with other folklore collectors made the older comparativist mode of proceeding insupportable. Yet introducing new strategies of description and analysis produced a kind of headiness, when presented in commonsense terms. Other scholars too often responded: "Of course, that's the way we should have been studying other peoples and their cultures all along."

Taxonomies

Criticism that emerged from the study of artistic representations developed descriptive categories from the neoclassical hierarchy of literary forms, which are far removed from vernacular categories. Using a taxonomy of forms drawn from a common language shared by various peoples, a *koine* such as Greek or Latin, literary folklorists conceived of their project as international and even universal. When collecting resumed after World War II, fieldworkers had the opportunity to talk with the bearers of tradition to discover just how they classified their expressive culture. Because collectors were, as often as not, themselves musicians seeking to add to their own personal repertories, they took to calling their discoveries by the names used by the folk. Songcatchers discovered that their collecting was facilitated by adverting to the folk terms, for singers and storytellers used their own categories as part of their way of remembering. As often as not, their categories referred not only to formal unities but to the social relations under which the songs and stories were performed.

Learning to translate between the technical taxonomies and vernacular terminology provided folklorists with a new place in the world. Every time the right term was used in print or on the festival stage, it drew attention to the experience and expertise of the collector. Audiences became aware of the friendly relations between folklorists and traditional performers and craft workers. The most beautiful of these discoveries also became remarkable illustrations of the principle of goodwill, which folklorists had been able to draw upon in so many unexpected ways.

The collecting experience suggested a new kind of comparative technique. Not only might songs and stories be studied in terms of their formal unities, but the ways in which they were used in actual social practices might be scrutinized. Looking at old-timey talk, music, and dance with regard to the relationships between the performer and listener and the places where the performance regularly occurred raised the possibility of using the models of structural analysis to examine performance *contexts* or situations.

This approach was a practical matter for those folklorists who were also teachers and felt the need to organize the materials of tradition for classroom presentation. The combination of macro- and microbehavioral analyses was borrowed wholesale from symbolic interactionists in sociology as well as ethnographers of performance in cultural analysis. The synergy of the many disciplines coming together to analyze real-life situations through vernacular terms profoundly affected the way culture itself was taught in these allied fields. This convergence called past analytic practices into question.

In the lively political climate of the 1960s and early 1970s, the old way of doing comparative analysis came to be identified with nationalism and empire-building. The new perspectives on vernacular customs and performances gave ethnographers a way of bringing together their professional practices with the politics of social concern. The larger performance forms might now be made a part of a systematic presentation that included the smaller vernacular forms of expression as well. All of folklore might be systematically presented in terms of the forms and situated uses of items of tradition. Epics or lyrics could be put together with proverbs or slanging contests. The textbooks that emerged from this excited environment stressed contexts. Barre Toelken entitled his overview *The Dynamics of Folklore* (1979); Eliot Oring called his *Folk Groups and Folklore Genres* (1986). Even a text-centered work, such as Jan Harold Brunvand's *The Study of American Folklore* (1968), used the organization of the field suggested by the range of forms ordered from the smallest to the greatest.

Teachers required their students to collect the smaller folklore genres themselves. Everyone was encouraged to view themselves as members of one or many folk communities. Gathering living traditions liberated the idea of folklore from its mooring in moldy, antiquated forms, even while it continued to celebrate the amazing resilience of vernacular cultures of all sorts. That these claims were essentially patronizing to those among whom we lived and worked was not yet clear to us. Students' encounter with new dimensions of customary practice was, and still is, sufficiently energizing that the problem of dominion didn't demand consideration. It was comforting to trumpet egalitarian virtue through carrying out field collecting, organizing the material in a local archive, and making it available to teachers, other students, and the general public.

With the ignominious end of the American military adventure in Southeast Asia and the impeachment of President Nixon, we became keenly aware of the failures in our system of government, its complicity with dictators elsewhere, and the baneful effects of the American Empire on people around the world. The New Ethnography, so called because it used technological devices to make ethnographic reportage thicker and richer, revealed the degree of complicity all fieldworkers would have to admit with regard to questions of patronage. Ethical issues were repeatedly aired at national and international meetings. Fieldworkers were called to account for their covert, and usually unreflexive, practices.

When previously subordinated peoples take us up on our democratic promises, the oppressor is easily embarrassed. More often than not, the result is not real reform, but a lot of hedging on the part of the former victims and their victimizers. Between that diffuse sense of guilt for arrogant stupidity and the admitted complicity of a few professional ethnographers in providing intelligence under secret government sponsorship in Southeast Asia and Latin America, ethnographic reporters were brought to their knees. However, ethnographers continued to publish their reports in the name of area studies, now enriched with the knowledge that they were writing for the restricted audience of others professionally interested in a specific part of the so-called developing world.

Folklorists were, in the main, able to shun or shed these feelings by giving credit to tradition-bearers and writing in coauthorship with informants, who were renamed "collaborators" (to the horror of those who had lived through the Nazi occupation of Europe). Folklore collectors who were active in the folk festival movement could claim exoneration because they brought fame and small but significant fortune to these performers.

The end-of-the-millennium malaise afflicted professional practices of all sorts. More important, the self-realization arising from such reflexive considerations called into question the scientific character and usefulness of cultural reportage. Work that had been regarded as part of a grand plan of cultural integration was now translated into evidence of naïve complicity in schemes of political domination and economic exploitation. What had been evidence of liberation was regarded in terms of victimization. From this moralistic cul-de-sac, it has been difficult to conceive of our work as socially useful. When gender and color were added to the discussion of agency and dominion, new kinds of moral claims might be made by those claiming an inheritance of victimization. The only way out of the maze seemed to be to build new models of social and cultural analysis which would take such matters into account. In the vernacular, this moral cleansing came to be called political correctness.

Yet, for over a decade, the promises inhering in communication based on goodwill yielded new ways of conceiving how culture operates. The very existence of culture was addressed as if it were systematic and arrived at by mutual consent. No longer just a congeries of institutions, culture engaged its participants on a moment-to-moment basis, teaching along the way what you should expect if you hang around with these people. The achievement of thinking in terms of whole cultural systems on the ground level has been maintained even through subsequent periods of self-castigation. Not that the sense of mutuality can be acknowledged openly; we have learned to maintain our ironic perspective.

Out of this moment of professional self-approval, the range of our vernacular expression seemed describable in consensus terms that leaned toward vernacular names for most expressive genres. Definitions could be approached in terms of contrastive features, including those that describe performer-audience relationships.

The *Folk* and Folklore Types

Folklore emerged in the nineteenth century as the collective term for traditional items of knowledge which were available to represent the spirit of a place and a people. Born of Romantic nationalism, the folk and their lore were used to represent the most antique ways to be found within the boundaries of a newly constructed polity (Abrahams 1993b). Folklore, as a concept term, gave gravity to old-fashioned ways, in contrast to modern contrivances. An epiphenomenon of the creation of modern metropolises, folklore was whatever was remembered from before the incursions of the printing press, assembly-line production, and the mechanical reproduction of cultural material. The collection and study of folklore was valued for what seemed to be preserved from that time when there was no nation, only a people who managed for themselves. Or, perhaps, the *folk* was the people as imagined in retrospect by the nation. Folklore was a collective term for all that was practiced among people tied to the land and speaking the local vernacular tongue. Collecting these relics of past practices and performances kept open the possibility of conserving the best of the past in the face of industrialization and commodification. This stuff was authentic, because it was closer to the temporal point of origin of the people and the landscape; it was also more natural and organic, less imposed and mediated, more vibrant (see Hymes 1975b). Folklore items were not subject to canons of reason, but the result of shared experiences and the values of endurance. For most of the public, in fact, this is what the term folklore continues to mean.

Folklore is treated as real because these remnants continue to carry a penumbra of pastness. They are, as Susan Stewart calls them, "evidence of distress." Each ballad or fairy tale bears signs of antiquity, even if it was written recently, by borrowing the marks of age from its genre. Speaking of the late seventeenth and early eighteenth centuries when folklore was "discovered," Stewart characterizes these "new imitations" of older forms as attempts "to bypass the contingencies of time." Catching the paradox of such imitations, she points to a "deepening historical awareness of the classical world . . . supplemented by a rising archaeology that demonstrated both the reappearance and disappearance of the past" (Stewart 1994: 67; see also Stewart 1991). With the historicizing of the discipline, folklorists acknowledge that they and other collectors rationalize their collections by invoking the "saved from the fire" story.

In the 1960s, as folklorists found it possible to get into the field more easily and more often, we found that these old songs, stories, and sayings were still a part of everyday vernacular existence for some country people in outlying districts throughout North America. While they were seldom called by the names used by folklorists, these old-timey forms of expression could be gathered in situ. Even stranger was coming to know that these tradition-bearers regarded the songs and stories, quilt patterns and herbal remedies as cultural resources kept alive because of veneration for their ancestral ways of life. Songs and rhymes were given material representation as they were written down and passed between friends and lovers as keepsakes or forget-me-nots.

Folklorists had already developed taxonomic distinctions by which they could organize and archive collectanea. In line with other antiquarian enterprises, the principles of organizing these materials were given scientific names in obscure languages. New names for old forms were developed for the purpose of controlled comparisons, conducted with the philological and archaeological hope that, through study, their geographic and linguistic origins would be recovered and the science of folklore would provide a key for understanding what was then called "the history of the race."

As folklore is made up of strips of interactions which may be stylistically separated from other realms of experience, the lifeblood of tradition is located in folklore's lack of novelty. It consists of items and objects which are phrased in memorable, and therefore repeatable, formulations. Folklore is subject to being recalled, replayed, and deployed in ever-renewable fashion. Identified through the process of invention, nevertheless folklore is collected, organized, and made into texts or some other kind of alienable object. This project is what folklorists do, and have always done since their self-invention. These cultural productions show their age, even when they were composed by individuals within collective memory. Waifs and strays, orts and shards just barely recovered from oblivion, they are trophies of time, the marks of cultural resilience carrying enduring values.

The concept of folklore is unthinkable without those compositions, for they are the channels of wisdom and entertainment. Yet folklore must be enacted, as it exists nowhere outside of a performance. For folklore to work effectively in performance, there must be a consonance between the situation that has arisen, the item that comes to mind, and the enactment. Competent performers recognize the situation as it arises, know the appropriate traditions, and have the ability to give voice and body to the replay. Such concerns are both constraining and liberating. The performer must pick an item that explores an appropriate theme, calls for the proper level of diction, and has a pertinent message. The item's internal characteristics must also make an appropriate, judicious, and economical comment on the situation.

Folklore performance may appear to impose delicate and difficult demands on the speaker, but in practice this is not the case. The group's conventions associate certain sets of problems with specific sets of expressive forms. In fact, the situation often calls for a particular performance, since such enactments encapsulate a problem and propose a solution. This almost reflexive response is apparent in the operations of devices like proverbs and superstitions. These short traditional statements emerge when a dilemma has come to notice and a conventional solution occurs to someone that at least deserves mention. Wise sayings, old saws, or tried and true remedies are recalled. Obviously, the vernacular provides names for these common conditions, and that commonplace phrasing suggests that the problem is not unique and there are courses of practice that have proven useful in the past. Of course, these sayings are couched in a form which suggests that the solution is as old as the hills.

The appropriateness of a given genre to a particular situation is most evident in thematic content. The subject of a proverb, superstition, or exemplary story will be judged to be pertinent or irrelevant to the problem at hand. For instance, proverbs and taunts are both overtly ethical in theme, and they address recurrent problems of interpersonal behavior with similarly economical means of persuasion. However, they differ considerably in the diction they utilize. Taunts are quite direct in their approach, commonly employing the pronouns *you* and *I* and other words of personal reference. Proverbs are more constrained because of the appeal to what our grandmothers or revered historical figures said. The openly aggressive content of the taunt makes it inappropriate ("untactful," we say) for most of the recurrent social or moral problems addressed by a saying.

Proverbs and moral tales such as fables both attack recurrent interpersonal problems, often confronting a conflict between individual needs and social necessities. Which genre is chosen depends on the situation and the relationships among speaker and listeners. What calls for an old saw in one situation may call for a parable if the situation admits a more lengthy case in point. Fables are recounted if the speaker is willing to take on the role and teacher and can presume the consent of listeners. The brevity of proverbs is part of their utility. In such discourse systems, fables are reserved primarily for the use of older people talking to younger ones.

In most proverbs, the descriptive terms in which this indirect talk is couched are commonly put to the service of clarity—that is, there is a sense of appropriate fit between the present talk and the trope involved in the saying. In riddles, the rhetorical effect is quite the opposite, for the aim of the riddler is to produce confusion and then to feel clever in producing the answer. The proverb is appropriate to situations calling for clarification of the problem, whereas riddles are more useful in contest situations which license interpersonal aggression. These are just two of the many fixed-phrase forms available to spice a good talk or deliver a message from on high.

The dimension of structuring most important to add to the discussion of genres is that revealed in the context, usually a social situation, in which a saying of one sort or another pops up. The *structure of context* directs us to the ways in which situational factors enter into the choice to offer a saying, an example, or some other indirect way of making a conversational point and giving it an edge. This structuring asks that we recognize the most important features of the relationships among those engaged in the talk, especially when the saying invokes archaic language.

A Spectrum of Genres

The *structure of context* provides a frame of reference for the comparative examination of traditional genres. There is a significant difference in form and technique between proverbs and fairy tales (*Märchen*). The greatest difference, beyond the obvious size of the forms, resides in the distinctive relationship between the proverb-sayer or the storyteller and their respective audiences. The proverb generally arises in casual conversation to make a point about the specific situation being discussed. The proverb-sayer appeals, directly or by analogy, to an approved course of action which has been effective in the past. He or she does so in order to solve an immediate problem and to influence future attitudes or actions. The tale-teller, on the other hand, calls into play verbal and instructive techniques and a dimension of aesthetic pleasure which is absent from the conversational situation of the proverb. The performance tends toward highly stylized words and actions requiring a distinct time and place, in which the performer can create an imaginary world with the approval and, indeed, encouragement of an audience. To be sure, the performer, like the proverb-sayer, is trying to persuade the audience, but this strategy aims at a less immediate effect. The narrative involves a psychic separation of performer and audience not observable in the use of proverbs.

The performance techniques of the proverb and the folktale do not exhaust the array of possible relationships between speaker and listeners. In fact, the range of performer-audience relationships runs from the personal interaction of conversation to the complete removal of performer from audience, for example, in the presentation of such objects of art as folk paintings. Between the poles of close involvement and absolute distance are four discernible segments of a spectrum into which folklore genres tend to group themselves in terms of describable traits of performance: *conversational* genres; *play* genres; *fictive* genres; and *static* genres. The progress from the more interpersonal to the more removed involves a passage from the smaller and more intimate forms invoked as part of direct and spontaneous discourse to the larger

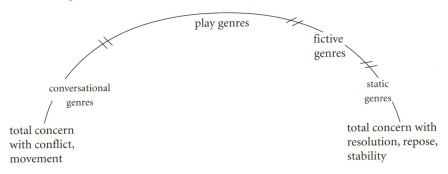

Figure 2. Range of levels of conflict in genres.

and more symbolic genres, which rely upon a profound sense of psychic distance between performer and audience. The shorter forms employ direct strategies that rely on the intensity, color, and concision of manipulated materials to convince listeners. Although all folklore calls for a sympathetic relation between formal object or item of folklore and the audience, the longer genres increasingly draw upon vicarious, rather than immediate, involvement to induce the sympathetic response.

Conversational Genres

In the conversational genres, one person directs his or her expression to a limited number of others as part of everyday discourse. The speaker does not need to assume any particular character role to make his or her point. The speaker is, rather, engaged in a spontaneous communicative relationship in which opportunities to introduce traditional devices of persuasion commonly arise. Nearly everyone in a group avails him- or herself of these forms, even if only in the clichéd and commonplace expressions of personal interaction.

Two groups of genres are conversational. The first includes the smallest elements of patterned expression common to a group: for example, local procedures for naming people, places, herbs and flowers, birds; jargon, slang, colloquialisms, and esoteric languages; and means for intensifying and hyperbolizing description. All of these devices are used in a conversational context to flavor speech. Genres such as colloquialisms and naming practices are special in-group vocabularies which serve to demarcate group membership. The intensifiers function adjectivally and are often called proverbial because they involve conventional extended units of composition. However, unlike proverbs, they lack an independent line of reasoning and contribute to the strategy of a larger argument. This group includes traditional similes ("as green as grass" and "as slow as molasses in January running uphill sideways") as well as comparisons ("like a bat out of hell" and "as good as gold"). Others, more complex in construction ("she's so ugly she'd stop a watch" or "he's so dumb he wouldn't know how to pour piss out of his boot if it had the instructions printed on the heel"), call attention to the speaker's wit.

The second group of conversational genres comprises formal conventions of the discourses of address, appeal, and assault, and includes proverbs, superstitions, mnemonics, spells, curses, prayers, taunts, and charms. Charms and taunts are a special kind of discourse based on the model of conversational back-and-forth and utilizing the same kind of persuasive devices. Although speakers need not assume a mask or role to make such an utterance, the occasion is more specialized and approaches the genres in the play segment of the spectrum. This play of wit is even more apparent in the use of a common type of patterned conversation one might term repartee of the "See you later, alligator! After 'while, crocodile!" sort. It is performed within conversation, but its prepatterned verbal exchange is akin to folk drama. Still closer to such play forms are longer repartee routines, for example: "That's tough. What's tough? Life. What's life? A magazine. Where do you get it? Down at the corner. How much? A dime. Only got a nickel. That's tough. What's tough?"

Play Genres

Traditional repartee resembles the simplest of the play genres, such as riddles or tag, for they too develop from the back-and-forth movement of interpersonal communication. Yet riddling occurs most commonly in a riddling session, a special occasion for performance somewhat removed from casual conversation in which an implicit set of rules and boundaries operates. Furthermore, the riddling occasion calls for a donning of roles as riddler and riddlee which are discrete—that is, they can be distinguished from one another because of the contest situation and the relative place each player takes at a specific time.

In this play world the spirit of license reigns, allowing for a playing out of motives we don't allow ourselves to express under ordinary circumstances. Any place may become the arena for playing, and any time the occasion, but in the more elaborate play genres the times and places are often as traditional as the pieces performed in them. Game-playing may arise anyplace, for instance, but the more complex play activities need a bounded field, stage, or consecrated place to supplement the rules and conventions of playing.

As with the conversational genres, the play genres divide themselves into more interactive and more elaborately removed groupings, but here three groups may be discerned. The first has less psychic distance and less role-playing than the others, and the genres found in it tend to occur more frequently and spontaneously. Types in the second and third categories tend to be more formal in presentation than the other play genres and thus demand more advance preparation. Included in the first group are riddles and joke sessions and other traditional verbal contests, nonprogrammatic folk dances, and most games. In the second are spectator sports and traditional debates and contests, such as spelling bees. The third includes rituals, folk plays, and those games

I	Less psychic distance among players, less role-playing
	riddles, jokes; games; nonprogrammatic folk dances
II	More formalized and less spontaneous, but still open-ended
	debates and spelling bees
	spectator sports
III	Progression of movement or narrative toward predetermined
	resolution
	rituals
	folk plays, folk dances with story lines

Figure 3. Play genres organized in terms of relationships among participants.

and dances that have a set progression of movement or a story and traditional role-playing.

The first group shares certain attributes of the conversational genres: emphasis on the back-and-forth movement of conversation, a near-identification of role and performer, and a fairly simple set of rules, boundaries, and conventions to control the course of play. Yet the total pattern of play in a riddle session or a game of tag is predetermined, even though the direction the play will take is not. This quality of dramatic confrontation without a predetermined resolution characterizes all of the genres in the first two groups of play forms.

In the more interactive genres of Play I, the players are each other's audience, and the activity provides little interest for spectators. Each person is potentially a participant. In the second group of play genres, there is a distinction between players and audience. This distancing movement is carried further in the third group, where the separation between actors and spectators is complete. In Play II, interaction is still viewed as interpersonal, but in Play III the personal element is sacrificed to the ensemble effect of the role playing, and the audience focuses primarily on the symbolic motives being reenacted. In the more interactive play forms, what removal there is seems spontaneous and temporary. The feeling of spontaneity diminishes in Play II genres with the addition of spectators, and Play III is characterized by a high degree of formality and conventionality. In the last set of genres, there is a greater feeling of artificial dramatic involvement, emphasizing that the resolution of the conflict is predetermined.

The distinction between games like tag in Play I and spectator sports in Play II involves more than the removal resulting from the introduction of an audience. In the Play I genres there are commonly only two discrete roles, like pursuer and pursued in "Hare and Hounds" and "Cops and Robbers," or riddler and riddlee. When spectators take a place in the structure of context, the spectators need a representative to guarantee that rules are observed and boundaries are maintained. In Play II, someone on the stage or field (master of ceremonies, timekeeper) begins and ends the proceedings, while others in the crew enforce the rules (referee, umpire, scorekeeper, judge). As the sense of removal felt by the audience increases, the more enforcers are needed to keep both players and spectators in line in and off the field.

In Play III genres, at least one more discrete role is introduced. It is convenient to view the change as a bifurcation of the representative figure and his role in Play II into one figure who introduces and ends the proceedings by direct address to the audience and another figure who serves to further or continue the action (blocking character, resuscitator, mediator). In the more active genres of Play III, such as folk drama, contact between performers and audience is almost completely severed by engineering both physical and psychic distance. Identification with the conflict occurs vicariously, rather than through the participation that occurs in games. In a game like "Hide and Seek" the actors direct their performances to one another, but in the folk play they coordinate their actions for an ensemble effect which is directed to the spectators viewing from a removed position. The actor may identify with his or her role and derive ego gain from the performance, but must still channel his or her energies primarily into the total effect of the piece in order for the play to work. The vicarious sympathetic involvement of the audience is an integral part of the technique of all genres on the side of the spectrum consisting of Play III and the fictive and static genres, dictating the organization and affecting the strategies of all items in these genres.

Fictive Genres

The fictive genres include myths, legends, fables, parables, fairy tales, and even examples (as in "for example, take the case of . . ."). These kinds of stories have received more notice and been subject to more theorizing than any other forms of folklore. With the further removal of speaker from spoken-to; all movements and motives are depicted fictively, through suggestive description in words and gestures. In the static genres, the performer is completely removed from the performance after the object is made; he or she has made something which becomes independent of himself or herself.

Genres and Relationships

Elaboration of the genre continuum provides an overview of traditional expressions in terms of the range of performer-audience relationships. This spectrum also casts light on another aspect of traditional aesthetic technique; the dramatic focus changes as we move along the continuum.

Genres are sets of performance pieces that performers employ to move the audience. This effect is brought about through the audience members' sympathetic involvement with the construction of the piece. Each item attempts to influence future action by appealing to past usage, but items differ in their connection with the past. Some performers choose items that highlight immediate consequences. Other performers take a longer view, searching the repertoire for illustrative anecdotes that cast light on the present and affect actions indirectly, by influencing attitudes. Conversational forms emphasize the potential immediately inherent in the present situation, but as forms grow longer the strategy of persuasion calls more for reenactments or descriptions of action already completed.

In all genres, a strategic articulation of conflict is intended to move the audience sympathetically with the movement of the item. But not all genres emphasize conflict and resolution equally. The balance between the conflict, with its emphasis on climax, and the resolution, with its emphasis on reconciliation, varies systematically. In fact, as one moves along the continuum from the pole of interpersonal involvement to that of complete removal between performers and audience, the embodiment of movement becomes progressively formal and performer-oriented, more reliant upon symbols, imagination, and the vicarious involvement of the audience. Moreover, the emphasis shifts progressively from the articulation of the conflict toward the embodiment of a dramatic resolution. Shorter genres focus on conflict, while the fictive and static genres focus on resolution. Play III and fictive forms have a dramatic structure—that is, they project dramatic conflict and resolution. This model is not available to the conversational or static genres, although for opposite reasons; the first makes no allowance for removal, and the second has no room for identification.

The conversational genres underline and intensify the conflict inherent in the recurrent situation they address. But we see no actual resolution, only an implied or proposed one. Conversational genres attempt to promote an action rather than specifically to produce it. In riddling and other interactive play genres, too, conflict is stressed more than resolution. In these activities, each component item is built on a miniature dramatic model, and only small resolutions occur within the totality of the movement. For instance, each time a person is touched in "tag" or each time a riddle answer is given, there is a resolution of the immediately preceding conflict, but the activity continues as the players switch places. These are serial conflicts without any sense of final and total resolution. Just as there is no winner in a game of tag, riddle contests do not end with a declaration of the best riddler. The central role of performer is passed around, like the "it" role in tag.

The more removed kinds of play activities place greater emphasis on resolution. Rituals have more dramatic structure than festivals, and folk plays offer more resolution than do folk dances. When narrative movement is introduced, the outcome of the story becomes as important as the original conflict situation in the strategy of the piece. Traditional stories are generally so well known to the audience and so stereotyped in construction that the resolution is foreshadowed from the beginning. This drift continues into the fictive genres. Lyrics, laments, and celebratory pieces are relatively static enactments in which the story behind the piece is either presented as having happened in the past or taken for granted by the performer or artist. Action is stopped in favor of a consideration of the emotional situation; the scene is generally depicted as occurring after action is completed. The audience's prior knowledge accounts for the strong retrospective and allusive feeling of such genres. The static genres present us with a fait accompli, an embodied resolution whose dramatic conflicts we must imagine and reconstruct. As we move along this segment of the continuum, we become more concerned with the design of the items and less concerned with the situations they are articulating. This focus on style and design commonly produces a feeling of potential repose, perhaps arising from the audience's greater sense of removal from the depiction.

The strategies of all these genres are directed toward influencing future action through the appeal to past usage. The conversational genres make a direct appeal, calling for an attitude that leads to action in the near future. The play genres shift rhetorical emphasis from future action to present reenactment. There is a sense of immediacy in a game of "Hide and Seek" or even in a hero-combat play like "The Moors and the Christians." To be sure, charter for play comes from past practice and establishes continuing patterns, but the effectiveness of the activity relies upon its here-and-now quality. Fictive and static genres are presented by describing or referring to actions that have taken place in the past. A myth begins with the formulaic "In the beginning . . . ," while a *Märchen* begins "Once upon a time" or "a very long time ago . . ." Nevertheless, by narrating actions, these genres work within a set of temporal references that remind the audience just what kind of fictional world is being depicted.

This change of focus and rhetorical technique is observable in different types of fictional narratives. Most fairy tales recount wondrous actions and startling transformations: Stupid Jack wins the money and the king's daughter; the scullery maid becomes the princess and defeats the forces of her wicked stepmother. Legends that explain how local phenomena came into being often echo the special feelings attached to that place. For example, "La Llorona" (The Weeping Woman) is told widely in Spanish-speaking communities in North America (Lomax Hawes 1968). The story usually begins with a description of the ghastly sounds and spectral appearance of a woman who, it is then explained, murdered her children or killed them through her neglect or absence and must search for them eternally. Although we are presented with both a conflict and a resolution, the ending is emphasized because we begin and end at the same place, dramatically speaking; the resolution is permanently indeterminate.

Strategies

Such shifts of narrative orientation clarify the relations among the techniques and strategies of different genres and genre groups, which is reason enough for constructing a hypothetical arrangement. However, this spectrum is not so much a typological formulation as an arbitrary frame of reference that may help the investigator understand the range of techniques used in traditional expression. It should permit fuller understanding of what diverse cultures share and in what ways they are unique. The ethnographer might discover that the groups with which he is most concerned favor one group of genres over another, or gravitates toward one segment of the spectrum.

In my own fieldwork, I have found a strong attraction (*tropism*) on the part of African American groups toward play genres. In these cultures, both conversational and fictive genres gravitate toward the center of the spectrum, toward formulaic exchanges such as pleasantries or toward traditional verbal contests such as "playing the dozens" among adolescents. Folktales and songs are performed with the expectation that the audience will become so totally involved that they make audible comments and exclamations to which the performers react. In some West Indian storytelling communities, members of the audience not only sing with the narrator in a *cante-fable* performance but also take the part of one of the characters in scenes with dialogue. In contrast to this tropism in Afro-American groups, white groups of rural plain folk commonly remove the performer from the audience while singing, playing, or telling a story (Abrahams 1966, 1967, 1968b).

This approach to the range of immediacy or distance in expressive forms begins to account for the ambivalence folklorists express toward forms which are commonly written. Among these peripheral folklore genres are such expressions as autograph-album rhymes, "latrinalia" and graffiti, chain letters, epitaphs, inscriptions and warnings, and epigrammatic printed signs such as those found in barrooms and restaurants. All of these are commonly found in recorded form; yet they are transmitted in essentially the same way other folklore genres are, carried in the memory of tradition-bearers and written down on the proper occasions. Since the performer becomes removed from his or her performance after the writing is done, these might be seen as static genres. In the process of removal they reinstitute an interpersonal approach, speaking to each member of the audience individually by using the first-person point of view. This address becomes especially evident in epitaphs:

Remember me as you pass by;
As you are now so once was I.

As I am now, so you must be,
Therefore prepare to follow me.

Similarly, in autograph-album rhymes each inscription is ostensibly directed toward the owner of the album, though it will obviously be read by others.

Other expressive genres with many traditional elements could also be usefully placed on this spectrum, but no one would want to designate them as folklore. The performer-audience continuum forms part of a larger spectrum in which all genres of expression, traditional or otherwise, could be placed. The difference between folklore and other expressive phenomena lies in the range of relations possible in performance. Essentially, we distinguish between folklore and *popular culture* on the basis of dissemination methods; folklore exists only in face-to-face encounters that lead to oral transmission. This distinction is even sharper between folklore and high art or *belles lettres*. These genres do not differ greatly in expressive capacity, in art, or even in the presence of traditional elements of composition. Setting folklore genres within the larger spectrum of aesthetic forms and rhetorical strategies reveals both its commonalities with other modes of expressive culture and its special defining features.

Chapter 4
Stories

A good part of our conversational life is given over to telling stories. Much of the vigor we find in the vernacular occurs because the words are animated by the process of the story emerging in everyday encounters (see Goffman 1963; Labov and Waletsky 1967; Ochs and Capps 1996). When we happen onto a scene, we often ask, "What's the story?" But only once in a while does the encounter make a good story—at least, good enough to retell. Even then, we are greeting with skepticism: "This had better be a good one for me to waste my time listening." So much for the goodwill principle in action.

Despite all this doing and telling and testing of one another, stories still come in abundance, and with them the renewed presumption of truth and a willingness to believe one another. The vernacular is enriched by so many kinds of stories that trying to order them taxonomically would be an endless project, for such a taxonomy would have to take into account not just the content and genre of the story but also the situation in which it is told. This chapter takes up the stories we tell on ourselves and on each other. I will not deal directly with gossip, except to say that these tales about others are given a bad name. Because gossip means malicious stories about others, the vernacular comes up with synonyms for many other ways we can talk about mutual friends without being accused of gossiping. Among elite young ladies, license used to be given simply by saying "tell, tell," but this practice seems dated. The scoop on gossip, good or bad, is that we do it night and day. One way or another, we want to keep up with the latest.

License to place ourselves at the center of stories may be presumed among friends and relations. Legend has it that this was not the case until recently; we wanted to keep our business to ourselves. But in the heavy information society, such secrecy, or even privacy, seems difficult to come by. Participants in the conversation have to ask permission to tell their stories, shifting from "he say, she say" to me-talk. Using "you know what they say" as a way to introduce a morality tale is to make a bid for oracular power, or at least for permission to use a fixed form cliché, like an old saw, or an old joke. The safest tales to tell in company are those which are heard from friends or friends of friends. But this indirection raises potential social problems as well, for relating someone else's experience is more than telling a tale on them; it may involve stealing their "storytelling rights" (Shuman 1986; Young 1987).

Old stories, like old habits, are best, especially if we find ways of recasting them for present uses. We take legends and translate them into personal experience narratives (Stahl 1989). We are entitled to this self-styling because when we offer such narratives we listen to others telling stories in the same vein, perhaps even variants of the same stories. "Tell me if you've heard this one" is insufficient in most situations; everyone wants to add their own voices, have their own say.

Anecdote/Story

"We tell ourselves stories in order to live," Joan Didion reminds us at the beginning of her book *The White Album* (Didion 1979: 1). The process of translating experiences into narratives is a creative response to fears that the unexpected will happen and we will not have a story already in the repertoire available for revision to align with the circumstances. We tell stories in the face of life's transitoriness so that we can *name* and *frame* those happenings as we relate them after the fact. But, storytelling is more than therapy. Didion recognizes that the vernacular has special capacities to make stories by transforming happenings into a form which can be understood in a conversational setting. When we see a situation that is not explained by its context, we immediately begin to draw upon stories of the type we have heard before, bringing what is seen into line with what might be told.

The point of this metanarration is that, in story-making, otherwise inchoate actions and random events are given formal unity of the fictional sort. In the process, vernacular order encourages us to join experience with artifice. By assimilating those stories into familiar types, we can dispose of the shock value by the déjà vu effect; that is, we feel as if we have seen before. After the acts of terrorism that brought such matters into our dens, where events are replayed over and over, the initial response of thinking what we are seeing is unbelievable is transformed into a horror story, a war story, a disaster worse than anything we ever saw on film, or anywhere else. We classify it as a tragedy or a comedy, a soap opera or a farce, leading the story into the realm of the barely believable but true. Through generic taxonomies, we understand better not only what the stories are but how also we are supposed to react to them. Heroes and clowns emerge from them, alongside villains and captains of the forces of evil. We also have scenarios for how those people may be cheered or booed, elevated or eliminated.

"We live entirely . . . by the imposition of a narrative line upon disparate images," Joan Didion intones, "by the 'ideas' with which we have learned to freeze the shifting phantasmagoria which is our actual experience" (Didion 1979: 1). Of course, this process of freezing occurs more often in the retrospective retelling than in the accounting going on during our solitary stroll through the city or countryside, when the isolated eye begins the story through people-watching. For it is the role of *flaneur*, the function of observing strangers, which Didion accepts:

The naked woman on the sixteenth floor is a victim of accidie . . . or is an exhibitionist, and it would be interesting to know which. . . . It makes a difference whether the naked woman is about to commit a mortal sin or is about to register a political protest, or is about to be (the Aristophanic view) snatched back to the human condition by the fireman in priest clothing just visible in the window behind her. (Didion 1979)

Like Didion, we look for some striking detail in what we are observing so we can report it later as a good example of its type.

We feel a need to make a point by telling stories—or, we make up a point for the stories we tell. At the very least, we want to be able to discuss what its point might be, looking for different interpretations. How frantically we try to match the point with the happening, especially for those events which command attention but which we cannot interpret for ourselves. We are convinced that the happenings themselves carry a message, and we want someone else to tell us the lesson it has to teach.

With breaking news stories, notable events which have an impact beyond personal and local networks of relations, there is always competition as to who can claim to get the story first and shape it into a tellable tale. In conversation or gossip, the story becomes "the latest," but in more public, mediated forms, getting first-hand reports most quickly is categorized as *newsmaking*. Personal and public accounts use the same criteria of ownership of story: who can provide in-depth, eyewitness testimony, and who has access to the most powerful communication networks and media for spreading the story. Speed is crucial to both, but so is the amount of detail, the determination of the important points of the story, and the teller's reputation for veracity. All storytellers aim to be seen as someone who understands, indeed, controls the story, whether they are professional reporters, ordinary people to happen to be on the spot during such events, or others who find themselves caught up in the story.

Barbie Zelizer's *Covering the Body: The Kennedy Assassination, the Media, and the Shaping of Collective Memory* brings to light the conflicts among various broadcast and print media over control of the story (Zelizer 1992). On-the-spot reportage carried the most weight, but the Zapruder film proved even more authoritative. Contestation for control over the story is played out at the conversational level as well, as each of us attempts to find a point of connection between ourselves and the catastrophe.

The Most Embarrassing Thing That Ever Happened to Me

With any tear in the social fabric, repair work begins immediately; indeed, it is already well rehearsed. A substantial proportion of what we tell has to do with people we know and things we and they have gone through. Once these happenings have been transformed into narratives, they become part of the repertoire of the everyday, subject to being retold in a number of contexts, each time potentially delivering a different message. For instance, embarrassment stories arise when a relaxed conversation turns to times when we have been caught "with our pants down." These anecdotes commonly testify to having allowed oneself to get caught in an embarrassing situation, especially as we are growing up. Here's one often-told story:

When I was a kid, growing up in a small town outside of Philly [Philadelphia], I was used to double-dating with my friend "Jelly-Beans." (His name was Jerome, a name that just didn't go down with his friends. We used to kid him about it and many of his other idiosyncrasies, as he walked around with one of those "what am I doing here?" looks on his face.) One New Year's Eve we decided, since there were no parties, that we would be very grown-up and go into Philly to the Bellevue-Stratford (the most formal place in the city at that time); we'd make reservations for a table. Just turned sixteen, both of us, and it was the first year we could commandeer a car for the evening. After many conversations about logistics, we picked up our dates and made the big trip down Broad Street to the hotel. After sitting for awhile, we were served, ate, and the dancing started. Jelly-Beans, not the smoothest of operators, found he had to take a leak but didn't know how to sneak away without being noticed. He finally snuck out, coming back with an embarrassed look on his face because he had disappeared without saying anything. When he came back my date whispered to me, "His fly's open." I couldn't resist. I leaned over to him when he sat down and whispered with appropriate gestures, "Your barn door's open!" As unobtrusively as possible, he zipped up. Meanwhile the band had started up again, and I asked my date to dance. We had just gotten out to the floor when we heard this awful clatter and looked back and there was Jelly-Beans with the tablecloth caught in his fly, and the dishes and silver all over the floor. Everything stopped and looked at what was causing the upset. Everyone in this huge room was looking. Eventually the waiters had to roll the tablecloth up and walk with J-B across the dance floor to the men's room on the other side of the room. And of course, as the waiter carried the tablecloth behind him across the dance floor, everybody applauded.

If the storytelling event were organized around "the worst date I ever had" stories, the dénouement would be to answer the implied question: "Well, what happened then?" with some remarks about slipping out of the men's room and going out the back way. On the other hand, if it were told in the context of a competition for the most embarrassing things that have happened to us, then the aftermath of the story would include walking back to the table to some more applause, a toast, or some other way of saving face, turning the affair into something that was planned, or that fitted beautifully into a first drinking occasion.

A typical response to this story is that it is too unbelievable, too formulaic, too neat, too much like a sit-com, or some other moaning reaction. Perhaps the story seems too familiar, too close to one we've all heard before. But no matter the direct response, it certainly can trigger the comeback: "You think that's bad. Well, you should hear what happened to me. . . ." Even if the even more embarrassing thing is not actually told as part of a series, then at least our own stories are replayed in our heads, triggered by the recollection of how disjointed the scene made you feel, and then the details of how it came about occur to you.

When I tell that story, I am often asked, "Did that really happen?" Or people say, "I've heard that one before, but not from you." So veracity is questioned, as is attribution. The story, after all, is a typical friend-of-a-friend joke and could have been taken from the ocean of stories out there that are referred to as urban legends, following the extensive work of the folklorist Jan Harold Brunvand (Brunvand 1981).

That such stories are as patterned and formulaic as any other oral narrative is clear from the laughing recognition that I witnessed as I have retold it over the years. Will they bear up under comparative analysis, and does the truth of whether or not it happened as it was told even matter? It is still a good story, a believable unbelievable tale of woe.

License to Tell a Tale

Folklorists have been concerned primarily with items whose historical depth and geographical distribution may be traced. This interest reflects the literary culture's hierarchy of forms, in which the most common sort of stories is deemed least worthy of extended analysis. On the other hand, analysts of narratives who come from various other disciplines see stories of this sort as useful in understanding the essential features of form that make *a story*, even *a good story*. Ethnographers of communication are as interested in the telling as in the tale, looking for those situating features which establish thematic relationships with the stories coming before or after, or how the story justifies the seizing of storytelling rights in the context of a conversation or an entertainment. The familiarity with which stories are greeted concerns as much a class of actions as it does the specifics of the story, judged by veracity criteria or by how successful it is in drawing laughter.

One criterion entering into the license to perform is obtained is to be a master tactician in the game of conversation—to know when to draw on a story, as well as how much time and, by extension, how much elaboration will be tolerated. Gauging such factors means assessing what kind of interactive scene you are involved in, as well as what your speaking status is in that scene.

In general, scenes which are, by common consent of the participants, defined as conversations live by certain flexibly interpreted rules, such as the I-talk-you-listen, you-talk-I-listen, one-speaker-at-a-time rule which obtains in most American talk situations. Another is the equal access rule, with the accrued appropriate ways to break in on the conversation. Another is apparent spontaneity, in which the participants in the conversation agree to disregard or laugh away anything which seems either rehearsed or spoken in an inappropriate code (as when we rhyme accidentally). As these conversations increase in intensity, the conventional rules are relaxed. The more "just talking" gravitates toward a "deep discussion," the greater the amount of time an individual is given to make a point; the more a discussion turns into an argument, the more voice overlap is countenanced.

Stories of this sort are exchanged in relaxed conversational situations as much as in formal presentations. Swapping experiences is a friendly act which permits one to talk about oneself—even make a fool of oneself, when the story is about shockers and surprises, disruptions of routine, having a brush with danger and death, reporting on a matter of gossip. Insofar as they follow other similar tales and lead to the recounting of others, stories elicit further stories using conversational norms.

Stories telling of something that really happened are usually believed. But the storyteller does not have to adhere to the flow of stories that closely. A really true story may be a set-up for one which is not true, but which relies on gulling the hearer into thinking that it is, until a punch line reframes it into a joke, or a ghostly presence transforms it into a weird story.

One kind of story of this latter sort has been singled out because it is susceptible to being studied through its actual reports, along the same lines as fairy tales. The named genre most actively collected and analyzed by folklorists is what Brunvand (1981) calls urban legends, a term which has entered the journalistic and conversational vernaculars. In fact, Brunvand has a regular column and website reporting the latest urban legends sent in for discussion. Other folklorists and reporters have followed Brunvand's lead. Before the adoption of this term, such stories were described by their tellers as scary stories or ghost stories. By whatever name, they were told as true, if strange, happenings.

Such stories live best as true happenings. They acquire, not antiquing in the telling, but contemporaneity in the retelling. In both theme and delivery, they differ in gravity and texture from tales, myths, and legends. In stories, as in other domains of tradition, age markers are an important dimension of their reception; no claims are made that these experience stories are as old as the hills. They depart from using archaic terms, getting that faraway look on the face of the narrator, and creating a temporal and spatial frame distinctly removed from the present. Yet such stories are as formulaic and as susceptible to being repeated, conventionalized, and coded with important cultural information as those narratives we recognize and study as traditional.

Many folklorists regard tales of bizarre happenings as too idiosyncratic to be worthy of being addressed using either the comparative or the performative methods of analysis. Dealing with such ephemeral matters has haunted the discipline, as folklorists are dismissed because we deal with such trivia. But it is self-evident that the more personal and conversationally appropriate a story is, the more important it is to discover what is interesting about it. It is not enough to study the most heavily resonant and symbolic activities, such as ritual and ceremony, song-singing, dancing, and tale-telling, for the most common way in which human sociability is expressed is by gathering together to discuss important matters.

Common sense reminds us that any experience may be used as the basis of a story, but that most of our doings are unremarkable and not worthy of recounting. Just as we make a distinction between experience, referring to the flow of life through the activities of individuals, and *an* experience, a happening which is sufficiently removed from the everyday flow of life that it may be used as a point of reference for later discussion, so too we distinguish among various kinds of retold experiences in terms of how typical they are and how fully they carry important cultural messages.

Consolidating personal experience narratives into one folkloristic category may not be as valuable as is taking notice of the variety of first-person stories as they are drawn on in different conversational and performance settings. We should not undervalue the differences between taking or giving testimony and bearing witness, getting off a good one and giving an example, a case in point, or an excuse for one's actions. They all call for personal recital and make an appeal for believability.

Not all recountings carry heavy messages; more often we tell our stories to clean up the past, or at least to eliminate some of the stronger aspects of transitory actions. As another native informant, the novelist James Crumley, asserted in his potboiler, *The Last Good Kiss*, "It's the story that counts." This maxim is uttered by one of his characters when, after telling a story of his love life, his hearer asks what happened to the woman. "It's the story that counts," but the other insists that most important aspect of the story is how it ends, employing different aesthetic criteria in dealing with real-life tales. The storyteller responds equally critically: "Stories are like snapshots, . . . pictures snatched out of time . . . with clean hard edges. But this is life, and life always begins and ends in a bloody muddle, womb to tomb, just one big mess, a can of worms left to rot in the sun" (Crumley 1978). His listener would like life, even in snatches, to have a point; if not an end, at least a sense of purpose. Surely, our native notions of story include the life-story, as well as reports of the more transitory activities that find their way into our daily talk. We like to hear of endings as well as meanings, messy disappearances or deaths along with good ones.

The stories we tell on ourselves are not necessarily clean and hard-edged, or even finished. Friendly relations are often defined as those in which we can confide in others—by which we often mean getting permission to tell our ongoing, unfinished, and halting stories. In less intimate situations, where we nonetheless fashion our self-image, we may define this self almost as the sum of the stories we develop to tell on ourselves. This is the stuff of literature, for such stories delineate each character in a novel and establish possible moves and motives within a contrived set of encounters. Recognizing that, in first encounters with others, we are what we have done, we all need to have stories ready on a variety of themes, especially who we have known under what circumstances and where we have been and what we have been careful to observe there. A fully socialized talker also has stories which can be linked to those of others about common situations, such as "the worst travel experience" stories, common as dirt, but essential if we wish to establish ourselves as travelers.

One of the conditions of modern life to which we must constantly attest is our equal exposure to becoming victims of outrageous approaches, invasions, and personal attacks. We add our voice to storytelling sessions on the subject of hold-ups, aggravated assaults, rapes, and other such unpleasantries that we or our friends and acquaintances have experienced. Insofar as each of us has a repertoire of such "you think that's something" stories, we make claims for ourselves as members of a speaking community. These personal anecdotes do a great deal of social and cultural work for us. We use them to testify to our having played a part in the ongoing drama we call life, having experiences which are sufficiently typical that we use them both to establish our humanity and to make a bid for group membership, even when the group is as evanescent as a queue or other chance encounter. In these interchanges, we find ourselves talking about, even dramatizing, our most life-testing experiences. We add detail to these conventional tales as a way of taking the edge off the lie, inducing some degree of receptiveness through the force of verisimilitude. Thus we are simultaneously typical in our experiences and individual, even idiosyncratic, by having lived to tell the tale.

Personal accounts which replay past incidents of disruption have a therapeutic function, drawing upon a shared, retold experience as a way of taking care of the problems they represent. Each time they are replayed, they are shared more widely, placed in ever-expanding categories of experience. We feel less threatened by the traumatic experience as we relive it, domesticate it, bring it under control. Native testimony confirms this power of retelling: the psychiatrist, the lawyer, the social worker, the teacher, the mortician each has a kind of story of anguish and disruption to which he or she is accustomed to listening and responding. And each has a repertoire of stories themselves which gives the message, "I know what you're going through."

Such stories thrive as shared experiences in the relatively egalitarian environment of conversation, not only in such hierarchical situations between professional and client. Among friends we engage in such very personal talk that we are given license to relate any stories to our life-story. Thus we make a bid for notice because of some virtue: as a hero, a stoic, a clown, or whatever conventional role we choose to take on at such tellings.

Our Native Notions of Story

Our vernacular system of storytelling includes at least three levels of storying: (1) the informal and ongoing personal storytelling in which the ending and its meaning are negotiable or still under negotiation; (2) the well-made story, capable of being retold because of its sense of a beginning, a middle, and an end and its implicit message or point; and (3) those stories which are so well known and central to the group that they need only to be referred to and not necessarily retold for their points to be made. The point of each level of story is actually a cultural lesson. The first of these is just a story; the second is an exemplary tale; the third approaches being a myth.

In *myths* we find accounts which are so widely known and so conventionally associated with the wisdom of a group that, rather than referring to them as conveying a point or even a lesson, they themselves embody truths—not ones available for verification, but assumptions that used to be called higher truths.

The presumption is that everyone knows the fiction which embodies the myth. Tales, in this sense, are formulated as if they need to be told to the unknowing, the child, or the stranger; myths register stories which go even deeper and rely on a richer cultural mix than can be delivered in singly narrated formulations. Myths, in this sense, are deep stories, weighted and often implied forms of narrating episodes which are so representative of human experience that they seem to epitomize some aspect of life in meaning and feeling.

These qualities are found not just in archaic myths but also in any gnomic referencing of a conventional, value-invested belief. These stories are not quite stories, for they are told in plotless, already-having-occurred fashion. In such a case, individual traits of character and the particularities of setting or situation are not important. Like religious and cosmological narratives, these myths carry a sense of developmental inexorability. We know them not only as myths (as in "The Myth of the Golden Age") in which the development is negatively regarded and we posit a falling-off in the quality of the natural and social environment, but also as dreams in which the development is positively portrayed and the ending is regarded as essentially unachievable (as in "The American Dream" or "The Impossible Dream") or a positive end is indeed possible (as in "The Great American Success Story"). "Idea" (or, properly, ideal) is a more neutral term in the same series (as in "The Idea of Progress"). Because myths impose value-orientations or ideologies upon a basic developmental pattern, they are capable of being exposed as reflexive fictions, and as such they may be regarded by some who do not share that vision as lies, sometimes even implicated in "The Big Lie." These contemporary secular myths are often pointed to as examples of gross human error, as devices as benign as wishful thinking ("The Dream of the Hereafter") or as malignant, life-defeating forces

("The Myth of Racial Inferiority"). We have other less ideologically encumbered names for differently rendered versions of these deep patterns: archetypes, representative anecdotes, fables, even paradigms or models. Whatever they are called, these deep patterns offer us matrices by which we may more energetically construct a social reality out of the details of our own experiences and conventions of presentation which make it possible for us to share these experiences with others after they are over.

PART II

Goodwill Tested

Chapter 5

Just Talking/Taking License

Most of the simple forms of folklore are imagined as performed in the comfort of home. But folklorists did not have to test such suppositions. This fireside comfort is idealized and granted authority within the vernacular because it carries the message of truths tested by time. Moreover, these tales, proverbs, riddles, or curses were slippery enough to deal with as they are discovered in different languages. When it could be presumed that these traditions were as *das volk dichte*, totally at home in a place and language that could be used as the basis of nation formation, then studying lore in transmission across borders undercut the nationalist enterprise somewhat. But carrying out intimately situated fieldwork generated even more challenges to the old paradigm.

Shifting the focus of folklore from the study of texts in transmission to the analysis of artistic communications in small groups relocates the discipline's primary concerns from the lore to the folk. This move enables us to characterize the sociocultural environment of traditional expression in ever-finer detail. But in the excitement of entering into this important discussion of humans' creative capacities, we have manufactured a number of problems which need consideration and clarification. In redefining folklore with regard to its artistic dimensions and the way in which the community enters into the creative process, we have forgotten that many of the forms which concern us are not artistic performances. Games, festivals, and rituals are not artistic creations held in small groups. To be sure, their expressivity has led us to describe these activities in performance terms. But a game is still a game, not a performance, and to regard the one as an example of the other is to commit an error of common sense. We need to develop a methodology for describing games, as well as festivals and rituals, that is appropriate to them while utilizing the insights developed by the performance-centered approach.

Performance

As the principal term folklore has undergone redefinition, questions arise as to what genres of communication are artistic. The most basic vernacular problem is how to regard the term performance itself in relation to other commonsense terms for communicative transactions. What is meant in general parlance when an activity is called a performance? How might we compare unselfconscious and apparently spontaneous role-playing with the more self-consciously stylized activities of planned social *occasions*, such as gatherings, openings, receptions, and shows?

Using *performance* as the central term for any cultural argument involves obvious problems, for in everyday talk and academic discussion we employ the term in several different senses (see especially Hymes 1975a; Ben-Amos and Goldstein 1975; Goffman 1974: 224; Bauman, Abrahams, Gossen, and Babcock 1977). One special difficulty comes from its appropriation as a term of art in transformational-generative or Chomskyan linguistics, referring to speech as generated from its underlying forms. Performance, in contrast to *competence*, is the capacity to produce meaningful utterances in any social setting. Language is thereby divorced from speech, which is reduced to the level of chit-chat or any way of engaging in face-to-face communication.

Ordinarily, a performance refers to the unique coming-together of a special occasion, a performer or performers, a tradition of open display techniques, and onlookers who interpret the performance. If folklore is successful, performers and audience share the same fictions of presentation. In this sense, performance describes a special mode of focusing interactions. A performance can be anticipated, replayed, and judged by the performers' effective control over the stylized occasion. Display conventions pervade these acts, so audiences know what to look forward to and how to respond appropriately should those expectations prove reliable.

When it is used on less specially licensed and set-aside occasions, performance operates by analogy to performance-proper. By calling this state of socioaesthetic excitation and celebration pure performance or performance-proper, I do not mean to ignore the self-conscious dimension of other kinds of scenes. To the contrary: I attempt to trace the continuities between behavior in other kinds of scenes and events and these more focused and stylized enactments.

Dell Hymes offers a useful contrast between behavior, conduct, and performance: "there is *behavior*, anything and everything that happens; there is *conduct*, behavior under the aegis of social norms, cultural rules; there is *performance*, when one or more persons assume responsibility for presentation" (Hymes 1975a: 18). These three terms vary directly with the degree of attention paid to the ordering particulars of acts, especially the ways in which they are carried out. Performance achieves its status because responsibility is assumed by designated performers and because of the openness of presentation by which the activities are underscored as morally and aesthetically significant. Responsibility, then, relates both to the level of self-consciousness in the form and subject of the enactment and to the social norms by which those actions are judged as good or bad, graceful or awkward.

In both behavior and performance, the rules governing interaction are observed and manipulated. But in everyday presentations of self, the rules serve as guidelines that facilitate participation and exchange. In the more restricted sort of presentation, a stage or sport performance, the rules are occasion-specific—that is, they are most in force and enforceable in those times and places conventionally set aside for celebrations, games, and spectacles. Playful transactions, of even the most serious fun, call for the players to assume a role separate from any personal identity, at least while play is in process. In ordinary interactions, each participant attempts to establish identity by controlling the roles he or she is allowed to try out or try out for. In play, roles are allocated using entirely different criteria. Performers are relieved of accountability for their actions and motives, except insofar as they extend beyond the play frame.

This distinction between the real and the dramatized self is a tricky one at best, for some performers use the license of performing to make speeches and commit actions which are potent but not attributable outside of the playground or the theater. Given the conventions of the closeted performance by which everyone allows writer and reader to address each other in seclusion, playwrights and lyric poets draw upon this subjunctive modality of presentation of self, speaking as if they are fictional and yet more real in that situation than in any other. Great performers find ways of convincing spectators that they control the boundary between the real and the play worlds by appearing, from time to time, to break frame with the ongoing presentation, seemingly calling up something like themselves in real life. This break is commonly engineered by a shift in voice and carriage, making the reentry to the play world seem imminent even while giving an "aside." Getting backstage or into the locker room provides a spectator with insights about the game or the show that would never be apparent from out front.

This strategy of presentation is not really confusing. In fact, the poetic system employs this ambiguity to create maneuvering space for performers, as a playful means of testing the boundaries between the real and fictive worlds while checking on the attention of the audience. In our most popular displays, the players are authorized to critique, not just playing, but also real-life situations. Although they follow a wandering lifestyle, jazz and blues players are repeatedly asked how they judge one another's performances and what relationship their art has to their life-situations. Bluesmen have proven to be especially articulate on the subject because of the audience's identification of the singer with the songs he composes and sings. The notable John Lee Hooker responded to the common question about the relationship between art and life:

You can hear a certain type of record be playin'. You can be feelin' very normal, nothin' on your mind, period. But it's somethin' that have happened in your life, and sometime if you can't stand to listen to the record you take a walk or take a ride or get in your car because you don't want to be hurt so deep that it cause heartaches and things. Because you'd rather not to hear it than to hear it. Because there's somethin' sad in there that give you the blues; somethin' that reach back in your life or in some friend's life of yours, or that make you think of what have happened today and it is so true, that if it didn't happen to you, you still got a strong idea—you know those things is goin' on. So this is very touchable, and that develops into the blues. (Hooker, quoted in Oliver 1965: 164)

The composer-performer finds his place, bringing focused energies and craft into the moment of performance. The reception accorded the performer relies on the degree of coordinated response triggered by the enactment.—not only how well the performer controls the medium and channels his or her energies, but also how fully the item resonates with recalled scenes from life—or, as Hooker puts it, how "touchable" a common situation is, and therefore how much it "hits you" as a human being who is also a member of an audience and a community.

In the dialectic between art and life, we witness the interplay of artist and genre and between the artist as the voice of tradition and as one who gives voice to personal experience. In nontraditional communities, performers must make the audience wonder how much they are singing of themselves and how much they are drawing on conventional observation and artistic fabrication. Even artists who perform works composed by others beg the question of originality and authenticity in their choice of repertoire, which works they play on what occasions, and by the intensity and stylistic nuance with they are performed.

This problem is not confined to sophisticated artists who express themselves reflexively, like Hemingway or Proust making their life into a work of art. Listen to another blues singer, Henry Thomas, holding forth on the "me, not me" speaking in his songs:

There's several types of blues—there's blues that connects you with personal life—I mean you can tell it to the public as a song, in a song. But I mean, they don't take it seriously which you are tellin' the truth about. They don't always think seriously that it's exactly you that you talkin' about. At the same time it could be you, more or less it would be you for you to have the feelin'. You express yourself in a song like that. Now this particular thing reach others because they have experienced the same condition in life so naturally they feel what you are sayin' because it happened to them. It's sort of thing that you kinda like to hold to yourself, yet you want somebody to know it. I don't know how you say that two ways; you like somebody to know it, yet you hold it to yourself. Now I've had the feelin' which I have disposed it in a song, but there's some things that have happened to me that I wouldn't dare tell, not to tell—but I would sing about them. Because people in general they take the song as an explanation for themselves—they believe this song is expressing their feelin's instead of the one that singin' it. They feel that maybe I have just hit upon somethin' that's in their lives, and yet at the same time it was some of the things that went wrong with me too. (Thomas, quoted in Oliver 1965: 164–65)

This is not to argue that life follows art or vice versa, or that to sing the blues you must experience them. A performer who gives voice to a feeling that seems to arise from personal experience is credited with having gone through the experience. Listeners often confuse blues singers with their songs, as the lyrics and delivery make it appear to be a life-testimony. On stage with bluesman Bukka White, a folk revival singer made a bold declaration: "You have to live the life you sing about in your songs." I turned to Mr. White and asked if that were true. He thought for a moment and then said: "Are you asking whether I sing for money? The answer is yes. I'm a scuffler like everybody else here."

Whether they are appearing on stage or off, performers like to keep the space between life and art open to any strategy of self-presentation, including the possibility of playing themselves being themselves.

Scripts and Scenes

The performer's self-consciousness of the relation between life and art is one of the defining characteristics of performance. Although scholars now understand performative action, the connections between performance and everyday life and the disjunctions between performative and vernacular modes deserve further exploration. There is a significant difference between the competencies and patterns of expectation carried in common into the interaction when the communication is conversational and when it is openly designated as a performance. In conversation, participants agree to cover over or at least take for granted the conventions that govern their interaction, while in performance these formal patterns are highlighted. Conversations mark those dimensions of communication which stress the relationship between the participants. Any elements of formal style in conversation must be made to seem to arise by chance and be explained away, or overlooked. Performances, in contrast, tend to cover over any notice of the exchange between performer and audience. Such metadevices maintain the focus on the stylized expression of the commonly understood genre. Still, a similar capacity for recognizing and rendering the scenarios or scripts of everyday scenes underlies conversation. The interaction may usefully be interpreted as a dramatic narrative which develops through accumulated experience, either directly or by reporting personal observations of others' activities.

Participants in sexual interactions, for example, are mutually aware of such scripting. By engaging in the requisite exchanges, they implicitly accept the roles and relationship the scripts suggest. Lovers or would-be lovers must make a whole set of moves, or this dance of life breaks down. Not that such interactions are wholly choreographed; there is a wide variety of ways in which seduction or other kinds of sexual coming-together may be carried out, and scripts contain many points where consequential choices are to be made. With the love-making script the differences between life and art are clear. Although the participants may recognize that they are following a script, they also maintain the fiction, refusing to acknowledge this recognition openly. "Just playing a role" or "walking through a scene" destroys the basis of trust on which the relationship is predicated. However, such accusations may be made if the lovers are not in full agreement as to where they are in the script.

Not only is learning to make love scripted, it forms part of a longer script, commonly called courtship, which is itself one drama in the larger epic movement of growing up. The relationship between the various levels of scripting is crucial to an understanding of the developmental pattern. A beginner in any developing set of scenes asks, "What do I do next?" This question indicates that he or she recognizes that the interrelation of the parts is vital to the overall pattern.

Communication events generally have a sense of beginning, middle, and end, and stylistic cues suggest what kind of interaction is being carried on and provide clues to where the participants are in the life-history of the event. These suggestions are intensified in performances. The exchange is marked openly, and the degree of stylization and predictability is acknowledged as a formal quality of the scene. This openness of framing, cueing, and underlining permits a higher degree of coordination and focus.

Self-conscious formalization is only one of the defining characteristics of performance. Some scenes and event-types which are notable for their high degree of formality and predictability are still not pure performances: for example, receptions, formal dinners, even saying mass.

We classify scene types with regard to their relative formality and singularity of focus. There are a variety of scenes which might be termed conversations because the register employed is conversational, and the basic rule governing interaction is the "I-talk-you-listen; you-talk-I-listen" associated with nearly all states-of-talk in Western culture. Ideally, all participants have permission to enter the conversation. The more formal the scene, the more such access is limited. We distinguish such conversational scenes as "just talking," "having a conversation," "brainstorming," "holding a seminar," "having a meeting," and so on, with regard to how overt the rule system is which guarantees access to the state of talk. Also, the more formal the occasion, the longer the period each participant is given to talk, the more careful the presentation must be (the point must be kept clear, and each segment of talk must be relevant to the point), the more visibly the spatial environment is divided, and the more fixed each participant's place becomes.

Other dimensions of conversation reflect increasing depth and intensity. For instance, the more fully an occasion is framed and prepared for, the more the interaction will be monitored for conformity to the governing code. We may feel that we are talking personally and in ordinary conversational ways when we bump into a friend on the street, when we meet at a cocktail party, a formal dinner, in a receiving line, or at a funeral, but we also are aware that this succession of scenes is marked by an increasing sense of formality and self-consciousness about our relationships, so we become more careful about how we speak and what we discuss. On some of these occasions, everyday roles are so intensified and interaction so stylized that participants make canned speeches, like those a father of the bride makes to even his best friends at the wedding reception. Such rehearsed or learned strips of talk are especially useful during stressful interactions. When we know we are going to "have a scene" with someone, we consequently go over what we want to say beforehand, in our heads, so that it will "come out right," even eloquently.

Dramatizing antagonists also induces the use of formulaic and formal conventions; especially in situations in which the conflict is controlled by common consent. Interactions progress (or decline) from "conversations" to "discussions" to "heated discussions" to "arguments" to "having it out." Other scenes of conflict which still maintain the conversational back-and-forth ways of talking are even more fully preformulated: debates, trials, and hearings, for example. In such events, not only are the rules of access to talk more fully spelled out, but rule-keepers are appointed to guarantee and protect that access.

As interaction becomes more formalized and self-conscious, scenes become more performance-like. The closer to the surface the marking places in the schema are, the more we judge behavior by the performance criteria of appropriateness of style as well as content. But so long as conversational rules apply, the fiction of spontaneity and open access to the state of talk must be maintained. Although such scenes may seem rehearsed, they are not in fact rehearsable in the same sense that pure performances are. Compare, for instance, real conversation with a dramatized conversation in a play. The staged interaction contains many cues which remind the audience that they are not just overhearing the interaction but being "let in" on it. These cues consist of a number of stylistic modifications of normal conversational patterns to help the audience "overhear" more clearly. There is considerably less voice overlap (a stylistic intensification of the "I-talk-you-listen; you-talk-I-listen" rule), slower pacing, amplification of voices, and modification of eye contact so as to include the audience. The pacing of the stage conversation allows for audience response, especially in comedy. Furthermore, the staged enactment is framed in a very different manner; the occasion, the set, and behavioral cues announce that the roles being enacted are not real—that is, are not to be employed by these players in any place but in this setting.

Intensification and formalization bring the everyday closer to pure performance. The same could be said for introducing playful motives into the encounter; joking makes participants more conscious of the formal dimension of any expressive transaction. When entering a play world, shifts in ways of speaking occur along with the role taken on by the player. Play, whether performance-play or otherwise, may deepen in response to a growing social investment. With performance, game-play, or even festive play, the more agonistic the motive of the playing, the greater will be the formality, the greater the amount of practice is appropriate, and the more self-conscious the rules and the stylistic niceties become. Given play's continuing endorsement of goodwill, or at least conflict avoidance outside of the playful agonism, the players expect more self-conscious adherence to accepted rules and practices. Though *agon* is the prime feature of game-play, it also operates in some kinds of performances, such as flyting, scolding, playing the dozens, and other formulaic yet playful castigations.

With song-singing we enter into performance-proper. Singing, with its shifting of vocabularies, codes, and conventions, is also available in less intense scenes; a song or a snatch of one may simply be used as a quotation in the midst of a more casual conversational interaction. Embedding a song in a conversation is certainly more strange-making than introducing a proverb into this kind of interaction, but the difference is of degree rather than kind. Both moves involve a shifting of the pronoun system and, by extension, a diminution in the degree of responsibility taken by the speaker for the words of the proverb or song. This shift of voice is one of the most common devices used to heighten awareness.

Taking License

Getting into the state of play calls for a customary departure from conversational rules, especially friendly talk. The very existence of personal talk within the play challenges the rules of both the game and the system of friendly manners. This is especially so if the players use the taunting language of "trash talk," demonstrating "attitude." How much do we allow each other to stray from the comfort of the predictable? How much of this wandering calls for special arrangements, a license to venture into a domain which will not be judged in terms of everyday manners? Each special zone of personal exchange seems to have different rules and expectations. How do we obtain permission slips to leave one kind of scene and enter another social milieu?

Dell Hymes has explored the dividing line between everyday talk and performance (Hymes 1975a). Looking at speech in terms of its relatively casual character, in which the flow of talk is regarded as central to the proceedings, there comes a moment at which the role of performer is accorded one or another speaker. The others involved in the discussion are implicitly requesting permission or *license* to change voice or register into one judged not only by content but by the style of delivery. At such a point, the speaker begins to take less responsibility for what is said and become more accountable for how it is delivered.

In the everyday, we are expected to keep a good part of ourselves to ourselves. In each kind of place, new expectations arise, licensed by what has been experienced there before. As most behavior is susceptible to being described in terms of acting, playing, or performing, we cling to those bits of ourselves that are reserved from notice without fear of having our cover blown. Once we accept the unvoiced norms of acting friendly in our culture, the number of tacit rules under which we serve seems unending. Thus the iceberg principle: most behavior is beneath notice, doing what we usually do.

How potentially embarrassing to hold everyday matters up to open discussion, or even to call attention in any way to how we do things mundanely. The most important dimension of the social fiction is that we agree not to notice the minutiae of our habitual and customary practices. How annoying is it to be told "I know you better than you know yourself," or to hear someone anticipating every word you say by actually saying it before you can? And these are only two of the forms of conversational talk that raise the question of whether imitation is friendly or not. Calling mimicry, or even empathetic verbal and kinesic (body language) responses to the level of consciousness is itself something of a mind-game, especially in those situations in which someone calls a gaffe to the attention of others. Even worse is when one participant in the interaction purposely plays with the rules in such a way as to catch other participants in a faux pas. When this happens, we provide a number of mechanisms by which the stream of friendly talk can be refreshed.

The most common type of a vocalized excuse is to switch into another mode of participation, cueing the others that a joke can be made or stories can be told concerning previous gaffes of the same sort. Any sort of repetition of the gaffe immediately afterward will usually be interpreted as a performance rather than just talking, which calls for the invoking of a different mode of judgment. We seem to agree to act conversationally sociable by helping one another get on track and stick to the subject. But, the more friendly and relaxed the talk, the more leeway we give each other to shift the subject. Joking is especially problematic in conversational environments. Thus the regular resort to phrases like "Just kidding," or "But who am I to tell you these things?" We might call this kind of scene "surprise," or "in and out of embarrassment," underscoring the friendly dictates of the conversational moment. Each departure from conversational interactions invokes an agreed-upon exit from the practices of everyday manners, even if the altered role being played is that of joker or mimic. Any move that calls attention to the style of interaction as well as the flow of talk moves the conversation toward performance. But to acknowledge most of what we do as playing a part is to pull down the walls of our own house of identity.

Bits of speech begin to recur which cue listeners that a quotation from someone else is being offered, maybe even a hoary piece of advice inherited from the wise people of the past. Talk is not supposed to be self-consciously performed in any way. If one person holding forth happens to rhyme a pair of words in the utterance, a break in the flow is admissible, with a voiced "You're a poet and you don't know it; you're a Longfellow." The same message can be given simply by raising an eyebrow or leading a laugh.

The flow of the most familiar forms of everyday interaction is faced with conventional interruption through circumstances dictated by passing from more private realms to more public places or by moving from just talking to storytelling. Accountability rules are constantly and often silently called into play as a conversation proceeds, for each segment of a good long talk may call for a cue of some sort that asks "Are you with me?" or asserts "I am not kidding." The adjustment is most commonly a conventional one, learned through earlier and repeated practice. To enter such other realms, permission must be sought—as with the children's game "Mother, may I?" At the gateway, a new pattern of expectation, a new compact, is brought to mind. In response, permission is granted to act and interact with a different set of conventions, which in play are called the rules of the game, whether their formalities are rigidly practiced (as in ritual behavior) or apparently drawn upon more spontaneously. In sports, as in business conferences, ways to check on whether the participants are all "on the same page" emerge. Power relations come into play at such points. If the prospective result of the interaction is regarded by all sides as important, whoever has higher rank takes it upon himself or herself to monitor and direct the flow of action. The difference may be as great as appointing officials or moderators ahead of time. The objective is to make sure everybody is playing by the formal or informal rules. Thus the presence of referees, judges, umpires, boundary-line men, or time-keepers in many sports—officials who are given the right to "blow the whistle." These points of passage within the flow of action in the everyday call for *license*, that is, permission to interact by different conventional rules.

Getting In and Out of Performance

In these high-energy encounters, the mutual investment makes participants aware of how the rules were drawn up and learned and how long the license to play lasts. Getting in and out of such states may be as easy as walking back through the gateway, saying "I'm going home and taking my bat and ball with me," or yelling "Ally-ally in free." But it may be more difficult to leave the agony and ecstasy behind through physically walking back through the gates; psychologically, we replay parts, scenes, and plot developments. In leaving the scene psychologically, the big moments in which the winning play or some other transforming event occurred come back to mind and may be replayed by the individual or by the friends who leave with us or draw on a different mode of voice and gesture for that moment. The bid for license to play or joke, to be ostentatious, to pull punches, or to play the fool seriously indicates how much leeway and how much room for negotiation there is in the system. But it also reveals the many ways in which licensing of this sort is carried out. Permission to switch codes calls for a deep mutual understanding of the communication system. When breaks occur between the usual flow of speech and another state of talk, another set of rules is invoked, at least within the frame established generically by the direction taken in departing from conversational mode. Whatever shift is asked for and accepted, it both identifies (*names*) and categorizes (*frames*) what follows. To be allowed to talk is to be permitted the entire range of such mood-shifting devices, in the absence of age or class markers that restrict speakers. To participate in this system is to be entitled to deploy all of these devices of talking and repairing or intensifying talk, or switching into one or another mode of performance. All these rules presume that everyone present has equal access to talk. They build on the norm of interpretation which says that truth-telling is going on between coequals.

Frames do not necessarily have a beginning and an ending. The process of licensing is tricky, because there are many cases in which everyone in a conversation will know that a bid for entitlement is being made and a frame proposed to interpret what follows. But it may take a few moments before everyone involved understands what the new state of talk is properly named.

It seems important to notice these fundamental matters, because extraordinary kinds of interaction call for extensive revision of these commonsense notions. That is not to say that no trickery occurs in these ordinary conversational encounters. Many cues indicate that participants are playing around. The wink reminds us that an alternative set of interpretative frames lurks just below the surface of the interaction. Even if the gesture is not picked up, friends may say "just kidding" or "joking, joking, joking."

Many joke-tellings rely on a similar shifting of conversational gears. To reframe backwards, after some violation of the frame has engendered discomfort, some cue has to be given of the "in all seriousness" sort, but even here the others have to decide whether a speaker means it when he goes for seriousness. One can say to a friend "I'm not sure if I believe you" and get away with it, because the question of trust is raised and disposed of simultaneously—unless your friend has other motives.

If a friend is, by definition, someone you trust, then perhaps you can't trust anyone, even your best friend—or especially your best friend, if he is also a joker. When a friend remarks, "that's interesting," you have to look closely at whether and how he or she means it. There are many ways to get away with dissembling among friends.

Confidence in this context comes to mean two things, both involving a compact. Friendly discussions rely upon the agreement that confidence between bargainers is called for. But in the public places which I call *zones*, the rules of friendly interaction are far from the norm. When in public, expect rudeness or worse. Defensive postures are produced on demand.

Each zone carries its own set of conventions of how to judge the veracity of one or another participant in the interaction. Being true to one's word becomes especially problematic in joking situations. Perhaps even more dramatically, while shopping, the question of trust arises, especially when the vendor avers friendship with the customer. "Buyer beware" kicks in here. The face-to-face style of market interaction works in a parasitic manner on the everyday by borrowing from friendly talk. Indeed, at the market almost every genre of talk and performance is kidnapped and redeployed to enhance the buying and selling experience. Lying, which is the enabling legislation for the bargaining that takes place in the market (and, now, online), is conventionally conceived and interpreted through the truths retailed in more familiar or friendly kinds of scripts. Anti-consumption advocates see this as a perversion of friendly persuasion.

The hijacking of friendly talk by denizens of the market zone is taken for granted whenever we go out in public. But there is a basic complication here, because earlier conventions of talk between service workers and their customers drew on the norms of politesse. Consider, for example, the routines developed in restaurants in which the "server" introduces himself or herself by first name and then brightly asks if anyone wants anything, which he or she will gladly bring. We expect that such servers are not actually in service, but have taken a job to get through school. (Pity the poor professional wait-person). If a customer takes up the invitation and asks a personal question in response to server-talk, the in-between character of the interaction becomes evident: more talk, more tips, but fewer tables and less time for others, and therefore less tips from others. Scrutinizing the serving process calls attention to the "fakeyness" taken on by servers in search of market rewards. A benign fiction emerges in which eating out is to be treated like family meal, especially at the point of greatest possible communication errors, taking and delivering orders and then presenting and paying the check.

Other regularly staged public situations also test the unstable region between a personal and a market transaction. At garage sales, flea markets, and country auctions, the seller does not have to take on the mantel of the grasping salesman. Rather, goods are passed on in a suspended-time transaction, during which a number of patterns invoked among family and friends come into play, especially the invitation to tell personal stories about the object being exchanged. Is all this dissembling a way to get around being or feeling accused of crass commercialism? Everyone involved in the transaction understands that what is bought cheaply may be sold dearly in more formal selling situations. The ghost of the dreaded middleman at those irregular places of buying and selling haunts many of the transactions. The customer presumes that this is not a professional situation, but rather a way of circulating goods and having a good time.

All this talk is an attempt to reframe market interactions away from the definition of the setting. This reframing is most commonly done by enlisting the most familiar of codes, putting them in the service of the bargainers. When successful, the interaction which promises a bargain feels natural or friendly. That this involves an acceptance of the possibility of artful deceit on both the part of the buyer and the seller is all too obvious. As ardent bargainers argue, it is "all part of the game."

In theatrical events, the rules of friendly interaction are suspended in favor of verisimilitude, the ability of the audience to suspend disbelief and of the players to build on this suspension by selectively mirroring the assumption of friendliness. Staged play is conventionally licensed to feed off everyday practices in a parasitical fashion. The most evident license of staged play is costuming—that is, borrowing the details of the everyday to induce the comfort inherent in verisimilitude. Staged play relies on the fiction that a player need not be responsible for his or her actions while in play. This is Diderot's paradox: realistic drama differs only in the greater degree to which it borrows from the details of everyday behavior.

In games, the saving lie is that competition lies at the center of the occasion, and all rules which underwrite normal decency are out the window, unless enforced by the conventional rules of the game and, in case of organized sports, by referees in distinctive uniform giving them power within the game to enforce the rules.

In rites of passage, the agreed-upon fiction is based on having ritual officers—shamans, ministers, big brothers, high priests, panjandrums, poohbahs—who are, by convention, given the power to issue the orders of transformation. The license to transform is the very power that is commonly called *performative* in the critical literature emerging from J. L. Austin's theories of speech acts (Austin 1962). Performatives may only be uttered by those accorded the power of office. Thus, the two-kings complex: the distinction between the person chosen to play the role, which departs from his or her everyday roles, and the figure vested with holy and transforming words, such as the judge, the king, the rabbi, those invested by the state to pronounce those standing before them "man and wife," or convict them of a crime and have them imprisoned, ostracized, sent away, read out of the community, courtmartialed, rusticated, rejected, banished, deported, exiled, extradited, or executed. Even worse, your credit can be taken away from you. You will have noticed that we have departed strongly from the licensing acts of the everyday to something very close to making a friend into a stranger, an outcast, one of the homeless. This is the basis of stereotyping in many of these domains, but that is well beyond the subject of the goodwill principle operating between communicating friends and family.

Chapter 6
Playing

Any discussion of play should begin by confronting the dilemma that Brian Sutton-Smith presents in *The Ambiguity of Play*. After spending his professional life studying the experience of playing, he (like everyone else writing on the subject) had presumed that he knows what play is, but now admits that no one has defined it successfully, and the subject is all the more interesting because of play's ambiguities (Sutton-Smith 1998). There seems to be general agreement only that we understand play in contrast to other states of experience. Play activities ask us to leave the "real" world behind and help construct alternative domains which define themselves by the ways in which they depart from the everyday. While play appears to involve liberation, players usually agree to act in accord with a much more restricted set of rules and conventions. Getting into play calls for entering an in-between condition where the new rules are agreed upon.

The most enjoyable experiences and high times come when we choose for ourselves how we expend our energies. Play worlds hold out the promise of such freedom because they depart so strongly from serious motives and workaday concerns. Playing does free players up, if only by contrast with the serious imperative to produce that controls us at work. Yet participation calls us to take on a conventional role, to become involved in activity which is highly redundant, and to take on a special mode by which activities are judged. Play gets us away from everyday routines but, rather than setting us free, it demands different routines. We play in order to reach a heightened awareness of our bodies and our minds and to center our attentions, along with the other players, on an object, on stylized practices, and on an agreed-upon result. Free exercise has no winner or loser. If game-playing is involved, we judge the game not only by the intensity of the contest but by deciding who wins and what counts in winning.

From the perspective of vernacular interactions among and between realms, playing is the most profound way in which the principle of goodwill and good manners is given expression. Fun is more often than not experienced among people who both keep one another company and break into play regularly without hesitation. Yet the rules ordinarily generated by the principle of goodwill can be suspended in play. Motives of competition, testing balance, taking risks, and making fun of others are not only permitted but allowed to drive the activity. Through different kinds of play, distorting mirrors refract light in some strange corners of everyday practices and motives. Going too far under cover of play, going overboard, going over the line, is always a looming possibility. Play does not operate very successfully unless that line is under constant threat. This test of balance raises the level of participants' anxiety at the possibility of confusion on the sidelines. That is why the deepest kinds of play so often call for nonplayers to make sure the rules of decorum unique to the specific play situation are maintained. Without the radical confrontation of the real and the play realms, the engrossing competition between fear and desire would not be sustainable. Being a good player not only takes practice but calls for clever testing of the rules from within the field of play.

The vivid conditions of play have been nicely described by the biological anthropologist Gregory Bateson within the vocabulary of frame analysis (Bateson 1972). He focuses on how a consensual coordination of actions can give rise to certain frames of action which appear as independent contexts for those actions. Outside ordinary social interaction, framed events are enacted in which a self-canceling set of motives is deployed. The best-known example is the classical paradox of Epimenides, also known as the "paradox of the liar." In its modern form, this paradox is represented in the statement "this statement is not true," a statement that cannot tell the truth about itself without creating a paradox and thereby rendering itself senseless. Bateson argued that, in spite of this logical prohibition, these kinds of paradoxes emerge time and again in communication between people and even among social animals. Two dogs baring their fangs while keeping clear of a fight are able to communicate a message that "the actions I perform do not mean what they mean." In other words, animals are capable of reinterpreting their own interactions, setting a context or frame in which those actions can be understood as something other than what they appear to be.

Common sense and self-protection dictate that, in play, everyone has to live within the same rules and boundaries. Without such an agreement, play cannot proceed for very long. Humans know play best through the introduction of some sort of break in the routine of daily life. At those moments of confronting difference, humans seem to be at our best in terms of open and unencumbered energy display, with consequences only understandable in a situation where everything marked as play within an articulated frame will be interpreted as play until behaviors are not interpretable by the suspension of good behavior practices. Bateson made some of the most interesting observations on the relationship between these worlds. When full-out play is taking place, an attempt is made to create metamessages that the activities should not to be interpreted as real in any way, moves that remind those in sight that play is taking place and motives are not to be interpreted by real-world standards.

This is not to say that play involves only energies freely expended. As Victor Turner pointed out in his discussion of liminal and liminoid worlds, there is often holy work going on in play precincts, and all rites of passage might usefully be regarded in the same way that play is, within its cultural contexts (Turner 1974b; see also Handelman 1977). Just as rites of passage are both risky and highly structured, so the free expenditure of energies in play is ritualized. As playing draws on an economy of motives and materials that are distinct from the everyday world, the more play expends resources, the more it takes place in milieux which are subject to rules and regulations and to boundary maintenance.

Although behavioral scientists would be happier if play could be described in terms of observable activities that do not necessarily lead to a result, nevertheless the term constantly overflows its own vernacular meanings. We don't seem to like being tied down to a definition that stipulates what is included in this most protean realm of activity. Along with the terms *performance*, *ritual*, and *celebration*, the term *play* suggests that it is a state that can be gotten in and out of. It might well be defined by what it is not. It is not productive. It is not routine. Its disposition of resources is more implicated in consumption than production. And, like other terms for expressive states of being, it will not stay within its own boundaries, because no one wants to delimit its domain. It is too useful in its indistinctness. All that we know is that it is not work and it is not serious, but even here there are some noteworthy exceptions.

Getting Away and Into Play

At our most playful, we are able to get away from it all, even into a parallel realm in which the motives of everyday life are replayed with no obligation to commit to anything but the flow of the play itself and the rush arising with the focused expenditure of energy. This is true of the entire range of engrossing activities that go under the banner of play, from peekaboo and tag to the sporting activities of adults. In the vernacular, we distinguish between play and games, while recognizing that games are simply one way of organizing play. Playing games suggests that some kind of contest lies at the center of that particular kind of play, but there are games with no sides and no winners and losers, such as crack the whip. And there is side-taking in activities that no one would call harmless games. While play may seem to promise the experience of letting go, the departure is not from the rules, but from one set of stylized practices to another, all in the service of participation by the players and an ability to follow what is going on. We must learn at least the basic idea of the event to be able to participate, much less play.

For play to be most effective, a certain degree of previous experience is called for. Being an aficionado, a devotee, a confirmed member of the fan club—all heighten the bodily engagement of playing. Knowing the plays or the conventions of judging good performances heightens the possibilities of sympathetic involvement. Real worlds and play worlds feed off of each other, both in terms of bodily involvement and of intellectual grab. The two worlds operate with magical sympathy, especially when the play is modeled directly after a repeatable scene in real life, as in "playing house" or "going to the doctor."

Beginning to play usually gives a name to the play world, and the registers of the voices of the players are modified to indicate that play is taking place. In this way, whether in child's play or at the theater, the viewer is reminded constantly that the players know that they are operating within highly stylized and severely restricted environment. The greater the expenditure of energy, the deeper and more diverting the experience may be. In games, the play motive is contained within the rules and playing field, the boundaries set out before the game begins. In theatrical or spectacular playing, similar conventions operate to maintain control over the players and the audience. Boundary lines are often a permanent element of that constructed environment. In sports and at the theater, the line between the two is usually clearly marked within the structure in which the play is taking place. However, in all of these play environments, the players often test the boundaries and attempt to involve the audience directly.

The vernacular has been immeasurably enriched by the language we use for play. As playing is so ubiquitous and calls for such a high consumption of energy, players have developed many ways of preparing, practicing, and talking about the play. Metaphors derived from play are employed to describe all sorts of eventful activities. Yet this vernacular talk may cause confusion. There are so many arenas in which serious political, social, or economic activities are described in terms derived from games or playing that the frame between the two seems to dissolve. But politics does not require the same suspension of everyday rules as word games or verbal contests; different sets of rules apply, and very few strategies are translatable in any way beyond the metaphorical. An "end run" in a business transaction or a political contest has only a limited correspondence to the football move from which the trope has been taken. In fact, confusing the two realms may lead to transgressors being accused of going crazy, carrying out an illegal act, or at best "just playing" at something that has serious consequences.

Whatever is serious within the play frame has to do with testing the rules and boundaries from within. The more resources from whatever source, internal or external, the deeper and more engrossing we expect the play to be. When a serious game comes up in the schedule, the degree of preparation is sufficiently great that, if there is any indication that the players are not taking the game as seriously as the spectators are, the play environment comes into question both on and off field. Because of this anticipation and investment, *serio ludere* is one of the most important dimensions of community activity.

When a city like Philadelphia or Siena holds its biggest civic festival, such as the Mummers' Day Parade or the Palio, the display is totally engrossing for most urbanites. Although the vernacular term play is often contrasted with serious as well as with everyday activities, seriousness itself is a constitutive dimension of the play. By this I mean that there are two kinds of seriousness: one has repercussions primarily within the everyday; and the other operates primarily within the groups involved in the playing. However, the more serious the play becomes, the greater the threat is felt among all those present that it will break into the real world, affecting business, civic pride, and tourism. No one wants a riot, unless it is those who set out to produce such an upset.

Play is used to describe every diversion or entertainment, from the casual conversation to the deepest ritual acts. As Victor Turner has urged, even a liturgical event calls upon the same sense of departure from the everyday and draws upon the same cultural resource bank as less sacred affairs. His work also traces the continuities between secular and sacred celebrations. Initially, he distinguished between liminal and liminoid experiences, those which embody holy work and those which are placed in the service of community and civic authorities. In his final years, however, the distinction seemed less and less clear to him as he observed various forms of Carnival (Turner 1974b, 1977, 1982).

Playing is often used in the sense of "playing around," not being serious or productive. Play is opposed to work and to seriousness at the same time. But, to the very good players, those who practice and rehearse, play is extraordinarily controlled. In fact, players are exhilarated at the process of giving in. Playing is closely related to having fun and to relaxing, but they are not the same by any means. Fun is a condition of body and mind in which few motives are closely examined. Relaxation, on the other hand, may arise from the need to expend energies, or from the ways in which play activity removes participants from the everyday. Play, like its kissing cousin, art, lives for and within itself, though the social, economic, physical and psychological benefits are patent. Indeed, many philosophers from Schiller to Hans-Georg Gadamer regard play as the defining experience of being human (Gadamer 1989).

Opportunities to play promise a contrast to humdrum experience. The specter of boredom is confronted with players' need to keep things interesting. In children's games, this commonly calls for the ritual of choosing sides. If the game is lopsided, the outcome is foreknown, and the play loses spirit. The rules or the style of play must be changed to introduce a further wrinkle, as when children graduate from tag to a similar chasing game with a home base or neutral place. This principle, which some play theorists call *galumphing* (following Stephen Miller's use of this term), has affected all types of play, from hopscotch to football, baseball, basketball, and hockey (Miller 1973). The rules committee is constantly at work introducing new prohibitions or licenses which encourage new practices. However, it does so by introducing unbalancing moves or a way of playing which is unexpected. Equilibrium is constantly tested, both within the activity and between players and teams. Professional sports teams and leagues call the principle "parity," an ideal they seek so that a good game should result. Of course, the individuals and the teams themselves try to upend this parity by recruiting better players and practicing harder.

Play doesn't operate successfully unless the activity draws on disorienting motives of chance, risk, and testing or even breaking the rules of the everyday. If tedium arises from repetitiveness, simply going through the gate of the playground triggers something like relief. Preparing to play, the next anxiety is getting into the game or the flow of play or the spirit of what's taking place. Entering into the zone of play may relieve the anxiety of being in a self-imposed prison. If, on the other hand, boredom arises from a lack of intense involvement in anything, play worlds—most notably popular entertainments or celebrations—may provide this contrast. A good part of playing may arise, then, through an in-common response of a community to outside anxiety-producing conditions, such as winter weather, or life in the trenches. Within our vernacular system of play, some activities carry pleasure because they contrast with all other experiences. Such is certainly the case with Big Times such as Carnival. When the play is connected with an annual festival cycle, the performers prepare their get-up for much of the rest of the year.

The passage of the seasons central to agricultural time and to the cycle of celebrations in premodern societies was supplanted by the calendar and clock of the industrial world, as workers punched in and out with time cards. Under such rigid time-keeping, working by the hour or by the piece, leisure had to provide the main break in the flow of everyday, and Sunday was taken away from the church and given to the playing field or the theater. Then, with the half-day relief on Saturdays, lo was the weekend born, and then the other breaks that "put a little weekend in our week." With the diminution of jobs in heavy industry and the shift toward providing services, usually of an episodic sort, another way of thinking about the uses of our energies came about. Flex-time has become more central to our plans. Work which used to be called housework or handiwork now looms large in the economy, especially since in the majority of households all adults engage in wage labor. In such an ergonomic environment, playing or just having fun becomes all the more of a necessity and an entitlement. Throughout the exindustrial world, increasing pressure is placed on enjoying oneself. As the incipient lassitude of drudge-work leaks into the play world, we insist on ever more intense pleasure-producing forms of play and spectacle.

Happiness arises from being surrounded by those activities which reach for the sensational. The payoff for everyone involved in playing is the possibility of being carried away by the shared activity. Play consumes everyone in its presence; even if we are not performing ourselves, we are so attuned sympathetically by bodily memories of past playing that we share the exhaustion and exhilaration. The overload of the sensorium which used to be reserved for celebrations and holidays now becomes the standard for all playing.

Each individual and each couple is given a day of exotic celebration surrounding the cutting of a cake. The whole affair is given permanence by cameras and video recorders. What had been a source of pleasure in the company of friends and family gravitates toward a display of consumption where play is no longer an entitlement but an obligation. We celebrate for our families now, as calendrical events serve as a magnet to bring them all together. We celebrate so our grandparents and our grandchildren remember the deep pleasures of family life. The government threatens to intervene when either the holiday or the family itself is threatened by the depth of consumption taking place. A bloc of national budgets is given over to fostering families and legislating holidays and vacation time. Now enters the desire of most of us to get away from it all. The anxiety level is too high. The best investment is the second home, the financial advisors counsel. Will that luxury now become a necessity, like owning more cars than there are drivers or having a television in every room? Perhaps that has already occurred as high-school students go to entry-level jobs rather than to meetings of the chess club or the Future Farmers of America.

In a consumer economy, play always seems excessive, useless, trivial, even deadening. Yet, the gatherings play creates can be commodified and pulled into the exchange economy. All of the devices of economic exchange enter into the play sphere; as shows are produced and sporting events are staged, the identity of humans as players becomes a paying proposition. Because play arises out of the optional side of life, paying for play or its inverse, playing for pay, seems anathema to many, for it commits the most egregious confusion of categories or genres. Play then becomes entertainment or spectacle. Somebody has to pay, and that somebody usually means nearly everybody. There are no tickets given which are totally free. Consumption always carries costs, however they are reckoned.

The play motive can be found embedded in any activity, but a play event goes out of its way to create a separate world, with different ways of apprehending and registering experience. Play stretches the body and the mind in a manner which has made it seem central to the most human activities. Because of the flexibility of body and mind which playing enhances, one strand of philosophy has seen it as the defining element of human life. But play involves more than physical or psychological departures from other states of being. When it is contrasted with work, play seems like activities that are under no obligation to produce anything. If anything, play consumes our energies and enthusiasms in a profligate manner. Play, in such an environment, serves as the point of liberation from official rules and other features which regulate our lives. Playing approaches shared experiences and energies as a kind of petcock, or pressure-release valve, through which our excesses may safely be channeled and let loose. Play is an effective way to divert attention from more threatening motives, especially when replay is included in the horizon of the term. Because playing may break out in any social situation, the vernacular tosses up the age-old questions concerning fencing in versus fencing out. Play can be wild, yet it is subjected to the kinds of controls that are employed to make anything natural into something cultural. Unruly motives can become divisive ones, calling for the exercise of control from within, by the rule-keepers, and from without, by the gatekeepers. The intensity inherent in play needs monitoring so that it doesn't get out of hand, either through rioting and mobbing, or by going beyond dizzy or risky behaviors into behaviors which society brands as diabolic, barbaric, or crazy. Play and its outgrowths in celebrations, sporting contests, and conflagrations are at the heart of the practice, for through flirting with danger, overdoing it, going overboard, playing gets close to the line of needless destruction. The deeper the play, the greater the need for the imposition of customary controls, through delimiting boundaries, creating play spaces separate from all other constructed environments, and having both formal and informal rules and rule-keepers.

Deep Play

The place of play in our culture can be understood as opposed to work. Its place as opposed to seriousness is a slightly different problem. The history of play theories suggests that no successful description has been possible because of the multiform character of the contrastive set of experiential states which produce fun and laughter and temporary relief from everyday anxieties.

Through the ubiquity of play, the concept of rules and boundaries is first encountered, and these limitations give meaning to acts of civility. As play is translated into display, as the activity becomes deeper and more rehearsed and preconstructed, play comes to serve those in power. Games, once useful for channeling the excessive energies of the group, now are deployed for civic and dynastic reasons. They can be owned and produced by powerful people in the community, who invite their friends to the spectacle. Displays of excessive wealth under chiefly and monarchical regimes, in the form of pageants and parades, become something else when directed by the representatives of those in power. Displays then include acts of subservience as well as hegemony. Even in our most economically informed moments, this subservience is read as enslavement or cooptation. Those paid to perform become the servants of those in control, and being in service to anything in a representative democracy carries contradictory feelings. When players are paid, they are accused of betrayal. Confusing play with the workaday world and making entertainment into a service industry seems like a violation, at least to the spectators.

Play worlds are engineered to encourage getting away from the rest of life. Entering a play space involves crossing a line, and the consequences of such transgression are not insignificant, even if the play is frivolous. Crossing the line invokes the twin incitements of fear and desire. Being enlivened through play always calls for giving into motives in which rehearsal, practice, even replaying afterward are part of the overall experience. Not only are repetition and other mimicry expected in play, but the highest experience, when one is carried away by the play, emerges from that point where moves have become automatic. How often do we hear players and spectators, aficionados, or fans attest to the experience of the play itself becoming unconscious? Players say they do it in their sleep. As a lifelong fan, I know the same holds true for the spectator. Try as we might, some of the time we just can't leave the play in the theater, stadium, or playground. The experience is so intense that it is vividly remembered in both body and mind. Because playing demands heightened experiencing, it is addictive. This condition is both psychological and physiological, having to do with secretions below the level of consciousness. Bateson was aware of just this in his study of play and schizophrenia. He reminds us that a bounded or framed area has to be set aside with the message that "everything within these bounds is play" (Bateson 1972).

Getting permission to play calls on previous playing, knowing the names of the positions on the team, practicing the moves—whatever is conventional, rehearsable, and memorable based on past play. Each play activity has its own names for the players and a set number of repeatable moves, steps, plays, ways of spelling out the rules and articulating the boundaries from within the frame itself, which are learned through practice and rehearsal. In command of the moves and the places where freeing-up occurs, we "get into the zone" and give ourselves over to the experience. Play becomes so deep and all-encompassing that the preconditions of total focus exist within the activity: a player may go with the flow, let it take over, give up self-awareness. A transformation of self emerges directly from the playing situation, in which players get outside of themselves or more deeply into themselves. At the point of transportation, the differences between inwardness and outwardness are without significance. Players may be identified by their ability and capacity for getting intense, at least while their playing days continue.

Grave social problems occur when this identity is taken outside the play realm, as when a boxer slugs someone outside the ring, or even someone of another gender or playing age. Alternatively, a player may use his or her identity to achieve license to play outside the stadium. At that point every act may be interpreted as being an extension of his or her identity into other play and display realms: a sports star becomes an actor, a politician, an action figure in an off-field drama, even a murderer. Or he changes gender styles, becoming she or queering pronouns entirely. What is one player's or spectator's social problem can be another's social commentary. If everyday identity is given over for that moment, the activity seems to exist by itself to the players, the team, or the cast of characters, beyond the disorientation of the noise, the lights, and the inhibitions called upon by everyday rules. This state is often called being carried away, totally into it, with it, out in space. As it gets deeper in its own vernacular vocabulary, play is capable of taking over. When I try to rest my argument on the terms native to the activity, I encounter a problem. Each type of playing generates its own vernacular terms. Wherever there are players and fans, there are elaborate ways in which everyone talks things over before and after playing. I call on terms from a number of different kinds of play, for the terms themselves have been drawn on in wide variety of play activities.

Describing the everyday world from within the unreal world of play is impossible, yet, of course, it feeds on habit and custom. Play operates in its own zone, on the stage, the field, the place set aside or recoded at the time of getting into it. The limits of play, the rules and boundaries, must always be tested, but sometimes playing has so taken over that going over the top is always possible. Play might not be successful without the looming sense of going out of bounds at any time. At such points the audience, the spectators, or an appointed monitor must reassert the boundaries of the frame and enforce the rules in the name of those attracted by the free display of intensely focused energy. Play draws upon the physical and psychological state brought on by the adrenaline rush and the flow of pheromones. Deep play occurs when the play and the players go beyond themselves, the roles, and the rules. The player, in testing the rules and the boundaries, can hide behind the rush which emerges from within and without at the same time, licensed by all as appropriate to the occasion in that time out of time and place out of place. Getting in and out of play differs only in intensity and focus from getting in and out of performance.

Places set aside for one or another kind of play suggest the kind of permissive activity both players and spectators expect. But they expect an attempt to break the rules and attack the boundaries as well, for to operate effectively play must contain constant reminders of the realms of the everyday which on which the play is feeding parasitically. For most involved, the experience of successful play is attractive in itself; it needs no justification. Play tests the sensorium in special ways that remind us why the experience is so deeply and conventionally framed. Each dimension of play involves tests of the boundaries between the real and the play worlds that threaten everyday order in some way. This balance is achieved through taking chances, defying gravity, getting so totally involved in the patterns of behavior in this separate world that to come back to reality becomes difficult. Of course, incidents may occur of such grave consequences that the rules of the everyday must be reinstated.

As Roger Caillois limned play and games—there is no distinction in the French, *les jeux*—each kind of play may invoke focus on one or more of these areas of bodily experience (Caillois 1979). The largest play events, such as rites of passage, invoke all of them at once. The deeper activities are closest to rioting. Even rioting might be better understood as play and display joining hands and spilling over. This conjunction is confirmed by the vernacular ways of making ruckus, tar and feathering , rebelling, revolting, taking to the hills, holding a kangaroo court, riding posse, going on strike, demonstrating—all of those occasions in which a group or club is transformed into vigilantes, rebels, or outlaws. Rebels engineer a confrontation by pitting behavior against the customary rules and practices, taking over authority, forcing a calling out of the troops. The authorities, whoever they are, enforce the law when play spills out of the frame. Here the vernacular is especially volatile, taking on terms for unruly behavior from other tongues: running amok, going berserk, having a charivari.

On the less wild side, many of our events are included in the domain of *festive gatherings*, all those goings-on in which people come together of their own free will to display themselves in a customary and anticipated manner. The venues in which festive gatherings are held affect how they are conversationally referred to. Usually they are connected to a season or an event marking a life-passage. The farther removed from home, the more public the event is likely to become. At the farthest extreme are those festive events held in the open, in a space where those in attendance are excused from everyday norms and manners: at carnivals, circuses, sporting events; parades, and festivals.

From a pragmatic perspective, participants in these shows, displays, and performance events seldom have any problem in recognizing and interpreting that something beyond the everyday is taking place. One seldom has to ask "What's going on?" unless the show itself engineers such bewilderment to induce focus-in-common and audience participation. Moreover, a sense of possibility arises because the events take place in already valorized public spaces such as theaters, arenas, or grounds. Finally, these are events that we are able to prepare for, anticipate with a combination of anxiety and hope, and recollect afterward.

Each type of festive gathering carries its own set of expectations that operate as guides to what kind of experience awaits. The nature of the occasion provides the focus for the event and the primary means by which expectations and actual behavior are intensified. These occasions fit into several categories: a performance or set of performances; a game, contest, or sporting event; a calendrical festive gathering, celebrating a time of year (harvest, midsummer) or a personal milestone (a birthday, a wedding); or a commemoration of a historical event. Performances mark the occasion by a mimetic, playful activity which calls attention to itself and which distinguishes participants as performers or audience. With games and sports, the focus is agonistic; conflict produces winners and losers. This kind of activity insists on distinguishing players from spectators. Festive gatherings draw from all the dimensions of the play experience: dizziness induced by oversaturation through ingesting, imbibing, having an adrenaline high. Much like rituals, they involve an experience of interruption from the everyday, a shared experience which mimics life in some dimension, and a return to the everyday world. Just as he described rites as liminal experiences, Victor Turner called these festivals liminoid, recognizing that something like sacred communitas is a defining feature of the experience (Turner 1974b, 1977). In them, the unexpected is as common as the expected.

By contrast, less playful commemorative events use the same techniques of playful intensification, but are usually framed by a ceremonial beginning and end, in which status distinctions are on display through controlled ways of talking and acting. Speech-making and other ceremonial activities provide the core of such intensive experiences. Of all large-scale festive events, commemorations are most like ritual, and rites also often have a strongly ceremonial component. The difference is that rituals are both obligatory and bring about, or potentiate, social transformation, while commemorative displays are optional and confirm rather than transform the statuses of participants and onlookers. Both sorts of events work to open up the senses and the social structure.

Such distinctions between types of events are commonsensical; we make them as a matter of course so that we can prepare to enjoy ourselves properly. The one overriding feature of all of these events is the ways in which they borrow the vocabulary of the play experience, now recoded in response to the occasion. While we recognize the general thrust of the event and carry into it a certain set of expectations, we also know that such festivities, like any other kind of play, can stretch whatever boundaries and rules are involved.

As festivities are altered into spectacular events, they borrow effects from one another to intensify the overall effect. A performance, such as a concert or circus, also involves standing up eating and drinking, as happens in receptions, picnics, or other pass-through events that are otherwise not enthralling. The response of the regular audience on such occasions may be that the producers have gone over the edge this time. Similarly, games or sporting events call forth parades, special foods and beverages, performances like half-time shows, cheerleading, and band-playing, and are often marked by opening speeches and an invocation. A commemorative event such as the Fourth of July or Juneteenth centers on the speeches which spell out the serious meaning of the day, but attracts all the paraphernalia of gatherings devoted to festive amusement.

The most memorable performances are those that really surprise, break frame for a moment, and force us to think about what the event has become. My wife and I went to a performance of "Sunset Boulevard" in London some time ago. Petula Clark, the fine singer, was starring in this production. At the beginning of the second act, the elaborate machinery used to raise and lower the set broke down. The curtain fell so repairs could be made in private. Clark came out in front of the curtain and apologized in an endearing fashion, talking about the vagaries of theater life. She then asked the audience if they would like to hear any music from the show while the repairs went on. Someone in the audience shouted out "With One Look," the signature song of the show. She replied: "Oh, yes, I really messed that one up tonight. So thanks for giving me a chance to make appropriate repairs." She brought down the house. Just a glimpse at the "real" Pet Clark brought a pleasure that a show which stayed within the frame would not reveal. The spectators felt they were right up there on stage. The awe inspired by theatrical magic was enhanced as the audience saw that these were fallible humans, not mechanical puppets singing mediated melodies with the aid of microphones and spotlights. How close to the edge theatrical playing is to real life even at its most extravagant. What a relief to be give up the burden of maintaining the suspension of disbelief. Few audience members realized that the singer was simply trading one kind of role for another, that she was suddenly back on the concert stage or in the cabaret. She changed play worlds, not really showing her offstage self but giving teasing hints about how she might be in casual conversation. This crazy breaking and remaking of frame made the occasion unique.

The framing that takes place when players enter into their special world is evident, as playing departs from real-world criteria of judgment and style. Performing is only one of many ways in which the intensity of stylized activities marks this break from the everyday. Yet performers know that they have to test these patterns of expectation by apparently breaking frame, reminding the audience that these are real people performing and that at any moment some element of reality may intrude. The degree of difficulty of the performance, an important dimension of any playing, is revealed as the frame breaks, the scenery topples over, the injured player or dancer is carried off. Some of the most memorable moments of my life as a spectator return to mind because of the breaking of the play atmosphere.

As Bateson noted, play has a paradoxical character; the play frame and the name it is given are conventionally accepted, but attacked from outside and within at many points in the proceedings (Bateson 1972). This presumption of acceptance is called into question at some point in the playing, as participants ask whether everything within the frame is play when things are obviously in a parlous state. The counter-message is also provided: "Is it really?" Play both relies on and violates the conventional dividing line between serious and playful ways of acting. Whistle-blowing draws attention to the fragility of boundary-making. Seriousness and playfulness, like real and unreal, truth and falseness, are regarded as opposites. But the practice in any kind of play is to allow the real to loom over these fabricated interactions, whose rules don't map well onto those of the everyday. Playing allows us to depart openly from the realm of responsibility and enter into a world that promotes a different system of accountability. In play, the repertoire of moves and motives which operate in the real world are subject to appropriation, but without necessary consequences.

Many observers regard play as basic to humanity in another dimension. Play is a means of experimentally trying-out and trying-on alternative selves. In play, we are encouraged to allow ourselves to be transformed and so to enter into the field or zone which only partially mirrors what goes on in the quotidian. In the very serious environment of war visited upon the Netherlands, Johan Huizinga considered such questions in his book, *Homo Ludens: A Study of the Play-Element in Culture* (1938). He parsed the human repertoire of motives and means to discover the relationship between these different states of being. In his view, the world needed to think about what combative play encourages. His theory of play focused on the spilling-over of agonistic motives and confrontative strategies into the mundane world. In play, manners and decorum become focused on the way the game is to be played. As those are stylizations of only one dimension of customary practice, the conventions for which the player is held accountable represent only a small and highly focused dimension of commonplace procedures. Accountability lies only in the agreed-upon rules and stylistic flourishes of play. Bellicose engagements occur when aggression and contestation spill out of the bounds of play and weaponry and ammunition are provided to those involved to affect the outcome.

The loss of self-consciousness is not registered as a failure of control so much as getting into the rhythm of the activity so fully that it feels as there is no necessity to question. It resembles the moment writers attest to, when an insight translates itself directly onto the page. In the days of pen and paper, it was said that the pen starts writing of its own accord. With the typewriter and personal computer, the experience draws even more mystical allusions, for now the words flow off the ends of your fingers, even though the pc is not always an automatic device. Aspiring writers are told not to resist this feeling, as it is part of our better selves.

On the other hand, consider the experience, reported by those addicted to games of risk or chance, of entering into a zone in which the player just knows what is about to happen. This is not precognition, sad to report. Rather, it is the addiction talking directly to the source of judgment, or so reformed addicts report. Organizations such as Alcoholics Anonymous and Gamblers Anonymous create groups premised on understanding the loss of self-control as the player enters that zone.

These moments of giving in to impulse are clearly related to what Clifford Geertz called *deep play*, in which the investment of personal resources is so great that the impulse to play operates independently of individual will (Geertz 1971). This condition is not only experienced by addicts; it is also familiar to die-hard fans, soccer moms, and impulsive punters. The recent documentary film *Strut!* focuses on one Mummers' club in Philadelphia, a set of working-class families who devote much of their energy and income to sewing a costume for the next New Year's Day parade and competition. The mummers and other members of their families discuss how strange and wonderful this expenditure of time and money is (Raab 2001). Studies of Mardi Gras bands and of Trinidadian Carnival underscore that these are year-round activities which totally engross the players and direct the passage of their year (Stuempfle 1995; Scher 2003).

The thrill of competition is so attractive that it takes over the gametime moment, and it is so fulfilling that, even if the deep player loses, players feel compelled to repeat the experience. In a rational society, deep play would never occur, because playing leads to a giving up of self-control. Resources are taken from everyday necessities and spent recklessly. When they work, these experiences take a player beyond self-consciousness and into a different realm of apprehension.

Getting carried away may lead the player into the state called the *zone*—that is, so fully into the flow of the game that something like second nature takes over. All the practice and the painful injuries retreat to the background. As one professional basketball player recently put it, "all the little things are suddenly in place . . . all the moves, all the plays, everything is there inside you, but they also are there outside, too. It's weird." It's like the muse that descends, enabling composing or inventing to find its own way.

This loss of self-consciousness within a play state has been theorized by the social psychologist Milhalyi Csikszentmihalyi. He appropriates the vernacular word *flow*, employing it to describe the state of creative abandon that emerges as the activity seems to take on a life of its own. The promise of achieving wholeness descends on the individual artist, game-player, or athlete in the flow experiences reported in Csikszentmihalyi's study of poets, mountain climbers, chess players, and participants in other activities that involve extensive training and practice and operate within a tightly restricted set of possible moves. Players themselves tend toward spatial metaphors to describe the feeling of connectedness (Csikszentmihalyi 1975).

What used to go under the banner of revelry or merry-making now devolves upon partying and raising hell. These events regularly shake those in official positions of authority and demand that crowd-control planning be put into place to maintain or reassert order. Celebrations of destruction and consumption are enjoyed in terms of how close to the edge they can get before riot breaks out. Carousing groups set out explicitly to threaten to turn the world upside down, in a move which culture critics, following Mikhail Bakhtin, call carnivalization (Bakhtin 1981, 1984; Clark and Holquist 1984). This set of practices involves the deepest of deep play motives; it gathers around moments of the year set off from all other times.

Where does play begin and the real end? Similarly, when does play become display, simply a spectacle?

Chapter 7

Events/Experiences

The word *experience* has such flexibility that it serves us well in tying together the ordinary and the extraordinary; so much of life is already enshrined in its circle of meaning as it is used in the vernacular. Experiences happen to individuals and are therefore sometimes regarded as idiosyncratic, but these very same occurrences might, under other circumstances, be usefully regarded as typical. The philosopher Charles Morris argues in such a direction by distinguishing between "private experiences" and "common experiences" (Morris 1970: 115).

All of us have a double consciousness and a sometimes self-contradictory value system about the meaning of these new experiences in the creation of ourselves and the needs and rights of others. For Daniel Schorr, the great newscaster, "reporting" and "reality" are deeply connected; he notes that as a reporter he was constantly confronted with the need "to discover the 'real story' or to extract it from the mists of vagueness and pretenses" (Schorr 1977: vii). This mighty calling demanded a certain amount of distance from the frantic events to which he and the people he interviewed were witness. This man, who could truthfully claim to be engaged directly in the action, nevertheless responded to the experience more as observer than participant:

It made me feel more real not to be involved. Participants took positions, got excited, shaped events for woe or zeal, but what a strange paradox that seems—to feel more *real* but not be involved—to be where it is happening but not to be engaged. To keep the action sufficiently distanced to be able, still, to call it an event, yet because that very distance provides the objectivity necessary to sort out important details of "the story." In fact, just being there, seeing the picture without being in it, qualifies the activity as an experience precisely because one is able to report, firsthand, what really happened. I remained the untouched observer, seeing the whole picture because I was not [actually] in the picture. (Schorr 1977: vii)

Schorr's description fits our work as ethnographers. Does not the field experience call for us to become professional naïfs, demanding that we self-consciously make ourselves invisible, and therefore supposedly remain untouched? A creative regression, if you wish, but a regression nonetheless. Placing ourselves in this position, we may observe, ask, and even imitate without taking the social risks such acts might produce were we taken to be adults.

This regression is carried out with the knowledge that, while we seem to our informants to act like children, because we are outsiders who come with devices of a powerful technology (such as cars and tape recorders) we can hardly be treated as less than adults.

Doing controlled observation reflects an approach to events as experiences that provides a kind of spiritual hedge against interpreting experience-at-a-remove as simple thrill-seeking or voyeurism. With our immense hunger for experience, having achieved this psychological distance while we make our professional observations, the feeling of noninvolvement—indeed, of the inability to involve ourselves fully—begins to affect the quality of our observations. Somehow we find a substitute with sufficient sustaining power to be able to say we were not actively involved. Being on the sidelines merely watching the big plays permits us to replay them later to those who were not on the spot; there is sufficient energy in such happenings for all those present to be recharged by the action. But those who are only looking on and reporting develop a double consciousness about the activity.

The problem of this double consciousness is far greater than I am able to get a handle on here, for it has much to do with our notions of what constitutes learning and to what extent and purpose we really do live and learn. Moreover, with the growing emphasis on the individual's control over his or her own identity, institutional ways of engineering personal transformations have lost much of their power. For such socially sanctioned transformations to occur, we must believe in the power of those invested with authority to mark these changes for us. But such authority has been undercut because of our belief that we should do such changing on our own. Authentication is substituted for authority. If success in life were a given, there would be little question that experience could be a useful teacher, if not always the best one. But a corollary of our American Dream is what might be called the American Dread of finding out that growing means eliminating some of our options. Failing in a task will do this, of course, but so will succeeding too well and being promoted because of that success. Our dread is always that we can't go back.

Many of the formative thinkers on the relationship between narrated experience and life and art have worked their profundities in witnessing failure. Donoghue discusses how American writers draw on the experience of personal failure, making it into "aesthetic forms and ceremonies . . . to take away some of its 'stress', thus entering into the all-too-human process of assimilating it." His response is that of the literary critic still adhering to the "wound and bow" approach by which great art is forged out of deep personal hurt. Donoghue discerns in American letters a pattern by which the genre "achieves its vitality by a labour to transform the mere state of failure into the artistic success of forms and pageants; it learns a style not from a despair but from an apparent failure—some, like Henry Adams, by making the worst of it"; others, like Henry James, "by making the best of it, and the best of it is the same thing as the most of it" (Donoghue 1976: 104).

These observations recognize in such a dynamic and often self-contradictory form both our attraction to experience for its own sake and our ambivalence about why we are so drawn to it. Both success and failure are useful outcomes, especially as the experience is talked about and written about later. Just how American this double consciousness of experience is becomes clear from the prominence of the contrast between the doer and the watcher in our classic works of literature: Henry James, who glories in the occasional moment of felicity in the midst of decorous, if frivolous doings; Henry Adams, who can only scorn the present because of its deep duplicities and its failure of nerve. Many American works of fiction are built around a pair of characters who dramatize the problem: one deeply involved in the action, whether successfully or not; the other a witness to it all and sometimes a judge as well. While one reading of *The Adventures of Huckleberry Finn* would make Huck and Jim into such a pair, the great example of this type of narrative is *Moby Dick*, with Ishmael being drawn unwittingly to the sea and to the voyage as a witness to Ahab's obsession. Other outstanding examples of such onlookers and reporters are Nick Caraway in Fitzgerald's *Great Gatsby*, Nick Adams in Hemingway's short stories, the more world-weary Jake Barnes in Hemingway's *The Sun Also Rises*, and Stingo in Styron's *Sophie's Choice*.

We identify all of these characters with the storyteller-author and his growing up through having experienced the energy and frenzy of these more charismatic presences, these larger-than-life figures, the Ahabs and Gatsbys who represent a mysterious power source which guarantees that wherever these figures are significant events will occur. These quintessential American novels are constructed around the interplay between the characters who instigate the action and those who are there to observe and record, who are caught up in the swirl of transforming events but emerge much wiser, perhaps bruised by events but relatively unscathed, so the story can be told.

Until the reflexive turn in ethnographic reporting (see especially Clifford and Marcus 1986), most formal field reports told us little about the experience of the fieldworker and little more about the experiences of the people being observed. Rather, we saved records of the systems and institutions that order the lives of people in groups, enlivened every once in a while with a representative anecdote. On the whole, the reflexive dimension of the ethnographic literature has not been well developed. While we have a number of fascinating autobiographical reports from the field, fieldworkers seldom address how cultural norms and professional expectations entered into the collection and reporting of materials, much less what was happening to them that might have made a difference (for a significant exception, see Rose 1982, 1987). As ethnographic reports get closer to the details of recurrent expressive behaviors, we seek to discover how individuals within a community learn cultural performances, prepare for and judge them, and feel about them before, during, and after their occurrence. With this shift, more ethnographic attention is being paid to native theories of emotions and feelings, as well as to the more objective utilitarian and symbolic orders provided for participants in a culture simply by having grown up within a specific milieu (Myers 1979; Lutz 1982; Feld 1982; Glassie 1982).

As I see it, this drawing on experience in anthropology is a part of the process of internal monitoring of basic terms and concepts that takes place in every professional discipline outside as well as inside the academy—among groups of doctors and lawyers, social workers, and even particle physicists. In the social sciences, especially sociology and anthropology, we have unique problems in taking stock of special terminology, as our keywords are derived from everyday talk (see Williams 1979: 180, for an indication of the importance of experience in his ongoing concern with keywords). As native interpretation becomes more and more important in our ethnographic reports, *experience* gives promise of tying together our everyday feelings with those encountered during Big Times. Experience addresses the ongoingness of life as it is registered through the filter of culture—that is, through acts we have already learned to interpret as experiences or, in the case of shock, surprise, embarrassment, or trauma, through acts we reprocess as experiences after the fact by talking about them and thus making them seem less personal and more typical.

Our commonsensical distinction between events—things that happen— and experiences—things that happen to us or to others—is important for a number of reasons, not least because notions of who we are as individuals are often tied up with those unique-if-typical things which have happened to us, especially when those happenings have become stories we tell ourselves. Individual experiences enter into the ways we choose to craft identities. Rose has consistently made distinctions between what "experiences we . . . recognize as meaningful as they are occurring"; the semiotic systems by which we are able to order experiences as we are having them; and an economy of experiences in which those we have are to be regarded as personal resources that may be used in interpersonal exchanges as a way of authenticating ourselves (Rose 1982: 220).

The ways in which we use our experiences as part of our personal economy are not well understood, or even directly addressed, by ethnographers. Stories about our own experiences provide an important resource not only for establishing a place in the community because of our special knowledge but also for establishing our identity, should that be an important feature of the culture. Such stories are commonly told to those who will respond in kind, or at least with some kernel of information regarded as equally valuable. If we kept such notions in mind, we would not be so surprised when many of the questions we ask of our informants are regarded as strange precisely because answering them calls for a giving-away of scarce resources.

The experience of being asked to give yourself away is far from unusual in our own most personal interactions. Examine how you feel when someone tells one of your stories about something you have experienced and told about in the past. You are likely to feel mimicked; worse, your ability to speak for yourself is put into question. This feeling is not aroused in all cultures when personal stories are appropriated, but a truly reflexive anthropology would make us aware of the possibility.

Such radical individualism, with its need to feel unique, is not held by the rest of the world. As Geertz cannily put it, "The Western conception of the person as a bounded, unique cognitive universe, a dynamic center of aware-ness, emotion, judgment and action organized into a distinctive whole is, how-ever incorrigible it may seem to us, a rather peculiar idea within the concept of the world's cultures." Nonetheless, he recognizes the draw that such a con-ception of personhood might have on ethnographic studies that attempt to get at the everyday experiences of those under observation. Geertz's caveat is a commonsensical one, even if difficult to abide by: "Rather than attempt to place the experience of others within the framework [of 'person' or 'self'] we must . . . view their experiences within the framework of their own idea of what selfhood is" (Geertz 1976: 225). This endeavor calls for the collection of native exegeses of the experiences regarded as meaningful; that is, discussion not only of the experience itself but of its value from the perspectives of the person to whom it happened and of others within the same interpretive com-munity—the *emic* way of describing culture. But, more commonly, we draw on our own metaphors—that is, we will use an *etic* perspective and the anthro-pological terms of art that go along with it—for interpreting the ways in which repeated actions within a culture are systematized and anticipated.

The notion of describing cultural activities in our own vernacular terms for goings-on—terms like "action," "practice," "occasion," "event," "experi-ence"—attempts to sidestep the limitations of the tropes derived from per-formance and play. We are pulled toward a vocabulary drawn from the exchange of energies for serious purposes with such terms. But this vocabulary is equally deeply implicated in our own very American and modern discourse on individuality and selfhood, our native notions of personhood.

The American pragmatic tradition of philosophy has brought this weight-ing of the everyday and transitional character of life as lived into the open (see Turner 1982 for another view of its genealogy; see also Turner and Bruner 1986). Anthropologists are drawn to this idea for many of the same reasons our philosopher-forebears were: to escape the imprisonment of using a priori ideal categories of the significant, such as the metaphysical tradition's notions of sublimity, virtuosity, and genius. The pragmatists sought to encourage a pluralistic cast of mind that would deprivilege the extraordinary moment of vision in favor of the more spontaneous chance occasions available to anyone, not just those who had refined their sensibilities and pursued their genius.

William James developed this point of view most fully and poetically. "Life is in the transitions as much as in the terms connected," he insisted in 1899. "Often, indeed, it seems to be there more emphatically, as if our spurts and sallies forward were the real living line of the battle, were like the thin line of flame advancing across the dry autumnal field which the farmer proceeds to burn" (James 1967: 212–13). The pragmatic tradition was set in motion by Ralph Waldo Emerson, especially in his later essays when he was extending his thought to the importance of the momentary (Emerson 1903–4, 3: 64). "We must set up the strong present tense against all rumors of wrath, past or to come." The only way to escape the hold of inherited moral precepts was "to fill the hour and leave no crevice for a repentance or an approval. We live amid surfaces, and the true art of life is to skate well on them" (Emerson 1903–1904: 3: 59).

James went even farther, giving moral weight to everyday experience as a way of putting such rumors to flight. He asserted in 1892 that we must find means for a "reinstatement of the vague and the inarticulated in its proper place" (James 1967: 21) and underscored the importance of "openness" in achieving meaning and purpose in our interpretive scheme. Repeatedly he asked us to contemplate the power of achieved relationships between things as well as people. However, what this perspective lost in the translation from Emerson and other transcendentalists to the pragmatic point of view was the importance of risk in the recognition of the moral weightedness taken on by our personal actions. Bloom evokes the problem as a gloss on Emerson's argument in "Self-Reliance": "American restlessness . . . puts all stable relationships at a relatively [low] estimate, because they lack the element of risk" (Bloom 1984: 20). Neither those who employ play analogies, such as Erving Goffman and Victor Turner, or those who drew on tropes from fire and other unpredictable natural processes, such as James and Dewey, have reinstated this Emersonian concern with the risk involved in valorizing the transitional, the vague, and the inarticulated.

In the translation from the Emersonian to the Jamesian perspective, personal moral probation is neglected in favor of emphasizing everyday life as the baseline against which other kinds of experiences are recognized and interpreted. We become more concerned with the human condition than with the questions posed by the morally tentative person in everyday dealings with others. James's vision encourages the equation of time and space in the experienced moments of transition. At such moments, when past time and present life most vibrantly come together, connections may be perceived and relationships established that "enable us to live prospectively as well as retrospectively. [Experience] is 'of' the past, inasmuch as it comes expressly as the past's continuation; it is 'of' the future insofar as the future, when it comes, will have continued it" (James 1967: 21). Just how deeply this concept is an invention of James's generation becomes clear in the writings of the commentators on the American language. H. L. Mencken, the most trenchant among them, noted that the verb form of "experience" was a recent American abomination, attributing the neologism to Henry James's friend William Dean Howells (Mencken 1919: 168).

James opened this subject up to philosophical speculation from the pragmatic perspective—that is, without tying it to metaphysical concerns. Dewey went one step further, placing everyday experience at the center of his philosophical concerns. He remarked that "like its congeners, life and history, experience includes what men do and suffer, what they strive for, love, believe and endure, and also how men act and are acted upon, the ways in which they do and suffer, desire and enjoy, see, believe, imagine" (Dewey 1925: 10). He encouraged us to link two notions of clear importance for anthropology: life is best conceived as carried on by individuals who have a capacity to remember and thus to build a future patterned on the doings of the present; and existence is describable on a commonsense level as an active and unfolding process. By understanding the individual's role in the process, we secure a place in the culture pattern for invention and idiosyncrasy. Experience as both a personal and a social construct looks on life as being made up of rules of thumb rather than of formal and regulated patterns of behavior.

This very notion of personal negotiation and play undergirds a pluralistic approach to the contrapuntal operations of the individual mind, on the one hand, and to the many interwoven voices and styles of society and culture, on the other. In the situation involving the coming-together of peoples of different cultures and historical conditions, this multiplicity of voices becomes the problematic facing any attempt to describe experiences adequately. Putting forth a theory of adequate description based on experiences under conditions of high mobility, especially in border situations, asks not for an all-out rejection of such notions as tradition, custom, or even rituals, but rather for a transvaluation out of the realm of authoritative practices and into the domain of socially devised units of activity, which are valued because they are agreed by all of those participating and because they embody patterns of expectation that can be learned, rehearsed, and practiced together. Emphasizing the common features of experience calls for a redefinition of culture itself away from the officiated practices, the regulated and obligatory behaviors of our shared lives and toward something more like the relative typicality of what happens again and again to individuals finding themselves in similar situations.

When an experience can be designated as typical, the doings of the individual and the community become shared, with regard not only to what actually happens under those circumstances but also to how people feel about the happenings. Simply stated, it is not just experiences that are shared but the sentiments arising from them as well; the doings and the feelings reinforce each other. This systematic typicality of event and sentiment provides us with a linkage between past and future, for the very recognition of typicality rests on others having gone through that experience or something like it before.

Thus enters the experience of experience—that is, the recognition, even while something is taking place in one's own life, that it is a replaying of things which have happened to others. This self-perception is especially important when the experience is not typical but intense and potentially disruptive. At that point, being able to recognize typicality becomes a means of recognizing how to feel and interpret what is going on. Through such reflexive activity we can recognize the difference between the more and the less ordinary, the every-day and the special event, as it is becoming *an* experience. Dewey pointed out this distinction: "Experience occurs continuously, because the interaction of live creatures and environing conditions is involved in the very process of living. . . . Oftentimes the experience had is inchoate. Things are experienced but not in any way that they are composed into *an* experience" (Dewey 1934: 35).

The distinction between levels of self-conscious apprehension achieved a place of such importance in Dewey's scheme because he wished to reveal the continuities between art and life. Therefore, he underscored those happenings in everyday life that are most like our ways of encountering works of art within the Western tradition: by the disjunction in the flow of experience that calls for a consideration of the event as a "thing apart." "Life," Dewey argued, "is no uniform uninterrupted march or flow. It is a thing of histories, each with its own plot, its own inception and movement toward its close, each having its own particular movement" (Dewey 1934: 36–37). His interests were in excerpted actions that have a sense of beginning, development, and end, like a well-crafted piece of the storytelling art. Perhaps he was guided by his own underlying feeling that *an* experience involves not only an intensity of feeling that takes it out of the flow of the everyday but also a framing operation by which the ongoing activity is translated into a reportable story—that is, suffi-ciently interesting that others to agree to classify them as *an* experience. But who will thereby listen to the recounting of the happening?

Even at the level of typicality by which experience becomes *an* experience, the term's semantic field is far from fully described. Indeed, an even higher and more general level of typicality enters into our discussion of how individu-als enter into happenings and feelings that are so characteristic of the larger developmental patterns we call Experience—the American Experience, the Jewish Experience, the Sixties Experience, even the Growing-Up or Growing-Old Experience. In a similar acknowledgment of differences of intensity and significance, we distinguish between events and something that becomes the Event, even the Big Event, most often through being marked by some rite of passage.

Although it is difficult to hold this range of meanings in mind while constructing an anthropology of experience, it is necessary to do so. For while *experience* is usefully employed to discuss meaningful actions ranging from the most ordinary to the extraordinary, we expect the more intense occasions to have a point, even to carry a message. Our native theory of action carries the expectation that we may be transformed by the intensity of the experience itself. To regard all activities making up an experience or part of a significant event as necessarily having such potential would severely undercut the usefulness of the idea of experience as a way of connecting the everyday with the special and the ordinary person with the representative human.

Yet just as surely there is a difference between the way we interpret everyday experiences and those that jump out at us as being significant. This difference is carried, in part, by the interpretive apparatus we use to discuss any experience. Between experience and the Big Experience, we impose a frame on the activity by calling attention to its extraordinary character. This attention commonly is elicited by the self-conscious stylization of the activity and by preparing for it, through rehearsal, warming up, or special kinds of anticipatory behavior.

This framework may be accomplished as simply as saying "Not it!" to instigate a game of tag. But it may be as complicated as the ways a family anticipates Christmas or a community prepares for a pageant, picnic, or parade. In those times out of time, an agreement goes into effect that everything taking place within that set-aside space will be judged by its own criteria of the permissible. This cultural device is so commonsensical that it can be evoked by the reminders of the subjunctive character of the practice, as Victor Turner named it, the hedging that occurs whenever we say, "We're just playing" or "It's only make-believe" (Turner 1974b). Whenever we agree among ourselves to enter these realms, we achieve a particular relief from responsibility for our actions. We are able to say that we are not quite ourselves when we are in such a state.

This suspension of the rules may be brought into play precisely because when we are within such frames we are involved not so much in experiencing things directly as in replaying them. The elements of preparation, rehearsal, and recapitulation introduce a kind of distance from the actions as they might be enacted in the everyday world. However, we must also recognize that any kind of replay involves the risk that the original will be so adequately represented as to dissolve the frame itself. Could any subjunctive activity operate effectively if the "as if" quality did not threaten to disappear at any time, the players jumping squarely into the spectators to strike them with their bats, or the firewalker pulling someone from the audience onto the coals with him?

Casting experience in these terms suggests that what we call *an* experience is of two kinds: those arising directly out of the flow of life, with little or no explicit preparation; and those for which we plan and to which we look forward, where the parts are precast and each role has its set of lines. The two share a scenic wholeness and a heightening of awareness, as well as the possibility of being repeated in form or reported on in substance. The greater the degree of self-conscious preparation and stylization, the more the experience may be shared, but also the higher the risk that the prepared quality of the event will be regarded as restricting rather than liberating. This becomes more problematic in those arenas in which the experience is ceremonial, an affirmation of traditional hierarchies and roles. The frame placed around the event calls for us not to take on alternative selves, as in play, but to be our best selves, to present ourselves in the best possible light, only more so. On such formal occasions there is no relief from being judged for what we do and how we act. Ceremonies celebrate whatever system is in place, as they elevate individuals who are being honored.

Despite these disjunctions between everyday experience and more openly fictive displays, a sense of continuity between these various realms is also guaranteed. Americans seek to ease the passage between Big Times and ordinary life. We value openness and apparent spontaneity, while we depreciate most expressions that follow form and convention. In our desire to optimize authenticating acts at the expense of authoritative ones, we seem to appreciate most those moments we can say afterward were big but which stole up on us and took us unawares. To encourage such moments, we expend a good part of our energies secretly preparing for these breakthroughs, for the spontaneous times in which we are overcome by the fulfillment of the expectations we hardly could admit to having—like those first-time experiences which, when successful, are so surprising because we hear about and even talk about them but they seem to sneak up on us anyhow. We are surprised only by the fulfillment of expectations.

Perhaps only the demystifiers in our midst, poets and sociologists, discuss such secret subjects openly. Paul Valery refers to these moments as "the active presence of absent things," when the accumulation of what we have already discussed and anticipated comes together with those experiences that occurred so early and were repeated so often that they became an unacknowledged part of our repertoire. This active forgetting becomes an exercise in what we used to call "custom" or even "habit": "The social world seems to us as natural as Nature, although it is only held together by magic. Is it not, in truth, an enchanted structure, a system found [in] . . . obedience to words, the keeping of promises, the power of images, the observance of customs and conventions—all of them pure fictions?" (Valery, quoted in Levi 1977: 308–9). Yet we have a number of ways of reminding ourselves of these cherished fictions, talking explicitly about what they mean and how they have come to mean what they do. We do this most during celebratory events. The discussion can be staged formally, when a ceremony is built into the event, or informally, when the occasion seems to come off with some degree of spontaneity. In that case, discussion after the fact turns on the intensity of the good time and what it takes to have such satisfying experiences. In spite of our distrust of formal practices inherited from the past because they are attached to a power system that seems to many to eliminate mobility and choice and, by extension, self-determination, we still enter, smiling and gracious, into such times when we ornament life by planning ahead, by getting dressed up and bringing out the best china and silverware. But also consider how much we value those times when a casual "drop-in" becomes a "get-together" and develops into a "party," a "blast," a "really great time."

Many events heighten our sense of life without requiring us to go through extensive formalities. We make our preparations for these in secret, for so much of our sense of self is predicated on appearing spontaneous that we cling to the idea that parties are best when they happen on the spur of the moment—which is about as true as the idea that lovemaking is best when unplanned. We have identified the appearance of spontaneity with our notions of the authentic self. But the value we place on authenticity burdens us: in our heart of hearts, how many of our acts are really spontaneous? Moreover, such questions of authenticity affect our perceptions of others, both as participants in a culture that privileges self and originality and as ethnographers constantly testing the behavior of our informants so as to judge whether or not we are being fooled. We must understand our own predisposition with regard to judging the acts of others if we are to stitch together an anthropology of experience.

All observers of human behavior seek a corner on the market of reality, for that is our profession, our way of managing our own identities. The project of all of the humanistic disciplines has been to discriminate between the real and the unreal, the genuine and the fake, the realistic and the sentimental or fantastic, the verifiable truth (all those things we call "the facts") and illusion, the misleading, the mystified, and the mythical. Humanists seek insight into life as a means of living more fully themselves, of experiencing more knowledgeably and more deeply, and thus being able to impart these techniques and this accrued knowledge and wisdom to others.

Goethe presents the Faustian dilemma to the reader in precisely this fashion. But the problem and the search are hardly reserved for professional seekers of truth. The drive to distinguish the real from the ersatz is part of Western common culture, used to develop the criteria by which we judge the behavior of others and ourselves. Repeatedly, our response to others depends upon how "real" they seem and how much we can "be ourselves" with them, how unguarded we can be in interacting with them and still feel comfortable.

Regarding someone as sincere or a fake, an original or a show-off, hardly exhausts the repertoire of ways by which we judge others. In fact, using the relative naturalness of a person's behavior as the basic criterion of what is real and what isn't would guarantee that we would be bored by all encounters and relationships. In many circumstances, the ability to pull off a role with spirit and in a manner to which we may respond in kind appears more important than whether the other is being sincere or even authentic. Our continuing fascination with those who openly perform, especially if they are willing to take on the role of the eccentric or the vagrant spirit (from Hell's Angels and punkers to hoboes and carnival spielers), reminds us that those who appear to speak and act from extreme experience often seem more real to us than those preoccupied by mundane pursuits. In fact, we seem to judge what "the real thing" is by how fully others are able to make us recognize the range of experiential possibilities, whether or not we undergo such experiences ourselves. Again, our double consciousness is brought into play: the value we place on centered action and on those who seem to engage life to its fullest calls forth our admiration and even adulation as well as our fear of taking risks.

Under such circumstances, reality is only understandable when we are able to contrast it with other kinds of experience, perception, and judgment. To William James's classic formulation of the problem—"Under what circumstances do we think things are real?"—must be added, "What do we contrast with what in developing our notions of the 'real'?" In some situations we distinguish between fanciful or poetic and real without judging one better than the other; in other situations we distinguish between "real life" and "just playing" without placing greater value on the real unless the occasion calls for high seriousness or a focus on work. Indeed, play may not only be appropriate to the occasion but actually heighten reality by quickening our senses. To be sure, ludic activities call for self-conscious attention to stylistic expression, and therefore depart from ordinary with regard to both preparation and actual play. But any activity that calls for us to act and react together at a high pitch can become a Big Time for us, valued for itself and in some cases used as a baseline against which everyday activity is judged—in which case the verdict is that life is boring for the most part.

Whether in the form of planned play, spontaneous celebrations, or even riots, some among us place supreme value on the action, on experience for its own sake. These breaks in everyday routines provide the measure of whether life is being lived to the fullest. Ever greater importance is placed on those experiential departures into the higher and deeper registers of feeling which emerge in rehearsed events and encourage us to get "deep." This quality is central not only to the experience of getting serious at the performance of a work of high art but also in having Big Times.

These two varieties of serious experience underscore the problems as well as the strengths of the pragmatist's approach to activity, a limitation shared by sociological phenomenologists such as Alfred Schutz and Peter Berger. Both schools use the quotidian as a representation of the "real" world from which all other states of experience depart. Schutz set up the world of experience in terms of a contrast between "the world of paramount reality" and all others: "the world of dreams and phantasms, especially the world of art, the world of religious experience, the world of scientific contemplation, the play world of the child, and the world of the insane," all of which he regarded as "finite provinces" of significance (Schutz 1970: 225). Yet, while noting the ease with which we may travel between these discrete worlds, he argued: "Within a single day, even within a single hour our consciousness may run through most different tensions and adopt most different intensional attitudes to life. . . . Furthermore [there are] regions belonging to one province of meaning [that are] enclosed by another" (Schutz 1970: 256).

We operate both within and between these various worlds and their realities. Clearly, one is no more real than another; rather, they differ in what is brought into them in common by the participants, how focused and intense and stylized the activities become, and how important such factors are in affecting the experience and our understanding of it. No concept of "a world of paramount reality," whether it comes from the pragmatists' idea of experiential flow or the phenomenologists' characterization of the quotidian, allows us to understand fully enough the role of play, of having fun and making fun; nor does it enable us to comprehend the process of celebration with sufficient fullness and clarity.

Both the flow of activity and distinctive, marked-out acts and events go under the name of experience. Moreover, the very flow of the everyday assures the continuity between routine activities and extraordinary ones. We have become aware of the continuities between the ordinary and the deeper or higher events through performed mimetic experiences, which openly imitate and stylize everyday acts and interactions. Far from exhausting the relationship between the ordinary and the otherwise, such imitational play only begins the discussion. Indeed, how the disruption of the patterns of expectation in ordinary interactions is remedied, even transformed, and used in play events may prove to be the most important point of connection between these different states of apprehension and understanding.

Each subjunctive event is more than simply a rendering, direct or inverted, of a social practice; it is itself an experience. Each draws on a community's concern with disruption, clumsiness, embarrassment, confusion, and conflict in the everyday. But in forming and stylizing the reported events, each develops a life of its own. Each performance draws on energies and patterns of expectation brought to the occasion not only because it embodies some life situation but because it departs from the everyday to the degree that it is self-consciously and artfully imitated, replayed, performed.

Consider, then, the complexity of the relationship between activity as it is practiced and the rendering of it as it is reported, reenacted, and intensified. Must life precede art for art to be understood? Can we comprehend a feast without knowing everyday eating habits? Too often the line of actual experience runs the other way: someone goes through hard times, yet to the extent that they are able to see the situation as typical, they maintain a sense of control over the situation. Is it not useful, then, to avoid drawing a hard-and-fast line between the finite representations of repeated events and any conception of paramount reality? In different kinds of scenes and interactions, there are various relational features that past practice enables us to understand and appreciate: levels of formality, of scenic wholeness, of intensity of frame, of calls on our attention, of reaction and judgment.

My argument may seem somewhat self-contradictory. On the one hand, we have a sense of disjuncture between the *flow* of everyday experience; *an* experience; a *typical* experience that is reportable about ourselves as a means of playing out our having entered, individually, into life's recurrent problem situations; and a large-scale Experience in which we recognize that the progress and pattern of our activities are part of a much larger story that began long before we were born and will continue after our death. On the other hand, the placement of the openness of experience within the American ideology of self-determination makes us conscious that the distinctions between the ordinary and the extraordinary commonly do not arise from either formal demands emerging from the ceremonializing of life or from any hard-and-fast distinction between the serious and the playful. Rather, we see life as organized around times, places, and occasions that encourage the participation of a greater or lesser number of people in a common activity. This approach sees both the larger and the smaller experiences as creative achievements; each experience, whether planned for or seemingly spontaneous, is interesting only insofar as it is able to enlist participation—that is, if the planning produces some sense of discovery, some spontaneous exchange of energies as well as information with others. For Erving Goffman (1967), the experience of even the smallest understandings (much less our larger mutual celebrations) seemed like a new rendering of an archaic holy act, which acknowledges the existence of others and signifies a willingness to be involved in the flow of vital cultural information and, on occasion, to be exuberant in passing on this knowledge as a way of tying together self, others, and the larger worlds.

By turning to one of our new holy terms, *experience*, and developing it into a moving term of art, what might we reasonably expect from anthropologists propelled by the desire to get down on paper what has been experienced in the field? First and foremost, such ethnographers carry into participant observation a recognition of their own culture's notions of significant actions and their related emotions and sentiments. This awareness yields a willing suspension of disbelief in the poetics of the new culture: the things that are regarded as being in the same category, the things that may be compared, and those that suggest other things in spite of not being in the same category. An anthropology of experience begins by noting the range of expressive means and affects, techniques and sentiments—that is, the most common and ordinary activities in the flow of life of the group under observation. Then it provides a calendar for the events that are already set aside as extraordinary.

Finally, an anthropology of experience looks for the ways in which the ordinary and the extraordinary coexist; how convention permits the framing and stylizing of activities, calls the participants to attention, and encourages a spelling-out of the meanings and feelings carried within these activities. In an anthropology of experience, the preparations for group display events are as significant as the means and messages carried within the events themselves.

As humanistic social scientists, then, our objective might simply be to demonstrate the flexibly systematic diversity of human behavior in groups. In moving *experience* to the center of our critical concerns, we elevate the representative anecdote and the personal experience narrative to the same analytic significance as the rite of passage. Our great discovery is not that everyone has experiences that are both unique and typical, but that everyone seems to have a way of organizing these doings so they may be shared. Just how this articulates with the elevation of individual identity is a matter for further discussion.

PART III

Social Imaginaries

Chapter 8
Zones and Borders

The tacit understandings that undergird privacy, friendship, and community rest not only on a substrate of commonplace expressions and experiences but also on an in-common typology of settings more complex than the simple contrast between private and public. The physical environment in which experiences-in-common occur provides a set of places in which certain ranges of behavior and scenes are expected by all who enter there. Following the contemporary social philosopher Charles Taylor, I call those marked spaces a set of *social imaginaries*: "A social imaginary is that common understanding which makes possible common practices, and a widely shared sense of legitimacy." Designating such zones is a part of our vernacular understandings learned through previous experience. Social imaginaries, as he puts it, are "deeper than the intellectual schemes people may entertain when they think about social reality in a disengaged mode . . . the ways in which [people] imagine their social existence, how they fit together with others, how things go on between them and their fellows, the expectations which are normally met, and the deeper normative notions and images which underlie these expectations" (Taylor 2004: 24).

In the vernacular, we tend to discuss such social imaginaries as generically marked spaces identified by the activities that are regularly conducted there. The boundaries between different kinds of places are constantly under negotiation. Every community-wide occasion carries with it rules of the day, which establish and maintain the borders within which familiarity and its vernacular practices hold sway. In many communities, an annual festive activity is used to mark the physical and experiential boundaries of the home country—a social imaginary if there ever was one, but a necessary fiction for those who seek order within the bounds. Indeed, at many points in the life of groups, such festive activities not only animate the social imaginary but actually constitute it. Variously called "beating the bounds," "ridings," or "perambulations," these annual events call together the central members of a civic entity to renew symbolically the physical boundaries of the place. They march around the perimeter of their common holdings, stopping at customarily designated markers to hold a small ritual of reconfirmation. Guilds, confraternities, or other organizations enter into the spirit of the occasion, often by donning costumes associated with their position in the local social order, and joint in the procession. The community reconstitutes itself through reconsecrating the boundaries between the civic entity and the outside world.

While the perambulation must be regarded as a serious ceremonial event, it is also a time of framed play. This is the moment when the sporty fellows of the community may seize the day and use it for their own antic entertainment (Abrahams and Bauman 1978). Ignored for most of the year, these rude fellows look for moments of celebration when they can act up, showing by their invective and often libelous behavior that they too belong to the community, no matter how imaginary it may be. By threatening to disrupt the order of the occasion, the players coerce the rest of the community into accepting, through the provision of cakes and ale, that this is their event too. On such occasions, at this time of the year, social inequities are redressed for a moment, and the poor are given their "wake"—the yearly treat which they have inherited by custom.

Ceremony and tomfoolery live side-by-side within this enlivened environment. They operate in contrast to and in combination with each other, confirming each other by the devices of mimesis. Together, they confirm the possibility of heterogeneity within the otherwise fixed social order. Through juxtaposition, they confirm that a life-world without marked differences in social status is imaginable, not through riot and revolt, but through tolerated acceptance and conjoined fear and hilarity. Deborah Kapchan calls this other side of mimesis "anti-genres . . . multi-styled and hetero-voiced," taking her critical position by revoicing Bakhtin's notion of carnivalization (Kapchan 1996: 35). These anti-genres mix high and low, serious and comic modalities, opening up the town to liberating mirth even as its citizens confirm its integrity.

A constant struggle for hegemony between these two worlds emerges on such occasions. The sporty fellows, unvoiced for most of the year except among themselves, are now elevated through their ability to mimic, to open up the other worlds and slither around in the mud they themselves create. Transformative possibilities emerge from this clash of order and disorder, cleanliness and contagion, hierarchy and rough equality. Even in the most closed and controlled polities, these exuberant times are to be found. The hubbub of the marketplace environment is used to trigger an alternative world of pure consumption, extending beyond the regular market day and the marked marketplace. The authorities respond to this outburst with riot control tactics, although forcible attempts to impose decorum may only provoke discord.

In those civic events which take place year after year, the proceedings are reined in by turning them into tourist attractions. The contest between various groups is made generic, classified, and controlled by awarding prizes to symbolic victors. The procession begins at one place, passes by a reviewing stand filled with dignitaries, and ends at another. If the rough and ready crew wants to turn the world upside down, they must go back to their home territory and put on an alternative ruckus. In this way, Mardi Gras is coopted and staged for tourists, amplifying civic pride and profits. So, too, Carnival in Port of Spain and Rio become tourist amusements through crowd control. Chaos is never far below the surface. The bottles are still passed between the players and the crowd, and the clowns and devils still scare onlookers through their frontal attack. The carefully constructed walls between players and spectators leak, and mirth overflows. Spirits are raised by overconsumption—and by subjecting the official world to satirical distortion and temporary inversion. Yet, the players become caught up in the officially sponsored competition. They must upgrade their acts to draw appropriate attention to themselves. The once unruly find it necessary to be costumed and made up by professionals, and their routines are planned, choreographed, and reach a climax at the moment the performers pass the reviewing stand. The merriment is fueled by competitive juices as well as the high jinks themselves. Participants no longer control their own transformation; it becomes a group matter and is negotiated with the authorities. When the chamber of commerce intervenes, improvisation and spontaneity are replaced by design and rehearsal. The players are pushed to the wall to reinvent themselves in the old style. They feel a sense of loss, as their control over what had been at their heart of their community enterprise is eroded. If they feel lost, they complain together, remembering the old days, looking at the old pictures, telling of the times that things really got out of hand.

Meanwhile, everything is amplified, giganticized, miniaturized, made into themes for the tee-shirt-seeking crowd. Spectacularity edges out the element of fun between friends and family, when the guys from the neighborhood used to mask and make fools of themselves. This development is not inevitable, but it is encouraged by increasing communication and mobility across zones formerly delimited and separated by time and space. The occasion is no longer a symbolic reenactment of community bounds and customs, or even a threatened dissolution of its boundaries and overturning of its hierarchies. Both the performers and the crows are faceless—and not simply because they are masked. But there is no reason to be cynical in the face of a takeover by the spectacular. This trend is just another adjustment in vernacular culture, part of a drift toward one-stop entertainment centers. In a parallel case, we go to the mall to shop, to window shop, to look and be looked at, and even, if we are young enough, to hang out with our friends, just as the evening promenade or drag strip used to operate.

Marketplaces

Public events create a highly charged time and space in which anything is to be expected, especially surprises. In public places, even everyday happenings may turn into events if anything erupts, transforming walkers and talkers into gawkers, focused watchers and listeners. A sudden noise might do, or turning on bright lights, or setting off an explosion. The greater the disruption, the more the onlookers come to be participants in whatever has erupted, and—if the crowd does not conclude that they are under terrorist attack—the interruption will gravitate toward spectacular performance. Fireworks, anyone? Visitors from the country to the city notice the noise and intensity of local life, just as urbanites do when first visiting a working farm. It is the break in the flow that brings life to notice and turns events into Events.

When noise and bustle of an unaccustomed sort frighten us, we run away, attempt to make a plan of escape, or, at best, look around to see how others are handling the situation. The more public the setting, the more we have access to others' reactions. Then the choice arises between individual and concerted responses. If police or other uniformed officials are present, we look to such figures as first responders. Barriers are called for, and the decorum of everyday life is reinstated to calm everyone. This scenario is not dissimilar from what happens in staged events, celebrations of civil order, even national holidays, where the sense of being startled to attention, pushed off balance, carried out of bounds, and absorbed into a crowd is used to enhance the experience.

A willing suspension of the expressive rules of privacy occurs at the door, on leaving our homes and venturing into the street, as well as on entering marked public spaces. In a variety of such environments, the air is heavily laden with pent-up energies; participants are there in order to sidestep the rules of long-term reciprocity operating among friends and family in favor of the risks and thrills of short-term and potentially duplicitous modes of exchange. The marketplace sets the terms for this place in our social imaginary. Here, the gathering of untrustworthy fugitives is taken for granted, as are the perils and pleasures of entering into negotiations with traders, entertainers, and those providing special services. At the market, the language by which the goodwill principle is commonly carried out is coopted, used to confuse buyers and to call out a reciprocity which encourages buyers to let down their defensiveness in favor of the pageant world of the exchange.

The boundaries of these markets are notably porous. No one seems to be guarding the gates, at least during the day. The chain of command of those in authority is purposely occluded, emphasizing that visitors are alone in the crowd and need to develop and deploy their own techniques for handling the disconnect from the rules of home. Indeed, buyers and vendors must constantly ask themselves who's in charge and how the authorities obtain and maintain their dominion. Markets which encourage a regular clientele rely on the repeated exchange to carry its own rules; the vendor looks for the returning customer, seeking to establish a reliable if not regulated pool of buyers. The liberation of these zones of trade is more manifest in fairs and festivals, in which both buyers and sellers are on the move and operate in an exchange system in which trickery without future consequences is a constant possibility. These moveable feasts are premised on the suspension of the rules of friendly exchange, without ceding the language of long-term reciprocity which undergirds friendly interactions.

Here, buyers are attracted by all of the apparatus and ambiguity of play: risk, chance-taking, costume pageantry with its eye-catching devices and exotic apparatus, and the ever-present possibility of conflicts breaking out. The boundaries between the real and the artificial are forgotten for the moment in favor of the pure involvement promised by the events taking place. Artifice is allowed to heighten experience. Entertainments, grotesquery, travesty, and surprise all add to the attractions of the expressive exchange. The market and the fair promise freedom, whatever that means in an otherwise highly regimented and policed society. Here, everyone is equally vulnerable to being conned. Advertising through the exoticism of their costumes, patter, and wares, the traders speak a language that buyers find intriguing but only half understand. The system of communication is stretched to its limits. Our linguistic guard is lowered, as is the law in other public worlds. Each fair or market has its own lord, its own kangaroo-court way of settling controversies quickly, its own standards which have to be observed—that is the rule of custom and commonsense (Braudel 1982; Stallybrass and White 1986; Agnew 1986; Abrahams 1988b).

This sort of phenomenon was on Fernand Braudel's mind when he said: "The market spells liberation, openness, access to another world. It means coming up for air." His point is a historical one, for he is concerned with the social and psychological concomitants of such freedom of exchange. "Men's activities, the surpluses they exchange, gradually pass through this narrow channel to the other world with as much difficulty at first as the camel of the scriptures through the eye of a needle. Then the breaches grow wider and more frequent as society becomes a 'generalized market society'." These markets, while described in archaic or exotic terms, are well known to tourists and travelers as sites of reconnaissance—looking into the most public segment of people's private lives, observing what they do when they go out of the house. Such places and the rules they authorize are never totally lost in the development of a metropolitan area and of modes of economic exchange. As Braudel put it, "there is no linear history in the development of markets . . . the traditional, the archaic, and the modern or ultra-modern exist side by side, even today" (Braudel 1982: 26).

These uneven developments have been unendingly fascinating to me as an inveterate flea marketer, a garage sale vulture, and an auction hand. In any conurbation, open spaces will be appropriated for purposes of exchange and entertainment, even as periodic fairs and celebrations continue in the center of town. Braudel described this developmental cycle: "Taken over by the townsmen, the markets grew apace with them. More and more markets appeared, overflowing from the small town squared which could no longer contain them." Each, as it became oversaturated with vendors, buyers, and vagrants, became a part of the movement outward from the center. "The solution adopted was to send them to the outskirts of the towns, outside the walls and towards the suburbs. . . . The new did not chase out the old. And since city walls also moved as the urban centres expanded, markets which had been placed sensibly on the outskirts found themselves locked inside towns, and remained there" (Braudel 1982: 30).

Zones

The marketplace and the home are the most extreme contrasts between the familiar and the public experience. Many other zones call forth scenarios which lie between the closed private and the openly public worlds. Each of these spaces in the social imaginary suggests conventional and repeatable expressive activities of a particular sort: playgrounds and playing fields, beaches and boardwalks, theaters and amusement parks, courts and churches, internment camps and prisons. Each suggests specific traditions of display. And each involves its own set of risks, secrets, thrills, ways of dressing and showing ourselves in other dimensions, ways of departing from the everyday and entering into a different temporal and spatial zone.

When everyone recognizes what kind of public display is occurring, they can derive their interpretive apparatus from the social imaginary they have learned through past experience. "What's going on?" operates much like "What's the story?" A recognizable set of conventions and expectations are put into play, making the event into an activity promising fuller participation. Players and onlookers come together as reactions and expectations are duly typed; the experience itself can now be identified.

Different places in our daily itinerary call for a range of distinct ways of acting and judging. The shared apprehensions attendant on entering a theater, a playground, a ballpark, or a fairground are different from the anticipations that arise when we enter a place of business. Going through any doors or gates reminds us of what changes we should expect to make. The more secret or potentially threatening the actions beyond the doorway, the more we want to prepare ourselves ahead of time. Leaving an accustomed place is just as difficult as entering terra incognita.

This dynamic is invoked even when leaving that place you call home. Custom may dictate a reckoning of where you are going, but in most situations locating yourself in relation to such a resting place begs explanation. Accountability to friends and family for where you're going and what you're going to do there may have become more common with the shared perception that "it's a cold cruel world out there," filled with all kinds of dangers and evil strangers. The popularity of the mobile phone, which facilities the coincidence of independence and interdependence, has made a licensed getaway easier for those who leave and for those who don't.

The old wisdom still applies: you are not yourself the minute you walk out your door. At the points of passage between home and other territories, we maneuver and negotiate in order to maintain our sense of stability. At the edge of the property on which we reside, arrangements have to be made so that we may pass out the front gate safely. Or, perhaps, we can navigate within our neighborhood without crossing into foreign, even hostile turf. What I call our *comfort zone*, the place we can let down our hair and "just be ourselves" without fear of conflict, encompasses more than the proverbial hearth and home. I use to term inclusively for those places in which people gather together for friendly discourse and joking: in the pub or rum shop and the barbershop or hairdressing salon. It is difficult to specify what practices really give satisfaction or induce pleasure, and, even at home, or sitting around with friends, kidding can quickly turn serious and confrontational. Yet the social imaginary nonetheless defines this as a zone of safety. Outside our comfort zone, confrontations occur when we judge ourselves to be subjected to unwanted approach. Going out in public, no matter how familiar, carries its own rules.

Many specialized spaces promise special experiences within. Pleasure gardens and palaces have not disappeared; they just got new names, and their reconstruction was carried out overnight. The commercial takeover of bourgeois life has created a plethora of places to meet, shop, eat, and enjoy other kinds of pleasures not found at home in the comfort zone. Even casual ethnographic observation of shopping areas demonstrates that the modern mall calls for as great a change of personal approach and avoidance rules as the archaic market did. In zones of economic and aesthetic exchange, wariness is coupled with a sense of adventure in the face of the entire range of public display forms.

In using the notion of zones to make such distinctions, I follow the dictates of vernacular mapping as it is presently discussed in the everyday. Zones are a part of the vocabulary of many agents of official life whose mass-media presentations affect the vernacular. Pleasure zones and tourist destinations have become interchangeable in the language used by whoever is packaging and marketing Experiences. As the contemporary perverted proverb has it, "When the going gets tough, the tough go . . ." "Shopping" is the most common reply, but "out of town" or "on vacation" are also common. Moving on, moving up or down, getting going, any generic form of locomotion carries its own set of concerns and expectations.

In public, the imperative to type and to draw on stereotypes is deeply embedded in our social defense systems; making quick judgments is necessary to keep our equilibrium and prepare ourselves for any eventuality. We must look out for ourselves even in familiar public places. There be not only monsters but exotic strangers there! Techniques of managing unexpected public encounters are passed on whenever people of one gender or generation walk around with those of another. Warning signs must become recognizable; we have to make constant physical and visual adjustments. Stereotyping of strangers, much less enemies, brings out a different second nature, a secret set of wariness procedures that closes in on the "open society." Slurs, slams, and racist jokes openly confront the norms of friendly behavior.

This distinction between private and public spaces, between going out and coming home, is commented upon more frequently by travelers than by ethnographic reporters. Because of our appetite for recording performances, folklorists and ethnographers of communication have left unquestioned the rules that others hold about how to get around safely and to move from one zone to another. This matter becomes especially complicated when homey entertainments are performed before a larger public who may not know the performer personally. Simply going about at Hallowe'en has made us aware of the perils of taking the show on the road. Carolers at Christmas no longer move from house to house; instead, we gravitate toward places less open to incursions. Fireside tales and parlor entertainments put into more public environments are performances of nostalgia, but they have been enacted in public places for millennia. Singing, storytelling, and other traditional entertainments are a perennial and ubiquitous feature of the marketplace.

In markets, singers and storytellers contend with other types of performances. Magicians and clowns, philosophers and preachers, healers and other masters of transformation add to the din. Teaching and preaching may occur, medications and healing services be offered, fortunes cast, and so on. Work itself often becomes part of the show, with admiring crowds watching craftspeople making their own kind of magic, transforming raw materials into objects for sale. Mumming and luck visiting have been transformed into street theater. With the growth of towns, the masked players who were let loose knew that their audience did not know the person behind the mask; so, as larger crows of more anonymous spectators gathered, luck visits became performance and busking.

In marketplaces, at fairs and festivals, and even in sports arenas, wherever there is a transient population, there is a need for rulings on the spot. Quick justice must be executed for small but invasive crimes, with officials meting out summary judgments; crowd-control techniques must be deployed if the gathering threatens to get out of hand. Social order and pricing may be regulated in this way. Short-term relations between those who are not familiar with one another mark these places of exchange, especially if the market is periodic and the clientele is drawn to the event from other environs. Here in public, buyers and audiences become indistinguishable from one another, especially when the vernacular of friendly conversation is drawn upon for reasons that are not always friendly.

As the crowd expands, different linguistic and cultural practices collide.

At flea markets, I have witnessed the conflict in styles of vending and bargaining cause problems as new ethnic groups come on the scene. The rules of friendly engagement are severely tested when so many strangers bring such a wide variety of buying and selling styles to these transactions. Performances in such settings demand a different way of projecting and modifying the voice, enlarging gestures, employing props, and making other physical alterations that take into account the size of the audience and the shape of the spaces in which the spectacle is contained.

In zones of one sort or another, one gives oneself over to the rules governing the marked place, departing from friendship norms. But this departure is not always noticed by everyone involved in the exchange. The experience is often felt to be natural, which may mean nothing more than what is to be expected in the particular zone in which we find ourselves. Yet it is also discussed as being *in the culture* of the designated district. The term *zone* emerges in many semantic contexts, all of which refer to a generic value-space, as in *comfort zone, combat zone, twilight zone*. Just as there are many conventional ways of apprehending situation-specific behaviors, many scenarios or scripts are colored by the mise en scène called into play.

This sense of the term *zone* is quite different from, but not entirely unrelated to, the way in which the term is used colloquially by players, which is discussed in chapter six. The phrases "in the zone," "getting into it," being "in the groove," or "in flow" are used by both athletes and musicians. They refer to those times which seem to soar above everyday time, when players enter into a different register of experience and are carried away, at least for the moment. Whatever is going on seems to run by itself. Just how "it" operates here is problematic, being so vague and insubstantial: "really getting into it" and being "in the groove" have no specific referents. The experience is sometimes put in spatial rather than temporal terms. Being "in the zone" or "zoning out" do not refer to a specific place, but to an experiential level where everything flows. The vernacular use of *zone* to define specific places in the social imaginary, each with its own set of rules and expectations, is more concrete and less fluid than this exalted state.

Each zone conjures up a special kind of intense involvement of the participants. Mihalyi Csikszentmihalyi, the theorist of play, calls these autotelic flow-states (1975). In his late work, Victor Turner saw a continuity between such states and those ritual states which he described in terms of communitas (Turner 1969, 1974a, 1982). While each of these states calls on intense involvement on the part of individuals, I draw attention to the associational and gregarious dimensions of the experience, its special kind of being-with, or being-together. Each of these zones calls on habits of the body in which focused activities are entered into, and each calls for a specific set of criteria by which they are judged successful or useful. The dimension of wonder, which first attracted ethnographers, provides the key to these other intense state of feeling.

Paying attention to named spaces and the kind of experiences that we can anticipate taking place within them parallels the argument about the relationship of the simple forms made in chapter three. To create some order out of the variety of vernacular cultural productions means departing from the usual way in which ethnography is centered. Outside the comfort zone, single performances become less possible except in the concert setting, but deeper and more layered presentations become the norm. Thus we move the focus of study away from the bounded domain of home and out into places where anything might happen. Here, as in my considerations of play and games, event and experience, I work with the vernacular uses of ordinary terms for unique terrains in order to understand how shared experiences are registered, made discussable, and judged. Approached in this fashion, zones relate performances to other kinds of intense experiences. In these spaces, more than one thing takes place at the same time. Our sensorium is both assaulted and expanded in such enlivened environments. Popular entertainments, ceremonies, even large-scale rituals seem to be animated by vernacular impulses and to exhibit similar degrees of internally generated order. I have ruminated too long on the supposed erasure of the face-to-face marketplace as a site of cultural production not to recognize that even in local imaginaries the interchanges that took place there were largely anonymous. Festivals and carnivalized entertainments usually were held on fairgrounds, in markets, and at the crossroads, rather than in the cottage, the parlor, or the great hall of the estate house. So we must recognize that the social imaginary has defined spaces for every sort of interaction, from the most intimate to the most public. We look to the vernacular to see how these places are marked, events are reported, and experiences are described to others.

Telling of one's experiences, even to strangers, is normalized. A group is tied together, even if just for the moment, by sharing personal experiences. The accumulated stories one tells on oneself, which Stahl calls "personal experience narratives," become the visible signs of personal identity (Stahl 1989). Alternatively, the stories one tells about others may be considered gossip or rumor when identities are being taken from the individual and subjected to group control. These states of talk commonly take place in the comfort zone, a sphere of expressive activity guided first and foremost by goodwill and the desire to be sociable. Contention as it arises within such a zone is regarded as contained or containable within the conversation. Within this zone, license is given to manufacture wonder without calling truthfulness into question. If there is a politics of this kind of interaction, it is that we agree to bury any counter-voices within the text and study it only after the interactive fact. Any contestation within this zone tends to be regarded as part of the negotiation for rights to talk, to take the floor, to interrupt. Contention is subordinated by both the speakers themselves and by those who analyze these narratives.

In clear contrast to such scenes are those encounters in which goodwill cannot be presumed because the interaction is taking place between performers and figures who take on the role of antagonists. This conflict is also socially constructed when strangers or potential enemies are identified and incorporated within the interaction.

Contact Zones

Let us explore that marked space of cultural production which Mary Louise Pratt calls "zones of contact," where interactions occur between "subjects previously separated by geographic and historical disjunctures . . . whose trajectories now intersect" (Pratt 1992: 7). Under conditions of first encounter between strangers, no principle of goodwill operates. Rather, there is wariness, "a testing of the atmosphere." The encounter is seemingly open, at least in terms of what expressive devices may be brought into the encounter. Pratt and James Clifford, who reports on her line of thought (Clifford 1997: 192–93), assume that those in power dictate the terms under which the interaction takes place. This may be true in some instances, but I follow Antonio Gramsci's suggestion that counter-hegemonic moves are often made in subterranean tactics of resistance. James Scott calls these "hidden transcripts," although in adopting his term, I do not mean to indicate that I accept his model of how these moments of resistance occur (Scott 1990).

The *contact zone* is just as available to description and critical scrutiny as any other cultural phenomena. The first encounters and the expressive activities that mark contact, in treaty-making, paying tribute, or more bellicose ways of ceremonializing conflict, are just as firmly routinized, rehearsable, and predictable as everyday friendly talk. The major difference between the two kinds of palavers is that the early encounters are carried between those who differ in almost every dimension of expressive culture. I would like to think that our friendly dispositions lead us to value stories of difference, even if they test the values and tastes of those involved in the talk. We seem to feel that if we could at least talk about differences, the problems arising from a conflict of cultures would evaporate. Making difference the subject of talk magically introduces a feeling that with personal experience and knowledge come friendly relations—or at least less defensive ones. Shouting matches at the borders are transformed into friendly, informative encounters, evidence that we can all live together peacefully.

Such an attitude, commendable as it is, tends to privilege the communication system of those already empowered. At the first meeting I attended with the Lakota tribal council in their home territory, it was clear within the first minute that I had brought my canons of tasteful and tactful talk, but talking about serious subjects in such an environment demanded a suspension of my own norms for conversation. In the Indian ceremonial way, we sat in one another's presence without talking at all for over an hour. Then the floor was given over now to one leader, now the next, until all had had their say. There was not much back-and-forth, and certainly no open appeal to air our differences or argue them out. Although we were in a classroom, council fire rules were in force. After I got beyond embarrassment and astonishment, experiencing another system personally made me aware of how much I had learned about Indian interactions by reading about historical moments of treaty or entreaty. In the colonial and early national periods, treaty-making moments called for Europeans to adhere to Indian practices, but the Anglos attempted to imitate Indians while putting forth their own ideas.

The social sciences as well as humanistic scholarship have been forced by circumstance to attend to extralocal and transnational ways of knowledge production. The insights provided by earlier attention to the differences between oral and written communication encourage serious attention to all communication media. Some of our best work has demonstrated that there is a constant flow between face-to-face, spoken practices and those which are mediated by script, print, or other forms of record. Moreover, the vernacular impulse that resonates in locally produced expressive manifestations is to be found just as fully in technologically driven cultures that rely on electronic and digitized communication. The system of manners in such new forms as email and the internet has had to be consciously worked out. Even when the rules are explicit and regulated by the users themselves, virtual faux pas are constantly being made, and devices for repairing misunderstandings are being developed.

Resistance to civic or metropolitan authorities often arises in these contact zones, where different rules are negotiated and prevail. Those who enforce ordinary rules may be excluded from the interior of the zone, although they may surround its perimeters. Within the zone, those who enforce the distinctive rules that prevail there may be less visible; indeed, freedom from surveillance and the unobtrusiveness of internal regulation may be among the defining features of those rules. Rather than seeing these zones in terms of their ordering, it is more productive to consider how they apply for and receive their license and involve the participants. Big Brother does not like them, unless they can be deployed to ratify the orders of the officers of the polity. Because these domains represent alternative worlds, entering one or another is a wholly human activity.

Naming and Framing Zones

Those forms of cultural production which are amenable to analysis as zones are mediated, but resonate with vernacular impulses. Each of these zones evokes a sense of wonder or magical involvement in unusual states of being, a wonder not unlike that experienced by our antiquarian forebears when they rediscovered folktales and songs, epics and laments.

Outside of comfort zones lie such generic spaces as playing fields or playgrounds; combat zones where shouting matches and other ritualized contests are held; and markets in which the rules of friendly exchange are challenged or suspended. If it weren't such an awkward construction, we could extend the jargon of civic groups and call these "enterprise zones" to bring to attention the kinds of license carried by free trade. Markets trade in other sorts of experiences besides buying and selling goods, raw or cooked. These places of quick-hit exchange are surrounded by pleasure palaces in which the appetites are satisfied by the exchange of services. An even more disturbing genre of places are those which fence people in or out, the two ways in which differences are most violently confronted: prisons, ghettos, internment and concentration camps. Each has different gateway practices by which the experience inside or outside the walls is differentiated from everyday life.

This schema makes no attempt to totalize either the field or the range of expressive activities which make a bid for authenticity. It is simply an attempt to make an orderly account of relationships between past and present folkloristic practices. This task is similar to what I attempted to do in chapter three regarding the range of performer-audience relationships implicit in the traditional forms commonly addressed by folklorists. Here, the generic features of performance to which I draw attention are the qualities of the spaces in which they take place. Each of these different kinds of named zones carries a restricted range of framed activities. While the license called for in each genre of interaction may differ, there are common features which reside within these zones.

Zones which are self-enclosed are often marked by a generic *name* and *frame* that announces what behaviors and practices are encouraged, by what social mechanism the rules are monitored, and how the plays or routines are rehearsed and played out. Zones are locations without center or periphery, in which activities with deeply encoded and compressed meanings take place. These meanings are spelled out in the vernacular terms specially fashioned for these activities, but joined with everyday discourse in a complementary fashion. All such zones involve a partial erasure of everyday modes of self-identification. This erasure involves an agreement—though hardly a contract—entered into by those cohabiting within the zone that the usual ways in which identity is proposed will be put off to the side, neglected for the moment. This agreement succeeds only as long as the intensity of the activity itself is maintained. It dissolves easily as skepticism or the everyday world intrudes. Each zone promises a kind of pure, authentic experience, although it is not always produced.

Combat Zones

Much folklore has been gathered in the comfort zone. Historically, indigenous or traditional cultures have laid claim to forms of expressive exchange naturally existing in a specific kind of space: the warmest spots in the house, in the parlor by the fireside, in the kitchen, or in the craft shop; at the places of congregation in which the small community entertained, instructed, and created objects of use and value based on the habits of the hand and the heart. Scholars and fieldworkers located in contact zones have spent much time discovering the worlds beyond the comfort zone, worlds as much tied to the past traditions of wonder, conflict, and struggle as the warm places in which stories and songs best live. Recognizing that many traditions focused on social and political confrontation, these folklorists saw in the practice of tradition ways by which group membership is celebrated while the political suppression and social oppression of the more powerful is criticized. This folklore of the *combat zone* is characterized by vigorous and playful resistance to the powers that be (Bauman and Abrahams 1981: 1–31). Many of the genres that lie at the center of our discipline contain reminders of social and political opposition which had been little noticed until folklorists ventured into zones of contact and conflict.

This perspective was deeply influenced by the political developments of the Civil Rights Movement. Members of our socially inspired generation sought to enlarge the model of public contestation to encompass streetwise modes of antagonism, which emerged in the cantina, the jook-joint, pool-hall, and barbershop, wherever identities were on display. These vernacular responses to marginalization, exclusion, and ghettoization were often carried out on the front lines; this was folklore *in* as well as *of* the combat zone. Shouting matches at the borders were not necessarily carried on in the open, or even with loud voices; often this was secret lore carrying hidden agendas. Intercultural jesting and jousting and competitive storytelling forms, such as *corridos*, *calaveras*, and *chistes*, toasts and jokes, work songs and stories, revealed a deeper politics of confrontation constituted in these performances. Consider, for example, the *corridos* of Gregorio Cortez or Jose Mosquedo and the toasts of "Shine on the Titanic" or the "Signifying Monkey."

The analysis of such lore from the perspective of ongoing sociopolitical inequality was couched in terms of macropolitical questions. However, these studies were informed by sociolinguistic and other microbehavioral concerns which discovered a dimension of negotiation in even the most everyday exchanges (Abrahams 1981a). This attention to the details of contestation in patterned interactions is sometimes overlooked by those who worry about the aestheticizing tendencies of this approach to performance. Those folklorists engaged in developing performance-centered analysis who were carrying out fieldwork among diverse socially marginalized and subordinated groups during the 1960s were forced to recognize these traditions of playful confrontation.

Folklore itself constitutes, as well as explores, such zones of historical memory at the borders where cultural groups collide and collaborate. As practitioners and theorists came to recognize, the discipline itself is deeply implicated in the construction of places supposedly removed in time and space where alternatives to the dominant metropolitan culture could be authenticated and authorized. Folklore's chartering narratives involve two linked stories: one featuring relics saved from the fire just before they were consumed by the conflagration; and another featuring ourselves as intrepid scholar-adventurers searching out memorial transmitters still living in wild places and bringing back their songs and stories. The two narrative moves were collapsed into one with the craft and the folksong revivals, as folklorists brought the songs and the singers, the pots and the potters to popular notice at exhibitions, demonstrations, and festivals.

The memorial traditions of our discipline trace this sort of discovery not only to the edge of civilization but also to the children's playground. William Wells Newell, the central figure in the formation of the American Folklore Society, reports his awakening to the presence of the past while observing children at play in Central Park (Newell 1883; Abrahams 1988c). Authenticity takes many forms. Certain roles, like certain places, make a bid for acceptance as points of emanation from which the authentic and the real emerge. These trip-switches of memory invoke a particular invented past. Getting a pass or learning the password to go through the gates and into the sanctum sanctorum of culture is a necessary rite of passage in our discipline, for the folk as well as for the folklorists. Dorothy Noyes has recently given an especially detailed and well-informed report of the dilemmas faced by folklorists in the field (Noyes 2003: 25–36). Through the invocation of authenticity, specific places or peoples are endowed as repositories of inherited wisdom. Places and celebrations are bestowed with a patina signaling pastness even when inventive novelty reigns.

Folklore has been treated with little respect by other social science disciplines because it is concerned with ephemeral cultural productions which arise from vernacular impulses operating in small locales. Yet, for folklorists, what evokes wonder is not the transitory quality of folk culture but rather the creative vigor visible in these seemingly unpromising sites for cultural production.

In the *twilight zones*, the gaslight and red-light environments where self-consciously ephemeral performances occur, radical departures from quotidian norms of interaction are encountered. The boundaries between the individual and the spirit of this other world are differentially dissolved. In this environment all experiences are potentially extraordinary, for not only the self but also the body is addressed in quite a different fashion. On these occasions, as Bakhtin described the carnivalesque world, all of the bodily orifices are susceptible to being opened (Bakhtin 1984). These carnivalesque devices draw on the entire apparatus of *mimesis*: costuming, masking, bodily adornment, and characterological remakings. In these zones, all of the ways in which experiences are registered are subject to transvaluation. The very idea of the individual and social body is put to the test. The world is redesigned and accepted through shared states of dizziness or disorientation. Here, too, experiences are tinged with risk-taking.

These areas of cultural production carried out in the intensive manner of the spectacle and the expansive modern forms of Carnival operate simultaneously as local celebrations and tourist attractions. Artificially controlled and illuminated worlds are constructed; memory theaters, botanical and zoological parks, and pageants, processions, and parades are confected. Here, too, are the *sons et lumières*, the sound and light shows presented at points of historical or geographical interest throughout the Western world, from the castles and palaces of Europe to American national parks.

Still other spaces in the social imaginary where different cognitive and corporeal experiences arise have been regarded as beyond the concerns of folklorists, at least up to this point. These zones are defined by the silence with which society surrounds them. Yet traditional forms of cultural expression are salient even there. In ghettos and other zones of containment, such as prisons, concentration camps, and refugee camps, the rehearsal and replay of tradition may be all-important for the maintenance of sanity. Until this uncomfortable fact is faced, the diasporic phenomena to which cultural nationalists call our attention will remain mystified for our profession.

Negotiations in the Contact Zone

Sites of cultural production in No Man's Land, where dislocated or dispersed peoples find themselves, would be fruitful locales for exploration. Robert Cantwell terms those marked places for the exchange of performances between individuals bringing with them desirable goods and exotic practices "unincorporated zones," areas outside the limits of the usual laws, interstitial zones often called "the liberties" in early modern England and America. A variety of in-between places exist where more bounded domains meet. At wide spots at the crossroads and in the customary markets, special days are enlivened by trade or treaty, pageant or public ceremony (Cantwell 1993: 13; Mullaney 1988: 38–55). New rules must be made by those producing these events and those seeking to contain them.

These contact zones are central to any effort to comprehend the varieties of ways in which peoples come together. Here difference becomes most important and most subject to commoditization. Here the habits of the whole body come into juxtaposition through representatives of ancient traditions, now in need of authentication through primordialization of a very special sort.

Contacts are engineered, produced, and carried out in a variety of ways. In the zones of most profound contact, such as tribute-paying, treaty-making, or the even more impersonal encounters in the market, bids for authenticity are confronted with other such bids; claims for truth-telling are produced within an environment of skepticism. Peoples from different places come together in expectation of amity, but with a mutual recognition that all acts of friendliness may involve lies or deceptive practices. Just as the face-to-face market brings together those seeking the confidence of each other while knowing that these claims must be discounted, so at treaties, while asseverations of friendship and peace are made, the wariness between the parties is never totally dispelled. A new set of rules of interaction must be established and routinized to govern subsequent encounters. In many circumstances of intense trade, the encounters are ritualized or ceremonialized, cobbled together from elements of ritual elaboration that are shared or exchanged. When longer-term agreements must be forged, as in treaties and alliances, the presentations of goods and the representation of respect and honor to each other creates an elaborate set of practices that operate under the rule of quick-hit discounting. The creation of face rather than social place predominates such encounters, for negotiations involving exchange are carried on with those otherwise regarded as strangers or enemies.

Folklorists have seldom addressed this sort of negotiation, in spite of the fact that these scenes of exchange involve an elaboration of traditional practices. Moreover, the forms of performance and celebration that emerge at such places of contact have a wonder and fascination of their own. When the "others" are so designated, the question of the alien or anomalous copresence emerges: are these "others" and their ways contaminating and contagious, or are they subject to being deployed symbiotically for the continuing health of the human social enterprise? Clearly, the presence of "others" introduces new resources of materiel and energy. A commercial economy focuses on cultural objects that are subject to alienation, but symbolic resources do matter, and in contact situations the "others" perform themselves.

Here the most artful, paradoxical construction emerges. The longer the contact continues and the more intensively it is carried on, the more the "purity" of the culture of those with whom one is in contact becomes valorized. Yet, purity is determined by how much the actions and artifacts of the "others" seem uncontaminated by that contact. Most strange. In a trade situation which raises the level of feeling, whether for healing or for fun, the sellers must aver the potency of their tradable by arguing for its connections with the uncontaminated tradition, or mystified place of origin. Often authenticity is established through significant contact with the originators' stories, or it is performed by the purveyor dressing exotically and speaking in some kind of authenticating lingo. Stranger still. Commonly this happens unwittingly, for the presence of outsiders always suggests the possibilities of exchange between groups, whether in war or in trade.

To gird themselves for this encounter, groups resort to their most intensive vocabulary of together-feeling—that is, their ritual and festival repertoire. Such activities are usually conducted within the group; now the presence of outsiders must be accounted for. Commonly this is done by ceremonial elevation—that is, by having the ceremonial superiors pay respect to their opposite numbers in the other group by playing as equals. Those involved in the occasion approach the interaction differentially: the "others" are treated as foils for self-glorification. They are taken to be pagans, barbarians, savages, misguided but potentially entertaining in the ways in which they costume themselves, stylize their behavior, perform themselves. Of course, the natural response is for the interpreters to put on their best clothes and to draw upon their high-style behaviors.

Folklore collecting itself may be understood as involving negotiations across lines of cultural difference. As in all ethnographically based disciplines, the folklorist as participant-observer is socialized into the ways of the subject group, and reflecting on the process of learning the rules is an important element in the analysis of culture. Their sometimes awkward discovery of cultural differences makes ethnographers more conscious of their own vernacular assumptions as well as aware of those held by their informants. My own experiences of collecting folklore while living in African American communities are a case in point. After I shifted my attention from people's textualized entertainments to their lived experiences, I looked back with horror at the judgments I had made so easily in my youth. In the rural and urban villages where I resided, in Philadelphia and the Caribbean, I was taught, sometimes the embarrassing way, what good manners and judgment were. The boundaries between yards and houses were the terrain on which the most important character judgments were made. In a world which most valued respect between people, the breaching of bounds was among the most disrespectful actions one could take.

Discussions of these unspoken rules often emerged during the run-up to a celebration in which the rules were deliberately violated. Especially in the old slave holidays of Christmas and Carnival, everyday rules of approach and avoidance were ignored for the sake of liberating nonsense. These celebrations were all about the body. Rules existed by which license might be taken to break the rules of everyday manners, to be rude, and to devise ways of doing so that drew attention from the crowds on the roads and streets. The readjustment of boundaries was a vernacular decision which could be talked about if anyone was offended. Discovering the rules of inversion was not difficult, as there was so much indigenous commentary. At the Saturday markets, too, an alternative set of rules was in play. Crowds of higglers and their customers carried on at a high pitch, full of invective. The seemingly contradictory messages I received applied to different zones, such as the yard, the crossroads or market, and the annual holiday. Every community has rules of the same sort, carried out in a vernacular that is commonsensical and customary.

Folklorists have to readjust boundary crossings going the other way—that is, to discover how to invade other people's spaces under festive conditions. Collecting songs, stories, games, speeches, and ways of costuming, dancing, and singing requires us to venture into places we know are sacrosanct. At fetes surrounding points of life-passage, the private worlds of the yard are thrown open. The performers of nonsense are invited in to carouse, tell stories, riddle with each other, and commit numerous other acts of rudeness as hilarious entertainments. As a folklorist, I could not examine these problems intellectually; I had to commit my body to indignities and risk becoming the target of abuse. I was told in no uncertain terms that if I wanted to understand their playing, I had to learn how to play.

The shared norms that govern behavior in these special zones strike folklorists in the field almost immediately. When we venture with pencil and paper, tape recorder, and video camera into the field, people tell us that we really ought to record their more public entertainments, where performances are at their very best. In African American communities in the United States and the British West Indies, especially, it was made clear that if we want the songs and stories, the riddles and speeches, we must enter into such celebrations as family reunions, keeping Christmas, playing Carnival, and moonlit-night nonsense. At a wedding supper or at a wake, our subjects assured us, we would find much more interesting and fully spelled-out performances.

In their houses and yards, people prepared constantly for these large-scale events. In much of the Caribbean, Carnival is a year-long affair for those who play. For many Trinidadians, being unable to play Carnival is regarded as a loss of identity, felt in the bones and viscera. For those groups who have been relegated to the margins and whose memories of the past are saturated with the pain of displacement, exclusion, and oppression, the performance of tradition in the service of national belonging is potentially transformative, liberating, even redemptive.

In Vernacular Vigor We Trust

Do the combined moves of decentering and demystifying custom and tradition undermine the folkloristic project? I think not. If we take such a process as exemplary of the congenial and protean capacities of humans in groups, then developing a sense of connection with the past, no matter how putative, is cast into a different and much more positive light. Folklorists are not faced with a disciplinary crisis. Rather, the theory by which folklore materials have been collected and organized in traditional folkloristics no longer accounts for the range of our interests—if it ever did. The times do not call for a new paradigm by which to understand custom, tradition, and other dimensions of vernacular creativity. Rather, we need an accommodating statement setting out and rationalizing the horizons of our disciplinary interests. We also could use a jeremiad excoriating the limitations of our past practices as a way of launching a renewed exploration of the entire range of vernacular inventions emerging under conditions of globalization. In accepting this larger enterprise, we need not abandon our commitment to small and often disempowered groups. Instead, our calling should be reconsecrated in the name of the conservation of human and cultural resources.

In one of the foundational documents of the cultural critique, the introductory essay to *The Invention of Tradition*, Eric J. Hobsbawm insists upon the distinction between custom—the unconscious and unreflective, but flexible passing on of past practices—and tradition—which involves conscious attention to the carrying out of practices said to be antique, leading to a ritualization of the activity and its attendant structural and performative rigidity (Hobsbawm 1992; see also Ranger 1992.). Like many of the distinctions offered by cultural critics, this distinction covertly expresses an antimodernist and anticapitalist impulse, which is an outgrowth of the nation-state and its bureaucracy and of the commercial and industrial world and the alienation of workers from products and products from consumers.

The ideal of the organic community is kept alive through the operation of practices apparently situated in one place and among one people over time. Studies of commemorative ceremonies and celebrations still in place show that custom is just as subject to hegemonic intervention as any traditional practice. This is not a cynical point of view, only a historically realistic one. Through these case studies, the nostalgic construction of the past and the exotic representation of the other achieve a different kind of fascination. In this view, a sociopsychological alteration in the mentality of Western cultures occurs at that point when the forms and social relations of bureaucratic government and depersonalized commodity exchange come to dominate the political economy.

Vernacular processes are our focus and our hope, not just the waifs and strays or the shattered remnants of past societies. As a discipline birthed in antimodernism and a rejection of capitalist, industrial, and bureaucratic excesses, we continue to search out places of resistance to these overwhelmingly powerful cultural forces. Our work bears witness to the spirit of cultural insurgency, where the saucy and the clever, the crafted and the respectful adherence to a useful past are given shrift. In vernacular vigor we trust. I recognize that this statement regards the vernacular with a nostalgia similar to that previously extended to distressed genres and their textual remnants. It obeys the same impulse which led to the invention of the folk. But I think it works in our own lives in potent ways that are worthy of study and celebration.

Chapter 9
Festive Gatherings

No form of traditional display activity owes more to an expansion of the goodwill principle than festive gatherings. Egalitarian principles and practices flow through parades and picnics, open houses and seasonal celebrations. The same festive devices of organization and display are available for ceremonies of dissent, especially political or social resistance, or simply to challenge all rules and regulations. Ceremonial elevation and elaboration confirm everyday status distinctions, but when a wink is given by the whole group, the very same practices can be used to make fun of any distinction. Liberation is just as exciting as patriotic celebration, although they are seldom thought of as twin motives except in their shared license to depart from the mundane world. Both use techniques of amplification and magnification to draw crowds and focus the energies of the community.

Celebrations

Much has been made of traditional exercises of the lords of misrule, the playing of rough music, and other topsy-turvy activities to which Mikhail Bakhtin and his followers have called attention (Bakhtin 1984; Clark and Holquist 1984: 299–320). This spirit of abandon still erupts into the present in many forms, most dramatically in Mardi Gras in New Orleans and elsewhere. In Pasadena, California, an alternative parade arose to protest the commercialization of the Rose Parade and reclaim the annual civic festival from the tourist- and media-oriented spectacularity that had overtaken the official celebration. Taking the same route through the city two weeks before the official event, this parade became known as Doo-Dah, and it has proliferated under that name all over the country. But this counter-event partakes of the same dynamic of spectacularization, as a recent incident reveals. When a fellow at a Doo-Dah parade in Pasadena was booed by the crowd, he broke all the rules of decorum and shouted out: "What do I care? I won't ever see you people again." The same anonymity that characterized the larger event prevailed—except, of course, that the performers and the spectators confronted one another directly.

As Susan Davis has shown for the Philadelphia Mummers' and Shooters'

eruption, the spirited opposition to official parades has been an important feature of urban life since the early nineteenth century (Davis 1986: 73–112). The
spirit of carnival bubbled up in fraternal organizations throughout the east,
although these events were held within the restricted membership of the voluntary organization. More public upside-down occasions based on Old World
traditions continued in festivities as diverse as the German *belsnickling* of
Pennsylvania and Nova Scotia and the Purim spiel wherever synagogues were
erected. This spirit animated the early blackface minstrel shows as well, aimed
at American prominenti, but delivered from the protective coloring of the
cork-blackened face in the mocking tones of whites' misunderstanding of slave
dialect. These North American versions of Carnival were in direct contrast to
the more formal celebrations of officially calendared holidays.

In the Americas, as elsewhere, newly formed polities generate festivals
that celebrate the accomplishment of nationhood. Monarchical regimes adver-
tised the power of the regime through displays. The theater-states of early
modern Europe became altogether more aldermanic, but no less dramatic.
Democratic republics rely on less garish effects, but attempt to gather the
whole populace in occasions which generate solidarity, proclaim continuity,
and bring dignity to the sacrifices that went into forming the nation. The
achievements of revolutions are marked by large celebratory statements
reminding the populace of the duties that citizenship entails.

Such displays are not a necessary component of nation formation. Rather,
they represent the self-confidence and gregarious enthusiasm of a people
actively involved in beginning a new regime. Inherited monarchies mount
public displays as a dramatic assertion of control over their realm (see Geertz
1977). Such statements of power are much more difficult to make in democratic republics. Leaders who rotate in and out of office cannot accumulate
power on such a grand scale. State power is transferred to objects and images,
such as the Stars and Stripes or the dollar bill, which embody the ideal of equal
and widely distributed access to the popular source of power. This spectacularity is a common outgrowth of democracy. Making a celebration into a display
of democratic spirit emerges seamlessly from declarations of independence.
The triumph engineered by the monarchy is not dispelled, but rather dispersed
to all of those who see and feel together.

Crowds reinforce whatever sense of community has remained in an
industrial and now a postindustrial world. The language drawn on for festive
events, we are constantly reminded, goes back as far as time, reenacting the
past achievements of the group as well as the solidarity symbolized by marching, processing, standing, eating and drinking, and by observing silences punctuated by making great noises together. Like all play activities, festivals
incorporate elements of the serious life, deploying attention-grabbing objects
in the central place of gathering. These objects spend most of their existence

in a secret hiding place, gathering unto themselves the secrets of the tribe, in many cases a holy set of secrets. They carry with them stories containing the eternal verities, as corny as that may seem to our heavily secularized society. In and through their presence, the group is encouraged to share those self-reflective moments that remind people of how things have been and how they are renewed. These sacred objects carry the enduring understandings which are explicated, whether through ceremony or through reenactment of the group's sustaining myths, for the consideration of all the members of the community.

Yet, like other forms of play, festivities also express the self-destroying motives that constantly threaten the existence of the group. These are times both of reflection and of abandon, though the two motives are not always expressed at the same moment. Just so, Christmas and New Year's Day play off against each other: the one underscoring consumption within the family and the renewal of the spirit; the other celebrating the destruction of the old year in the creation of the new, which is amplified through the consumption of mood-altering substances.

In our consumption-driven societies, some bewail the ways in which the old celebrations have been contaminated as their staging has devolved upon specialists who derive their income from producing these activities, violating the communal spirit of the occasion. The current celebration of birthdays throughout much of the world typifies this drift. Children are no longer part of the productive economy; they are now recipients of a surplus economy in which just being young creates an entitlement to a momentary elevation of spirits and monetary reward. Family resources are used up on such occasions. The planning and execution of special days are given over to new ritual specialists: clowns and magicians, deejays, wedding planners, funeral directors, and always caterers and servers. The few celebrants who are deeply invested in the ceremonial moment, but witness the depletion of resources taking place, are not uplifted; they feel depressed afterwards and need an accounting in order to register whether the event was a success or not. We take photographs so that we remember these as joyous occasions when we look back. A vernacular cynicism has emerged that does not always harmonize with the announced traditional spirit of official holiday celebrations.

With the growth in size of spectator groups, whether on the spot or witnessed via the media, the theatrical effects become louder, more closely scripted, and designed to evoke whatever warm sentiments have survived into the twenty-first century. The scripting emerged from festive programming, but now the punctuation points are provided by advertisers, and spectacle and consumption keep company. All celebrations, archaic and modern, draw on effects of intensification, amplification, and hypertrophization—that is, the grotesque enlargement and distending of images. Those festivals that have persevered draw on the most colorful and boisterous vocabularies of celebration

in order to dazzle and overwhelm the senses. As presentations become more
spectacular, they tend to borrow from each other, so it is difficult to tell the
difference between a Thanksgiving parade and a Super Bowl production. Successful local festivals develop larger effects over time; for example, pageant
wagons are turned into parade floats. Dragons remain perennially popular, as
do big heads and the effigies used on saints' days. Massive models of symbolically significant buildings and ships, and even military displays including tanks
and rockets, are marshaled in moving formations through the center of the
crowd's field of vision.

Festive celebration has become an everyday affair. Each civic entity
mounts its own celebration, often seizing on a local staple crop as the theme
of the event. No commodity remains unheralded; indeed, festivals are held in
the name of local products long after the mines, fields, or factories have been
abandoned. Historical turning points are also fair game, especially if they have
been turned into legends—broad-brush representations of affairs which, if
they ever happened, were originally small-scale. Events which are celebrated
are commonly shorn of most of the hostile motives out of which they emerged.
Carefully choreographed reenactments of bloody battles don't involve real
blood (or fake blood either, for that matter); dead soldiers are magically resur-
rected, bodies intact, after the smoke has cleared.

Distrust lies in wait at all times during festive gatherings. But the vestiges
of predemocratic power displays are in decline. Everything, including mar-
riages and jail sentences, is subject to endless appeal. The lawyers and politicians have the last say, but even that isn't final or fully transformative.
However, church and state public affairs continue to seek formal legitimation
through hoary archaic practices. Our love of ceremony has not abated, only
the powers of those who would lead.

Group Displays

What are the assumptions, or givens, that members of a group carry into life
which maintain group membership? And how do those change when the
group appears in public as a group, dressed in some official costume? Certainly
the shift in the ways folklorists and anthropologists define culture has had an
effect. When ethnographers turned their attention to everyday practices as
illustrations of the ways a group's institutions are taught and made manifest,
the importance of celebrations became apparent. When in-group activities
experienced at high pitch come to the notice of the fieldworker, he or she is
often accompanied by a person from the group who explains what's going on
and what being a member and a celebrant means. Although this practice
amplified the importance of "key informants," as they were then called, the

terms they employed could be used for conversations on the subject with other celebrants.

I think particularly of discussions I had with West Indians responsible for organizing part of a festive gathering. In this part of the world, one seldom is able to carry on a one-on-one conversation. In trying to get off in a corner with a self-styled sporty fellow who was captain of a Christmas masquerade group, I discovered that, if other people were in the general vicinity, making private talk was discouraged. Everyone wanted to have a say on how this man saw himself, asserted leadership, trained the young performers in how to present themselves within the *mas'*, arranged for musicians, and carried out all the myriad dimensions of organizing the merry-making. I went into his yard to find him alone so that we could *lime and blag*—sitting shoulder to shoulder, talking informally while fixing our eyes in the same outward direction. But, as soon as we began to talk, others overheard and joined in excitedly. As other scholars have discovered about Trinidadian Carnival and the Philadelphia Mummers, a good part of the pleasure of these celebrations came from the year-round discussions that surround the actual fête (Stuempfle 1995; Scher 2003; Raab 2001). Performers and audience members did not want to talk about the textable or objectifiable parts of their *mas'* playing. Although they rehearsed songs and stories and invested resources in masks and costumes, the performers' focus was on the overall experience, along with the pride in making a good show (Abrahams 2003). In each village, the imperative to celebrate together permeated local life. Each celebration called for discussion of the past, when a good time was not hard to come by and there was no trouble finding others to play *mas'* with you. Working and playing together was a full-time concern.

These experiences changed the emphasis in fieldwork and ethnographic writing from treating celebrations as if they were self-contained to understanding how participants talk about their experiences, before, during, and after the festival. This shift opened up a new set of questions which seek to establish, in the group's own vernacular, the connections between everyday activities and "the rite side of life." Field workers took note of this native exegesis, as well as the ways in which times of celebration selectively broke the rules of everyday interaction. The social roles, statuses, or memberships that are articulated and confirmed in ceremonies yield insight into the ideals of the village regarding how groups assemble, at least ideally, and how often the captains or masters of ceremony were not able, on specific occasions, to keep appropriate order among the players.

My West Indian experience was echoed by many others working in the field during the 1960s and 1970s. In addition to taking a census of group members and discovering how they organized their religious, social, sexual, and economic lives, ethnographers regularly attended to "native categories" and "indigenous exegeses." By such notation, the experiential differences between the everyday worlds and the fêtes made it possible to observe how cultural capital was exchanged in those sites and what the rate of exchange was in economic and social terms. Our own commonsense system made us conscious of any distribution of capital, economic or otherwise. We made distinctions between what to expect in work and in play, on weekdays and at the weekend, without sufficiently considering how these concepts map onto the ways of the others we are studying.

Our distinction between work and play rests on the modern, capitalist system of making radical distinctions between productive and unproductive practices. In our vernacular, a major question is how the expenditure of energy is regarded by individuals in our society, with an emphasis on decisions based either on investment or on the achievements of happiness, pleasure, and relief from care.

Rituals/Festivals

At the center of our vernacular discussions lies the keyword *experience*. As defined in chapter seven, *experience* is the flow of happenings as they are registered by individuals, whether or not we are highly aware of what's going on, while *an* experience involves the recognition that this flow has intensified in pressure and volume, and thereby become more significant to us. Such experiences may sneak up on us and enliven us as they produce thrills, excitement, fear, or dread. These events become our stories insofar as they are interesting, typical, and retellable. When their intensity and significance are shared by others, an *event* is upon us.

All cultures build upon anticipations of moving experiences, especially events tied to life-passage. When these occasions reenact the way in which the world has been put together, we interpret them as *rituals*, not simply as festivals. Rites build upon memorable moments, tying together past and present through personal bodily involvement. In fact, rituals are heavily layered with foundational acts as they have been interpreted in the past. Shared meanings are turned into messages to those new to the occasion, lessons explicitly spelled out by the gatekeepers or their surrogates. Rites actively encompass, through naming and framing, the approved meanings and feelings. The interpretations can be discovered through direct physical involvement, in which mistakes are made and embarrassments endured, rather than through mere verbal instruction.

When festivities take place in what is normally a market zone, they achieve a different way of commenting on life and its passage. High seriousness is delegated to the priests and other officiants. Low play and the license to act outrageously become the devil's duties, led by the sporty fellows of the community who are not given such transforming or confirming powers in the everyday world. Now we enter into situations in which confirmation of past orders may conflict with the dispensation to play, even to turn the everyday world upside down.

Festival motives are transparent: they are dedicated to passionate principles of consumption, excess, even waste. Sounds dissolve into the ambient noise. Sparkling objects divert and distract the gaze, with so many things going on at the same time that eye-catching is not tied to personal relations but rather to contrived effects. Explosions and conflagrations advertise the destructive impulses coursing through the crowds. Everything is subject to being broken and discarded. Costumes are pieced together, often very carefully, but made of many colors and textures. Processions and parades seem to emerge from nowhere and then disappear over the horizon or into the crowd.

Today, parades involve a congeries of festival formations inherited from past power displays, but only put into serried ranks to parade by a reviewing stand. The objects which in the past were constructed in larger-than-life forms now appear ballooned, floating without anchor above the crowd. Techniques of hypertrophization change, but not the effects of such enlargements on the crowds. Through it all, the special festive devices for making noise and detonating explosions carry the deepest of the mysteries of self-consuming artifacts. Firecrackers are the most ubiquitous of such devices, appealing to many of the senses simultaneously as they explode.

Just as ceremonial moments borrow from the vocabulary of rituals to frame the festivities, so buying and selling activities common in fairs arise at the edges of festivals. *Fairs* and festivals are so often found together that these terms have become almost interchangeable. Fairs were developed to attract outside customers for local crops and craft products, using the values and practices of the market to bring in the crowds. Festivals center on fun and consumption. In fairs the products bought and sold are usually carried away by buyers after the event, as opposed to festive objects which are intended to be used and their remains left behind. The ethnographic study of festivals has shown that the biggest secrets lie in the clean-up that occurs afterward, on the quiet.

Yet, over time, the differences between fairs and festivals have been elided. Seasonal festivities connected to the agricultural year are recoded from celebrations marking the cycle of production in the crops or manufactures of the locality into orgies of consumption, drawing on imported commodities and techniques to achieve maximum visibility. The very word season now refers primarily to temporal changes in clothing, coloration, and the display of new lines of manufactured consumables. Each holiday carries its own expectations of what will take place within any exchange. Stores and mail-order sites key their stock to the season, but keep two or three seasons ahead in order to have a salesworthy inventory.

These times of change in the annual cycle now become intensely nostalgic, marked by reunions, get-togethers, and theme parties. If such ceremonies remain public, two kinds of festivities emerge, one for the natives and returning natives and another for tourists. When outsiders are involved, the festival has to rely on spectacular effects, for the performers cannot rely on the audience understanding local references. Family holidays, by contrast, are now produced primarily for children. These are often the only times of the year when several generations are gathered in one spot. Discomfort over the alterations in family life that result from geographical mobility, the necessity of having two wage-earners, or divorce make these reunions more imperative, although more difficult. Similarly, local rituals once marked on the sacred calendar have been secularized and commercialized. Hallowe'en, the holiday when youths could get out of the house and away from adult supervision, mutates into a children's begging holiday, but without even having to perform a trick to get a treat.

Riotous Occasions

Our vocabulary of celebrations registers the change from an agricultural and then an industrial economy to a way of life that keeps people on the move. No longer do the seasons or even the calendar tell us of lulls in production that make gatherings possible. We have been led away from vigorous vernacular entertainments and put in the hands of entertainment specialists, who remind us how we are supposed to feel on these occasions. Producing such events in the name of carrying on traditions seems like a bit of a stretch. The new customs do not make festive times experientially different from the everyday; rather, they are indicia of a never-pleasure land that expends our resources without stimulating exhilaration. Play now serves neither the players nor the community. Instead, it creates a new player class and a new set of events simulating moments of joy issued through a loudspeaker or in projected images. The result is exhausting rather than exhilarating. Lost in this system of experience production are the feelings that previously made play so vivid: risk, testing balance, inducing a sense of community in the universe of the celebration, creating muscle memories as well as sentimental souvenirs.

Community life in the early American republic was punctuated by a variety of display events, whether the populace hailed from the British Isles, Germany, the Low Countries, or France (Abrahams 1998a). Bees and frolics in the countryside and pageants and parades in small towns both had a fully worked out set of riotous traditions: noisome charivari celebrants, "anticks and horribles," "callithumpian bands," "skimmington" riders, "whitecappers," and self-styled "Mohawks." Rural folks regarded the more controlled bee or frolic as the most characteristic and representative community custom.

In such frolics as barn-raisings and quilting parties, individual enterprise and community cooperation were conjoined and made palpable through performance. Developed from Old World festive forms, the bee differed from its progenitors by drawing on freely shared labor among neighbors, without the organizing force of status differentiations based on land ownership. In this respect, early American yeomen self-consciously departed from Old World practices. While work parties were regarded as customary, they were not carried out because of any archaic, inherited and transplanted traditions celebrating the land and its bountiful yield; they were not even spoken of as traditional. And, in contrast to the more boisterous charivaris and skimmingtons, these community gatherings were not rationalized by arguments from natural rights.

The most obstreperous festive traditions found in American rural communities were derived in part from European forms of adolescent gregariousness, such as those attached to guilds in the building trades and religious confraternities. While the Puritans rejected the impulse to have mummings and maskings at church holidays—witness the famous reaction against the Maypole at Merrymount (Abrahams 1998a)—nevertheless occasions arose in which the same kinds of public dressing-up occurred, even at Plimoth. These occasions were tied not to any calendar, but rather to local sociopolitical conditions.

In times of struggle between those exercising power and those subject to it, groups which felt deprived of power deployed the disruptive and subversive ritual techniques of rough music or the skimmington ride. Squatters and renters organized claims clubs, often carrying out their activities in secret, taking on masks and other paraphernalia of the *posse commitatus* (Kulikoff 1992). Confronting the representatives of landlords or civic authority, they attacked a house or a warehouse representative of power wielded in absentia. These were not disorderly riots, although victims as well as onlookers reported them as such. Rather, these well-rehearsed events drew upon the traditional devices of rough music, uproar, and upset that participants had inherited from Old World antick or topsy-turvy practices. The attacks were waged by well-organized groups, masked in scare garb, which gathered before and surrounded the house of the target, made noises and speeches which called out the figures within, delivered a message, circled and howled again, and then rode away into the night.

The more decorous term bee came to refer to all social gatherings, named as if they were organized to carry out difficult and complex labors. Often they were more play than work. But the communal character of these events was always central to their meaning, and in circumstances of social conflict they readily became politicized. During the American Revolution, for example, Patriot women held spinning bees to manufacture thread and yarn for "homespun" clothing rather than purchasing commodities imported from Great Britain. Boycotts and the whole panoply of forms of revolutionary rioting were deeply rooted in the European past even as they proclaimed change in the present (Abrahams 2002).

In Europe, too, the politicization of community rituals had a retrospective cast. Europeans had developed differentiated identities through the formation of what was called "national character"—now called "national identity"—and a sense of historical and geographic distinctiveness. Romantic arguments based claims of sovereignty, whether local, regional, or national, on a unique relationship among the land, the customs of the people living close to it, and the vernacular language in which they celebrated their past. These arguments rested not only on the local place legends addressed to the earlier inhabitants of a region but also on the cycle of celebratory activities as they articulated those locales. In the form of festivities or ritual beating of the bounds, a locale inscribed and reinscribed meanings upon a landscape, symbolically uniting the celebrants with the history of the land and the coming of the people.

Each locale had its annual course of festivals marking out the ways in which those living within its bounds achieved prosperity. In agricultural communities, these festivities were commonly attached to the passage of the seasons. They carried with them moving symbols of plentitude intended to bring good luck and fortune to the celebrants. These were also times of license, drawing on the powers of disorder and wildness. In-between figures drawn from the wild and unmarried young men were designated as leaders of these revels, their unattached status serving the community as an alternative source of energy.

In much the same way as the procession that "beat the bounds" of the locality, performing groups of mummers or serenaders went from house to house presenting performances, giving and getting the blessings of the season. This group activity is commonly called the good luck visit, for it called for goodwill as much as it requested good fortune for the in-dwellers.

In communities where several different peoples came together in calendared festivals, outside figures might come not only from the young bravos but also from the less sedentary groups found in the region: shepherds and other animal tenders involved in transhumance; gypsies and other roving performers; and those involved in the maritime trades. These unlanded and unbound figures might bring their special styles of performance, like the bagpiping shepherds, along with the social license that arises from being unfettered.

Mumming was identified by New England Puritans as a pagan observance, especially since the practice had been encouraged by the official church, which was associated, by extension, with Rome. But the Puritans were surrounded by other colonies which were not to be stripped of all of these house-visiting practices, from Newfoundland and Nova Scotia through New York, Pennsylvania, and Maryland. In the more densely populated portions of the mainland South, a serenading tradition was maintained, or at least taken over and transmuted by the slaves into the John Canoe and Christmas Gif' traditions. In places with substantial German populations, the cognate tradition of *belsnickling* continued.

The gentleman banker Samuel Breck, when he still lived in Boston, noted a luck visit of this sort. He and his neighbors were clearly not aware of the tradition, and he was upset at the ways in which rudeness was scripted into the day.

I forget on what holiday it was that the Anticks, another exploded remnant of colonial manners, used to perambulate the town. They have ceased to do it now, but I remember them as late as 1782. They were a set of the lowest blackguards, who, disguised in filthy clothes and ofttimes with masked faces, went from house to house in large companies, and thrust themselves everywhere, particularly into rooms that were occupied by parties of ladies and gentlemen; and they would demean themselves with great insolence. I have seen them at my father's, when his assembled friends were at cards, take possession of a table, seat themselves on rich furniture and proceed to handle the cards, to the great annoyance of the company. The only way to get rid of them was to give them money, and listen patiently to a foolish dialogue between two or more of them. One of them would cry out, "Ladies and gentlemen sitting by the fire, put your hands in your pockets and give us our desire." When this was done and they had received some money, a kind of acting took place. One fellow was knocked down, and lay sprawling on the carpet, while another bellowed out, "See there he lies, But ere he dies A doctor must be had."

He calls for a doctor, who soon appears, and enacts the part so well that the wounded man revives. In this way they would continue for half an hour; and it happened not unfrequently that the house would be filled by another gang when these had departed. There was no refusing admittance. Custom had licensed these vagabonds to enter even by force any place they chose. (Breck 1877: 211–12)

The customary license to which Breck refers is that of the antick perambulation of the Old World, in which maskers went from house to house bringing the luck of the season with them. These groups of young people rehearsed an entertainment of some sort, in this case the widely performed melodramatic dialogue of St. George and the Turk, undoubtedly brought to Boston by recent immigrants from Ireland, where it was (and still is) a common seasonal entertainment. Luck, in these cases, arose from the freely liberated energies emerging from the breakdown of everyday manners, the wearing of disguise, and the mock battle. That this was still a statement of class differences comes clear in Breck's description of the contrast between the mannerly card-playing gentlemen and the obstreperous "vagabonds."

In towns like Boston, the politically driven *house attack* and what came to be called the *tea party* draw on this kind of masking and tomfoolery. The one British occasion which made its way to New England and the Maritimes was the bonfire night, which was attached to the anti-Catholic Pope's Day. This name was given to Guy Fawkes Day, a celebration in which handing an effigy of "the old Guy" was reenacted every November (St. George 1998: 250–69). Commonly, the effigy would represent not Fawkes but someone who had committed a political or social affront. Songs and speeches were prepared and even written out and affixed to the effigy's clothes, and a parade route was worked out to call attention to the procession. The event ended in the house attack. Such demonstrations were often directed against British officials and multiplied in the years leading up to the Revolution.

The most common form of *ruckus* involved white-capping, effigy burning, tarring and feathering, and riding someone on a rail (Young 1976, 1991). These Old World social punishments were given new direction and ideological focus after the introduction of the English and American constitutions. Dressing in rags, blankets, or sheeting, wearing the tall, conical hat, or elaborating the head with feathers, midnight warriors emerged during times of stress well into the twentieth century. The post-Civil War nightriders and later the Ku Klux Klan adapted these techniques to terrorize African Americans, but this time the victims were no mere effigies (Fry 1975). In the West as well as the South, hanging and burning became an important weapon of vigilantes.

These groups invoked the same spirit of voluntarism as bees, although they commonly involved leadership, internal organization, and ways of maintaining the secrecy of membership from outsiders. The difference between the activities of the skimmington riders and the *posse commitatus* is obvious enough, but instructive: one involved the symbolic carrying out of justice, while the other called for the establishment of a kangaroo court and the abduction of a human who was then lynched.

Memorializing Moments of Amity and Loss

Nothing illustrates the value of amity and the failure of goodwill so clearly as people of different cultures encountered each other, especially over issues of land ownership. For good reason, many places celebrate the achievement of amicable relations through treaty encounters with local Indians. Commonly centering on the achievement of friendship between the leaders of the two sides, the treaty scenario was, and is still, replayed all over the continent at the officially designated moment when peaceable relations were first established. Central to these occasions is the proffering of the gift of corn to the newcomers, usually through a representative donor figure. Some native mediators, such as Pocahontas, are nonthreatening characters who, despite their premature demise, are rewarded by historical notice. Others, such as Squanto, were classic culture brokers, Indian spokespersons who had learned the language and the ways of the White Man and agreed to help the two groups make a ceremony and feast together.

These figures are commonly described as brave warriors who, in the face the imposition of private property, fencing the land, and tilling the soil with plows (not to mention in the aftermath of repeating rifles, which with which whites killed Indians and exterminated the buffalo), recognize that the day of Indian hegemony is over. Breaking the arrows, burying the tomahawk, and smoking the peace pipe while standing under a massive tree which provided the destination point for both sides, this Indian, usually referred to as a chief or sachem, then retires to his wigwam or longhouse to live out his days in peace. These moments of supposed amity are marked throughout the landscape by reference to a treaty oak or elm and by the report of a great oration made by the chief testifying to his sadness at being the last of his tribe.

Insofar as these treaty scenes actually took place, they dramatize the willingness of those colonists seeking title from the Indians to play the scene by the rules of the indigenous peoples. Is there any doubt that this is the master narrative of Thanksgiving feast? So, too, is it the story being told in the images of the Penn Treaty at Shackamaxon, enshrined in the *trionfo* painting by Benjamin West and repeated in the works of Edward Hicks of Peaceable Kingdom fame. Europeans sought validation of their cultural superiority and entitlement to the American continent from the native people themselves.

Nowhere is the nostalgic tenor of American life more deeply expressed than in the holidays that maintain this tradition, reenacting the feast at the conclusion of strife. Many of the most fraught occasions in history serve as the subject of annual reenactments. Such places in the landscape are marked by the memory of confrontation and triumph, or defeat. Dates once observed with patriotic parades are now animated by historical reenactments. In living history museums, these moments become repetitive scenes, with a set scenario, scripted dialogue, period costumes, and even attempts to revoice the speech of the past.

Thus do enactments become regular reenactments, and finally spectacles in which anyone can play any part. Patriotic Americans assume the costumes of Revolutionaries or Loyalists, Unionists or Rebels. All roles are, in principle, interchangeable; only white and black persons, and male soldiers and female camp followers, do not commonly exchange roles. And, of course, there are no real Indians in our mournful commemorations of the "last Indian."

Festive gatherings continue to play a central role in American family and community life, no matter what ethnic group celebrates them. They create occasions for reunions, homecomings, patriotic celebrations, and a plethora of other social events. Developments in communication and transportation have not only dispersed kin and kind; they also make it possible to keep in touch, to plan and calendar events, and to travel from far and wide to attend them. A note of lamentation for past inequities and separations makes its way into many of these events, but joyous celebration in the presence of so many relatives and friends tends to ameliorate these feelings of historical rupture, loss, or guilt.

Chapter 10
Facing Off at the Border

To live fully, freely, and happily in our consumer culture, we must come to grips with the contradictory forces of fear and fascination as they are evoked by venturing out of the house. Once we are in public, we put up our guard—"for good reason," say the cautious among us, who stand ready to believe all the horror stories we hear. Leaving home, even briefly, elicits a scintilla of panic. In its most extreme form, fear becomes agoraphobia. Impelled by our desire for difference, the widest variety of things for sale, or the thrill of the experience itself, we carry with us instinctual fears of encountering weird, rude, and often unruly people from outside our community. We gravitate to those places of public interaction where a gathering becomes a group, a group may transmute into a mob, and a mob may turn riotous.

Buying strange goods or services is often the easiest way to experience difference, to encounter the exotic and begin to incorporate the "others" who show up one day at the gate with products and performances that promise us the liberating force of variety. We also fear not venturing, not having the regular high arising from going shopping, to the show, or whatever else we do to partake in sociable pleasures. Isolation and deprivation are counterpoised against encounters with the abundance brought by strangers.

This combination of fear and desire undergirds all play to some degree, but especially strongly if the price of admission has been costly. Tickets you can buy, but a license to confront the public world is not subject to purchase. Who would retreat from a chance to meet Death or some other stranger in a public place, surrounded by onlookers? Think of all the screams we have heard, and how very few of them arose because of actual mayhem.

Permission to scream in public is not hard to come by, although perhaps more readily available to children than to adults. Screaming, like percussive laughter, is encouraged as a signal that a good time is being had by all. Experiences out of the comfort zone promise encounters with the exotic, even shocking; more profoundly, they offer us the possibility of release.

We have a good vernacular explanation for such behavior: it is only human to "let off steam." But it is not those dressed or decorated with death's heads who provide the greatest thrills, despite the designs of tattoo artists and others who alter the body. Marking the body is a common way of conquering fear and experiencing difference at the same time. We know that best from going to parades and pageants, raves and dance marathons, or other occasions calling for costumes. Costuming itself seems to provide the ticket to this realm of enjoyment. If you have the right clothes, you can go anyplace in public, even if you can't quite pull it off. Little girls playing dress-up provide the model for all such behavior. Going out in public in fashionable or formal dress, in drag, or in grunge or hip-hop garb calls for the same kind of licensing. You can wear anything as long as you live up to the obligation to be on show. This impulse is also manifest in street theater and the most recent developments in cabaret, where you get to tell your stories from a little stage in front.

Being "it" is found not only in tag or hide-and-seek, but in all playful public displays that involve altering the body or assuming disguises. Such public shows carry immense risks because they also involve getting high. Almost any public outing can lead to a freak show or monster's ball, especially around holidays. Making a flash doesn't just involve going to the beach, though that's a good place to start.

Going out puts you in the way of rude behavior and trash talk. These offensive routines are just as rehearsed as movement theater, and the channeling of hostilities is no greater. Whoever is walking tall must have the right responses already prepared; you don't want to go to war out there. If you accuse someone of rudeness, you had better be prepared for a response that says, in one way or another, "Hey, it's a free world, isn't it?" Hostile encounters yield as good a high as a demolition derby. Self-exoticization is the key to the vernacular lives of the young. Any uniform will do: dressing as a pimp or a hooker, wearing a kimono or a biking outfit. What used to be called blending in with the crowd might involve carousing as an alien, or dressing as one of the homeless. Go figure.

Insults

The vernacular contains a myriad of terms for arguments that veer toward hostility without the cover of joking. The ancient words for the art of making fun at someone else's expense reveal just how socially capricious these practices have been. Discussions of the literary texts of ritualized arguments in English commonly call them by the Scottish term, *flyting*: conflicts voiced and expressed in formulaic insults which contain aggression through stylization and wit; these were brought to a high art by well-schooled bards singing praise and scandal. The archaic practices of *scouring*, *scolding*, *slander* (an extended curse impugning someone's actions or motives), or the more rehearsed *libel* (a play or song focusing on a local disagreement)—all provided community entertainment. In entering the vernacular, they lost much of their wit but retained the danger of provoking community intervention. Indeed, some of the best evidence we have of such words and action comes from court records of local libels, tarring and feathering, hangings in effigy, skimmington rides, rough music, charivaris, and other forms of informal justice. In this way, crimes are disposed of and punishments imposed on the local level, sometimes with the intervention of the courts, sometimes through the formation of a *posse commitatus*.

Ethnographers have noted such traditional forms in many cultures: playing the dozens among African American youths (Abrahams 1976) or the slanging and slurs traded between rival sports teams. Studies of kinship devote a good deal of discussion to what are technically called joking relationships—the compulsory insulting of relatives, usually of the opposite sex, which voice otherwise forbidden words. In many festive occasions, insult and aggression are channeled into a performance, and experts of invective are employed to represent the honor of their community. Song and dance forms of stylized competitions which emerge into the popular arts are as various as calypso, the samba, or *capoeira*, which grow out of staged encounters in festive competitions.

When these competitions erupt at the boundaries between rival groups, shouting matches ensue, and animosities can get physical. What may begin as entertainment quickly turns ugly under conditions of intense competition for turf, or where females are regarded as property and males compete for sexual partners. Even formal competitions assume a different place in the expressive economies of the rivals. Once borders and boundaries are crossed, unfriendly words and actions follow. When fighting breaks out, all actions betray the licensing system, questioning the viability of playing by the rules. The difference between playing around and issuing a challenge which chills the spirit is immense.

These arguments carry us as far away as we might conceive from any territory in which the presumption of goodwill is in force. It is difficult to discuss the subject in general conversation, because it challenges the norms of friendly encounters so fundamentally. Even the most highly stylized duels and shootouts polarize and destroy social groups. This potential for irremediable division certainly accounts for the lively contemporary public discussions being carried on regarding racism and colonialism. So long as these are discussions rather than more violent confrontations, they seem to be a necessary component of an open society. But historical precedent demonstrates how quickly such discussions turn into arguments, which in turn become demonstrations and riots.

Many civic entities in plural societies subject cultural difference to public view by staging multicultural display events. Performances connected to home and village life skip-hop onto the festival stage, food stands, and craft stalls. Festivals, like county and state fairs before them, become good business under these controlled circumstances. Decisions about who should be represented and how may cause some internal dissension before the event, but the ideology of friendly and shared experience is internally policed by attendees obeying the spirit of goodwill.

The values of family and friends remain with those who go out of their way to share ethnic identities and experiences in public. Displaying oneself as *an ethnic* may test the boundary of the permissible as members of a group joke with each other about their ethnically marked behaviors. Derogatory terms used by those so stereotyped in the historical past become cozy words when used within the group. But outsiders who overhear such in-group slanging may take the wrong cue; these slurs are regarded as improper coming from an outsider. "Honky," "spic," or "yid" evoke the shared historical experience of prejudice and disempowerment and teeter on the edge of appropriateness any time they are employed, either within or outside the group. The more neutral terms *paisan*, homeboy, *compadre*, or *landsman*, used within in-group conversations, mark an ethnic alignment without embarrassment, insofar as the banter suggests that there are still secrets of the tribe. But with the growing volatility of inter-ethnic relations, even these may prove dangerous.

What my Texas *compadre* Américo Paredes calls "neighborly names"— words like "gringo" and "greaser"—imply continuing power struggles between these groups and signify that ethnic border disputes are still present, even when these terms are used jokingly. These openly derisive words may lose their fangs if used in friendly conversations between groups, though less easily than when used within them. But the vernacular always reveals other and more secret terms for historical foes. Paredes points out that hardly anyone uses "gringo" any more except to refer the dolorous history of border conflict in the Rio Grande Valley. But in his neighborhood such terms as *paton* (big foot) and *godemes* (English speakers who are always saying "god damn it") are the hidden or esoteric terms for the others (Paredes 1961). Here the slur and the slam, the stereotype joke and the big games held between the rivals are all part of a conflict that everyone knows exists and expects at any time to turn into a battle.

When a shouting match across the border arises, it can easily turn into something quite unneighborly. Vernacular competitions within communities encourage the honing of verbal powers, which may then be drawn upon when members of rival groups find themselves in a face-off. Demonstrations of "bad attitude" account for a lot of hurt feelings on both sides of even the most casual interactions.

At the perceived boundaries between territories, no man's lands may be created, and just walking through these zones resuscitates apprehensions that hostility is in the air. Appointed or self-appointed guardians patrol the bounds. The best competitors from each group are given the privilege of representing the rest. Competition may take many forms, from trading clever rhyming slurs to ritualized demonstrations of a martial art. The vernacular commonly argues that these practices are imbibed with mother's milk, passed on by whatever passes for the spirit or soul of the group. Groups marked as ethnically different draw on these slurs, eliminating any hope of dealing with the combatants except as a foe: hotheads daring each other to commit the first act of a seriously deepened fight. Private antipathies explode into open antagonism and threaten to become public events as the onlookers and overhearers gather to find out what's happening. Unfortunately, experience says that "Everybody loves a good fight," even though a fracas or a mobbing may grow out of it.

Cultural Displays in Multicultural Contexts

The tensions engendered by conflicting expressive systems are employed by performers and artists. The artist-hero is revitalized by this ongoing contention, and the exile artist plays a special role as "the conscience of the race," as James Joyce had it.

Planned events capitalize on such antagonisms and energies, constraining them and using them as fit materials for a show, spectacle, festival, or fair. These are times when anything goes, at least in principle—times when people give themselves the license to play, to drink and eat and shout and dance too much. Or they willingly enter into inchoate worlds where they may be taken in, or do some taking-in on their own; they may fool others or be made the fool.

At these very points of confrontation are found the most creative responses to social tension and intercultural strains. In the neutral ground of the stadium or the arena, or in the highly charged symbolic movements of the dance, parade, pageant, or ball game, accumulated feelings may be channeled into contest, drama, or some other form of display. Here I outline a morphology of such planned-for public occasions in which ethnically marked objects and performances are put on display. These events are as disparate as expositions and meets, games and carnivals, and auctions.

In the public anonymity of display events like fairs and festivals, masks are worn and dramatic roles played out. The stereotypical neighborly names can be employed to exorcize, at least for the moment, unneighborly feelings. The ideal of a civic celebration is to make space for every segment of the community that wants representation. And in the uncivil celebrations, the topsy-turvy events like Carnival and the mock parades in which anything goes, the event is animated by those who maintain an outsider status in their home communities. Civic celebrations beget counter-parades of dissidents.

Perhaps the most telling of these trends has been the development of the folk festival. When organized with the resources of all groups within the polity, they serve as advertisements for diversity. Cultural differences are dramatized as a means of maintaining separate identities while joining in an inclusive celebration. Folk festival displays produced with the aid of ethnographers serving as both insider and outsider—as culture broker, if you will—plumb the expressive resources of the group and come up with an authentic presentation. The displays are judged by how well they maintain the everyday character of traditional practice even when transformed into a rehearsed scene carried out in a public place. How much is the spontaneity and integrity of the practice when carried out within familiar places compromised by this move, especially when there is an implied competition between the presenting groups? Success is judged not so much in terms of authenticity, but in the performers' ability to reframe the traditional practice for popular presentation alongside demonstrations from other groups. Festive events tend to homogenize displays, so each group is satisfied that its old ways are being adequately represented.

Each group's display is framed in homogenized performance terms by a person, often an outsider, who narrates what is taking place "in front of your very eyes." The perceptions of both those entering into the display and those who watch it are conventionalized in such a way that any present tensions within the polity are erased at the moment of performance. Each group relies on the common understanding that each represents a "folk community"—a term ripe for a variety of interpretations, but perhaps, in contemporary vernacular, a code word for cultural pluralism on show.

As they are developed into public presentations, customary local practices advertise the principle of ethnic diversity, even as the presentations begin to look alike when they are performed together in the festival format. For many ethnic communities, much of the lore put on display comes from the customary practices already geared toward presentation. Courting songs and dances, wedding music, show quilts, prize-winning dishes—all are regarded as celebratory of family and community values and thus fit easily into the festival format.

In the formal parades organized from the early nineteenth through the late twentieth centuries, each ethnic group displayed itself through the uniform of the voluntary organization that had sprung up within the ethnic neighborhood, often based in a church. These groups organized themselves hierarchically and marched in serried order, demonstrating community purpose and vitality. The folk festival works on a similar principle, although the participants are not all men, they are not organized by rank, and the costume creates its own scenes that demonstrate the uniqueness of the ethnic community.

The folk festival form is more colorful and varied than the parade, but after awhile the cookie-cutter effect flattens the presentation. Groups borrow styles and techniques from other organizations. Folk dances repeat the same figures, even as their movement styles remain distinct. With both forms of community celebration, the primary rule is equal opportunity for all groups to show themselves at their best. But the setting of the display remains the same for all, which tends to homogenize the performances. Groups are brought together in the overall conception of the event, while maintaining their own collective identities within the umbrella of festive time, space, and movement.

In the parade of ethnic notables and the festival demonstrations of the old ways, both neighborhood and civic pride are displayed, often in the face of the historical animosities of two or more of the groups involved. Many of the older members of the community, smiling on the present celebrations, find it ironic that traditional enemies in the Old World find themselves playing next to each other in the New without reminding onlookers of the horrors of past battles. It is always ironic for the historically informed to see peoples who killed one another for ethnic honor singing and dancing alongside one another in joy. For both sides, happiness seems to lie in the dramatic forgetting of past wars and destruction. All the groups involved give forth the message that they not only represent the ancestors but have gone through the same dislocating experience together and lived to tell the story.

The idea of the folk community has been a useful fiction for rationalizing certain attitudes toward social structure and cultural diversity. Such a frame of reference contributes to vernacular discussions of the way society is and ought to be. It also highlights difference of style and substance that promise to be socially useful under peacetime conditions. If public-sector folklorists operate on the assumption that recognizing and representing lore contributes to the maintenance of the community and of its sense of boundedness, they can hardly be faulted. This fiction is more than a convenience for putting public display events together; it represents a continued groping toward equal opportunity practices. However, to continue to regard something which draws on a traditional style as real, in contrast to fake, is making moral claims of the sort that no audience or collector should make. Any reconstruction, now matter how marked with an old sound, invites potshots from those who say that the backstage managers are using the idea of authenticity for reprehensible purposes, taking economic advantage of performers who don't know any better.

Customs and traditions of the sort that are displayed at folk festivals are put on show in a wide range of social settings, not all of which are associated with ethnic groups. The songs, stories, and handmade objects to which we assign value as folklore because they are crafted using traditional technology for the use of others within the community can be found, often in greater abundance, outside the self-conscious folk festival. Such objects are featured at open-air markets, fairs, and auctions—indeed, at all public displays where people from contiguous and often antagonistic communities participate in a neutral setting. We can gain access to the texts and objects which folklorists seek to study more easily and in greater abundance at places where there is none of the usual sense of community that arises from shared lives and values.

Observing and analyzing the small homogeneous community has dominated vernacular conceptions of how culture operates for so long that it can be assigned to a system of nostalgia which is held in common by all involved: academics, revival performers, cultural conservators, civic leaders, and members of ostensibly closed communities as well. Politicians accept that collecting and presenting past practices under the aegis of cultural preservation and heritage maintenance helps them to identify constituencies that are otherwise opaque to officials. Formerly, folk traditions were synonymous with ignorance and illiteracy. Now a wholesale revaluation of such matters is taking place in public and in the academy. The ghettoized and the previously disempowered can be grouped together as subalterns, and our consciousness of past injustice comes into clearer perspective.

This process does objectify or textualize cultural forms, making them into consumables. It also contributes to a potentially debilitating longing for a past that never existed. The distinction between oral and literate worlds reifies the notion of modernity and progress by championing the forces of antimodernism without questioning the repercussions of such a sociopolitical position. Promoting the vernacular in the name of diversity must—or, so the argument assumes—be all to the good, no matter how much it is anchored in the past and learned from hard experience.

Folk festivals are only one outgrowth of the heritage industry. Schools and settlement houses used to promote education to bring about cultural assimilation. Making this point today in any metropolitan center would invite laughter, as differences in vernaculars come to be prized and exhibited. But folk festivals are public events that gravitate to spectacle, which dazzle audiences and increase the number of paying ticket-holders. That transformation runs counter to the politics of culture espoused by most social scientists and humanists, who wish to enter into and perpetuate the variety being celebrated.

In large-scale fairs or festivals, people gather in an open, neutral, and licensed space for less familiar give-and-take engagements in which all the participants are not known in advance. Under such conditions, everyone is fair game to be contended with, conned, lied to, dazzled, entertained, exploited. This way of looking at life is much less settled, more open-ended, and more subject to constant reinterpretation because participants are in constant negotiation for something—even if only to entertain and be entertained.

Fairs and festivals may be more effective as ways of maintaining the appearance of amity and diversity than of encouraging the diverse practices of distinctive cultural groups. One way or another, we are all involved in a process of creating those saving lies and convenient fictions that feed the spirit. Festive entertainments are as different from the usual performances studied by social-scientific participant-observers as one can imagine. By harmonizing these different voices, the festival setting encourages the idea that no community can represent itself. Rather, diversity is put at the service of variety for consumerist purposes. The more the variety, the greater success of the festival, especially if all groups are given the same amount of presentational time and space.

At least ideally, any segment of a plural or stratified community can play itself within this licensed context. This multiplicity produces a practical acting-out of ethnic or other social identifications, as both a contrast and a complement to the self-presentations of others. Games and performances operate simultaneously as ethnic displays and as part of a larger statement of multiethnic cooperation. Whether this pluralism works within the vernacular domain or is too highly planned and canned to imitate the spontaneous and energetic elements in that particular presentation remains problematic (Price and Price 1994). Ideally, of course, those involved are able to simulate this impression of spontaneous revelry. But how could anything spontaneous arise in the programmed and calculated festival space? As one of the producers of a large annual festival put it, "the interesting stuff really goes on backstage, or wherever the performers are housed."

Cross-Cultural Exchange

Most festival traditions include a clown figure to give the message that "it's all for show." Pulling things out of shape, the way clowns do, is so deep a part of old ways of celebrating seasonal changes that no one questions the festival producer's use of such figures of fun.

The use of pratfalls and travesty crosses ethnic and cultural boundaries without carrying any of the animosities from the cultures in which they were embedded. Indeed, expressions of animosity are discouraged in these touristic or civic celebrations. The audience and the authorities need assurance that intergroup hostilities will be buried for the moment. It is difficult to remember that groups of Balkan singers and dancers regularly brought together Croats, Slovenes, Serbs, and Montenegrans in performances and celebrations, not just at festivals but at social clubs in the old neighborhoods. No reenactments of civil wars are permitted in these climes. Ethnicity may be translated into political competition in the neighborhoods, but not on the festival campus.

Various interest groups, especially hobbyists and recreationists, form organizations with their fellow "freaks," ranging from birding and caving to owning gear—vehicles, short-wave radios, hunting and fishing paraphernalia. Like serial monogamists, we chart our passions through our latest craze. Of course, the gatherings that arise as enthusiasts act out their passions are about as authentic as the uniforms, equipment, and costumes they purchase. Reunions, rallies, and conventions serve devotees. From the ethnographer's perspective, these activities pose extraordinarily interesting and socially pertinent questions. The address to tourists and seekers of big experiences and the lure of the authentic remain.

The appeal of the popular and the vernacular gives old practices new audiences and new performers. In Philadelphia, as in many metropolitan areas, Chinese New Year holds an important place in the civic calendar. For many onlookers, the celebration focuses on the dragon, as this figure leads the procession around the bounds of Chinatown. With the growing popularity of Asian forms of martial arts drawing so many people to the neighborhood for instruction, members of other groups are often found there. But it came as something of a surprise to those observing the festivities to discover that the young people in charge of the dragon were African American martial arts students. Tradition and cosmopolitanism find themselves in uneasy but vivid encounters.

In a public event, it is often difficult and sometimes impossible to "be yourself" without losing yourself in some way. People commonly go into such events expecting to be swept away by the experience, to take on new and totally different roles. Nowhere is this difference so fully spelled out as in pure festival. A successful event creates a perfect balance of excitement, poised between hilarious or ludicrous behavior and the highest seriousness. Studies of community festivals suggest that they are capable of epitomizing the most cherished ideals of the community, along with the most highly valued symbolic movements by which the community as a whole defines and celebrates itself. Surely, investigating such displays in other cultures would reveal patterns of spatial and temporal organization and movement which epitomize the ways in which the group gives value to itself and to life, even while the event summons forth the most derelict characters and diabolic motives.

Fairs differ from festivals precisely in the relationship between the show activities and the sale of products and services. Both types of occasion intensify experience by creating quality times and spaces to carry out extraordinary activities and by staging a large number of acts simultaneously, which contributes to an overwhelming experience. But festivities focus on the exchange of energies among participants in play activities, while fairs center on the exchange of goods or services. Fairs may have a playful component, but they are primarily concerned with displaying work techniques and products. Merchandising is relegated to the periphery of festive events—things are sold at the door. When play arises at trade and trading events, it is relegated to the margins and placed at the service of the flow of merchandise.

This subordination of play to the exchange of goods is strikingly visible in that most performance-like of trade events: the auction. Many people attend country auctions because they are such a good show, and great auctioneers know that they must perform to draw a crowd of bidders. But the business at hand is selling things at the highest possible price. Country auctioneers, like carnie pitchmen, develop their routines much as bards do. They stitch together set units of expressions, or formulas, with fluency and even eloquence. Their routines force the audience of potential buyers to pay them the kind of constant attention accorded a virtuoso performer. The performance consists of cadenced calls for bids punctuated by jokes about the goods on sale or persons in the audience. Much of the effect of their sales technique is predicated on building up a wall of sound in order to stun prospective purchasers into silence and immobility.

This intimidation is intensified by the feeling common among the audience that any movement may be interpreted as a bid—a belief which is in fact a misapprehension. Indeed, one of the major problems for someone wishing to buy is learning how to establish oneself as a bona fide bidder and how to sign one's bid correctly. A successful auctioneer increases the distance between himself and the audience by placing a crew in front of him. These intermediaries hold up the object for sale, pick up bids from the audience and relay them to the auctioneer with a yell, make jokes, coax prospective buyers, and contribute to the noise and bustle among the sellers, which contrast so dramatically with the fixity and silence of the buyers. If ever there was an unequal shouting match over a dividing line, it is at such barn and open-air auctions.

The tremendous popularity of such auctions is paralleled in other merchandising events, such as bazaars, flea markets, and sidewalk and garage sales. These are less boisterous, but they are held for the same reason: to attract a buying public with the possibility of getting something for practically nothing. The objective is to make a sale through bargaining well, or at least to find a bargain.

Both festivals and fairs involve scenes of intense exchange, the passing of significant objects and actions across a high-energy field in which participants are involved, knowingly and willingly, in negotiation. When play is taking place, the negotiation is usually for intangibles. But how different, really, are a trophy and a bargain? Ultimately it is the display and the intensity of the experience that count, not what we take away from the event.

The effect of festive play and celebration, as of games and performances, is made possible by the license the occasion affords. The rules of everyday life are surrendered in favor of ceremonial practices, the rules of the game, concert-hall decorum, or arena manners. This license is only sometimes licentious; rather, alternative rules of behavior and judgment govern an intense and focused exchange. There is little question what kind of license prevails at a ball game, concert, circus, or picnic. Each frame produces its own way of looking at the goings-on, its own way of anticipating what is to come, enjoying the activity, and judging whether it is successful. The license which governs all play is the license to engage in actions for their own sake without the need to produce anything.

On first blush, this set of criteria would not seem applicable to fairs, exhibitions, or any other type of trade event. Yet the two extraordinary worlds comment on each other in interesting ways. An auction calls for the abrogation of the buyer-seller code of decorum which characterizes everyday commerce. Licensed departures from the everyday conventions governing exchanges are evident in hyping items, misleading, and conniving. Trade events use the principle of *caveat emptor* to keep participants, especially new ones, on edge. Those who enter such events realize that truthfulness itself is under negotiation. In events that focus on quick-hit commercial transactions, everyone must adopt the code of the marketplace not to trust anything that anybody says. Veracity is a rare commodity when alluring objects are offered for exchange.

The customary permissions that enter into these transactions are to speak expansively, to make claims for the object being traded that will not hold up in the commercial world outside of the display event. The success or failure of the experience is predicated on the appreciation of the risk involved in getting caught up in the spirit of the occasion, or in the ability of the auctioneer, spiel-meister, or vendor to make a good pitch. All face-to-face business exchanges have a performance dimension. We look for good service as well as for goods. And sometimes, at country auctions as well as other kinds of markets, the service we look for is a good shouting match, which quickens our sense of life and makes us forget about the rest—at least for the moment of truth-and-consequences.

Play and Display

We have strayed from performances traditionally carried on within the comfort zone around the fire for the sake of establishing a larger frame of reference for vernacular activities. These display events have maintained a counterculture of far more revolutionary potential than the radical tactics that energized the social and political movements of the 1960s.

The most subversive display events produce intense moments of pleasure and even communitas. In the bargaining or bidding and the actual purchase, the most important dimensions of play are brought to bear in an environment that otherwise would engender seriousness. These events maintain the momentum and flow of life in palpable, yet often scary, terms. Obsessive is not too strong a word to describe the typical participants in these exchanges. These mad moments in the set-aside worlds of commerce held on the margins of time continue to provide us with highly charged experiences that are usually associated with models of revolution, as many commentators have pointed out. But more than this, the trade fair, in league with the festival, maintains our sense that there are alternatives to commodity fetishism. In these extraordinary road marches and parades, these shouting matches and shooting matches, the possibility of hanging on to the use value of things and acts is defended, in the face of those who would turn all of life into acts of consumption. Such occasions openly draw upon and subvert the machine-made, die-stamped elements of our material lives. But they do not quell our competitive spirit. We tend to remake, to customize ourselves under such circumstances.

These trade events become entertainments, but not of the warm and fuzzy sort. They involve risk, fabrication of various kinds of verbal performances, dizziness as the spirit of the occasion spreads throughout the assembly, contests over objects and ownership, and a good deal of play-acting even in the most serious of them. Their vernacular naming and framing is consistent and consistently resisted. We want to be friends with someone we buy from, though common sense reminds us that being that close would ruin the fun.

PART IV

Terms for Finding Ourselves

Chapter 11
Ethnicities

The term *ethnicity* was added to the social science vocabulary as such terms as national traits and character, as well as the racial categories, lost their explanatory vigor and political usefulness. It was proposed during the 1950s by voices representing the party of toleration and assimilation when the specter of genocide hovered over all discussions of stereotyping. As late as 1963, when Nathan Glazer and Daniel Patrick Moynihan wrote their influential book, *Beyond the Melting Pot*, ethnicity as a term for historical and social difference still marked a trouble spot for those seeking to put the forces of inequity behind them. The *Oxford English Dictionary* points to its first usage as a noun by the sturdy American social critic David Riesman in 1953. The adjectival form *ethnic* is somewhat older, and the root word is ancient; in Greek, *ethnos* means culturally backward or pagan (Williams 1975: 119). The term was used in this pejorative sense in English until the mid-nineteenth century, when it was rehabilitated by Romantic nationalists to serve as a synonym for racial or national characteristics.

Americans recognized their own ethnic diversity through their experience of World War II, when the range of different people in the armed services was trumpeted as a patriotic statement about how assimilation actually works. Even then, of course, some groups remained beyond the pale; only those white immigrants and their children who were recognized as Americans were deemed ethnic. Indeed, the term became a sort of racial honorific, excluding Japanese Americans and African Americans. But the diversity it did include was amusing enough. Comedians still draw on the clichés of war movies featuring an ethnically mixed cast of soldiers: the Italian, who was usually a casualty of war; the Jew, who (in sharp contrast to actual events in Europe) was never killed; and the Irish Catholic, who remained a clownish figure whatever his fate. The Roosevelt administration promulgated the image of an army with three chaplains: priest, minister, and rabbi. At this historical juncture, the term ethnic came into play as the polite way of referring to members of white minority groups whose accents were audibly different from the majority of English descent. Recognizing "backward" groups who were geographically separated from the centers of industrial progress encouraged Americans to envisage themselves as tolerant of diversity. Indeed, if being old-fashioned represented sturdy self-sufficiency and resistance to the excesses of modernity, such historically isolated groups represented homely and quaint alternative ways of life, useful reminders of the virtues of the Age of Homespun.

With the massive movement of rural populations to urban centers seeking employment opportunities, many previously isolated groups joined the urban working class and became part of the metropolitan mix, alongside various immigrant populations. Both Scotch Irish plain folks of the Southern Mountains and African Americans from across the Deep South gravitated north and west. Their presence in the cities threatened those already encamped, especially when longtime residents and new arrivals competed for employment. These groups of culturally distinct working people could not be accommodated by the older methods of assimilation. No longer could the schools and settlement houses "Americanize" them; indeed, some were already distinctively American. The new elements being added to the urban crucible did not melt so readily. *Ethnicity* came to be associated not only with difference but also with problems of accommodation within the larger polity. In most cities, a small, exclusive group of locals exercised power and enjoyed hegemony, inviting resistance by ethnically distinct groups. One group after another developed its own voluntary organizations and used them to confront those who were running things. Social science adapted to this drift by drawing on ethnicity as a term with more positive meanings, referring to groups maintaining their own sense of integrity through continuing to observe their own ways of organizing and expressing themselves.

With the triumph of the Civil Rights Movement in the 1960s, *ethnic groups* and ethnicity became the approved terms in the social science literature, journalistic reports, and public discussion for white people of immigrant descent. African Americans, Asian Americans, and Latinos remained outside the ethnic fold; the hyphenated term *racial-ethnic* had not yet emerged. The rapid expansion of mass production that continued into the postwar period generated a multitude of new manufacturing jobs, drawing large numbers of ethnically diverse people together in industrial cities. Competition for scarce housing and for jobs led to ethnic conflicts, especially during recessions, while consumption of a wider variety of foods and clothing styles made visible cultural differences more acceptable. *Ethnic* has never returned as a term of opprobrium for immigrants and those of their descendants who continue to identify themselves through accounts of family migration. Occasionally, when referring to such groups collectively in public discourse, the generic term *hyphenated Americans* is used in place of specific ethnic identifications. In the face of this usage, we must observe that most people who double their identity terms are not white and no longer use a hyphen: they are African American, Asian American, Native American, etc. Few people actually speak of themselves as Norwegian American or Jewish American, for example; the defensive assertion of Americanness no longer seems necessary. Nor do they necessarily think of themselves as more like other American-born descendants of European immigrants than like Americans with quite different ancestries and migration histories. Indeed, many people remain uncomfortable with all of these marked terms, choosing to continue to regard the assimilationist mode of thinking as the American Way.

Multiple Meanings

The definitional survey by the Norwegian anthropologist Thomas Hylland Eriksen continues to be useful in rehearsing this history. However, he worries about the multiple, sometimes conflicting uses to which the term *ethnicity* has been put (Eriksen 2002).

Ethnic studies done by social scientists around the globe typically focus empirically on some, but not all, kinds of ethnic groups. This set of four types, while not exhaustive, suggests the contours of the field.

(1) *Urban ethnic minorities* include non-European immigrants in European cities and Hispanics in the United States, as well as migrants to industrial towns in Africa and elsewhere. Research on immigrants has tended to focus on problems of racial and ethnic discrimination by the host society, problems of adaptation, and issues related to identity management and cultural change. Anthropologists investigating urbanization in Africa have explored change and continuity in political organization and social identity following migration to entirely new settings. Although they have political interests, these ethnic groups rarely demand political independence or statehood, and they are as a rule integrated into a capitalist system of production and consumption.

(2) *Indigenous people* is a blanket term for aboriginal inhabitants of a territory who are relatively powerless politically and only partially integrated into the dominant nation-state. Indigenous peoples are associated with nonindustrial modes of production and a stateless political system (Minority Rights Group 1990). The Basques of the Bay of Biscay and the Welsh of Great Britain are not considered indigenous populations, although they are certainly as indigenous as the Sami of northern Scandinavia or the Jívaro of the Amazon basin. The concept *indigenous people* is not a precise analytic term, but rather draws on broad family resemblances and the configuration of contemporary political issues.

(3) *Ethnonationalist movements*, or protonations, resemble nations more closely than they do urban ethnic minorities or indigenous peoples. In common parlance, these peoples are "nations without a state"; Kurds, Palestinians, Sikhs, and Tamils exemplify this type. Ethnonationalist movements proliferate as empires and federations break up. By definition, these groups have political

leaders who claim that they are entitled to their own nation-state and should not be ruled by others. They are always territorially based, although some have important diasporas; they are differentiated according to class and educational achievement, and they are relatively large in population. Anthropologists have studied such movements in a variety of societies, including Euskadi or Basque country (Heiberg 1989), Brittany (McDonald 1989), and Québec (Handler 1988).

(4) *Ethnic groups* in plural societies—states with culturally heterogeneous populations, which are usually artifacts of colonialism—exhibit distinctive characteristics (Furnivall 1948; M. G. Smith 1965). Typical examples of plural societies include Kenya, Indonesia, and Jamaica. The groups that make up a plural society, although compelled to participate in uniform political and economic systems, are regarded as (or, regard themselves as) highly distinctive in other matters. In plural societies, secession is usually not an option, and ethnicity tends to be articulated through group competition. As Richard P. Jenkins remarked, most contemporary states could plausibly be considered plural ones (Jenkins 1997: 25–30).

Prevailing definitions of ethnicity include all of these kinds of groups, no matter how different they are in other respects. Ethnicity is a comfortable term for discussing an uncomfortable condition: the persistence of potentially unpleasant confrontations over the allocation of scarce resources. This set of divisions opens up a discussion of differences that can be coopted in order to rationalize a system that in the main wants to get rid of difference, although not of inequality. In vernacular usage, the word *ethnicity* still has a ring of "minority issues" and "race relations," but in some semantic environments it has been transformed into a word for variety and choice, where cultural variation might be turned into a social good. The term can refer to practices whose distinctiveness is unproblematic, or even contributes to the idea that human variability is a necessary evil in the conservation of the pluralistic ideals of representative democracies.

Not much explanatory vigor has arisen from the continuing use of Israel Zangwill's metaphor of the melting pot, although the alternative metaphors suggested by politically concerned ethnic groups drawing on their own lexicon provide some amusement: salad bowl, bouillabaisse, jambalaya. With William Petersen, "we must ask how (rather than why) it was that ethnicity has become a more important organizing principle" in popular accounts of social difference (Petersen 1980: 240; see also Peterson, Novak, and Gleason 1980).

Most scholars in this field are concerned that the hypothesis proposed by Marcus Lee Hansen of a three-generation process of assimilation renders ethnicity a passing phase in the development of a national consensus or standard culture (Hansen 1940; see Gordon 1964). Racial politics throughout the world has cast a pall on any straight-line model of cultural amalgamation. Because both governmental and nongovernment funding agencies in America and throughout the world remain challenged by groups who insist on maintaining their cultural distinctiveness, social scientific attention to the maintenance or the disappearance of ethnic practices in cosmopolitan nation-states continues unabated.

Food, Talk, and Sex

While ethnic conflicts, rationalized as arising from ancient enmities, continue to provide the downside of contemporary discussions of ethnicity, the mood becomes celebratory when food is the subject. While differences in food choice live at the heart of a good deal of stereotyping, street fairs and folk festivals provide opportunities to confront the fear of opening up the body to other people's practices. At events which advertise cultural diversity in specific locales, having the widest possible array of foods is regarded as a key attraction. While variety democratizes difference, fear is addressed by presenting ethnic dishes as foods to taste.

The mystery of sampling ethnic foods is that family dishes and home cooking are presented in more public settings. The experience of eating while standing or walking around and using the fingers seems to diminish the sense of risk. The adventure relies on the idea that what is being eaten is really someone else's comfort food. Ethnicity is acted out within the home as traditional foods are prepared in "the old way, using grandma's recipe." This continuity is disrupted when someone doesn't want to cook or eat that way any more. But tradition operates as a cultural resource that can always be resuscitated as long as someone in the family knows how to do it. These dishes often remain part of the holiday meal long after they have vanished from the everyday diet. In neighborhoods that continue to identify ethnically, stores develop something resembling that dish as a carry-out. Commonly, the dish is accompanied by a presentation story about someone who used to make it, or specific occasions on which it was eaten.

Three currencies of exchange are of primary importance in culture: food, sex, and talk. Each activity and recurrent scene involves a repertoire of distinctive foods and an etiquette for eating them. To learn how and when the natives eat these foods is to accrue cultural capital. In the same way, ways of talking or of making love as well as eating are laden with repeatable scenarios that are learned from earlier experiences and discussions of appropriateness. In all three realms, symbolic objects and actions are laminated with personal and shared meanings. This palimpsest is endowed with messages of the most profound, if conventionally phrased sort. Discerning with whom one may engage in talk, shared food, and sexual approach or avoidance is crucial to belonging.

Moreover, the three domains share a set of animal references which comment on the styles of the interaction. In some circles, referring to someone as a pig-eater is hardly enough to banish him from the table. But the euphemism "pork" is still preferred to calling a pig a pig as you eat. It is of greater consequence to think of a person as a pig, and especially to call him that; perceiving someone acting like a pig around food or sex often terminates the exchange. Eating and similar classes of interactive exchange enter into how we type others and how we treat them in intimate situations.

Animal categories used metaphorically are often found at the center of stereotypic categorizations, especially when it comes to the foods typically associated by one with the other. For instance, being known as an eater of critters sends a potent message to those who don't like the taste of anything gamey or wild, much less anything that might be thought to carry germs. Association with *menudo* (tripe), tamales, chittlins, fried fish, or watermelon serves as a negative cue, embodying stereotypical images of the others in our midst. Nevertheless, given the opportunity to sample one of these dishes on a festive occasion, we might regard ourselves as adventurous enough.

Folklore and Ethnic Cultures

The study of folklore began with a special focus on small, rural communities, but this emphasis on country people and their ways did not entirely delimit the perspective of American folklorists. The 1888 charter of the American Folklore Society mentions American Indian tribes, descendants of African slaves, and other ethnically distinct communities as appropriate sites for study, along with relics of agrarian life. Such disparate groups were presumed to have two crucial characteristics in common: the sense of community that arose because of their social or geographical isolation; and the relative intimacy between makers and users, performers and audience in their material and expressive culture.

To the extent that verbal lore both instructs and entertains, it puts into words the most important shared values of group life. In this way, folklore reminds us of how life ought to be lived and cautions us about the consequences of not following these precepts. Thus, folklore outlines basic patterns for the expression and enactment of group norms and ideals. To see the folk arts only from this instructional perspective, however, is to reduce such verbal formulations to kernels of wisdom or, worse, to clichés. When such playful forms as riddles, parodies, lampoons, jokes, and jibes are performed, the world view of the group may be tested, or even turned upside down. The study of the folklore of a group opens the possibility of revealing the deepest feelings of its members and, at the same time, of illuminating their ways of testing the boundaries of the community from within.

In giving voice to values and entering into the celebration of ethnicity, oral traditions are a major component in establishing the boundaries and contours of an ethnic group. A cultural performance may distinguish between members and nonmembers; it may also distinguish separate and even antagonistic segments within the community. Further, the same item of performance may on one occasion be drawn upon as a way of excluding a person or a group by designating them as non-persons (devils, animals, crazies) and on another may publicly proclaim the community as open to view and even to voluntary membership. Publicizing previously private ethnic ways is the primary thrust of many folk festivals, which self-consciously celebrate cultural diversity by displaying different culinary, musical, dance, and craft styles as styles, not really as alternative ways of life. The difference may simply be a matter of translating and explaining what is going on to outsiders, but in sociological terms that different is crucial.

Verbal lore is primarily tied to inherited patterns of language use. Linguistic acculturation to mainstream American English norms has undermined foreign oral traditions. Until relatively recently, collecting ethnic lore has been a retrieval project, preserving lore from tradition-bearers who have survived confinement on a reservation, a ghetto, or an immigrant neighborhood. Collecting ethnic lore often proceeds on the assumption that the songs, stories, proverbs, superstitions, and other practices of the homeland will inevitably be lost as soon as linguistic acculturation has taken place. This assumption is not without foundation, even with English-speaking immigrants who are adapting to the American varieties of their tongue. But recent studies of the expressive dimension of ethnicity based on more developmental principles have elucidated the various perceptible stages of Americanization (Gleason 1992). These stages are actually definable by the oral traditions that are maintained, modified, forgotten, or newly developed as a means of coping with novel and complex cultural situations.

Evidence is accumulating that acculturation to the mainstream is far from unilinear and that social assimilation must be distinguished from acculturation because it represents a different process and obeys a different timetable. Groups that have begun to assimilate politically and economically often strive to maintain culturally distinct forms and prefer to live in separate communities or neighborhoods. As this distinctiveness has become an asset rewarded by access to political leverage and economic opportunities, ethnic differences have to be self-consciously maintained as a means of making common cause politically or economically. This form of ethnic identity does not demand radical stylistic alternatives as much as it requires a display that carries a minimal message of cultural uniqueness—as superficial as drinking green beer on St. Patrick's Day. Such practices often draw upon an ethnic stereotype and turn it into a kind of self-conscious performance; that is, one's identity changes with the role and the relationships one takes on, whether willingly or not. In such a case, one's ethnic heritage, whether real or derived from a stereotype, becomes simply a role which is available because of the circumstance of one's ancestry and upbringing.

The dynamic of stereotyping is one of the most important forces in the development of ethnic consciousness. Whether an ethnic group decides self-consciously to assimilate, it develops a self-consciousness about language and cultural difference as experienced in the everyday world by the immigrant or refugee. It is not just life in the old country that is remembered, but the shared experience of the newcomers. Stories recount the recurrent embarrassments of greenhorns ignorant of the ways of the new land and probe the deeper confusions sometimes labeled *culture shock*. Leaving home, even for the "promised land," involves great psychological dislocation, compounded by inevitable failures of expectation. Out of this experience comes a kind of in-group lore, stories of personal experience that one shares with one's shipmates and others of the immigrant generation, and perhaps on rare occasions with younger members of one's family. Immigrants commonly have formulaic hardship stories or remembrances of funny or awful experiences while going through the port of entry.

As Barbara Kirshenblatt-Gimblett argues with great common sense, culture shock places the migrant or the refugee in the temporary position of a cultureless being, analogous to a child (Kirshenblatt-Gimblett 1972). The newcomer is forced to assume the role of one who doesn't know how to perform the most basic life tasks. The first experiences may operate in a manner similar to those of an initiate, but without the careful and extensive preparation that commonly goes into the traditional initiation ritual. The culture broker, the appointed or self-appointed member of the ethnic community who leads new arrivals through the worst spots, is a fascinating, insufficiently explored feature of the lore of all minority groups, including not only immigrants but also Indians and country folk who find themselves in strange cities. Like all migrants, the newcomers look for "homeboys": relatives, acquaintances, coreligionists, *landsmen*, anyone they can find who speaks their language and has made a place in the new society. Kin-groups often engage in chain migration, as husbands bring wives, brothers bring sisters, and cousins bring yet more cousins. Those who have already made the transition provide help in finding housing and work, are usually bilingual and often literate, and have learned whatever is essential in order to get along in the new environment. As a way of dramatizing and humanizing this transition for newcomers, ethnic brokers often develop a repertoire of stories, illustrative anecdotes of common embarrassment that provide lessons in getting through crisis situations with self-respect intact. These stories often float from one ethnic group to another, demonstrating that the sense of embarrassment is shared by many who come to a new country and have to learn new codes and languages.

One story, which appears in many forms in many communities, tells of the attempts of a newly arrived immigrant to get something to eat during the lunch break at his new job. His relative carefully coaches him to say, "I want a piece of pie and a glass of milk." On the first day, he successfully negotiates the purchase and is immensely proud of doing so. He repeats the order each day for several weeks thereafter. But one night he says that he would like to eat something else for lunch once in a while. Accepting the new task, his bene-factor teaches him to say, "I want a ham sandwich and a cup of coffee." The newcomer, after practicing, walks boldly into the restaurant and renders his order. "I want a ham sandwich and a cup of coffee." "White or rye?" is the response. After a long pause, he answers, "Gimme a piece of pie and a glass of milk."

In a situation of enforced acculturation, the person who has become accustomed to the new language, new foods, and new patterns of living becomes something of a hero or heroine. The ability to switch linguistic and behavioral codes provides the clever immigrant with the power to resolve inadvertent dilemmas and unavoidable conflicts. Enabling newcomers to learn these solutions and carry them out with good humor makes this role so impor-tant that the culture broker often figures as the central character in stories that recapitulate the embarrassments of the newly arrived long afterward.

The collection and contextual analysis of ethnic folklore has proceeded from three often overlapping strategies: first, showing how the devices of tradi-tion are used to maintain a sense of connection with Old World life and estab-lish a new sense of community in the alien New World setting; second, looking closely at the content of the lore, especially responses to displacement and its attendant social problems, such as being marginalized, stereotyped, or ghetto-ized; and third, collecting and analyzing the lore that emerges from the new environment, with special focus on the stages of acculturation and the manner in which lore is used first as a device for surviving and then as a way of achiev-ing a new sense of ethnic identification within a self-consciously pluralistic population.

From Remembered Cultures to Emergent Traditions

Studies of ethnic lore have typically followed the value preferences of the host culture. Early collections of folklore were carried out in an antiquarian spirit, as a means of collecting lore before it died out. From this perspective, texts are analyzed as a gauge of the extent of ethnic persistence and as a test of the cul-ture-wave theory, which argues that internationally distributed items are often to be found at the peripheries of a culture area long after they have been lost at the center. Folklorists have often been concerned with such lore collected within culturally conservative communities, including ethnic enclaves that self-consciously preserve their distinctiveness by maintaining a separate town or neighborhood or by clinging to an ethnically particularistic religious or social organization. In such studies, the baseline against which the material is placed and judged is the Old World repertoire. Indeed, the mainstream of American folklore studies searched for relics of British traditions—ballads, songs, and folktales—in every area in the United States and found especially rich resources in Appalachia, New England, and the Ozarks. A hierarchy of forms was established in the late nineteenth and early twentieth centuries, but actual collection of such items in North America was not carried out extensively until the 1920s and 1930s. The reference works that resulted from this collecting effort focus on the oldest and most widespread texts of ballads and folktales, noting where and in what range of versions and variants the item has been found.

A number of Old World verbal traditions have been widely and deeply collected by employing this essentially antiquarian approach in ethnically distinct communities. Especially notable in this regard are studies of Pennsylvania German (*Deutsch*, but often dubbed "Dutch"), Louisiana French (Cajun), and Mexican American lore. These traditions are commonly presented as evidence of cultural continuity in these linguistically conservative areas, especially those that remain in rural isolation.

Studies of immigrant and ethnic folklore are still being carried out using the body of Old World traditions as a point of departure. The point of these studies, however, is no longer antiquarian; rather, they attempt to epitomize, in the content of the lore, the complementary processes of tradition maintenance and change. Community studies elucidate the social and cultural dynamics of transmission and transformation and draw upon folklore as a gauge of acculturation and community stability. This approach underscores the selective maintenance of traditional forms and practices as immigrant groups adapt to their new environment, a phenomenon that social historians call "putting old wine in new bottles." The pressures to conform are counteracted by keeping up some of the old practices in family, church, and community, but the new (and, often, newly ethnicized) forms they take vary from one group and setting to another. Important internal variables that shape this process include the relative size of the immigrant group, the type of friendship and kinship networks that are maintained, and the degree of development of the ethnic enclave newcomers enter. Both open-country farming communities and dense city neighborhoods are susceptible to a high degree of language and culture retention. Tradition-maintenance is also promoted when newcomers are concentrated in an occupational community—mining, lumbering, or the cattle trade, for example.

Robert Georges's studies of the Greek community in Tarpon Springs, Florida, where the traditional employment is sponge diving, may be usefully compared to Gregory Gizelis's analysis of the Greek community in Philadelphia, where immigrants were involved primarily in service work (Georges 1962, 1964; Gizelis 1972). Both folklorists examine the narrative lore of a Greek-speaking population. Georges shows the ways in which both traditional stories and personal experience narratives maintain the system of belief and practice revolving around the sea and the sponge-fishing trade, as well as revealing a range of responses to the pressures generated by being surrounded by non-Greek-speaking Americans. These Greek Americans came in family groups from one small area of Greece and depend upon a traditional occupation they brought with them and pursued in America. Gizelis, on the other hand, collected folklore from individuals who came from diverse backgrounds in the Old Country and share only the experience of dealing with dislocation in their new city. Gizelis interviewed Greek Americans about how home traditions combine with ethnic awareness in an environment where newcomers are both establishing a sense of community and pursuing individual identities. In contrast to the Greeks of Tarpon Springs, Philadelphia's Greeks had changed their occupations and lifestyles almost completely in making a place for themselves in the urban environment. The verbal art displayed by Greek Americans there includes stories about Greeks who have been successful in America, emphasizing those aspects of Greek character which made it possible for them to succeed. Gizelis also analyzes stories that present the stereotypes Americans have of Greeks and provide folk rationalizations for why these misunderstandings arose. Many stories, both personal and jocular, recount the cultural and linguistic misunderstandings that the immigrants encountered. Gizelis underscores the variety of ways in which these narratives are used: normalizing common anxiety-provoking situations; making jokes about newcomers, sometimes to share their anxiety; and offering reminiscences to emphasize how hard times had been. In this emergent New World lore about an Old World group, Greek tradition has become subordinate to Greek-American experiences and perspectives.

A fascinating study carried out by Elizabeth Matthias and Richard Raspa addresses a corpus of Italian folktales recorded from one immigrant informant during the 1930s. Matthias and Raspa collected stories from the age-mates of the original storyteller in the town in which these stories were first told, exploring their performance in the stables, the warmest part of the house on winter evenings. In both cases, however, the stories emerged from the memories of the performers, not from actual situated performances. The researchers then discovered that the woman whose stories had originally been recorded in the 1930s was still living, although she had moved to the American Southwest. They visited her and asked for new renderings of the old tales, but this effort proved futile; she had not performed them for many decades and simply could not recall them. On the other hand, they discovered an active tradition of stories about the immigrant experience, personal experience narratives told among immigrants from all over Europe (Matthias and Raspa 1985).

The selective maintenance, rejection, and modification of traditional practices among those who undergo similar dislocating moves are governed by situational conditions. For culinary traditions, availability of foods and fuels might be crucial; for healthcare practices, the role of healer and protector might be challenged by the dominant culture's medically trained personnel, and traditional remedies such as herbs might not be available. Sometimes parameters of age and sex are central. For instance, in her study of memorial occasions, especially storytelling events, in Roseto, Italy, and Roseto, Pennsylvania, Carla Bianco found that traditional tales had maintained their usefulness in the new setting, serving as important forms of entertainment among both the first generation of immigrants and their grandchildren (Bianco 1974).

Documenting the persistence or adaptation of Old World traditions in *mestizo* or *creole* cultures poses very different problems than studying the development of ethnic lore among immigrants (Dégh 1968–1969; Klymasz 1973; Danielson 1977; Stern 1977). Strange academic biases have entered into the study of the culturally distinct communities that emerged in the wake of the plantation, hacienda, barrio, and ghetto. Studies of both African American and Mexican American folklore emerged in reaction to many of the same conditions of social segregation and subordination as did sociological and historical accounts of these racial-ethnic groups. Although folklore studies underscore the creative process that occurs in response to these conditions, it is nonetheless the conditions of exploitation that command our attention.

In the attempt to relate social conditions to the cultural bases of creativity, collectors and analysts commonly accepted the argument that folklore emerges in response to conditions of oppression. In North America, African and Native American repertories and styles were supposedly eliminated by the process of colonial domination. Where specific items or practices were reported across cultural lines, folklorists presumed that Africans, African Americans, and Indians learned them by imitation from their European or European American masters. This bias arose in part because scholars collected and organized European traditions much more fully than they did African or Native American lore, but it also evinces the assumptions that shaped the emerging social sciences. Folklore, along with sociology and anthropology, was pervaded by an assimilationist bias. Applying the theory that all culture rests on the institutions of community life (family structure, the economy, the political system, and religion) to subordinated groups, scholars reasoned that, since the maintenance of African and Native American institutions was discouraged by the dominant Europeans and European Americans, all the other features of African and Native American cultures would be fatally undermined as well. They then concluded that these essential elements of culture would be replaced through imitating the dominant society, or through a shared reaction against domination. This view, which shaped many studies of Afro-American culture, is most closely identified with the Chicago School of sociology, including Robert E. Park and E. Franklin Frazier (Park 1950; Frazier 1939).

The deculturation hypothesis prevailed in approaches to black folklore until the revolutionary work of Melville Herskovits (Herskovits 1941). One of the best-informed collectors of folktales, Richard Dorson, maintains this Euro-peanist point of view, arguing that the great bulk of Afro-American narrative lore in the United States, when it exhibits Old World antecedents at all, dem-onstrates a derivation from European rather than African sources (Dorson 1972a). In rebuttal, a number of scholars have noted that this theory defies both common sense and the empirical evidence (Dundes 1976; Crowley 1977). Studies of the distribution of specific stories, especially of the Uncle Remus variety so widely collected in the United States, demonstrate a strong mainte-nance of African narrative lore (Baer 1980). Morphological analyses of a variety of expressive forms—tales, dance, song, practices of worship—indicate that, even when specific items are derivable from non-African sources, the deeper patterns of both construction and performance are demonstrably African or pan-Afro-American. Herskovits's model of acculturation distinguishes three modes of continuity and adaptation: straight *retention*; *reinterpretation*, in which forms are maintained in new environments with new uses and mean-ings; and *syncretism*, in which similar elements of two or more cultures merge (Herskovits 1941, ch. 5).

Herskovits describes a variety of ways in which cultural forms and prac-tices change. Those who study expressive culture in Afro-American communi-ties sometimes begin the analysis on the level of traits and practices, making attributions to specific points of origin in Africa, Europe, or the New World. But most scholars continue on to explore the deeper level of aesthetic and cos-mological organization, or examine the microbehavioral level (styles of walk-ing, running, and dancing, ways of greeting and making eye contact). The most fruitful discussion of African retentions has been carried out not in rela-tion to texts or traits but in the concrete practices in which these deeper pat-terns may be observed most clearly—as in, say, hand-clapping and drumming, dance, sermons, and call-and-response liturgies (Abrahams 1992d, 2001).

The cultural dynamic by which such deeper structures of organization and attitude operate is profoundly complicated in cases like Afro-American lore, given the very real possibility of new cultural elements being introduced from contemporary Africa or from Afro-American communities outside the United States. For instance, Afro-American dance in the U.S. has produced a great number of indigenous styles, from "Jump Jim Crow," the "Buzzard Lope," and the "Turkey Trot" to the "Charleston," "jitterbug," and "boogie." But equally important have been the Afro-Latin dance crazes: Mambo, Limbo, Samba, Congo, Bossa Nova.

During the 1960s, when such practices became entwined with the soul movement, display forms took on special meaning. Dashiki shirts and love beads came into the black American repertory through the Cuban Yoruba community newly moved to New York and Miami from Havana and Oriente province in eastern Cuba. The Cubans from this community had never lost contact with their Nigerian cousins; they often sent their religious leaders to Africa for training. When they moved from Cuba to the U.S. they found fertile ground to grow in, and many of their practices came into wider fashion. In addition to the dashiki and beads, the multi-unit handshake and plaited hair decoration were reemphasized. The corn-row (or cane-row) had been one of many traditional styles in the U.S. South as well as the West Indies. Rejected as a reminder of slavery times in favor of hair-straightening techniques (which also are found in many parts of traditional Africa), plaiting reemerged in this era of self-conscious cultural revitalization. Perhaps even more important is the fact that throughout this history hair styling remained important, especially having a family member or friend do the hair in public. This point is dramatized by the widespread African saying, which is also found in the West Indies: "Nothing is sadder to think about than a person with no one to take care of his hair."

Indigenous and Boundary-Making Statements of Verbal Art

Concern with the maintenance of relics of the past became less central to the study of the folklore of American ethnic groups in the post-World War II era. The indigenous forms became increasingly important. Many studies concentrate on folklore that expresses strong attitudes toward and images of self and other. Here we can reasonably make a distinction between the *lore* that dramatizes one's stereotypes of one's own group and of contiguous cultural groups and the *forms* and *styles* of traditional practice that are unique to the group. In both cases the lore is of an esoteric sort. The lore of self-typing and stereotyping projects and reinforces intragroup and intergroup conflicts. The in-group character of such stereotypical material derives from highly biased content features that reveal the attitudes held by one group about another. The expressive forms and styles that develop are so idiomatic to the group, so full of slang, jargon, or other special vocabulary, that they are virtually unintelligible to nonmembers. Perhaps more to the point, such esoteric lore is subject to constant intercultural misunderstanding, increasing the sense of in-groupness as well as intensifying the sense of exclusion felt by nonmembers.

The ways in which ethnic lore explores the subject of social and cultural differences have been especially useful as an index to the intensity of social stratification and the dynamic of intergroup relations. This lore about self and others has been analyzed in terms suggested by William Hugh Jansen and expanded upon by Richard Bauman and numerous others (Jansen 1959; Dundes 1962; Barth 1969; Bauman 1971). The esoteric-exoteric (s-x) complex concerns the techniques of boundary-marking and the dynamic arising between the bounded groups as it is revealed within the corpus of an oral literature.

These boundaries arise not only from the integrity and sense of shared experience, language, and values within the group but also from that group's image of the degree to which it is regarded as distinctive by nonmembers and how these differences are, in fact, regarded. Thus, the s-x factor would include not only the stereotypical depictions of self and other but also the ways in which the lore functions as a cultural means of fighting against the negative effects of stereotyping.

Recent studies of African American and Mexican American lore underscore this dynamic of stereotyping. For example, Américo Paredes explored the relationship between "gringos" and "greasers" in the joke-lore of Mexican Americans, emphasizing the real antagonism between Chicanos and Anglos recorded in events that dramatize social inequities. In-group jokes draw on the Anglo stereotype of Chicanos to establish counter-boundaries, directing both laughter and derision at those who would otherwise be regarded as socially superordinate. Stereotypical traits are inverted: laziness and virility become devices of manipulation in cross-cultural encounters (Paredes 1961, 1993). This same process of' inverting stereotypes has been found in urban Afro-American lore (Abrahams 1970; Bauman and Abrahams 1981).

The expressive forms that arise within these ethnic enclaves, especially in Hispanic and Afro-American cultures, have received more critical commentary than virtually any other area of folklore and expressive culture in general. Studies of the blues—classic, country, and city—characteristically focus on the role of the bluesman as a social representative, or even culture hero, of African Americans during the post-Reconstruction period. This view reflects the social concerns and political commitments of the predominantly white commentators and their fascination with emergent creative forms. Innovative forms of verbal art also attracted a great deal of attention: the sermon, the spiritual, jiving, playing the dozens or mother rapping, and the toast. Commentators relate these forms, the nature of these performances, and their subject matter to the sociocultural conditions of contemporary African American life.

As the focus of folklore studies shifted from text to performance, examining traditional practices in new environments became a way of probing the core cultural dynamics of the community. Esoteric lore permits insights into the features of shared identity as perceived in different ways and at varying intensities by individuals within the community. This extension of the s-x argument underscores the centrality of folklore as enacted to the typing of self and others.

In essence, this shift in approach transforms the way we perceive ethnic enclaves. It calls us to reject the prevailing assumption that so-called minority subcultures remain separate only so long as power is unequally distributed and that the elimination of inequality would jeopardize the cultural distinctiveness, or even the very existence of these groups. According to that view, assimilation and acculturation are inevitable so long as equal access to power and resources is assured. Conceiving of development in such a linear and unidirectional way fails to recognize that cultural as well as economic exchange relationships arise as cultural forms come together, even when the exchanges are not entirely reciprocal. The recording of performances within black communities and their reproduction in print, on records and tapes, and in movies made it possible for European American imitators to draw on those cultural forms without ever attending a live performance, much less visiting their remote places of origin in the trans-Atlantic African world. Such forms as blues, tap-dancing, and skiffle-music have become popular rather than folk forms, for their audience extends far beyond the ethnic community, yet their folk roots are widely acknowledged.

These dynamic, community-based analyses of folklore demonstrate precisely the ways in which certain enclaves resist assimilation because of differences in ethos, world view, and secular and religious practice. A self-consciously different religious community may maintain its deep sense of separateness not only through traditional religious practices but also in language, and it may recreate a sociocultural sense of community by performing the old stories and songs in the traditional fashion. Although most ethnographic studies are not primarily concerned with the processes of oral transmission and dissemination, the lore reported there often undercuts the assumption that assimilation is inevitable. The uses of the lore and the folkloric items themselves must be regarded not as relics of past practices but as examples of a lively emergent tradition. Such a process of cultural revitalization has been widely observed in immigrant communities and among American Indians and mestizos.

Folklore and the Concept of Creole Culture

Folklorists ask the same questions about ethnic enclaves as about regional cultures: to what extent are their ways unique, and how much do they share with other communities within the American polity? This question becomes increasingly problematic as the most marked features of regional and ethnic cultures become part of popular iconography and, by extension, part of mass culture, the most widely shared expressive and symbolic vocabulary of the United States. Just such a process occurs as regional and ethnic cuisines are developed into national franchise operations. Going public in such a way often involves drawing upon the very stereotypes that have operated as exclusionary techniques in other times and other intercultural situations. The way in which the masters of popular culture manipulate images of sleepy, sombrero-wearing Mexicans to sell tacos and burritos, of white-suited Southern colonels to market fried chicken, and of pearly-toothed Uncle Bens to brand rice is fascinating, if a little fearsome, to behold.

Considering culture from this perspective highlights the interaction between cultures, especially the coming-together of expressive elements from a range of traditions. Studying this synthesizing process would underscore the privileged status of those forms shared by the larger society, and would therefore involve a study of lore and language as it gravitates toward national norms and forms.

From a sociolinguistic point of view, individuals who belong to ethnic groups in multiethnic settings draw upon a variety of speech codes, ranging from the most archaic or ceremonial to the most recent slang or jargon. Speakers within ethnic enclaves might be studied in terms of the range of codes in which they have developed receptive (understanding) and/or productive (speaking) competence. In the language-contact situation arising from mass movements of peoples, one language or code within that language is commonly accorded high prestige, often because it is employed in radio broadcasts. Other codes are given lower status, especially when they represent the languages of old and illiterate, backward, or defeated and enslaved people. Individuals are judged by their ability to control the high-prestige form or, alternatively, to switch at will between different codes (Ferguson 1959). Some seek to gain a place of importance in the community by enacting the widest variety of speaking styles; others will make their mark by their total mastery of one form, whether high (such as oratorical English) or low (such as slang or jargon).

This range of interactive and expressive codes has been seldom addressed even by sociolinguists and ethnographers of communication. Clearly all speech communities share a range of ways of speaking which are commonly attached to the situations in which they commonly arise. Individuals within such communities attain popular notice because of their ability to switch between registers, adapting quickly to the dictates of the situation and the audience. For example, Fiorello LaGuardia, mayor of New York City from 1933 to 1945, was widely hailed for his ability to read his audience effectively and to switch to the register most appropriate for the crowd. In addition, he spoke both Italian and Yiddish and could spice his speeches by drawing on expressions in either language.

Politicians and other public speakers prosper when they adapt their codes of communication to the variety of situations they encounter and audiences they address. Since the development of academic programs in ethnic studies, the practice of switching back and forth between academese and street talk or other argots has produced star performers on the lecture circuit who are virtuosos at shifting registers. A very wide range of codes, from exalted preacher-talk to the rap routines that pervade popular culture, may be maintained within the same community as a means of dramatizing the (usually) playful opposition between the value systems expressed in these varieties of speech.

The person who can control all of these codes in their appropriate places, or can even pull off the act of mixing them, is given very high status indeed.

Recognizing that a number of historically distinct forms are maintained for expressive purposes within a single community runs counter to the usual ways in which the language and lore of ethnic communities have been studied. Immigrant groups have been observed and judged with regard to how quickly and effectively they acculturate from the Old World language to American English. But when the racial-ethnic group and its alternative languages have been in this country for some time, as with African Americans, Mexican Americans, and American Indians, the immigrant model of change does not pertain. Sociolinguistically oriented ethnographers have sought to document the alternative system of expressive culture of those groups who chose not to go through the normative pattern of linguistic and cultural assimilation (Hymes 1974). For African American communities especially, the group's maintenance of multiple codes dramatizes both its resistance to mainstream expressive culture and its creative responses to varying conditions.

When expressive resources are reported and analyzed by members of the speaking community themselves, extraordinarily subtle observations often result. For example, the work of Zora Neale Hurston has excited so much interest because she drew upon her own wide range of speaking abilities and self-styled biculturalism in her literary and critical writings (Hurston 1963, 1984). Similarly, Américo Paredes reports the expressive system of Mexicans on both sides of the Rio Grande from his dual position, as a member of the speech community he recorded and as trained ethnographer and literary stylist (Paredes 1959, 1993). Both have served as important exemplars of how ethnic communities might be studied, bringing previously stigmatized ways of speaking to the attention and the respect of the outside world.

Barbara Kirshenblatt-Gimblett also drew upon the insider's perspective in her early work dealing with the Eastern European Jewish community of Toronto, in which she was born and raised. She demonstrates that in the midst of pressures toward acculturation, a complex of verbal traditions arose which draw upon a receptive understanding of both Yiddish and English. In this labile language situation, a hybrid code she dubs "Yinglish" emerged. Not only were Old World verbal forms kept alive while new ones were emerging from the immigration experience, but a large body of lore arose which turns on the active and usually witty commingling of these languages and cultural forms. Much like the interethnic stories reported by Paredes, stories are told in English with contrasting Yiddish punch-lines and vice versa. Kirshenblatt-Gimblett underscores the fluidity of the cultural milieu as the language of the host culture is incorporated into an already developed system of joking (Kirshenblatt-Gimblett 1972).

This emergent lore is, in the main, metacommunicative—that is, it comments on the nature of communications in a new social environment. Becoming multicultural is not a matter of shedding one culture and donning another, but rather of fashioning a new cultural and linguistic repertoire adapted from the common experiences of immigrants. Through cultural contact, verbal lore becomes increasingly self-conscious as it draws upon an ever-widening range of expressive resources. Narrative lore especially comes to be employed as a means of asserting, testing, and rehearsing newly learned competencies. In this situation, the multilingual narrator becomes the model for successful accultur-ation. Capitalizing on otherwise dying language resources, the narrator main-tains the usefulness of the old vocabulary and sayings, even finding humor in situations of language change.

When ethnic difference is put on display for both insiders and outsiders in such events as festivals, the entire activity is interpreted as a friendly gesture by everyone involved. These celebrations of difference amplify only the non-threatening dimensions of interaction, subordinating experiences of misun-derstanding in the service of establishing an environment that foregrounds the goodwill principle. Those attending learn explicit lessons about accommodat-ing difference. When outsiders are invited to witness how life is lived and tra-ditions are carried on within the ethnic group, the group is on its best behavior. Those from the outside attend voluntarily, congratulating them-selves as they advance intercultural understanding and responding to each act with uniformly polite enthusiasm. The self-conscious dimension of these cele-brations of ethnic difference inevitably compromises the spontaneity scripted into the event. The most interesting things happen off stage as performers and craftspeople representing distinct traditions interact; the vitality to be found in diversity is noticeably absent within the display. In fact, a culture of display commonly overwhelms the stylistic differences represented by the performers of ethnicity. A kind of homogeneity settles in, which is made more palpable by the limitations of the venue, especially if it involves a stage. Presenters, often folklorists who have researched the traditional styles and performers being exhibited, find themselves adopting an appropriately stagy and rehearsed style of introduction.

Family and community festivities are translated into ethnic representa-tions performed for audiences who are hungry for the kind of variety charac-teristic of spectacles. Traditional representational forms such as dance, clowning, acrobatics, song, ceremony, decorative arts, crafts, and cooking are most easily understood across language differences. Consequently, it is in these realms that traditional ethnic expression most readily goes public. What used to be *immigrant folklore* and then became *ethnic folklore* has now become the *folklore of ethnicity*. Community-wide events feature multiethnic performances as a means of drawing in participants who do not necessarily belong to the ethnic groups involved. Events and enactments which formerly were employed as a means of asserting and maintaining ethnic boundaries become the very instruments by which the boundary is opened up, at least for the moment of celebration. Even the more private forms of expressive culture may become available for public exposure.

Living history museums and folk museums increasingly attempt not only to re-create everyday activities such as preindustrial work and food preparation but also to present performances of the games, riddles, stories, and songs associated with the hearth. These public demonstrations make distinctive ethnic behaviors available to anyone who chooses to learn them. Thus, ethnic styles as well as items of performance become detached from the folk communities that gave rise to them and are employed for entirely different popular effects. In fact, this dynamic of appropriation has characterized American entertainment since the development of the blackface minstrel show, which drew on African American traditions but turned them into caricature for white audiences. Removed from their sources within culturally homogeneous communities whose members meet face to face to entertain and instruct each other, these ways of performing are deployed in venues that assemble crowds only for the occasion of entertainment. Amplification and recording technologies vastly increase the audience, and individuals perform in front of people they could never know personally.

Folk traditions provide the materials for a celebration of stylistic diversity that often has been distorted and lost its vital connection with the members of the ethnic community it is purported to represent. What was once learned through everyday observation and repeated experience now has to be taught in a more formal fashion. The performance of ethnicity no longer serves as a statement of cultural continuity and rootedness, but rather as a set of stylistic options taken on by those seeking the experience of learning new styles and techniques. At this point, everyone can learn how to play a banjo or a koto, just as they can take lessons in how to cook grits or sukiyaki—or, at least, how to eat them properly.

This process of making the private public involves dramatizing what heretofore has not been dramatic and performing acts that are not inherently performative. Figuring out how to present craft skills and work techniques at folk festivals has always been difficult. Audiences are as interested in the process of craft-making as they are in music and dance, and craft demonstrations are transformed into performances. Since artisans often prefer working to talking with onlookers, presenters are needed to explain the process while it is being carried out. Such mediating figures often employ traditional narratives, such as jokes, hero tales, and personal anecdotes, as an important feature of the framing performance. Although the texts of the items of verbal art may be the same as those found within the folk community, their context and thus their meaning is substantially changed. With the tremendous growth of ethnically based folk festivals, the figure of the presenter takes its place beside the costumed tour guide and the folksinger as a popular role in the business of purveying ethnic folk culture. There is little distinction between such staged events and the "native and authentic" displays of ethnic difference that are routinized as tourist entertainments.

Ironically, although such public presentations keep alive the ideal of ethnic differences and the preservation of the old ways, they do so in a cultural setting as removed as one can imagine from the small, face-to-face group in which they originated and persisted. The very event which most opens up family and community to outside observation and participation has elevated the tradition-bearer to eminence, bringing together several generations of family members to perform or demonstrate traditions that seem to have been dying when carried on only within the home. Unlike the American-born children of immigrants, younger people in later generations more readily enact ethnicity in public than in private. In fact, the folk festival movement has consciously sought to bring public approval to these old-fashioned ways so that the younger members of the community will find more than family reinforcement for learning traditional performance practices. On the other hand, in seeking out traditional performers, festival planners often find themselves honoring individuals who have been regarded as eccentric or deviant within their local community or ethnic group.

There is another irony here, in the differences between ethnicities that are kept as a form of family nostalgia and those carried on in private because the ethnic group has been forced by sociopolitical circumstances to be isolated and kept on the move. In diasporic situations in which the travelers are considered outcasts, as with the Rom (Gypsies) or Jews, maintaining a distinctive culture has to be done secretly. The irony is further compounded as the host group often draws upon the guests as entertainers, asking their performers to draw on what is perceived as an ethnically distinct style in the host's festive gatherings. In such situations, two kinds of culturally different behaviors are found: those developed for entertainment of the hosts, and those which are used within the encampment of the people on the move. While this pattern is not characteristic of either the Rom or Jews in America, we see similar instances of dislocated peoples being called upon to entertain those in power: Native Americans playing Indian in the Wild West Show or carnival side shows; and African Americans singing the blues or tap-dancing for white audiences.

The public occasions at which demonstrations and performances are carried out run contrary to ethnic persistence, for they are aimed at a popular audience. This tendency undermines the actual social base of ethnic distinctiveness and relegates ethnic identification to that strange place in the possible repertory of roles in which to be "an ethnic" is to be a purveyor of stylistic alternatives—interesting, no doubt, but without the sense of alternative values held in opposition to the dominant culture.

Chapter 12
Identities

The term *identity* has become the encompassing term for cultural, social, and spiritual wholeness. It also emerges in ethnonational turf battles premised on the historical significance of territorial integrity. Such fictions invite questions, but not so much about their truth value as of their usefulness. *Identity* draws on a conception of individual and social life that has infused modern life in the West, especially in the United States. I have attempted to employ the term in my writings on African American culture, but have come away dissatisfied because *identity* gravitates away from the concrete ways in which self-identification works and both respect- and reputation-seekers set out to achieve a sense of social place. We need more ethnographic accounts of people's self-conceptions and image projections.

The term identity presumes the uniqueness of each named whole (Köstlin 1997), even as it draws on typical, or stereotypical, conceptions of those we call strangers, enemies, outsiders—all those others dwelling on the fringes of what we regard as civilization. So it must surely be useful to anatomize the body of this particular beast. The wholeness posited by identity is a longed-for state of being, which emerges within a romantic rhetoric and the invocation of nostalgia. Like authenticity, it rests on ideas of the real and the enduring that do not bear up under much weight in understanding either everyday practices or extraordinary experiences (Bendix 1997; Gilroy 1996). It does provide a blanket term for anxieties recorded on both the personal and the sociopolitical levels; the same word is used to get at incommensurable states of being.

Identity seems to build upon notions of an ideal life-plan or an archetypal map of the actual world. Few discussions of identity manifest the sense of play, or recognize the multiplicity of personae that any individual can adopt in different settings. The discourse on identities carries this burden because it emerges from perceptions of social and cultural difference which contend that bounded wholeness can be maintained in a culturally plural environment.

Claims for the uniqueness of these markers of difference overwhelm the commonsense notion (borne out by research in genetics) that human beings throughout the world are more alike than otherwise. Observations of difference have been the lifeblood of popular and professional social orderings long before our present age. However, the intensity and degree of cross-cultural contact recently triggered by the massive politically and economically inspired dislocation of populations have heightened public awareness of diversity.

Differences become visible as cultures come into contact in border zones within cosmopolitan and nation-state settings. Distinctions are made, for social and political purposes, on the grounds not only of geography and language but also of felt differences in lifeways, sometimes by the group so identified but more often by those in power, between their group and the others who are within their ambit or at its borders. It is almost impossible to discuss identity without invoking deep stereotypes of those designated as strangers or enemies. Issues of power, segregation, and even subjugation are often at stake in such discussions.

Observations of social and cultural identity and difference come to a head in urban marketplaces which act as magnets for diverse and highly mobilized peoples. But just how important these markers are in marketplace exchanges deserves some scrutiny. Observations of cultural difference do take place, especially as expressed in divergent styles of interaction. But social leveling occurs at the moment of exchange as well. Within the marketplace world, even when bargains are made face to face, the salience of identity tends to be subordinated to the power of the goods and services being exchanged. The burden of meaning lies not in the interaction but in the objects obtained or services provided, which may themselves be exotic to the consumer. For example, the haircut as an identity marker takes precedence over the conversation with the stranger who cuts one's hair—although only in arenas where such rituals of bodily adornment are not central to the in-group culture. In the market, too, assuming roles, even disguises, is taken for granted. The rehearsal of cultures that appears to be built into sites of commercial exchange has produced a popular literature on the different types of figures found at the crossroads, documents which both celebrate diversity and attempt to give it order.

In the form of national and occupational stereotypes and conventional stage-figures, maps of the marketplace have been projected since the early modern period. In Europe, these acts of mapping were prominent among initial responses to the dispersal of peoples driven by economic necessity or drawn by desire. Such trading diasporas (Cohen 1971; Curtin 1984) present an array of life-choices based on the observed stylistic differences dramatized at points of exchange between different peoples. This willing movement must be contrasted, of course, with the many displacements of whole populations occurring with displays of military force or the transformation of persons into articles of commerce.

Ethnographers examining expressive culture attempt to understand more subtly these concerns about achieving and maintaining identities within the polities in which diasporic peoples find themselves. Questions relating to the maintenance or disappearance of cultural forms, or the invention of new forms of expression, are highlighted in situations of the host/guest sort and with the creation of isolated sites in which peoples are concentrated and fenced in, ghettoized, or imprisoned. The dispersals that arise in response to market forces are also being reexamined by cultural critics, though often in league with terms such as postcolonial which draw on the rhetoric of victimhood. *Cosmopolitanism* is now replaced in the main by the less socially marked terms *creolization* and *hybridity* (Hannerz, 1987, 1992; Canclini 1995; Kapchan and Strong 1999; Baron and Cara 2003). The question that arises from this altered perspective is whether one can conceive of a creole, a hybrid, even a diasporic *identity*.

Multiple Meanings

Identity has been drawn into discussions of other loosely employed keywords: folklore, ethnicity, tradition, authenticity, heritage, even culture and context. All have been designated as inventions in the sense used by cultural critics— that is, socially constructed concepts, with the hint that they are used to mystify rather than clarify in public debates. All of these terms have undergone extensive tugs and pulls as the tourist and the spectacle-seeker have come to dominate our modern condition and the inventions of popular culture have caused us to rethink the very nature of vernacular creativity.

Identity-seeking is not new. Rather, it involves renaming and recasting older notions: of *genius* as it was employed in the Renaissance; and of *race*, *blood*, national and personal *character* as conceived during the eighteenth and nineteenth centuries. In contrast, Locke and Hume used the term identity primarily as a way of designating the basic features of an individual or a people otherwise constantly being altered (Dundes 1983: 236–37), as what persists through the process of change. Identity carries the burdens of these earlier terms and usages even as it has displaced them in contemporary debates. The ghosts that lie hidden in the ideological arguments about identities, nationalities, ethnicities, and other related terms require examination. Identity, in its various formulations, has entered discussions of the public sphere at the postmodern moment in which increasing urbanization and its byproduct, cosmopolitanism, have undermined the foundations on which particular social, occupational, and political identities have been constructed in the past. Cosmopolitanism is an epiphenomenon of globalization. The changing nature and speed of information storage and transfer, accompanied by alterations in cross-cultural market exchanges, have brought stylistic differences in music, dance, and other display forms to the notice of the commercial world.

In the main, this expansion of consumer values has been regarded as a threat to traditional cultures. Many politically engaged social scientists embrace the approach of the antimodernists under the rubric of cultural conservation (Lears 1981; Hufford 1994). For folklorists and other analysts of expressive culture, the transformative effects of these global processes on particular peoples underscore the fragility of inherited traditions.

For many psychiatrists and sociologists, as well as folklorists, one's identity emerges from the stories one tells on oneself or one's community (however that term is defined). The sum of these stories constitutes the life-history of the individual or the group. Each incident, each report of past experience, is transformed into an emblem of the uniqueness of the individual (insofar as it replays a unique experience) and a badge of group membership.

The primary present formulation of identity emerged when the Freudian narrative of the guilt-inducing family romance was being displaced by the psychosocial development narrative put forward by Erik H. Erikson. A psychoanalyst turned social psychologist and psychobiographer, Erikson described a pattern of eight age-related stages in which individual identities were constantly reformulated in the face of a particular characterological problem, which he called an identity crisis (Erikson 1950). Erikson worked out his ideas through conversations not only with other analysts (he studied with and was analyzed by Anna Freud) but also with cultural anthropologists, including Margaret Mead and Gregory Bateson (Friedman 1999). Following Erikson, the discussion of life-stages defined the transitional periods in crisis terms, a rhetoric deeply in tune with the social and political ambience of the 1960s (Abrahams 1992a, 1993a). At each stage he underscored the possibilities of personal renewal in the face of crisis. After Erikson's progressive scheme became widely accepted, the term identity came to center on life transitions. By 1972, Erikson's fellow psychiatrist and public intellectual Robert Coles was saying that both "identity" and "identity crisis" had become "the purest of clichés" (quoted in Gleason 1983, 913).

The way in which *identity* has been incorporated into the discourse on nationalities has produced much discomfort. Given the cataclysmic developments of the twentieth century and the use of racial and ethnic identities as rationales for massive displacements and bellicose engagements, ethnicity and the process of "purification" and "cleansing" have once again raised the specter of genocide. On the more positive side, however, ethnic identities have been used in more benign political environments as the basis of official attempts to achieve political, social, and cultural equities in plural societies. Dundes surveys the forms of folklore in which these more benign arguments are located (Dundes 1983).

Because *identity* enters into a variety of specially coded environments, there is substantial diversity in the usage of the term in different discourses:

1. In bureaucratic life, it is used to refer to the unique features of individuals as they are subject to official identification.

2. In political science, it becomes involved in arguments about localism, nationalism, and chauvinism.

3. In social and political history, the terms class, caste, status or standing, and locale or nation are used synonymously with identity, as in "American identity."

4. In cultural history, it is used as a synonym for national formation, or it features in the discussion of patterns of domination and resistance as they are spelled out in particular practices, such as local and national festivals, carnival, shivaree, guerilla warfare, and social banditry.

5. In ethnic studies, it becomes synonymous with a group developing a greater sense of common history and a delimited set of cultural practices.

6. In the discourse on gender and the body, sexual orientation comes to the fore, often in parallel with ethnic identities as a way of focusing arguments concerned with historical conditions of invisibility—that is, political and social erasure or discrimination.

7. In discussions of cosmopolitanism and the consumer economy, it tends to be deployed in Romantic terms as a descriptor of personal development by individuals making radical choices: as artist, consumer, member of the counter-culture, and so on.

8. In cultural studies, that strange hybrid discipline, identity has been turned into a shibboleth term in contrast to *subject*. One perceptive commentator suggests that "identity could be seen as dragging cultural studies into the 1990s by acting as a kind of guide to how people see themselves, not as class subjects, not as psychoanalytic subjects, not as subjects of ideology, not as textual subjects but as agents whose sense of self is projected onto and expressed by an expansive range of cultural practices, including texts, images and commodities" (McRobbie 1992: 730).

9. In the religious realm, spiritual identity is the descendant of terms for belief and soul. This secularization and liberalization of the spiritual dimension of life is much discussed in both the popular literature on social change and that of individual development of spirit.

Surveillance

Folklorists often find ourselves conflating the most individual and private identity concerns with the public display of sentiments of belonging to a group, neighborhood, or nation. I have been especially concerned with the idea of individual and cultural wholeness within our disciplinary discussions. The study of folklore, once singularly focused on the inherited beliefs and traditional practices of a group whose members share a body of custom and manners and who seem to achieve a sense of community through the replaying of age-old practices, now focuses on the production and uses of the stories that a group or its members tell on themselves. Often, these stories are invoked by festive celebrations in which individual and group experiences are coordinated. Representative anecdotes evoked in friendly conversations as well as times of reminiscence emerge as badges of both individuality and group membership. The widespread introduction of *identity* into this discussion represents an unexamined attempt to maintain the importance of communities, even if the group under examination comes together only to tell these stories.

Given the commodification of cultural forms by the entertainment sector of the service economy, local and regional styles and hand-crafted products attract a great deal of attention and personal investment. These representations of past practices carry a heavy burden of nostalgia, including the ongoing dramatization of the experience of loss. Cultural study has been deeply affected by the bourgeois disease of nostalgia. We have all been engaged in creating and consuming objects and performances whose attractions arise from their ephemeral and insubstantial nature. In an attempt to reject the excesses of the commercial economy, we have been drawn into equally consuming passions, but for things and moments which celebrate a sense of pastness, representing life before the development of capitalism. This chapter reveals some of this trace-work which lies just beneath the surface meanings of identity and its predecessors. It rehearses the Renaissance and Enlightenment habits of mind that enter into discussions of social identification and shows how these processes have been maintained in the present usages of the term. It dwells on the changes which occurred in the 1960s throughout the West as they were manifested in broad alterations of vocabulary and sensibility. My objective is not only to parse this semantic shift but to consider it in relation to the more flexible and heterogeneous ways of approaching cultural representations which emerged at that time. In contrast to the implicit theory of (actually or potentially) integrated identities, I suggest the greater usefulness of recognizing the play among and between identities on cultural terrains subject to constant readjustment.

The multiple uses of *identity* developed from Renaissance and Enlightenment notions of how to give order to a world of increasing diversity. As travel and trade extended beyond the familiar, different ways of marking identity in the public realm emerged. Identity was used not only as a synonym for name or as a means of identification in the emerging bureaucracies of the nation-state but also as a pointer to the social, political, and spiritual place of individuals and types in the order of things. Thus humanity and representative individuals were located in relation to God. Perhaps more important for the present argument, that ordering involved depicting the many types of humans by nation, locale, and occupation. European popular publications illustrating this inventory of the world include the Book of Trade, the Dance of Death, the Ship of Fools, and the various modes of describing the World Turned Upside Down. This colportage literature, also referred to as anatomies or cosmographies, gives voice to wonder and social satire at the same time, ironically pointing to the vanity implicit in making such orders (Amman and Sachs 1568). Moreover, these orders are celebrated in their fragmentation in cultural manifestations such as *Wunderkammern* (cabinets of curiosity). The process of assembling these anatomies is brilliantly analyzed in Elizabethan terms as "the rehearsal of cultures" (Mullaney 1988; also Stagl 1995; Daston and Park 1998).

Encountering heterogeneous populations engendered problems of surveillance and governance, especially for expansionist regimes concerned with creating spaces of trade and communication that followed their rules of exchange, including the tricks of the trade of rogue mercantilists. Out of this experience emerged tales in which traders reported the naïveté of those with whom they came into contact. They did not tell stories about being taken advantage of, because they did not want their shortcomings to become evident to those at home who were monitoring their activities. There are some deep conceptual problems here that cultural historians have not yet faced. In early contacts between Europeans and Native Americans, trade was carried out in the oratorical fashion typical of native peacemaking. European traders acknowledged this fact, and most did not think that they had gotten the better of the Indians. They learned by painful experience that, if they wanted to trade, they had to adjust to their desired partners by adopting some native ways: techniques of time and space management, the system of expressive gestures, and symbols for prestige and standing. The terms and style of negotiations were evanescent, but each side saw the other as clever. Trade took place because both parties knew it was in their best economic interest to keep it going. Only in retrospect does the purchase of Manhattan Island seem like robbery on the part of the Dutch. In fact, it was not the natives who impugned the financial acumen of the Dutch; Dutch merchants and officials acquired a thieving reputation because they were Great Britain's primary trading rival. Nevertheless, the achievement of some form of hegemony in structuring trade relations became imperative as great investments from powerful individuals were negotiated at home. It became increasingly evident that colonization required a mode of surveillance, although attempts to establish them were seldom successful. Governments tried to impose control devices over both those with whom they were trading and the traders whom they had empowered to enter into exchange in the name of the colonizing nation. One of the most important ways that European powers promoted development was authorizing their agents to collect information about the colonized while carrying on colonial trade. Accumulating, storing, organizing, and transmitting knowledge became an important tool, at least from the perspective of those in power in the home country. They employed agents to collect as much information as possible about the cultural equipment and practices of the colonized folk. This information was sent back to the various scientific academies established in metropolitan centers of knowledge, creating national and imperial archives.

There is little evidence that the information so painfully gathered was ever consulted by the civic authorities and used for its intended purposes. Even modern forms of this enterprise, such as the archives of folksong and ex-slave narratives compiled in the U.S. during the 1930s, were not mentioned in official congressional records or policy reports. Regina Bendix uncovered a trove of cultural riches from a survey sponsored by the government of the Austro-Hungarian Empire in the 1890s which does not seem to have been consulted by that government and remained buried in forgotten publications (Bendix 1997). Many of these archives still exist in the forms in which they were first assembled.

This body of information constituted the colonizers' attempt to develop techniques for surveying these diverse populations, paying special regard to the ownership of real and personal property, religion, and healing practices. That these inventories of subject populations were neither accurate nor based on a coherent schema for cross-cultural observation and analysis is almost beside the point. Indeed, their very disorder and obvious biases make them a fascinating record of the dominant group's own cultural categories and its misperceptions of those groups it sought to subordinate. What is most important for ethnographers to recognize is that such reportage, which laid the historical foundation for the anthropological project, has always been a part of the imperial scheme.

At markets and in travels arising from the expansion of material exchange, cosmopolitans throughout Europe developed an eye and an ear for difference. In fact, judging by the literature of the streets, colportage—the visual rendering of the various orders, native and exotic—had become a fad by the late seventeenth century. Although the street literature has been mined for traditional texts and variations, the visual record has been relatively neglected. Colportage constitutes a profuse representation of vernacular life and performance, especially festive displays. Reflecting the variety of costumes found at cosmopolitan markets and celebrations, these comic-strip, map- or chart-like renderings convey the color and texture of street life in the centers of emporium culture.

Diverse nationalities and their distinctive styles were not simply commoditized; they were made into a resource for elites wanting to dress exotically. A craze for Native American garb and artistic embellishment has continued through the Western world for three centuries. Indians themselves have often been put on show: at court, in the circus, and at world's fairs. In theaters and other places of illusion, the various types became conventional stage roles identified through costumes and props. At Carnival and other festivities that feature dressing up, they became part and parcel of the roles available to the celebrants. In such environments, all roles become accessible to those would so array themselves. Other kinds of illusionist trickery flourished

in those environs. The street literature concerned with types spawned a plethora of reports of thieving techniques, crimes and criminals, and hoaxes.

The growth of the public sphere encouraged the development of street
literature in which social and stylistic differences were given a visual and
orderly—if also playful—accounting. When Jacques declaims on the Seven
Stages of Man, he is evoking the clichés of the Renaissance moment and putting them in conventional stage terms. Describing life in theatrical terms had
already become a common trope; over a lifetime, each person would play
many parts. The contradictory history of identity formation is suffused with
the possibilities of upward mobility inherent in self-fashioning. While high-
status dignitaries could parade themselves on state occasions dressed in their
official garb, the playful and the ambitious could cobble together equally elevated identities through personal initiative. Dressing up ceremonially provoked parody, inversion, and travesty. Under festive conditions, the exalted
might dress as a stranger or outcast, while the lowly might become price or
queen for a day.

Invisibility

Most discussions of identity are still strongly affected by the panoply of discrete public roles. Insofar as students of expressive culture have looked for
texts, objects, and figures that represent such larger wholes, identity has been
used more to refer to groups than to individuals. But, unlike other such keywords as tradition or authenticity, the semantic domain of identity is tied not
to styles but to apparent matters of substance, states of being, or existence in
its display.

Valorizing openness, freedom, liberty, and other such terms for exercising
options, the emporium economy places choice-making above all else. Making
choices relies on observations of difference and attributions of value within
the setting of public exchange. Folklorists and other students of expressive culture have staked out our professional claim by observing and cataloguing stylistic differences in material and expressive realms. To this extent, we operate
within the expanding enterprise zone of free trade.

This perspective naturalizes identity formation, presuming it is a common element of all cultures. But this perspective must be resisted. Ethnographers of all persuasions have assumed the mantle of the invisible participant
observer, a role inherited in great part from the *flaneur* of early modernism,
the cosmopolitan stroller in the city who follows Baudelaire in celebrating "the
ephemeral, the fugitive, the contingent." The wandering viewer paints himself
at the edge of the picture, recording the varieties of life as it comes together in
especially energetic places. The figures at the edge of the picture represent not

only the artist who observed the scene but also the viewers—us—who observe the painting. Invisibility thus involves a double and duplicitous suppression of self-consciousness in the act of representation. Playing the role of the observer makes claims for invisibility—that is, without a recognizable identity, at least within the environment in which happenings are experienced and reported.

In his presidential address to the American Folklore Society, John Roberts pointed out some of the ironies which arise because of this unexamined and ambivalent professional stance. The field of folklore, Roberts argues, has a special take on the literature on identity. Like Ralph Ellison's eponymous hero in *Invisible Man*, folklore has benefited from the anonymity of operating without an identity recognized by the outside world. A lack of clearly stated purpose, while raising embarrassing questions among adherents of other disciplines, has proven to be a conceptual strength, freeing us from the necessity of developing fully shared understandings of the basic terms of our discipline, much less arriving at a common theoretical perspective. Roberts suggests that historically this has placed us in the social position of the protagonist of Ellison's novel, largely invisible to those around us and therefore given the mobility to shape-shift and adapt ourselves to changing conditions (Roberts 1999).

This voluntary invisibility is a self-conscious move, which has provided a useful rationale for pursuing and celebrating vernacular creativity wherever we encounter it. The appearance of engaged disengagement has proven seductive, not only to folklorists but to cultural observers in general. When folklore was primarily the study of fragments of the constructed past, a poetic congruence between subject and scholar provided comfort to scholars and collectors. Both the folklore and folklorists were presumed to engage with the most transparent, if mysterious, side of human expressive capabilities. Our objectives included assigning meanings to the stuff of tradition, even the hidden meanings buried in historical reference or in the unconscious.

The sense of wonder with which antiquarian-style folklore study began has recently been revived in innovative forms. New theaters of memory and cabinets of curiosity are revealed wherever peoples congregate. There is a shadow-identity here, or at least a historical identification on our part with marginal and often neglected peoples. Not only have we rescued the peasantry and their expressive culture from anonymity, but we have been drawn to the outcasts of the roads and the cities.

Identity Politics

Identity resides within another set of terms which are less positive and even less useful in developing a critique of postmodern culture. These concept terms are most commonly employed by the intelligentsia to describe the problems associated with questions of cultural equity: inferiority, subordination, dispossession, disempowerment, marginalization, even counter-hegemonic—all null terms defined through loss and displacement. All of them presume the existence of groups who have come into being as epiphenomena of imperialism through the deployment of negative stereotyping. How much do students of expressive culture attain our own sense of identity by setting ourselves out as intermediaries or representatives of the dispossessed?

Let me further compound the question: like so many keywords, identity contains contrary meanings within its semantic field. When used to refer to self- or group identification, the word seems to emancipate; when used with reference to others, it too often imprisons. Recent political usage of this complex of terms takes away the element of choice from the process of self-identification.

In those parts of the world embroiled in ethnic conflicts, identity formation is not optional. You are what you are born into. The belligerent employment of identity has resuscitated the very idea of Balkanization, extending this concept to include many of the republics formerly in the Soviet sphere of influence. Here self-identification is accompanied by racial stereotyping and deployed to explain and rationalize the displacement or murder of those regarded as enemies and strangers.

Attributions of savagery and barbarism that underlie the media's description of ethnonationalism as a resurgence of tribalization and the intrusion of warlords into civil society have provided the shorthand terms to explain local conflagrations, sometimes as a rationale for outside intervention. Conflicts in Somalia and Sudan were weighted with supposedly objective reporting couched in these terms. Journalistic and political discourse on Afghanistan, Iraq, and Kurdistan furnishes even more recent and chilling examples.

Borrowing from longstanding Western attitudes, the popular press continues to report the awful displacements and massacres among Balkan peoples as evidence of the continuing backwardness of essentially uncivilized tribal peoples who are governed by crazy and despotic warlords. Hermann Bausinger offers valuable insights into these identity questions as they play themselves out in the modern world. Folklore and ethnicity, he points out, become implicated in dangerous political operations. In discussing identity in terms of ethnicity, there is an inclination not to accept people just as human beings and neighbors but to look at them as members of another ethnic group, with a clear tendency toward fencing-off and demarcation. The only way out seems to be the homogenization of politics and the erosion of ethnic boundaries. When the autonomy of ethnic groups is extended from cultural to political goals, this attempt exposes minority groups to grave deprivations, or even deportation and war (Bausinger 1990: 75).

The Slovenian cultural commentator Slavoj Žižek points out the intensity of this stereotyping as it affects the politics of the region. The Balkans, he notes "are portrayed in the liberal Western media as a vortex of ethnic passion—a multiculturalist dream turned into a nightmare." But this modality of thinking is not restricted to those living elsewhere. Slovenes themselves "say 'yes, this is how it is in the Balkans, but Slovenia is not in the Balkans; it is part of Mittel-europa; the Balkans begin in Croatia or in Bosnia; we Slovenes are the last bulwark of European civilization against the Balkan madness'" (Žižek 1999: 3). Others in the region adjust their responses along the same axis of relative civility or barbarism.

It is not difficult for those on this side of the Atlantic to call all Balkan peoples barbarians, throwbacks to those times in which control over land provided the primary impetus for nationality. Why, we ask implicitly, would anybody give themselves over to such thinking when it delimits the possible directions in which individual potential may develop? In the United States, the term identity lies at the heart of how each of us confronts the equally slippery and falsely opposed concepts of individuality and community. That neither individuality nor community is a fixed state of being but contingent on the historical moment when it is invoked seems clear in the early twenty-first-century environment of deep skepticism. These concepts are employed as if they embodied god-given rights, but that is patently not so. Both individual and group identities are contingent on the construction of the power relations that characterize liberal, representative democracy. As the philosopher Richard Rorty notes in *Achieving Our Country*, "We raise questions about our individual or national identity as part of the process of deciding what we will do next, what we will try to become" (Rorty 1998: 11).

Identity, in such a formulation, seems to mean the sum of the self-classifications taken on by an individual who recognizes alternatives. But, as David Hollinger has forcefully suggested, is not this process of choice-making better referred to as a process of affiliation? In his work of special social pleading, *Postethnic America*, this eminent historian attempts to recuperate the promises of social and cultural pluralism without falling into the pit of the present multiculturalism debate. Says Hollinger: "The concept of identity . . . can hide the extent to which the achievement of identity is a social process by which a person becomes affiliated with one or more acculturating cohorts" (Hollinger 1995: 6–7). Building on the distinction made by sociologists between achieved and ascribed mechanisms of role allocation, he is confronting one of the most troublesome vernacular ideas that oozes through American lifeways: that each of us has an identity independent of its social construction. This notion may have become a necessary fiction for ideological reasons, but the fiction is a dangerous one. Individual autonomy simply doesn't bear up under sociological scrutiny.

Surveying the various usages of the term identity, the historian Philip Gleason located a major shift in the 1950s, between the publication of Oscar Handlin's *The Uprooted* in 1951, when identity was not yet the reigning term to organize perceptions of diversity, and Will Herberg's *Protestant, Catholic,*

Jew of 1955. Herberg argued that religion had become "the most satisfactory vehicle of locating oneself in society and thereby answering the aching question of 'identity'" (quoted in Gleason 1983). This meaning of religion has little to do with traditional and inherited church practices; by the time Herberg made his analysis, belonging to a religious community had already become a matter of individual choice.

Identity has recently passed through an equally profound reconfiguration, although the politics involved are still in dispute. Even which discipline in the academy controls the discussion of cultural alternatives and change is a matter of controversy. The growth of the materials and processes of production of popular culture scholarship is paralleled by the more heavily theorized Cultural Studies literature (Grossberg, Nelson, and Treichler 1992). While folklorists and cultural anthropologists attempted to assert their place in this negotiation, the claims of morally elevated and semiotically intensified theorists stole the march on ethnographers. Yet folklorists continue to call attention to how the discipline might cast light on this and other hot topics of the early twenty-first century.

The Politics of Identity

The introduction of the idea of identity was part of the reassessment of the biases contained within previous models of society and culture. The social upheaval of the mid-1960s was paralleled by a shift in the central words and metaphors of public discourse. The political activism and social concerns of that era were part of an expansion of educational opportunity and access to knowledge, alongside the development of an ironic disposition, that has continued to dominate our lives until today. Proving one's humanity required one to demonstrate the existence and the uniqueness of one's culture and one's folklore. Every group came to be designated in terms of its distinct lifeways, a habit of argument which is still very much with us in popular discussion.

When the New Left proclaimed the New Politics, within the cultural sciences the New Ethnography was proclaimed, along with New Perspectives in Folklore (Paredes and Bauman 1972; Hymes 1972; Bascom 1977; Limon and Young 1986; Shuman and Briggs 1993). The cultural and historical disciplines adjusted their research agendas to give historical depth and geographical range to the traditional modes of resistance that were being displayed in marches and sit-ins. Reinterpreting the idea of types, the pluralistic notion of alternative lifestyles was brought to high visibility in those volatile times. Stylistic difference was articulated by self-consciously taking on the appearance of "the Other" by dressing as a peasant, farmer, or working-class stiff. African Americans involved in the movement, however, pointed out again and again that the white-bread people who were marching alongside them could go home and wash out their coloration when they wished. The point remains a good one; as far as the underclass is concerned, this stylistic appropriation is a weekend leisure activity. That this practice was an extension of the archaic idea of travesty was forgotten for the moment; up-ending official structures was too potent a way of operating to relegate it to a historical process. It had to be reinvented as rites of inversion, processes of cultural reversibility, and evidences of resistance and counter-hegemonic acts.

The idea of the folk had been substantially set in twentieth-century America primarily with reference to socially or geographically marginalized groups. But the term continued to imply technological and educational backwardness as well. In resisting the system, the military-industrial complex, and an unresponsive government, white young people were inclined to identify with these marginalized folks. Identity was achieved through altered patterns of dress, hair style, and social activity (the new equal-opportunity eating, which stressed peasant foods); in political action (through demonstrations, marches, and other working-class techniques of protest and resistance); and even via economic activity (selling on the streets, from blankets thrown down in front of the major local emporia). It became important to many people involved in counter-cultural work to identify as a member of a folk community. In this manner, the term folklore itself was democratized, removed from its earlier nationalistic deployment.

When folklore was redefined during the 1960s, the range of groups considered folk who produce and practice lore was greatly expanded. The most significant change in identity has been its employment as a shibboleth term in the discourse of difference—that is, the apprehension of self-and-other, especially as individuals cobble together personal identifications. This frame of reference emerged out of American pragmatic philosophy as initiated by William James and pursued by George Herbert Mead; indeed, the very idea of reflexivity in current cultural theorizing emerges from the same point. This position holds that the self is a human capacity for reflection upon actual situated practices. The achievement of self arises from a dynamic of interaction between the "I"—the subjective, creative, emergent dimensions—and the "Me"—the more known, outer, determined, the social phase. Using *identification* as a name for this process, those writing from this perspective argue that humans are involved in a constant process of naming and renaming self. Sociologists pursuing role theory and symbolic interactionism have approached this process in terms of a fit between selves and socially constructed categories. In his later, more political writings, Erikson called attention to this troubling problem. Lamenting the development of a "pseudo-species" in which ethnic or national differentiation became more important than common human concerns, he called critical attention to the process by which "one nation or group feels that it has the right, the power, even the obligation to denigrate those who look or act differently" (Erikson 1969, quoted in Gardner 1999). As this term and way of thinking has moved to the center of the public discussions of society and values, identity has seemed not simply a desirable state of being but one endowed by nature, a human right, or at least an entitlement in a truly civil polity. By this rhetorical move, personal choice itself becomes the buried concept in the praxis of self-identification. Here self-presentation becomes subject to discussion both in historical and contemporary forms of public display.

From this liberal democratic perspective, identity has replaced pride of place and station as a civic duty. Having an identity and using it as a way of creating a sense of self-worth becomes an obligation. Exercising the right to make one's own choices replaces the plebiscite in our national imagination. Choices are no longer regarded as irreversible; each choice seems to be arrived at for the sense of possibility it brings, which heightens and deepen experience or well-being. The inadequate achievement of identity is associated with being unhappy and feeling unfulfilled, the bugbears of contemporary existence; failing to attain such elevated states is a sign that we have individually and collectively lost our way. Thus the need to step out of life from time to time to "find oneself." In this structure of meanings, each time a life-choice is made by or for us it is attended by a sense of loss. If we feel our options have been foreclosed, we lament being victimized by historical circumstances.

But the basic irony of attaining freedom through making choices is undercut in the personal realm by those who actually choose to make a life-change. Committing oneself to a new identity through marriage or divorce, moving jobs or domiciles is not regarded as irreversible. We have devised many different ways of dissolving contracts to which we have solemnly and seriously dedicated ourselves. Such proceedings for getting divorced from commitments seem to be regarded as entitlements which restoring possibility. This attitude toward choice is not necessarily found in other parts of the world. In those systems in which identity arises from family, national, or religious obligation, the achievement of an identity is not presumed. What could be more threatening to Western society than "fundamentalists," "dictators," or any leader who would make choices for others?

In the politically energized environment of the late 1960s and early seventies, exiting from "the system" was symbolically enacted by self-consciously imitating previously despised or disempowered peoples. African Americans and Native Americans had served as models for imitation by the disaffected since the beginning of the nineteenth century. Other excluded peoples now became models for serious or comic emulation. In response to such forces, the definition of the folk was self-consciously altered. The groups that came to the notice of the discipline were those which engaged in intense activity in common and in which membership was voluntary.

Folklore came to be taken as the constitutive elements of the group; knowing, performing, and participating in group activities conferred membership. By extension, individuals could belong to a number of such groups; indeed, one's life-story could be conceived of as a record of taking on such allegiances. Historically distinctive groups who shared specific conditions of oppression and resistance achieved high status in the national dialogue on cultural equity.

The Politics of Difference

In a commercial economy, playing different parts and learning a variety of lines are a way of life for those in trade. Difference is inherent in the roles and relationships of sellers and buyers, not just in the exotic products brought from faraway places and displayed for consumption. Duplicity and mutability become second nature in the marketplace. The practices that become traditional in that site are central to the study of expressive culture, not least because they spill over into large-scale festivals and popular entertainments, on the one hand, and leak into and reshape personal interactions, on the other.

Capitalism and its associated bourgeois values have been ascendant throughout the West since the seventeenth century, and its mercantile, colonial, and imperial projects have been redrawing the map of the world for a century longer. At the remote beginnings and the present end of this great transformation, the cultures of the West and the rest of the world come together in the form of persons, practices, and objects, creating and reconstituting difference in remarkable ways. Profound changes have come from the massive displacement of peoples in the wake of capitalist expansion, the uprooting of whole nations from their lands, and the accelerating circulation of wage labor as well as commodities. Now, as Americans who had thought themselves privileged face the unfettered mobility of capital and employment, the exemption that some classes were promised from the relentless dynamics generated by the international market has clearly been abrogated. Newly alert to the continuing presence of the unprivileged in their midst and to the arrival of immigrants from stunningly numerous and various elsewheres, Americans attempt to come to terms with globalization, locating themselves in relation to all those others in unaccustomed ways.

Responses to dislocation are manifest in the display activities of those who have had to move and feel the effects of cultural distance. What were once domestic traditions carried out within a home community become devices of solidarity among the displaced, and private practices become public gestures. The stranger is made into the good neighbor willing to share cultural riches. Putting them on display in exotic forms transforms these activities into performances. When packaged for public consumption, performances of ethnic identity resemble one another, undercutting the message of cultural distinctiveness. Showing off becomes a way of blending in, without acknowledging the motivations for such a cultural move.

Folklore practitioners and folklore as a discipline are implicated in this entire process. The awareness among public folklorists that they compromise their own values when participating in the commercialization and homogenization of cultural difference is a belated beginning of a whole chain of salutary recognitions. Folklorists' focus on traditionally landless and newly migrant peoples—two antitypes of the bounded communities which are taken as the type by which culture itself is constituted—dramatizes the equation of land, language, and lore that emerged in the wake of Herderian thought. That equation remains powerful even its signs are reversed to register dispossession, dispersion, and linguistic and cultural rupture. The global economy increasingly calls the usefulness of the Romantic nationalist paradigm into question, especially as media of communication break down local, regional, and national boundaries. World music and dance drawn from the practices of traditional peoples are available around the globe. Rumor mills and gossip networks which used to be local and personal now extend to anyone in the world with access to CNN, the Internet, or any other "mediascape," as Arjun Appadurai calls these means of instant communication (Appadurai 1990).

The drift of immigrant-driven bourgeois cosmopolitanism resulted in profound changes in attitudes toward expressive culture of all sorts. Different clothing styles, body decoration, food—all provide a panoply of choices that underscores the centrality of choice-making in the achievement of personal identity. In such an environment, certain dimensions of traditional practices are seized upon and used in extralocal surroundings, gathering momentum as they are constituted as different and marketed for health, spiritual, or touristic entertainment purposes. In everyday vernacular usage, terms suggesting age and authenticity continue to be highly valued—none more highly than identity—because they embody the possibilities of connection with the past and the promise of individual integrity. Nostalgia is at the center of such an enterprise, to be sure, but that recognition need not lead us to undervalue the experience of consuming differences.

Hijacked Identities

Enlightened acceptance of cultural difference has become a core principle of all capitalist democracies. What was during the 1950s called tolerance in the vernacular has become the acceptance of diversity, which goes by the name of multiculturalism. Cultural difference has received sufficient notice that few want to be accused of being inflexible in such matters; exhibiting tolerance is a necessary element of social acceptability. Not much has changed with regard to home visiting, much less sitting in the same schools. Contemporary prac-

tices of segregation, desegregation, and resegregation simply have new rationales, including obeying the rule of law. And they are covered over even by
the discourses most hotly disrupted in the "culture wars" of the 1990s.

The most valued life-strategies arise from the equation between political
and religious liberty and the marketplace notion of freedom of choice. The
Marxian insight that these crucial choices in bourgeois society are based on
fetishizing commodities has become such a commonplace that it no longer
carries much intellectual weight. Even those students of situated expressive
culture who have entered the field searching for alternatives to a consumer
mentality find themselves unable to ask interesting questions of this world
view except by taking notice of how local traditions have been adapted into
products or productions aimed primarily at tourists and other cosmopolitan
consumers.

"The overbearing self-sufficiency of modern civilization" that concerned
Franz Boas (Boas 1907) seems to be built on the notion that everything in culture can be recycled, used to produce moments of nostalgia without the pain
of dislocation commonly carried by this dis-ease. Even the process of rehearsing and repeating significant experiences becomes useful to commerce. Master
narratives can be revised so they have a peaceable ending.

Discussions of identity visibly contribute to rationalizing violations of liberty and the taking of human life. Here students of expressive culture have
insights to offer, though little apparent inclination to do so except to point to
the lore of stereotyping and cultural cooptation. The lure of taking sides and
of attempting to represent the underrepresented is too great. Yet recognizing
representative narratives and calling them by their proper names is, or should
be, the business of the ethnographic professions.

In the future, new metaphors will be imagined by which vernacular culture may be more fully understood. Certainly, if the pace of population displacement holds, while the rest of the world is bound together by technological
means, we will have to forego any claims for critical understandings of culture
by focusing exclusively on small-group aesthetic engagements. What will happen when questions of identity actively take into account the many diasporas?
Diaspora itself has come to be naturalized, used in a neutral sense in descriptions of whole groups of people in motion carrying extensive cultural equipment with them. As these populations-on-the-move begin to be seen not only
as a display of difference but also as a cultural resource, discussions of identity
will be altered.

This alteration is being felt already at those points where cultural differences are subject to commoditization in the increasingly global economy. The
association of vernacular creativity with the equation between land, language,
and lore is questioned and undermined by those with an investment in the
commercial movement of goods and services. Peoples involved broadly in the
import-export business of culturally diverse products and practices now

choose to underscore their stylistically marked national identities. Under such conditions, identities are ethnicized and marketed in the plural environment, where they become imbricated in tourist economies and the heritage industry as well as trade. Under such conditions, processes of *hybridization* and *creolization* achieve a more positive status in nationalist cultural theory. It is surely time to reexamine the concepts of culture emerging with the embrace of cosmopolitanism and the culturally plural character of the city and the market.

Although identifying and showing the widespread narrative typing of self and other remains central to our task, realistically the discussion must begin by recognizing the contingent character of this lore and the rhetorical contexts in which typological attributions are made. We should examine how folklore enters into the characterization of self and whether it is useful to regard selfhood as being the same as identity. This sense of identity will simply not hold up as a container of meaning under the conditions of the postindustrial world in which people move or are moved at a moment's notice. Vernacular creativity under adverse conditions now provides the public with sustenance even as the middle class continues to fear and segregate the very people who consistently produce these marketable other remains central to our task, realistically the discussion must begin by recognizing the contingent forms. The process of engaging consumers' fears and desires, especially with public entertainments, maintains the social derogation of subject populations even as those who are subordinated continue to produce different and marketable vernacular styles. Questions of truth, justice, and authenticity have little place in this discourse except as they serve the fluidity of the market. A critical folkloristics and ethnology, now beginning to emerge, should provide some insight into our role as commentators on the process and the ways in which our discipline should expand its subject.

Chapter 13
Creolizations

So long as cultures were regarded as being linguistically, geographically, and institutionally distinct from others, neither the movement of peoples nor the way in which they expressed themselves was problematic. This presumption was called into question by the recognition that historically a great many peoples were uprooted and entered into relations of some sort with indigenous peoples wherever they moved. If the natives had not been annihilated, the two groups developed an exchange relationship. For students of culture, the situation was complicated by the ongoing interaction between the two groups, especially because exchange almost always involves a transfer of cultural practices as well as material goods.

When war or some other form of hostility erupts between the two groups, expressive differences are amplified. Hostility toward enemies is commonly rationalized by depicting them as subhuman, uncivilized, and ignorant of the proper way to talk, to eat, or to maintain a family. Differences in manners are implicated in the ways in which the two parties address one another. We constantly learn the prosaic lesson that good fences do not make good neighbors. Under conditions of war or enslavement, breaking down the barriers between the groups through eating, drinking, or having sexual relations confuses the situation. Such border crossings occur more frequently in a stable situation of political stalemate, or when one group colonizes the other.

Civil order and ritual purity are felt to come under attack from both sides in most encounters. In extreme situations, the defeated ones are relocated elsewhere, or simply ordered to move away. Boundaries are reinforced when the losers in a conflict are imprisoned or put into internment camps. More commonly, the defeated ones are forced to labor for the victors and used to carry out demeaning activities. Subject populations are feared as a source of potential contagion, or even dreaded because they are regarded as capable of mounting a counter-offensive at any moment. Surveillance and extreme forms of control are developed to protecting citizens from these invasive or subversive forces.

Yet the commingling of cultural forms between the two groups is inevitable if the defeated ones have not been disappeared or entirely displaced. Such conditions are the source of most situations referred to diasporas today, even if the idea of displacement and dispersal has lost its edge among the survivors.

Simply living in contiguity establishes a kind of exotic distance between members of two communities, which diverts hatred into the creation of neutral zones, or no man's lands.

In-Between Zones

Exoticizing carries with it the creation of objects of desire, which is usually sexual in nature. From this dangerous attraction comes a system for communication across the divide, including an imitation of one another's performance styles. As performers emerge from within the subject population, even stronger desires of a sexual sort arise. Call it human nature, or call it rape: a highly charged semiotic zone emerges in which something like expropriation occurs, whereby the women of the subjected group become sexually available as a continuing demonstration of the superior power of the dominant group. The sexualizing that occurs in this situation encourages other kinds of expressive contact. The conquerors soon learn the styles of presentation of the defeated ones. As each group imitates the other, points of contact going beyond Checkpoint Charlie are elaborated. Cultural performances, especially those invented by the newly displaced peoples as a defense against total oppression, cause a further mixing of cultures, though without altering their social statuses.

An in-between entertainment zone commonly emerges in these conditions, spaces in which these transactions can now take place. Styles of music, dance, formal speaking, and food and drink consumption, as well as sex, become a part of the modus vivendi of the two communities. In such mutually agreed-upon zones of interaction, official rules of approach and avoidance are subject to renegotiation, and entertainers find themselves playing the role of culture broker. Whoever has learned the ways of the other acquires a new position of power. In exchange for becoming a cultural nobody, the entertainer is given the power to articulate the displays in which exotic performance occurs and the twin emotions of fear and desire are put into play.

The propinquity of peoples produces a highly charged and volatile social space, which results not only in sexual congress but also in styles that combine elements of the two sets of representational forms. Here hybrid forms of life emerge, along with a hybrid population of mixed parentage. Both groups develop an ongoing wariness of these contact zones for many of the same reasons: the confusion of realms, the dilution of canons of purity and cleanliness, and the violation of social rules brought into the encounter by each of the groups. In places where the two groups meet regularly, a distinctive liberating force begins to operate. A consensus culture emerges, worked out under distressing and unequal conditions, but achieving a kind of stability as the groups continue to live in close proximity.

In the New World, these areas betwixt and between took on a life of their own, for all of those who found themselves in this volatile situation found ways to accommodate themselves to its instability. In such zones, new peoples and new cultural forms emerged. These peoples and these expressive styles were often stigmatized by the dominant group and ostracized by the subordinated one, yet they thrived—not only within these in-between cultural niches, but eventually beyond them.

A mixed population, composed of those conceived through cross-cultural sexual congress who belonged to neither the community of the oppressors nor the community of the oppressed, gradually developed its own society. In the great Iberian world, these new people became known as *mestizo*; in the francophone realms, they were called *métis*. Although they sometimes served as mediators between groups, they were not the only carriers of the new cultural forms that emerged in these in-between zones.

The communication systems developed to make mutual intelligibility minimally possible—the contact pidgins—were quickly absorbed, especially by subject peoples, and soon they were used not just in contact situations but also in other precincts of their exposed lives. Because of the constant need to broaden the ways in which quick-hit transactions are accomplished, this hybrid way of speaking and acting soon became customary beyond the marketplace. These expressive forms became the lingua franca, and their best performers embellished the codes used between the two groups. Commonly the translators were market traders and members of their households who used these abilities to further their fortunes. Those who were successful developed into a new social stratum composed of those living betwixt and between. From this process emerge all of those expressive formations referred to as *creole*— that is, growing out of the process which for the last few generations has been referred to as *creolization*.

Creole/Hybrid

With the collapse of European markets for the staple crops produced by slave labor on colonial plantations in the Caribbean, emancipation was declared. The creole populations, along with the *mestizo* or *métis* populations with whom they overlapped, found themselves the inheritors of status in the colonies. As these complex, stratified societies achieved national independence, these new people often became political leaders. Where large cosmopolitan populations had emerged during the period of successful trade, creoles found a niche much more quickly than in those areas in which colonial identities persisted because of metropolitan indifference. As creoles became leaders of independent nations, creolization slowly lost its sense of opprobrium and became legitimate. In some cases, it was celebrated as a source of national identity (Devonish 1986; Bolland 1992).

The terms *creole* and *creolization*, which once connoted contamination and degradation, are now used in a less condemnatory sense. They and their near synonym, *hybridity*, receive a more kindly reception in the contemporary world of global trade and cosmopolitan sensibilities. A growing number of cultural observers have turned this set of terms into positive descriptors for the pluralistic communities that are emerging under current conditions of exchange and interaction (Hannerz 1987). This shift has been reinforced as the artistic styles developed under the old orders have proved to be marketable through new forms of mediated communication. Artists born into creole communities redeem (although not unambiguously) the words for colonial resilience and combinatory genius. These expatriates and cosmopolitans see the possibilities of maintaining the viability of creolization as a term of art, even as they are able to draw on the reservoir of historical experience found within such ex-slave formations.

Other commentators within the ranks of the postcolonial brigade urge the use of hybridity. That term sidesteps some of the semantic drag accruing to creolization, but hybrid forms are far from uncontaminated by past usage. The sense of illicit and uncontrolled breeding maintained in creolization is bypassed, but not the implicit meanings of forced interbreeding. Perhaps the appeal of the term hybridity has as much to do with the critical success of the work of the Russian language philosopher Mikhail Bakhtin. By his definition, hybrid forms involve "a mixture of two social languages within the limits of a single utterance—an encounter, within an utterance, between two different linguistic consciousnesses, separated from one another by an epoch, by social differentiation, or by some other factor" (Bakhtin 1981: 358). Drawing on the term from this perspective, critics have been attracted to the usefulness of hybridity as a way of drawing attention to the idea of kidnapping cultural forms, translating them into the colonialists' language, and putting them into print, which formerly colonized peoples recognize in this postcolonial world.

All literature does this doubling, through the introduction of descriptors with self-canceling meanings. The postcolonial critic would agree that this doubleness is not necessarily duplicity, but rather a way that writers use intrusions to complicate the flow of their words. The author shadows her characters in order to attain an ironic perspective, to maintain both the framing of the world being depicted and *la vie quotidienne*. Endless mirrors are inscribed into any narrative, not only the postcolonial text. To be sure, a special ironic stance is always called for when a writer enters into the discussion with a chip-on-the-shoulder sense of having been taken advantage of historically. Mimicry alone opens up these doubling, tripling, quadrupling tricks of the writer's trade.

The act of authoring invites the kind of distrust and ironic distancing that the reader must read as "don't interpret anything that follows as being real, even if it has an authentic feeling about it." This infinite mirroring effect is sold as a serious topic, a record of the deception of the colonizer, the warden, even the pitchman. However, I confess to feeling pushed around by the critic who attacks the veracity and usefulness of his readers. The only possible pleasure that might come of this is that the reader shares in the bullying of the author through allowing his ventriloquation rights. It's pretty painful stuff, which demands that the reader sit there and take it with good spirit—as if invoking the proverb that suffering is good for the soul. "Kill all the professional liars, especially the children and grandchildren of those who have abused power." That is certainly a strange charge made by those who most prospered under colonial rule. The spielmaster in the marketplace is always able to coopt everyone else's lines. But does he have one of his own?

On numerous occasions, when I was speaking about different cultural styles in our midst, someone has asked to see my license. But even this is not so offensive as when the questioner also claims that he is one of the historical victims, who had to make the joke to slip the yoke himself. To do this, he must demonstrate control over the ethnically identified vernacular, becoming a preacher, a teacher, a hipster, and then a tipster. Everyone can do it if they apply themselves. At one point, I fell back on a rehearsed line that asked explicitly: "Are you claiming to have a pimp or a hick license? Are you lining up with the kinfolk, the brothers, or the graduates of the university of the streets yourself?" This riposte does not bring a stop to the proceedings, or quiet the residual anger of the questioner and those sitting next to him on the mourners' bench. It may hold them up to laughter from others, but that is a mean laughter.

Contemporary Americans have not resolved, or even adequately addressed, the difficult issues arising from the long history of asymmetrical cross-cultural interaction as it intersects with present and persistent socioeconomic inequalities. Coming to terms with the legacy of cultural difference in this postcolonial world means facing highly charged memories of fear and loss, longing and desire. Our society's confused sense of the contradictory meanings of this legacy finds a telling sign in the propagation of days, weeks, and months dedicated to commemorating victimization. In a consumer society, everyone has the same trouble: nostalgia for a past that never existed. But why be nostalgic for field hands yoked by slavery on land that was never their own? This act of usurpation of the local by cosmopolitan intellectuals who have received asylum in the academy is especially galling for those who have kept up the good fight for the preservation of the vernacular back home, wherever home may be.

All peoples who have lived through the experience of achieving political independence and subsequent devolution are lumped together in this act of commemoration. When emancipated from imperial governance, oppressed peoples are defined in terms of the heritage of victimization. Yet many indigenous cosmopolitan intellectuals born and raised in colonial situations are uncomfortable with being put into the same cultural pot. The term obscures or even eliminates historical specificities, ignoring the nuances of the achievements of different postcolonial societies.

Creolization

Before creolization became a glamour term used to describe all cultural conjunctions, the word was employed to describe the linguistic and social process by which different peoples came together under the harsh regime of export-oriented plantation agriculture.

In the first reaction against structural-functionalism in cultural analysis during the 1960s, fieldworkers studying the expressive production of plural communities were increasingly unwilling to impose a model based on a standard way of interacting. Instead, behavior and performance were described and judged in terms of their situational appropriateness. Local norms of interaction were given primacy in such a view, which was called *emic*—that is, native or indigenous—by contrast to *etic*—that is, externally derived. Ethnographers working in Afro-American and Afro-Caribbean communities embraced this shift of view. In creole cultures, especially, beginning not by normalizing standard language production but rather by recording and analyzing local varieties of speech in context seemed essential.

Creolization suggests that internal variation and continuous historical and situational change are necessary dimensions of language and culture reportage. The number and range of language codes in any creole community are remarkably wide—so much so that speakers and performers often discuss the matter among themselves. Good talk and other kinds of artful presentation are an ongoing topic of conversation in daily life; audience reaction during performances often centers on the quality of speech as well.

Ethnographers working creole communities discuss the range and intensity of various kinds of interaction: orating, bantering, singing and dancing, and performing the many ceremonies that percolate through creole life. From these reports, alternative perspectives on language were proposed which account for the range of situation-specific styles of communicating. Using the visual image of the spectrum as a model, scholars proposed a creole continuum. Some form of Standard Broadcast English or School English was posited as one end of the spectrum; the other end was broad or broken talk, *patois*, or old talk. These ways of speaking derived from historically distinct moments in the process by which Africans and Europeans were brought together. Taking the power structure of the colonies within the empire into account, the broadest or most quickly performed codes were presumed to be closer to African antecedents and to contain, at least potentially, secret messages.

Creole linguists, attempting to reconstruct how this *patois* developed, posited the existence of an African-based creole used throughout the maritime world. In such a view, variety and change are to be anticipated in any expressive environment, especially in areas with populations constantly on the move. Each language and culture in any contact situation was presumed to enter into the expressive mix, even in situations of forced dislocation and enslavement. Fieldworkers discovered that the more intense the occasion of interaction and performance, the more the creole populations drew upon the most archaic expressive resources.

One of the greatest problems facing creole-speaking peoples in the modern world has been that those forms closest to their African antecedents are socially stigmatized by the education system—that is, regarded as bad or broken talk. Folklorists and ethnographers emphasized how mixed, mobile, and adaptive these populations have been. While attempting to sidestep the stigma, this approach still elicits the old problem of language and cultural legitimacy. As the dean of Caribbeanists, Sidney Mintz, argued in his Huxley Memorial Lecture:

Creoles were people who moved beyond the cultural and conceptual confines of their migrant parents, and became, for better or for worse, hemispheric Americans of a new sort. . . . The new concept of creolization has been borrowed . . . without serious attention to what the term meant, or to what historically specific processes it stood for. What typified creolization was not the fragmentation of culture and the destruction of the very concept, but the creation and construction of culture out of fragmented, violent, and disjunct pasts. (Mintz 1994: 302)

Certainly, the continuing vitality of contemporary creole cultures is hardly debatable.

Another major figure in the field of creole studies, Michel-Rolph Trouillot, described the changes in cultural theory called for in order to approach plural societies whose "boundaries are notoriously fuzzy." Referring specifically to the Caribbean region, he describes the analytic problem succinctly: "Long . . . the open 'frontier' of cultural anthropology, neither center nor periphery, but a sort of no man's land where pioneers get lost, where some stop overnight on their way to greater opportunities, and where yet others manage to create their own 'new' world amidst First World indifference" (Trouillot 1992: 19). This indifference is inherent in Western theories of culture which have privileged small, bounded communities, on the one hand, and the cosmopolitan modernism of nation-states on the other. What is new is the mixed character of the populations regarded as worthy of observation, raising the question of when a population become a people.

Once these questions are bypassed by developing more adaptive models of cultural flow, these expressive styles, genres, and languages become available in developing a national literature (Brathwaite 1971, 1984). In those communities most historically marked as creole, a new, more rambunctious history is pursued in which creole languages and musical and dance styles form the basis of local pride. As industrial societies mutate into global figurations, creolized representations become attractions ripe for touristic exploitation. They even make their way into the festivals and concerts produced in the name of the folk by foreign folklorists.

As an active force, creolization is a process occurring of zones of trade, where peoples of different stylistic presentation encounter each other in the exchange of goods and services, including performances. Within these zones, the enslaved population's Sunday markets and holidays operated independently of the larger staple-crop economies of the plantations. The Congo Squares found throughout the creole world were sites of expressive innovation which drew upon the performances and spectacles of Western Europe and the Mediterranean, as well as the remembered skills and bodily dispositions of the displaced performers of African ancestry.

Forms that illustrate creolization arise out of particular historic and cultural matrices in which artistic invention is highly valued, improvisation is customary, and the performances comment directly on historical inequities and ongoing social and political conditions. These events often are called to public notice because they depart in some dimension from customary practices. Under conditions of the political instability, they provide a means of expressing social discontent, often through replaying historical injustices.

The civilizing mission of colonialism itself came to be suspect from this plural perspective, recognized as the invention of power elites seeking to justify expansion. But the more interesting story has to do with those who were actively involved in inventing a way of life adapted to the intensive staple-crop agriculture that drew upon a mixture of customs and practices which went beyond the techniques of control and surveillance of the plantation. What is too seldom remarked upon in discussions of creolization is the degree of cultural transfer that occurred throughout this plantation world as a matter of course.

Within creole performances, improvised and often inversive social behaviors became the norm, especially during slave and ex-slave holidays. Here, those otherwise considered to be social outcasts could find a place of importance in the celebrations. Following the Russian language philosopher, Mikhail Bakhtin, many observers have located Carnival at the archaic marketplace rather than at sites of official power and surveillance (Bakhtin 1984; Stallybrass and White 1986). At fairs and on market days, rules and regulations gravitate to the more egalitarian norms of quick exchange. Even social misfits and illegals were permitted there.

The problem of disorder is made all the more extreme in those situations in which a new language develops at that point of contact, freed of the constraints of official or standard forms used by nation-states in their communications. These ways of speaking and interacting have commonly been branded as mongrel or bastard forms. Yet, throughout the plantation period, agents of empire and travelers found the situations in which these otherwise stigmatized enslaved peoples exhibited themselves immensely attractive. A profusion of new and lively display forms arose in these cultural borderlands.

It is the fear-inducing dimension of creole productions that have provided the greatest degree of fascination for onlookers ever since creole cultures were first observed in the seventeenth century. Deep anxieties about disorder and dread of contagion overflow in the texts written by observers of African America for three centuries and more. Terms such as "dunghill," "cesspool," and "shit-heap" resonate through the early descriptions of those outposts of empire. Such catch-phrases reflect a complex reaction to the formation of trade communities which were out of the regular control of those bureaucratic and cosmopolitan centers of civilization that were involved in overseas expansion and the creation of plantations. Creole encampments were met with revulsion by the very people responsible for their coming into being. Whatever culture-building took place under such inhospitable conditions contains a history of human despoliation and iniquity, which I am loath to abandon or ignore—even though the process term, creolization, has recently been transvalued to underscore its secondary characteristics of artful conflation, improvisation, and spontaneous creativity.

To be sure, adaptive mixtures of historically distinct styles and systems of practice have been discovered now in one place, now another, in the creole communities of the New World. The honor due these developments is surely appropriate, but not at the expense of eliminating the historical lamination to be found in creole performances and celebrations. The processes through which various African and other cultural elements were transmuted in American circumstances are not an explicit part of the script that governs the presentation and interpretation of these events by the participants, although it can be discovered by historians. Once the cultural continuities between Africa and the diaspora are accepted by scholars, an African substrate of meanings becomes evident to those who know the cultures on both sides of the Atlantic. But, in this way, history is replayed through stylistic points of reference, not through the meanings that creole people themselves make of their past in their performances.

These historically coded inventions elicited little interest until recently because of their characteristic mixture of styles. Such conflation and confusion carried the stereotypical message usually put forward concerning what was perceived as mixed forms: they were regarded as degraded, bastardized, confused, contaminated, degenerate, and only vaguely human. The congeries of people brought together for the production of commercial crops was considered corrupt simply because it was such a hodge-podge. The wide variety of languages encountered there led to a sense, among Western commentators, that there was no real language to be found, but a non-system of expression made up of bad, broken, and incomprehensible sounds.

These people, whether slave or master, were too far removed from metropolitan power to maintain the sense of social order and practice which was beginning to go by the name of culture or civilization. People in these creole encampments were not subject to any effective law except what was created and imposed there. Whatever order existed was based on the masters' naked power over the bodies of the enslaved. Masters and slaves, to say nothing of overseers and other intermediaries, were all bloodied in the process. These were passionate and unruly people, purported to be given over to bestiality and uncontrolled sexual liberty. Their eating habits were beyond strange; not only did they eat unrecognizable foods, but they ate the overabundant foods with their fingers or in some other bestial manner.

Equally important, planters were regarded as the most extreme and least trustworthy representatives of the mercantile system. An experiment in industrial production, plantations were carried out at a great distance from consumers. This gap intensified the distrust between the entrepreneurial managers and those toiling in the fields and boiling houses. The workers were not to be trusted, but neither were the business people involved in curing or processing and distributing the product. Markets, always the gathering place of vagrants and scoundrels, now became the center of new unscrupulousness by those engaged directly in making fortunes. To the skullduggery and lying endemic to market traders were added the complications of double bookkeeping. Those engaged in business took advantage of the huge social and geographical distance between those working on the land and those distributing the product. The riches so derived were enormously troubling to the elite social structure of European cosmopolitan centers. No one knew what to make of these colonials, to say nothing of their slaves.

Finally, the most distinctive feature of creole societies to outsiders was the inventiveness of the enslaved peoples. Seizing upon the plots given them to provide their own subsistence, the slaves produced surpluses which they sold at periodic markets in town, creating a shadow economy. They demanded and were given time off at Cropover, Christmas, and sometimes Carnival. They expanded these into the holidays that were even more wildly celebrated after Emancipation. On Emancipation Day, as in Carnival and Christmas entertainments, the theme of expressive liberation is remembered and often reenacted in contemporary terms. This creative explosion lies at the heart of the process of creolization as it has been discussed during the last half-century.

Memory and Commemoration

These festive observations involve a number of historical ironies. The languages and styles which emerge at the most intense moments are those which were regarded as especially aberrant and corrupting, even diabolically inspired, under the plantation regime. Descriptions of these moments were especially troubling insofar as they obviously employed African styles of song, dance, and enthusiastic display. Complicating matters, such occasions draw upon more deeply African styles as the expressive occasion became more intense (Marks 1974; Abrahams and Szwed 1977; Malone 1996; Gundaker 1998). Secret understandings are hinted at and revealed to those within the circle of celebrants.

Today, these festivities have been translated into homecoming events for people who have emigrated from the community. They also have become national holidays, which amount to tourist attractions. These reenactments commonly call for singing, dancing, and costuming regarded as unique to that particular place, time, and occasion. Here are born some of the most enduring forms of vernacular expression by which the creole world has put its stamp on international popular culture. These celebrations have provided the impetus for the development of song and dance and other display forms which have subsequently been adopted throughout the global *oecumene*.

The quintessential creole events involve serious play, an investment of time, money, and sentiments. They are marked by excessive consumption, but they build upon the labors of the rest of the year: planning the events, designing the costumes, rehearsing, composing new songs or speeches on the patterns of past performances. At Carnival in Trinidad and Tobago, Mardi Gras in New Orleans and Memphis, Christmas Sports on Nevis, St. Kitts, and Jamaica, and the Bahamian Jonkonnu, enslavement and liberation are replayed. The cultural rupture created by the Middle Passage lies at the heart of these events, minimally submerged in the official prize competitions and old *mas'* mock battles.

Such national celebrations are not unique to the anglophone areas of the New World. Similar stories are told of Rio and Bahia, Port au Prince, and Buenos Aires. As the results are often successful for nation-builders and for tourism, their narrative tends toward a triumphalist interpretation. Those promoting local civic pride give the message that, even in the face of a brutal past, the people have been able to persevere through creative expression. But for those who have played these festivities throughout their lives, the story also carries messages of loss of the old ways of celebrating, as the events have grown in scale and attracted outside investment. Individual performers and neighborhood groups attempt to keep the traditions alive. In the most extreme formulations, they conduct counter-festivities that comment negatively on the official ways of celebrating.

All-consuming high times engender the songs and dances which embody the signature styles of each locale: scratch band, steel band, beguine, belaire, calypso, or wining, to name only a few. This singing and dancing, relocated to dance halls, rum shops, and juke joints, endow the entire year with reminders of the high moments of the festival. The year is threaded together through the replay of the victorious road march or calypso from Trinidad (Rohlehr 1990; Hill 1993). In the yards of many neighborhoods, next year's productions are conceived, new tunes and songs written, the stories of previous years' presentations retold as the paraphernalia of the big time is repaired or made anew. Here renewal and replenishment provide the tone for the rest of the year.

It would be a mistake, however, to see these uproarious big times as the only events in Afro-America which signal this invocation of the past. The more solemn oratorical and orderly marching display events, like Emancipation Day in its various apotheoses or the activities of the burial societies at the death of a member, all testify to stylish gravity. The two styles—the slow, stately and ornamental, and the riotous and freewheeling—are often juxtaposed, as in the Second Line in New Orleans, or the Tea Meeting and Shakespeare Lessons in the ex-British Lesser Antilles. In the Second Line, the marching group accompanying the dead body of a community member is led to the graveyard by a brass band playing songs directing home the spirit of the departed. With the interment, the mourners become the celebrants, and the brass band plays with greater freedom and even abandon as the group wends its way back to the neighborhood via a purposely meandering route. With the Tea Meeting, the two styles of speechmaking, orderly and the farcical, are juxtaposed within the same event and often performed against each at the same moment (Abrahams 1988d; Kinser 1990; Burton 1997).

Historical reminders are contained in these events. Overt memorial references occur within the performances themselves to Africa, to slave times, and to emancipation; the performances also remark on the activities of politicians and other leaders in more recent notable events. Far from reveling in the outrage of historical victimization, these celebrations remind the participants of the resilience of people of mixed parentage who repeatedly invent and reinvent display forms which are portable and exportable. Indeed, the particular genius of creole performance and celebration arises from that combination of protean inventiveness and mobility.

The sauciness and swagger of many marchers command everyone's attention. No wonder that some outsiders have been troubled by this expansive display on the streets wherever these practices have been deployed in national celebrations. These forms have become part of the cultural equipment for living of many New World peoples seeking a usable past. Holidays observed by the descendants of slaves have embedded within their practices traces of historically identifiable motifs that were well understood to refer to Africa, the experience of the Middle Passage, and enslavement. Carnival and other representative African American holidays—Juneteenth, August Monday, the Family Reunion, the Million Man March—explicitly reenact a commitment to significant subversive possibilities. Coursing through the countryside, the town, and the city, these events underscore the adaptive and portable character of these gatherings and their potential to fuel social movements.

The power of performers and celebrants to knit together various styles and traditions into one moment of celebration stuns onlookers unused to such propulsive displays. In these acts, the history of the creole world is embodied, rehearsed, and replayed. Here are found the newest old creole styles of moving together: jumping up, surging, strutting, jamming. These mass dance-frenzies are commonly accompanied by groups of clowns and by more serious groups, such as the Landship sailors or the Army Nurses, who perform drill maneuvers in a stately manner as they march by the reviewing stand.

The early reports of New World crossroads resonate with the profusion of noise. These worrisome sounds resisted sense; they seemed to communicate and be interpretable, but were never quite understood. The cobbling-together of styles of song and dance, marching and competitions within these new creole worlds promised the possibility of social and spiritual renewal. But this dizzying world also elicited anxieties surrounding its challenges to civilization: sexual abandon, eating strange foods prepared in an alien manner, even hints of cannibalism. Most important for the present argument, creole societies seemed to spawn the alteration of systems of expression.

The New World venture brought fears of contagions of all sorts: failure of all those involved to live by the simplest rules of custom; failure implicit in risky business carried out by piratical adventurers and land speculators able to claim license to carry out actions of a dubious nature. The denizens of creole worlds were duplicitous people living at the edge of metropolitan surveillance and control. The mixture of European, Mediterranean, West and Central African, and indigenous peoples coming together in these enterprises created a culturally unstable and economically unfeasible milieu after the first phase of the sugar and tobacco crazes.

The term creolization seeks to capture the recombinatory power of the cultures of what I dub *mixteryi*, which the forced dislocation of Africans and European peasants translated into those mixed forms and styles which animate popular culture throughout the contemporary world. Without the agonizing history of dislocation taking place as the modern emporium economy emerged, the process of creolization becomes just one more name for the modernist or cosmopolitan project, which encourages the coming-together and superimposition of peoples from many different parts of the world in a metropolitan polity. I fear any erasure of the harsh history of the massive dislocation of peoples, whether enslaved or emancipated. These emergent vernacular forms can only be fully understood as they comment and reenact this often violent past. That these reenactments are also carried out in a sea of laughter and celebration makes them especially interesting for those interested in exploring the range of human expressive possibilities.

In sum, *creole* has undergone a transvaluation. The term has gravitated away from a sociopolitical set of meanings toward a more neutral, global term for the many ways in which different cultural forms are fused. The overtly confrontational attitude arising from the conditions of creole communities does not effectively get noncreoles to listen to overloud messages reminding the reading world of the ways in which the history of dislocation and enslavement, economic hardship, and political marginalization is connected to any mixture of styles achieved through entertainment forms of display. We pursue the very idea of creolization at our own risk if we forget the more deleterious attitudes toward racial admixture which heretofore have been implied by the term.

Creole Degeneracy

Conditions in the marketplace magnified the instability of creole outposts. In the Old World, both in Europe and Africa, trade was carried out at periodic fairs and markets, often through bringing together merchants from many places, alighting in a locale for a few days, and therefore not subject to the legal systems of the sedentary members of the host community. Markets were filled with noise, tumult, lying, high theatricality, loose behavior, and a recognition that people of many different sorts gathered there.

The market gathering draws upon the fiction of what Marshall Sahlins called "negative reciprocity": "the unsociable extreme" of exchange behavior in which attempts may be made "to get something for nothing . . . [not only by] 'haggling' or 'barter,' but through outright chicanery and even theft" and other varieties of seizure (Sahlins 1972). It thus contrasts clearly with exchanges carried out within the family or the community, which are often surrounded with ritual gestures to confirm or transform relationships.

Acts of negative reciprocity do no more or less than other enactments of exchange relationships; the act of exchange is carried on within a licensed environment in which there is an intense awareness of the event. But more than face-to-face trading is carried out at the places in which diverse peoples gather; other kinds of suspect intercourse and secret undertakings occur there as well. Such matters are especially salient in addressing the question of creolization, for at marketplaces all kinds of expressive activity take place in which the performers cannot rely on mutual intelligibility between themselves and their audience. The subjects and topics of local enactments must be universalized, or at least made more general. Large-scale eye- and ear-catching devices are employed to build what is called today an audience or consumer base.

Wherever trade was carried out in these distant market zones, one would find members of traditional trading cultures: Levantines, Jews, Portuguese, and representatives of the great Italian broker families. New World markets included sailors on shore, that most volatile of mix of exotic and feared men. On shipboard they might be tightly controlled by a rigid hierarchy, but on shore there was little to contain them under colonial conditions (Hugill 1967).

The peoples that followed the privateers and the first European colonists knit themselves into European markets, even as they changed the way in which production was carried out. Both fear and wonder were contained within the profusion of goods and the mixture of peoples engaged in these practices. A very real social and physical fear of contagion centered on actual sites of market exchange throughout the expanding emporium economy. The presence of traders in exotic garb further intensified this sense of strangeness.

Under conditions of enslavement, both on the sea and in the new colonies, an even greater set of fears was introduced. The greater the number of languages drawn upon in carrying out this trade, the higher the possibility of secret cabals which might betray the order of the official worlds. Getting rich and consorting with the Devil often seemed the same thing, as planters and their agents were enriched by their ventures. White creoles came to be associated with not only with vast wealth but with spiritual slovenliness, physical laziness, insanity, brutality, and double-dealing.

The social historian Karen Kupperman points out that "Criolian degeneracy" was "a theme of transatlantic discourse almost from the moment of settlement" (Kupperman 1995: 23). Characters like Lady Rochester, the mysterious madwoman in the attic in *Jane Eyre*, are stock figures in British literature. The Grub Street pamphleteer Ned Ward pointed to the conditions that produce such figures: "Jamaica . . . the Dunghill of the Universe, the receptacle of vagabonds . . . the Sanctuary of Bankrupts, and the Close-stool for the Purges of our Prisons." The place is "As Sickly as an Hospital, as Dangerous as the Plague, as Hot as Hell, and as Wicked as the Devil" (Ward 1700: 13). Such a gathering of appalling traits, while not always phrased in such lampooning language, revealed a common European stereotype of New World settlements, especially those in the tropics.

The promised New World riches dreamed of by European investors and adventurers were often overshadowed by the anxieties attending overseas settlement. Both French and British tropical and semitropical enterprises were described by travelers in such terms. One source of this fear and fascination with depravity and decadence lay in the traumatic engagement with conditions at the edge of the European colonizing efforts (Abrahams and Szwed 1983). Plantations may have been conceived as rational agricultural enterprises. In practice, however, the civilizing process itself underwent a test as a new breed of humans came into being, the issue of an unstable blend of upward-striving dislocated metropolitan Europeans, indentured servants, native peoples, and enslaved Africans.

Few of these freewheeling figures developed any love of the land or allegiance to a *patria* in the New World. Both Europeans and Africans continued to look to places in the Old World as home. The historian Ira Berlin calls the ambiguous figures who emerged within this system on both sides of the ocean "Atlantic creoles," designating their point of origin as the west coast of Africa where commercial go-betweens of various sorts came together. "Many served as intermediaries, employing their linguistic skills, and the familiarity with the Atlantic's diverse commercial practices, cultural conventions, and diplomatic etiquette to mediate between African merchants and European sea captains. . . . Others played fast and loose with their diverse heritage, employing whichever identity paid best" (Berlin 1996: 254–55).

New World colonizing experiences were accursed. Market traders were feared not only for their habit of keeping multiple account books but also for lying and fast talking in face-to-face encounters. The actual processes of trading strained the limits of language and other modes of expressive exchange. Within the strange lingua franca endemic to the market, new ways of interacting developed. Sometimes these modes of communication were regarded as a secret held by the masters and overseers, but often enslaved peoples participated as well. Different kinds of exchange emerged as those carrying divergent modes of expression intermingled.

Peoples with various ways of expressing themselves, both within and outside the market zone, participated in the formation of new expressive forms in a range of locations. The diversity and admixture involved in this process was especially clear in creoles' self-generated entertainments. The creole world generated a whole range of zones and modes of mixing, from more or less secret sexual and social intercourse to public imitations of other groups' stylized festival enactments.

Europeans often found themselves in situations in which their inherited customary practices, especially the family, were not responsive to their altered circumstances. Most plantation settlements were established without European women and children (Kupperman 1980). Just as the technology of cultivation appropriate to the climate and crops spread from one plantation to the next, so too were domestic practices of housing and food cultivation, preparation, and consumption altered for both slaves and masters. The darkest side of this social experiment, the shockingly brutal treatment of slaves, must also be regarded as a cultural development of the New World. Techniques of surveillance and control were conceived and implemented under such newly unequal conditions that punishments found throughout Europe were made much more severe as Africans came to be regarded as property. The result, from the perspectives of all involved, was regarded as unique and widely referred to in terms of its creole character.

The degree of direct control required to maintain plantations led, on the surface, to the dissolution of most vestiges of Old World cultures. Europeans were especially conscious of the deterioration of civil norms among their own kind. White creoles, especially in the anglophone parts of the Caribbean region, were seen as contaminated by the system, taken to laziness, barbarity, and licentiousness in eating, drinking, and matters of sexual congress. The cultural dislocation was even more profound within the slave populations. In the face of this deracinating principle, however, slaves developed a new mnemonic system in which both Africa and the plantation found a place.

The ongoing historical and geographical disjunctions of the creole experience continue to animate the present. Agents of empire and commerce created outposts on both sides of the Atlantic, audaciously mixing a wide variety of transient peoples and asking that they forge a society which would wrest tangible riches from these lands. It is no exaggeration to say that African forms were as deeply coded in their most intense moments of song, dance, and parade as were English forms, when colonials saluted visiting dignitaries, celebrated the King's Birthday, or conducted religious observances. Each group witnessed the other's public performances, so imitation went both ways across cultural boundaries.

Travelers were dispatched to judge and report on these enterprises in the expansionist experiment. This appraisal focused not only on economic matters but also on the relative success of carrying the benefits of civilization to these outposts. Whether the observers saw the enterprise as successful or not, all commented in one way or another on the customs and mores of the creole people they encountered. Some, like the polemicist Ned Ward, used the occasion to play on fears of cultural difference. Others attempted to woo Europeans to the colonies through the promise of material and social gain.

For Europeans, unmooring subjects from their homeland and setting them up at the perimeters of the European sphere of influence tested the viability of the rationalizing and civilizing processes. The test became all the more intense as another dislocated population, enslaved Africans, was added to mix. Using the style of social thought inherited from the European manorial system, slaves were to be slotted into the position of serfs or peasants—or so the theory went, before realities on the ground reshaped social relations.

Markets and Festivals

Localized markets, run by female slaves who were often called higglers, operated entirely separately from long-distance colonial exchange and almost independently from white control (Mintz 1971, 1974a, b; Simmonds 1987; Jordan 1993: 86–124; McDonald 1993: 29–30, 2001; Dayan 1995: 133). Not only were the higglers independent, but they held both land and personal property legally, a fact that was not fully taken into account in the classic scholarship on the Black Atlantic. The literature on the opposition of respect and reputation, which emerged in the early 1970s, was based on ground-level observations of categorical moral distinctions (Abrahams 1983; Burton 1997). To be sure, the markets were found in the same districts as storehouses and factories used in transshipping the cash crop. Not only was there a good deal of secondary and often illicit trade between those involved in transshipping, but certain liberties were taken by the slaves that were widely recognized by the masters even if they did not like to acquiesce in them.

All forms of material exchange in the New World, but especially marketing itself, were affected by this alternative system of exchange carried on by the slaves. I do not mean to ignore the presence and importance of indigenous marketing systems in Mesoamerica and the South American continent. But one of the most remarkable features of African American forms of expression, much remarked upon by visitors to the areas of African enslavement within the plantation world, was the development of periodic markets by the slaves. Encouraged to produce their own provisions in their off hours, the slaves raised surplus crops and livestock which they sold in these recurrent local trade-events. These might be enslaved peoples, but they maintained their African-based traditions of hoe agriculture, kin-based labor, and weekly markets.

These markets became zones for the development of other creole forms of expressive culture as well. Creolized holidays came to reside at the center of the annual production cycle from the slaves' perspective. Christmas in the Eastern Caribbean and seaboard states and Carnival further south provoked licentious displays of the most bizarre sort, in which the vocabularies of both Old World culture areas were drawn upon and combined with practices arising from the plantation experience. The songs and dances, costuming and music-making emerging from the slave quarters on such occasions first attracted notice to creole identities. Here a vernacular impulse operated even under the most severely restrictive conditions. From this openly improvised and protean concoction, positive attitudes toward creolization emerged.

Such liberties were developed from the system of allowances given slaves in the face of the tight surveillance and control exercised by planters. In many areas of the Caribbean, as well as the Carolina and Georgia Low Country and Louisiana, it was common practice on large plantations to provide slaves with plots of land to grow their own provisions, as well as to raise goats, sheep, cows, pigs and fowl. These plots of ground were one of the most important entitlements to the enslaved population. Here slaves produced most of their own daily fare; they sold the surpluses to town-dwellers and even the planters themselves. Both provisions and livestock were regarded as the property of the slaves. In addition, the production of woven and field-baked ceramics was encouraged in some areas. These items were then entrusted to a higgler, who carried and sold at the Sunday markets in town. Whether or not these figures were adaptations of African practices (Mintz 1971 and 1974b argue otherwise), the very presence of women marketers in a slave society confounded common-sense notions of European traders and other visitors, contributing to the conviction that in the New World social travesty was a constant possibility. Not only were these slave entrepreneurs; they were also women selling the products of male labor and craft (Abrahams and Szwed 1983: 23–24, 93–95; Dayan 1995: 133–34).

To this day, these market women are regarded as the sharpest tongued representatives of those living in a village economy. They are delegated the role of intermediary in taking the provisions to market and selling aggressively there. Held in great fear as well as high regard by villagers, they are known not only for their abilities to contend in this tumultuous environment but also to perform with high wit and strident voices.

The importance of this small independency was noted by many travelers, at least in passing. Typical of such observations is the document written by Eliza Chadwick Roberts, wife of a working sailor with whom she sailed to Jamaica in 1805. Contrasting the exertions of the slaves with the indolence of the planters, Roberts noted: "I do not wonder that the people in general loose [sic] their health for want of exercise is enough to Ruin their Constitutions. they pay no Regard to the Sabbath, but keep it a day of Mirth."

The slaves shared in this disregard of the Sabbath, but did so for other reasons. Roberts reported:

the negroes on that day have ther market and Carry to town the produce of the island, they all have some little spot of ground allotted to them and Sabbath they Cultivate it and bring the produce ass itt is fit to Sell to the shipping in the harbor, and with the profit arising from there small sales, they deck themselves out with trinkets and other finery. they assemble Large partys in the Orange and pomento groves, some with bells, others with Callebaties filld with Seeds and little pebbles which they shake and make a noise, the same as with tamborens. they all play there own tunes and dance for hours together. this is all there Recreation, and some are so active that they will dance with burdens on there heads for hours and not dislodge it. (Roberts 1805: 68, quoted in Klepp and MacDonald 1997: 11)

While Roberts was clearly fascinated by the twin tumults of the market and the dance, she saw both as evidence of the continuing ignorance of the slaves: "for they are never taught that they are Rational beings and have a soul to be Saved."

The Sunday markets deepened the apprehension of strangeness attached to slave life even among those attracted by this demonstration of independence in the midst of enslavement. It was widely acknowledged that something secret must be going on that provided the occasion for any congregation of the slave population. This fear was intensified by the sale of the herbs and roots used in *obeah* healing and spell-casting, which suggested that markets were frequented by conjurors, rootworkers, or practitioners of *obeah*. Bringing together this fear with the tumult of the market and the exuberance of the entertainments afterward begins to account in some degree for the dreadful fascination with similar events which developed after emancipation.

The life of enslaved Africans and African Americans on the plantations provided the entertainment forms of these societies, and the protean capacities of the slaves to adapt to commercial conditions proved a source of fascination and anxiety for Western observers. In forms of performance and celebration arising within the greater plantation world, these observers uncovered a cauldron of creativity which confounded European notions of artistic production. Virtually each New World area developed its own festive and ritual display forms and its own song and dance styles, which became synonymous with the creole peoples found there. The offerings in each area are vast, typifying the emporium economy as it entered into the imagination of the rest of the world.

Developing within political and economic structures dictated from European centers and with access to the discourses and ideologies of nation-state and empire, these colonies seized upon the European apparatus of Romantic nationalism in arguing for independence. They adopted the land/language/lore framework for asserting national character differences. But the creole language clearly doesn't come from the land, and the relationship between the creole peoples and those who represent the indigenous or aboriginal peoples is far from relaxed. Creolization as a process is acknowledged by creole peoples at the point at which they must engage in differential identity formation. Two moves are fused in this moment: differentiating the nation from the colonial metropole, and forging a national cultural unity among diverse peoples. It is only in the postcolonial era that the transvaluing of creole is accomplished (Condé 1995). Under these conditions, the acquired historical guilt of the imperial or colonial states may be used within the context of the argument from victimization, and creole forms become signs of resistance to European domination.

The stylistics of creole forms of performance and celebration come to represent the cultural independency of these overseas outposts, thereby herniating the hegemony of the *patria*. The blend of peoples at these points of convergence developed unique styles, based in some part on the amalgamation of the vocabularies of celebration developed in the new climes. New ways of eating and drinking, singing and dancing not only confected but soon become icons of local identity. As they begin to receive metropolitan exposure, these new songs and dances, new foods, and transformed ways of speaking create fads or even addictions.

Those able to capitalize on this once-strong sense of removal relocate arguments for identity into expressive cultural forms: dances, songs, stories of endurance and creativity under the yoke of historical conditions. This is especially notable in festive productions and presentations, where the same themes of All We Be One emerge, even in foreign climes. In Trinidad, Carnival becomes an image of cultural confluence for the creative moment, especially as historical victimization and the achievement of a sense of community through performance is reenacted in a variety of celebratory moments (Kinser 1990; Stuempfle 1995; Burton 1997; Tokofsky 1999).

Creole Memories and National Futures

Creole cultures and the process of creolization remain mystified. Creole peoples share with other dislocated and socially marginalized peoples the stigma of having to emigrate constantly. When they do make a place for themselves, their space is bounded from without, lest the disorder they bring spill over into the dominant society. Yet from mobility and mixture comes creative innovation. Many of the emergent creole forms of display and celebration emanate from the streets and yards of the most hard-bitten urban neighborhoods; the barrios, favelas, and ghettos which those in power continue to regard as contaminated and potentially contagious. Finally, the results of creole vernacular creativity come to public notice through their commodification—that is, their employment in a cosmopolitan literature intended for noncreole-speaking audiences (Brathwaite 1984; Chamberlain 1993; Condé 1995; Price and Price 1997). Postcolonial communities situated within the New World Order and its global economy find themselves living at the unraveling edges of empire. The creole world begins to capitalize on its culture in the development of both a tourist economy and a diasporic manner of arguing nationality. Here visitors on holiday enter into the local economy and the stylistic forms engendered within the creole world are exported, the two movements occurring simultaneously.

The historical remnants of colonial enterprises left behind as the various Western imperial projects collapsed now insist that within this experience lie the roots of their new cosmopolitan nationalism. The creole languages and expressive forms which were the products of their vernacular genius become the basis on which a new, vitalized national identity is formulated. If the imperial nation-states are able to imagine themselves into being and generate their own rights of eminent domain, manifest destiny, and their own rationale of divine sanction for pursuing empire, why not those who inherited the ruins of this dream?

Chapter 14
Diasporas

Diaspora, according to the *Oxford English Dictionary*, is defined generally, as the condition of being dispersed among an alien people, and particularly, as the scattering of the Jews among the Gentiles since the eighth and sixth centuries B.C.E. *Diaspora*, according to contemporary culture, is defined metaphorically as all of life outside the walls of your own home. Diaspora created a new religion of a demolished temple, a disintegrated past. If Talmudists are to be believed, the temple will remain in ruins till kingdom come. Judaism became the religion of permanent waiting, of marking time and whiling away the years in a land that is always foreign, pressed in between packed suitcases. Diaspora expresses, not only longing, but also fear of returning to your people's lost past. Diaspora is the refusal to go back home made sacrosanct (Zinik 2004: 12).

The Contradictions of Diasporic Consciousness

A secular Jewish American, I grew up in a family of talkers, but not arguers. Our tense dinnertime conversations were relieved by ongoing family jokes and punctuated by whisper-terms, names for mysterious, intimate subjects that one would never presume to discuss outside the family. These charged terms included any word given in Yiddish and the word Yiddish itself. Yiddish was the language of refugees—a word that my parents whispered as "refuges," as if it were a set of welcoming places rather than a homeless condition in which people found themselves. The discourse of the Jewish charities that both my parents supported used "refugees" as if it were a shameful condition. These newcomers brought with them a way of thinking about possessions that had those involved in the giving very uncomfortable. There were a bit too many schnorers (entitled wheedlers) involved, and thus, especially for the German Jewish segment of the community, people who did not know how to say "thank you." Many well-established American Jews of German descent had regarded new immigrants from Eastern Europe with a mixture of charitable condescension and anxious concern, providing them with assistance so that assimilated Jews would be seen as taking care of their own and would not be stigmatized by the enthusiastic religious observance and working-class or peasant ways of their coreligionists from elsewhere. So the arrival of desperately needy refugees from the supposedly more civilized parts of Europe was doubly fraught. Ultimately, the existence of refugees reminded Jews who felt secure in America that they, too, were part of an involuntary diaspora; more immediately, the new arrivals threatened the social acceptance that those who had immigrated generations before smugly enjoyed.

My parents, like many of their class, kept the family seats in the synagogue but never attended, even at the High Holidays. Nevertheless, their active involvement brought them into contact with the problem on an everyday basis. There was a lot of talk about what it meant to be the "chosen people," but that subject was Americanized; my parents and other like-minded people of their generation talked about ghettoization as a failure of enlightened Americans to make the free choices to which we were entitled. They spoke *sotto voce* of the disparity between the ancient wisdom regarding the return to the "promised land" and the redemption of the world, on the one hand, and the mounting pressures among Jews to translate this dream into an argument for a Jewish state located in the Middle East, on the other. Because my parents were accommodationists and assimilationists politically, yet public Jews when non-Jews would ask "the big question," even the word Jew was half-whispered, as if the identification should always be qualified, at least within the family circle.

Whatever edge of survivor guilt my parents may have felt was assuaged through the narrative poem that my father wrote and published in the *Saturday Evening Post* called "A Shopkeeper Dies: Vienna 1938"; its publication resulted in the magazine being banned in Germany and Austria. Acting on his assimilationist beliefs, my father served as the local honorary consul of the Dominican Republic and negotiated an arrangement with the government of the dictator Raphael Leonidas Trujillo for land and transportation to be provided for thousands of Jewish families from Poland who emigrated to that Caribbean outpost. The dispersal of the Jews was visible in our reading of the news virtually every day. But the word diaspora was one of the whisper-words, along with "beyond the Pale." *Diaspora* appeared to be a shorthand term for the inability of Jews to obtain sufficient power to confront repressive European regimes.

Although all of the children went to public schools, we inhabited a ghetto of our own imaginings, for we lived on the same street as many of our cousins and their cousins. Branded as Jews and self-identified as Americans, we were also at risk of being condemned as anti-Semites by our neighbors because we were anti-Zionist. This set of multiple identifications made all of us prematurely and defensively aware of the array of arguments against the idea of a Jewish homeland. In our dinnertime conversations at home, the goodwill principle of family interaction was self-consciously enforced. Each of us was expected to act on our individual right to enter into the discussion, whether we knew anything about the subject or not. We needed intellectual armament for the intense scrutiny of other Jews.

As assimilationists, we were supposed to go on record as being Americans first, and then as Jewish if anyone asked. Here, all of the erasures of the European and Mediterranean dispersals of the Jews were subsumed under the principle of its being good to move, especially to a better place. After the war was over, family trips were organized around the sites where American freedom was made, moving outward from Philadelphia to Washington, D.C., Mount Vernon and Monticello, Harper's Ferry and the rest of the John Brown and Abraham Lincoln trail (the two were often elided in our imagination), and the Civil War battlefields with the ritual incantation of the Gettysburg Address. If the family table-talk was intense, imagine the car-talk carried on by the many Abrahams. These long trips challenged family ideals and the goodwill principle for our generation, yet they were also a bonding experience. As we undertook pilgrimages to honor and reenact the sacred American past, we learned the legends of the Founding Fathers and of the ongoing struggles Americans endured to attain emancipation in every generation.

Our difference from our ancestors and our counterparts in Nazi Germany and occupied Europe was that our trips were vacations planned in advance and replete with choices, not the result of forced migration or dispersal. We were not fleeing for our lives. We children were always acutely aware of that difference, even while we were taught never to speak of it directly.

What American Jews first imagined as prison camps and then recognized as death camps informed us, as it reminded all Jews of previous historical expulsions. The horrors that we could not prevent dwarfed the numbers we could deliver from bondage. My parents talked elliptically about the deaths of distant relatives. We did not know exactly what had happened to them, but we knew full well they had perished. Since we had not kept in contact with them anyway, the sense of guilt and loss was overwhelming, but muted. Highlighted by the peril faced by those who had remained behind, our consciousness of being safe in our new home in the New World was a matter of comment on every family occasion. My father had more immediate reasons for identifying with this pervasive sense of loss and disaster, since the 1929 crash and the ensuing depression had led to the suicide of his father and his inheritance of what was referred to as "the family responsibilities."

When my father bought his first house for us, the poet-prophet in him decided that he would call it "Henceforth," for the Bible said that "Henceforth the name of thy house shall be Abraham." Tellingly, this pronouncement comes when God ordered Abram to leave his father's house and changed his name. "Henceforth" is still the home of my first imaginings, but within a year of my mother's death it was put up for sale, proven to be a white elephant, and finally sold without a murmur of protest from the rest of the family.

So it is with many Americans: we look back nostalgically to the idea of home while looking out for the next chance to get a move on. The land of liberty, opportunity, and freedom to choose has often meant escaping in search of—who knows what?—somewhere else. Non-Native Americans, even those whose distant ancestors arrived on these shores many generations ago, are people with itchy feet. The ideal of the self-sufficient family homestead is a memorial to a promise or a delusion. The broken promises return to haunt us like absent or missing relatives at family reunions; the shattered delusions shadow our memories of the past, when we imagined a future redemption that has not come.

The Tangled Roots of Nostalgia

Nostalgia began life as a term for a minor characterological problem which, when medicalized, might be treated like other psychosomatic conditions. It originated in the late eighteenth century as the diagnostic term for the home-sickness suffered by young Swiss men who were commandeered to military service and sent to foreign parts, which included places within Switzerland that lay beyond the soldiers' natal villages and valleys. But the Swiss were hardly the first to experience this longing. Nostalgia is as pervasive as "the good old days." Seeing it in pathological terms, even in the nonmedical vernacular, obscures the positive energy and commitment to utopian values involved in looking back longingly and lamenting the passing of a simpler time and friend-lier community. In retreat from the tendency to see such feelings as debilitat-ing conditions, other terms for a more usable past are elevated in public discussions: patriotism, tradition, heritage.

Nostalgia may be simply a displacement of the feelings of voluntary emi-grants, especially those who felt guilty for leaving home and family behind. Perhaps the act of moving on always carries with it a complex set of abandon-ments. The children and grandchildren of European immigrants who left their rural homesteads for the city expressed most acutely their ancestors' sense of loss at coming to America. So, too, those who moved West voiced their long-ing for the long-settled East, with its dense kin networks and close communi-ties. Nostalgia seems an inevitable outgrowth of a commercial economy and a cast of mind which valorizes individual and social movement in search of a better life. Every move intensifies this yearning for the familiar people and home places left behind.

Ironically, the figures who embody our lamentation for the lost past are precisely those who arise from the historical ruptures inherent in "taming the wilderness." We honor most deeply, not those who were "moving up by mov-ing on," but the sole surviving representatives of all those peoples who were pushed off the map by this relentless imperial westering. The quintessential figures are the Native Americans who represent the last of their tribe: "Who will mourn for Logan when he is gone?" Even the vestiges of the old plantation regime are objects of nostalgia: Joel Chandler Harris's Uncle Remus; Old Black Joe, whose refrain is "I hear the voices calling"; and Dilsey in Faulkner's *Intruder in the Dust*, whose repeated life-lesson is "I seed de fus' and I seed de last." This perspective also lies at the center of "Home on the Range," which was erroneously purported to be F. D. R.'s favorite folk song. The lyrics celebrating the place "where seldom is heard a discouraging word" also lament the disappearance of the buffalo, another symbol of dissolution and loss.

If such nostalgia arises even from voluntary departures, what are the consequences of involuntary exile? Those who were captured in Africa, transported across the Atlantic, and enslaved in America suffered a soul-death more profound than even their descendants can imagine. Sundered from village communities, they were bereft not only of husbands and wives, mothers and fathers, siblings and cousins but also of ancestors whose spirits offered protection and guidance. No wonder that some Africans threw themselves into the sea during the Middle Passage and that so many kidnapped women refused to bear children in the New World. The miracle is that their creole children recreated kinship ties, often based on the generous fictions adopted by shipmates and covillagers, and became attached to new home places, from which they were again uprooted and sent south and west to settle the Cotton Kingdom. In moving and mixing, enslaved peoples of African descent forged a common culture knit together with loss and longing.

"Welcome, Pilgrim"

Exile, involuntary migration, and voluntary transplantation are not the only conditions that elicit nostalgia, nor are repeated, restless, and self-reinforcing patterns of movement its only byproducts. Land enclosure and the highland clearances also amount to a banishment which surely creates the root condition from which the impulse to collect folklore arises.

Nostalgia is the familiar companion of ethnographers. Whenever I have gone away to do fieldwork for an extended period, even when I identify strongly with those among whom I seek to live, I nevertheless feel isolated and forgotten by all the important people back home. And then, when I return, I receive letters from the new friends I left behind asking for help in escaping their insular situations. The photographs I send recording our friendship and the crafted objects that we exchange maintain the feelings of hope and fear attached to such lost and found connections. As Susan Stewart has argued, almost every object carried away from such sites is a container of longing; indeed, the practice of putting together a collection emerges from the wellspring of nostalgia (Stewart 1984).

Change over time as well as movement in space gives rise to nostalgia, and in a settler society like America these two dynamics are often powerfully coupled. Such fears and longings tinge even our characteristic appreciation of the sublimity of the wilderness. If we Americans have a pride of place, it resides not in the geographical vastness of the New World but in designated national monuments. More often than not, these places are the gifts of nature formed long before human settlement (Sears 1998). The national monuments make a claim, contra Old World values and vanities, of a patrimony as old as time, the creations of a beneficent spirit who shed his grace on the land and its present inhabitants. We conveniently forget that these natural wonders were created eons before the achievements of any Western Empire and even the first human footsteps on this continent. We put boundaries around them, lest we be over-come by their sheer vastness, and we interpret their historical depth in terms of their recent "discovery" in order to assimilate them to national purposes.

If the sundering of intimate ties based on shared experience is the com-mon legacy of becoming American, then how is a new sense of group identity constructed? A convenient fiction must be reinstalled constantly to remind those coming together through conversation and citizenship that the ideal of equal access and universal belonging is achievable among those who act in a friendly manner. Commonly, stories of uprooting, moving on, leaving behind, trying to keep in touch, and having to live in alien lands would hardly be con-sidered *success stories*. Yet that is exactly how they are viewed in the wake of a voluntary mass migration, after they have been transmuted into tales of endur-ance and ultimate triumph. Such stories contain lessons about the setbacks experienced and sacrifices made while on the move. But, even more often, these stories of cataclysmic events carry strong messages of historical victim-ization. They hold such things on account, like money in the bank to be drawn on in the future, creating a fund of stories centering on the hard times and especially the ever-present missed opportunities.

The goodwill principle and the success story may well have emerged from the privations and loneliness of early European settlers in America and their hunger for company whenever a friend or stranger passed by. From the seven-teenth century through the Revolution, *Pilgrim's Progress* was second only to the Bible in importance. This poem's image of the pilgrim stranger wandering lonely, the wayfarer who can only stay a little while, was echoed in the nine-teenth-century custom of calling strangers "pilgrim." The vernacular greeting, "Welcome, pilgrim," comes from the verse of a popular hymn: "I am a pilgrim and a stranger/wandering through this wearisome world." In this sense, his-torically, we are on a constant pilgrimage through a worrisome and uncertain world. Dreams are made to be dreamed, not to be realized, except from the retrospective distance of generations. We dream of going to new places and starting new lives, but—at least before transoceanic flights and satellite trans-mission—those who do pay a terrible cost in the loss of connections with kin and homeland. The diaries and letters of European American settlers on the Prairies and Plains reek of loneliness, dislocation, and longing. But they also tell of the pleasures of protracted visits and the times when the far-flung community gathered to celebrate their accomplishments by working and playing, eating and drinking together, at a corn-shucking, barn-raising, harvest bee, or frolic.

Americans are inclined to call one another by our first names and to open up to other wayfarers on first encounters. Climbing into a long-distance bus, plane, or train entails inviting conversation. Casual friendliness is the norm, whether we like it or not, and if we don't want to talk, we have to develop strategies of silence. If we bury our heads in a book or assume a vacant look, our new neighbors will get out a mobile phone and force us to overhear their very personal chatter. Keeping in touch while in motion has become an obsession. A quick ethnographic survey of phone-answering messages, especially those which reassure us we have reached someone when we obviously haven't, reveals how upbeat we are even while missing a connection. The dynamics of disconnection and reconnection with intimate friends and of close encounters with complete strangers which arise from mobility shape our everyday lives.

In this drama of continuous departures and longings for return, family secrets swirl around personal ruptures and social disjunctions. Many stories concern who lost a fortune in the crash and committed suicide out of despair; others name those who ran away, were cast out, or just disappeared. Such tales are not linear; they offer no causal explanations; what endings they have resolve nothing. Every family has a black sheep, but how would we know? They are seldom discussed within the fold except in whisper-words. The migration of intact families was far from the norm; many wives and children got left behind as the men simply decamped. If we share a cast of mind on the dark side of the vernacular, it arises from such sudden encounters with the abyss. We discover many stories that go untold, absent kinfolk who are only mentioned in passing at family gatherings.

The most repeatable stories are not those accounting for family successes, but those recounting the dramatic failures and ruptures occurring at critical times. Such tales of lost fortunes and fractured relationships underscore the notion that freedom resides most fully in being able to start over. The stories that stick with most families are not those of finding a vocation or location in life, but of what we might call the American Dread, stories about how we account for our lives and what causes relationships to dissolve. Stories of endurance, yes, but also of strange diseases of body and mind that just might be carried in the genes. How often do these stories color our lives as we assess our present situation and our inheritance of the anxiety of displacement?

Tales of Longing and Belonging

Nostalgia was carried in the trunks of our ancestors from abroad, at least by those who had possessions to bring and the time to pack them, and in the minds and hearts of those who brought no physical baggage. Across oceans and continents, such baggage was transported by women in defense of whatever civilities they had been able to accrue before the move. For enslaved Africans, the problem of leaving cultural artifacts behind was even more profound, but a cascade of recent scholarship demonstrates that Africans carried on their bodies as well as in their minds traces of memories on which they based African American practices of dance, music, speech, worship, and healing (Herskovits 1958; Abrahams and Szwed 1977; Gundaker 1998). Native American practices, too, were based on stories that still percolate among displaced peoples, most notably the Trail of Tears. Within some ethnic communities, narratives of how people came here are connected with expulsion rather than with the desire to "follow one's star." Jews, Armenians, Scots, Irish, Chinese, and many others remember experiences of captivity, displacement, and homelessness in their native places and then at Ellis Island or Angel Island, Galveston, or Boston, where new selves were invented, often by gatekeepers who were not entirely welcoming. The parallels between these immigrant stories and those of Americans who moved west—of their hostile encounters with landowners, blizzards, and dust storms—are outgrowths of the lives of restless people moving on, or being moved unceremoniously.

These ubiquitous stories achieve the status of myth: a mere mention of one disastrous time will bring the rest of the story to mind without the necessity of filling in the details. They often reinforce the goodwill principle because, although they tell of rejection, they also remember those who helped people get through trying transitions and hard times. In the United States, this dynamic animated the Horatio Alger novels (Rodgers 1978) and the Little Orphan Annie complex, providing subsequent generations with a name for getting ahead with the help of such benevolent, even paternalistic figures. Ironically, the Horatio Alger idea has been shorn of the helping figure, becoming a tale of self-improvement through one's own efforts.

In the most remembered version, *The Wizard of Oz*, the orphaned Dorothy has her new home taken from her by a tornado and is transported to an alien land. She soon meets her helping figures, who first get her to the Wizard and then propel her back home. This plot is not just a figment of the imagination of L. Frank Baum writing at the very end of the nineteenth century. When Stephen Spielberg retells it in *E.T.*, the draw of home works even in a jerry-built contemporary suburb, far from the settled life imagined on the family farm or in a rural village. The idea of being taken from home, even a broken home, is as threatening and fascinating as ever. In many contemporary family-fun productions, as in the early English novel, the story is driven by the fact that someone is missing in the structure of the family; orphanhood, a stolen baby, and the need to leave home prematurely to support oneself put such plots into motion. Characters take the quintessential temporary jobs that called for relocation as early as the late seventeenth century. Many protagonists become servants in—between, a nurse, governess, amanuensis, traveling companion, or tutor, outsiders allowed into the family circle but not quite admitted there. Such plots shift subtly as they are translated into modern and postmodern settings. While Dorothy is able to assemble a group of helper friends, E.T. is a total loner, but he becomes a part of a family at this place that just isn't his home.

In such paradigmatic stories, we discover just how central the idea of home is to the constant reproduction of nostalgia. Having a wanderer come into such an environment is still fraught with the fear of estrangement and expulsion. And the retelling reinforces the idea of home, reminding us that life is all about loss. Of course, these are true stories, but their truth matters little. More important are the nostalgic feelings which telling such tales rekindles.

Diasporas and the Forces of Globalization

The difficulty of finding adequate key terms for naming and framing such experiences and perspectives remains, even long afterwards. Social and cultural critics, who in the 1990s shifted their focus from the class structures within the boundaries of polities sharing a language, tradition, and territory to questions of cultural exclusion and cross-cultural encounters, have developed new terms for the diversity generated by a transnational marketplace (Hall 1993; Babha 1993). But the cultural critique has not yet produced the organizing terms for an adequate account of postmodernity. Such terms as *global oecumene*, *mediascape*, and *glocalization* address this terminological void, and self-confessed geeks thrive in the *virtual worlds* of chat rooms. Now we await the judgment of the culture mavens who decide what words become dictionary entries. Neither the scholarly nor the technical jargon has made it into my computer's dictionary or thesaurus, although more up-to-date programs are doubtless for sale at Staples. Those who compiled the word bank on my p.c. are still concerned with maintaining the old line between jargon or slang and real words. They don't include any of the old "neighborly names" like "wop," "Dago," or "Yid," either. This practice is one of many reminders that the rules of thumb of the pre-postmodern world are still very much with us, bumping into the instant inventiveness of those on the cutting edge who attempt to keep up with the ways in which mass-mediated business is transacted. Local cultures are clearly under siege in these open-market milieux, and gross domestic products and balances of trade are compared and discussed as if they had some descriptive and comparative power.

To develop terminological systems that transcend the confines of nation-state analysis, account for the impact of translocal devices of communication, and trace culture flows, critics must transform previous concepts of exchange and hegemony. Disappearing from such discussions are not only the devices of citizenship and bureaucratic organization but also the need to have native exotics within the boundaries as a contrast to urban gatherings. Under the sway of the globalized marketplace, the relationship between maker and user is altered so profoundly that the old ways seem to disappear—rather than simply become encapsulated—in the wake of postmodernity. The study of culture, long defined as the expressive dimension of tightly circumscribed groups with a common language and set of customary practices, can no longer account for the persistence and maintenance of traditional practices, except as relics of past small-group production. The allure of the family and the community is cast as a cultural invention, but one shared by all peoples facing the dislocating circumstances encouraged in the global state that seems to be emerging.

What is left to us is the reassurance of humans still guided by principles of goodwill as they come together to exchange goods, services, and sentiments. As the range of travel grows, nothing becomes more important than the practices continued from the past and the products which carry the stamp of authenticity. Nostalgia for the familiar small group remains at the center of our affections, conveyed primarily by the continuing presumption of goodwill in personal exchanges.

Of the many words used to describe globalization of the work force, *diaspora* has become the term of choice among the attending generations of people who have moved, en masse, away from anywhere they might call a homeland. Heretofore used by Jews to describe their characteristic stance of perching where they are while remaining ready to flee persecution and maintaining their religious customs, the term has been appropriated by many other ethnic groups on the move (Hall 1993). If diaspora were employed simply to describe the dispersion of one or another African, Middle Eastern, or Asian population, one could hardly find fault with such terminological hijacking. But, in its usage among Jews, diaspora also carried the implication of a forced emigration and a continuing history of being ghettoized, forbidden to own land, and cast as willing sufferers when economic conditions demanded their elimination or removal (Boyarin and Boyarin 1993).

Diaspora has lately been attached to the entire range of migratory acts, taken from its original context of describing the "Jewish problem" from inside the Jewish community and employed as a term of art by those in the business of promoting what used to be called "racial pride," "homecoming celebrations," or even "family reunions." Now the term is not only a declaration of a people's shared sense of identity but also a basis for advertising ethnic tourism.

Sometimes, too, it becomes a term for a dislocated and vagrant population, such as Gypsies (to themselves, the Rom), who pose problems for host communities wherever they have migrated. So diaspora and an ironic reading of the meaning of "the chosen people" were conjoined. As Barbara Kirshenblatt-Gimblett observed, the term has always been twinned with *ghetto* as representing the Hobson's Choice for European Jews. "The terms diaspora and ghetto form a linked pair. What is not blamed on one is attributed to (and often entailed by) the other—stranger and marginal man flow from them" (Kirshenblatt-Gimblett 1994: 340). We can add *holocaust* to this list of linked terms.

Diaspora, then, began its life as a term of art with a good many now-silenced voices accusing the critical community of subverting a historical condition for use as a general and unmarked term for any ethnically identified group involved in the global dissemination of work and workers. As with *creolization* and *ethnicity*, this historical two-step seems unentertaining for social observers. Yet, because diaspora is now tied to celebrations of ethnic pride and *ghetto* is tinged with the nostalgia which is also attached to tenement, pushcart, and peddler, the term is certain to remain in general usage. Terms for dispersal call attention not only to social movement but also to historical victimization, so they serve as shorthand for a particular kind of forced emigration.

Using such a portmanteau term tends to erase a folkloristic dialogue, born under late nineteenth-century pluralist realities, which continues to argue that every group's traditions are worthy of collection and dissemination. Particularly in North America, folklorists have brought cultural diversity into the service of intercultural display and celebration. Diversity, difference, and other such terms have had their negative features expunged, and the terror of such forced movements of peoples has been turned into a singular story of "the immigrant experience." Stories relating to African Americans' experiences of enslavement have undergone a similar transformation, as ex-slave narratives, spirituals, and the blues are presented as evidence of resistance or at least an adaptability that made it possible to endure. The old ways of scraping by under conditions of deprivation and duress become evidence of creativity under fire. Traditions are deployed to demonstrate cultural continuities from the Old World to the New through which the past might be recuperated.

Much of my previous work has been dedicated to such a principle: to documenting the continuities of ancient cultural practices in the face of adversity as a way of paying tribute to the human spirit. I have directed my professional capabilities to tracing these old ways into the present in order to acknowledge the numinous qualities of spirit which make them worthy of respect and conservation. As I suggest throughout this book, I continue to be stunned by the resilience of human beings through talk, performance, and celebration with friends and family. Life according to the principle of goodwill continues even in the face of shared terrors. I, too, have dined out on tales of misfortune. As a Jew, how could I ever retreat fully from assigning woes to the cyclical history of expulsion and reception by the anti-Semites who controlled our movements?

Along with many others of my generation, Jews and Blacks and Plain Folk of the rural South, I have found my way to becoming an advocate for those who have been kept in this despised and alienated condition. I have sought to empower "the people" themselves. Why, then, am I so angry at those who now argue for reparations for past inequities? Victims surely are in need of recompense of some sort, as well as an acknowledgment of the burdens of the past. I have the consolation of the new old proverb: "Be careful of what you ask for, as it may be granted." So soon brilliant, so late smart?

This quandary is not uniquely my own, nor is it confined to folklorists and political activists. The problem is embedded in the prevailing vernacular liberal ideology. Many social observers who themselves were born into such a community of past sufferers have urged that awareness of the past be deployed to promote greater tolerance for difference in the present.

A move to make *diaspora* an honorific term is endemic to liberal democracies. For the heritage of dispersals seems to lead inevitably to essentializing geographically and historically distant longing-places and deploying cultural continuities to advertise our plural selves. By demonstrating continuous contact with our hosts, which highlights the cultural borrowings between the powerful and the powerless, hegemonic regimes are legitimized, even prized for their openness. The presumption of goodwill that undergirds our vernacular now seems compromised, even complicit in rationalizing social and economic inequities. Henry Higgins's outrageous question "why can't a woman be more like a man?" doesn't seem so outré when phrased as "why can't they keep their yards as clean as ours?"

Public-spirited folklorists and other ethnographers have been especially adept at finding communities which have maintained the old ways, seeking out the representative artists and exegetes within that community, and putting them in display in the alien setting of the festival ground or the museum. I am not arguing that we should not be doing this, but only that to feel virtuous in so operating in this way is not very attractive. Kirshenblatt-Gimblett has provided a purchase on the problem which draws on her historical reading of the past in the present. "This bankrupt language of influence and imitation, which is endemic to a largely philological preoccupation with cultural genealogy, is central to legitimizing discourses of nationalism"—or regionalism or localism, for that matter. All use the criteria of authenticity, precedence on the land, and ancient rights that rationalize reconquest in the name of purification or cleansing. "Where difference is positively valued on the powerful side of the distinction it marks" she continues, "stigma [may] become . . . the ground of transvaluation," especially when the marks of stigmatization are embedded in particular objects or places of ethnic tourism (Kirshenblatt-Gimblett 1994: 341).

The development of endurance narratives adhering to places and objects of torture, subjection, or enslavement has a serious undertow. Not only does it encourage the commodification of emblems of past misery, but it also creates an ambiguous heritage for succeeding generations. This discursive practice is especially ironic when many people are enduring similar conditions today in detention or relocation camps. The bodies of the disappeared are still being excavated, even while new secret burials are being carried out in Europe, Africa, Asia, and elsewhere. There is no positive side to these stories of displacement. Reparations sidestep the problem, and even put a monetary price on human lives.

European social critics have been forced to acknowledge that in their passion to define class they ignored other power relations based on gender, generation, and ethnicity. Leftist cultural critics castigated the blindness of Marxian theorists to the discriminatory dimension of social and cultural diversity. This critical lacuna has been dramatized especially strongly by European ethnographers trained in North American social science, who serve as brokers of ideas and carriers of goodwill between cultural communities. When Barbro Klein returned to her native Sweden after studying folklore in Indiana and working among immigrant groups in New York City, for example, she recognized how folklore and folklife research might be put to use: as a bridge between the dominant national culture and the alien cultures of new arrivals, and to reveal the adaptive mechanisms of immigrant groups. In the path-breaking work reported in *The Organization of Diversity*, Klein showed how such overlooked activities as gardening might illuminate the larger questions arising as dislocated peoples come to grips with a new environment (Ehn, Klein, Rönstrom, and Sjögren 1990). Through an analysis of various diasporic passages of peoples into alien environments, Klein recognizes how the study of vernacular forms of culture might create conditions of greater understanding in situations otherwise thought of as social problems. Inevitably, dislocated peoples invent an array of stories or adapt old ones to their new situation. Such narrative forms come to the fore as apt subject for folkloristic analysis, as Richard Dorson, Linda Dégh, and Américo Paredes reported a generation ago (Dorson 1952; Dégh 1969; Paredes 1959, 1993).

Whither Folklore?

The discipline of folklore carved out a special place in the bourgeois economic and cultural dynamic. For *the folk* were a construct of the developing nation-states, often as a counterpoint to the banal uniformity of life in a commercializing society. Under these conditions, the folk emerged full-blown as a conglomerate term for those peoples who maintained a sense of connectedness to the past, especially the land. The price of the mobilization of the workforce was reckoned, among other ways, by the stereotypical delineation of those who were presumed to have stayed on the land after the enclosure laws and the consolidation of realms all over Western Europe. The folk were depicted as people who lived by a simpler set of technologies in accord with earlier (and vanishing) social values. Taking on an antimodernist stance, folklorists looked for peoples little affected by the contaminating forces of the commercial and industrial city. Simply by being identified with the land, the folk were constructed as communities responsible for maintaining the active presence of the repositories of the ancient wisdom of place. And to encourage national claims to natural rights to this territory, all of the vernacular forms found in place came to be valued in and of themselves as vestiges of this national past. (For British examples, see Dorson 1968; Hufford 1977; Levine 1986; Parry 1996; Swann 2001.)

Through designating certain peoples as folk, it became possible for Romantic nationalists to reveal what they called national character. Ironically, the tradition-bearing folk themselves proved to be some of the most indigent and marginalized peoples in the polity, but that dismaying fact could be obscured in the excitement of the discovery of the authentic (Bendix 1997). Another contradiction forces itself into our consciousness. For now we must acknowledge that the nostalgic origins of the folk in previous scholarship leads to the idea that stories move, rather than populations, performers, or audiences.

The traditions of dislocated peoples have been the subjects of folklorists' scholarly interest. In North America, the earliest and most pervasive remnants of tradition were discovered among the most mobile and marginal elements of society: "frontiersmen," "pioneers," enslaved peoples, and those who pursued extractive industries, such as cowboys and lumberjacks. The United States, Canada, and Mexico defined themselves differentially as nations by the ways in which they recognized or denied the mixing of peoples that took place during and after colonization. Mexicans celebrated themselves as mestizo; Canadians were bicultural, became bilingual, and are becoming pluri-national. Only the United States established an exclusionary and hierarchical biracial system that denied the experience and legacy of multicultural intermixing. Yet all these North American nations proclaimed an identity that distinguished them from their European antecedents.

The American Folklore Society (AFS), at its founding in 1888, offered a model of how an American social science might serve the needs of an increasingly diverse citizenry. The American character of the new professional organization was spelled out explicitly in the chartering statement. Collection of folklore in North America would be carried out, recorded, and published in the *Journal of American Folklore*. In addition to the "relics of Old English Folklore (ballads, tales, superstitions etc.)," the charter called for collecting "Lore of Negroes in the Southern States . . . Lore of the Indian Tribes (myths, tales, etc.)" and the "Lore of French Canada, Mexico, etc." These etceteras were as important as the groups actually named, for the AFS charter left open other gatherings of indigenous and immigrating peoples, including those just then forming themselves into ethnic communities. Newell pointed out the number of new "nationalities" that might be encountered and how the traditions they brought with them might assist in adapting to their new situation. "Germans, Irish, French Bohemians, and Russians" all "bring to our doors the spectacle of the whole civilized and semi-civilized world," he noted (Newell 1888). Civilization would be served through such collection and publication.

To ensure that local cultures would be addressed, the charter proposed that meetings be held in cities which established chapters of AFS. One of the first, located in Philadelphia, published a charter that mentioned even more immigrant groups in the "various quarters" of the city, including outcast groups such as "roving tinkers, tramps, and Sailors Haunts" (AFS 1890). Philadelphia was then one of the great ports of call. Social scientists there were confronted with a good deal of social ferment, which they approached with the care of those wishing to further the civilizing and Americanizing project. As an 1894 article in *Popular Science Monthly* pointed out, "What our folklore scholars are driving at is the importance of the unwritten tradition . . . while there are time and opportunity" (cited in Abrahams 1988c). While the charter was written by Newell, this perspective reflects the position on race and cultures then being developed by the new immigrant from Berlin, Franz Boas (Boas 1906, 1907, 1938). (The same perspective was voiced in the charter of the American Anthropological Association four years later.) Successive issues of the *Journal of American Folklore* were to focus on each of these groups. The results were mixed, to say the least, but the pattern held for a few years into the twentieth century and remained in the minds of the collectors as an ideal to which they subscribed.

The practice of holding national AFS meetings in various localities to encourage this pluralist agenda continued into the early twentieth century. After initial meetings in Cambridge and Philadelphia, the third was held at the Hampton Institute, and later meetings convened in St. Louis and New Orleans. Most of the literary figures of the time who were devoted to recording local vernaculars were early members, including Samuel Clemens, Joel Chandler Harris, and George Washington Cable. It is only in the last hundred years that these orts and shards of past practices have been taken into account in the development of American culture. In these nations of constantly moving peoples, mobile and landless populations are susceptible to being studied as the repositories of a fiercely distinctive body of traditions. In the U.S., as in many European countries, such groups emerge as the object of study—Jews, Rom, Sami (known to others as Lapps), Szeklars (Transylvanian Magyars who speak a distinctive dialect)—because they provide a thrilling, dark presence in the otherwise sedentary nation.

Other forcefully displaced groups have received a good deal of critical attention, though more often by cultural historians than folklorists. These groups retreated from official centers of power, were often identified as outlaws or renegades, and created outsider communities living in dynamic tension with those from whom they separated. Called "social bandits" or "primitive rebels" (Hobsbawm 1959) in the Old World and "maroon communities" in the New (Price 1983), these groups of fugitives pose some of the most interesting and profound challenges for those attempting to create a unified cultural theory. Under the old dispensation of power within nation-states, these groups are treated by those in control as contaminated and as living in a parasitic relationship with landed people. Jews, Gypsies, and groups of runaways who would not be enslaved are all defined in such terms. Little wonder that, as Richard Price discovered among the Saramakka maroons, they carry secret histories and occluded practices within the group, and bringing this knowledge into the open might result in the dissolution of the spirit of the community (Price 1973).

Such groups of runaways were "discovered," even "invented" as a category by Marxian cultural historians as evidence of popular resistance to the powerful. This dynamic includes what the political theorist James Scott calls "hidden transcripts," the submerged records of subject peoples as they develop techniques of resistance (Scott 1990). Discovering and parsing such transcripts has been the major means of recovering the African element in New World black communities. From W. E. B. Du Bois's idea of "double consciousness" to the voluminous writings on Rabbit or Spider and their kindred spirits, the subversions of an animal trickster have been constructed as representative embodiments of politically useful deceit. Using a trickster figure in this way, or even more dramatically, portraying an animal symbolizing uncivil behaviors in ground-level celebrations, such as Carnival, carries even greater potency in making such statements of semisecret resistance.

The work of Benedict Anderson suggests that these outposts are one kind of "imagined community," cultural inventions created by the ongoing dynamic and symbiotic relationship between the outsiders and the official forces at the center of power. They are real insofar as they live and define themselves in terms of their historical resistance to hegemonic forces. These groups commonly create a hidden history of themselves that establishes the priority of their natural rights to those of the dehumanizing power-brokers from whom they have managed to escape. That they exist as groups only because of their ongoing resistance to such dominance is patent. Anderson explains they "always regard themselves as somehow ancient." In response to the regimes resorting to a history created through the agency of print culture, it proves too "tempting to decipher the community's past in antique dynasties" (Anderson 1983: 101–2). These dynasties must almost always find place in the unofficial and usually oral history of the despised—not only the "first time" narratives of the Saramakka (Price 1983), but the deep literature espousing the Nilotic, Trojan, Roman, or Arabic point-of-origin arguments espoused by now one, now another people.

Recent critical studies of globalization have not been unmindful of the history of both complaint and resistance embodied in the term diaspora. Analyses by James Clifford (1994), Barbara Kirshenblatt-Gimblett (1994), Paul Gilroy (1987, 1992a, b, 1995), and William Safran (1991, 2002), among others, have been widely consulted by theorists concerned with confronting the confusions of what the social philosopher, Jürgen Habermas, includes within the confines of "the post-national condition."

Hijacking Diaspora

Bringing these strands of our study together, let us admit to the possibility of developing ethnographies of dispersals and forced removals that call attention to the improvised traditions of group maintenance, or resistance, of techniques of torture and execution. Such studies have already been carried out for many immigrant populations. In North America, this was one of the major means that folklorists entered into the discourse on pluralism, for each such study demonstrated what a rich cultural repository was to be found here. For example, the American Dream is discussed as a myth of expansive inclusion, in which shared opportunities lie at the center of the life-worlds of all Americans. But parallel to this, though seldom discussed, was the American Dread, the story of individual failure, the loss of family homestead or fortune, and the need to go even further west. Alternatively, the Dread operates in contrast to the communitarian Romance, in stories of moving on to escape the constraints of civilization. We tell stories of moving to where the jobs are, disrupting family and community ties. Both the Dream and the Dread are narratives of disruption and the necessity of adaptability.

One of the many responses to this suppressed narrative of loss and longing—buried to view from the national level, at least—has been the development of massive community homecomings and family reunions. Another response is the reenactment of historically decisive battles. These commemorations, reunions, and homecomings are receiving a great deal of attention from American folklorists and anthropologists.

To refer to other such mobilized communities as diasporic, then, carries with it the strategy of claiming historical victimization and projecting the promise of return. Diaspora has come to the fore as a term for a specific kind of shared nostalgia as manifested in stories, songs, and holidays which highlight the plight of the exiles and the courage of the survivors. Exile and survival are at the heart of most of the historical uses of diaspora, a perilous strategy even in times of apparent accommodation on the part of the host country. In the present negotiation for claims of historical victimization and restitution, the term quickly becomes rancid, especially in situations where two or more peoples are making the same kind of claim and using it to shame those who continue to feel some sort of historical guilt (Slyomovics 1998).

In a way strangely reminiscent of the adoption of *creolization* to get at questions of stylistic amalgamations, recent treatments of diasporic processes have been dehistoricized, used to describe the inventive coming-together of cultural styles without the burden of history, exclusion, and inequality. The rulers of this establishment would, of course, be the artists and cultural critics who understand the process best. Under the sway of the internationalist search for a positive way to look at the absorption of traditions in contact situations, critics such as Paul Gilroy see the possibility of a truly nonnationalist culture based on what seem to be the norms of old-line cosmopolitanism (Gilroy 1995, 1996). Kirshenblatt-Gimblett points out the ironies in this development, in which diaspora is transvalued "from a negative state of displacement to a positive condition of multiple location, temporality, and identification" (Kirshenblatt-Gimblett 1994: 340). I share her concern with this sort of drift.

Robin Cohen tries to get around these problems by distinguishing between different kinds of diasporas. She posits distinctions between victim diasporas, trade diasporas, labor diasporas, and cultural diasporas, each with a different dominant cause for dislocation (Cohen 1997). What is a homecoming to one element of a diasporic community is a vacation to another, and a family reunion with still others.

Cosmopolitanism has been appropriated in this direction as well. This word retains most of its earlier meanings associated with the cultural liberation awaiting those who embrace the international side of city life. Used by commentators with a strong adherence to cultural nationalism, going cosmopolitan was regarded as threat to the establishment of a national literature and language.

By couching my argument in such tones of admonition, I am not advocating a purposeful forgetting of past crimes. Rather, it seems useful to parse the meanings of such complex terms so that the past is not replicated in terms acceptable to any hegemonic forces who want to claim a pluralistic agenda. I worry, specifically, about any nation which acts in the name of democratic virtues but forgets about the ways in which those virtues were first cultivated and refined. To kidnap the idea of the diaspora to advance a political agenda feels like an abomination. Of course, a major difference exists between a people mobilizing themselves to go where the jobs are and those who are forced to move in the breadline. Virtue in a democracy is based on principles of optimizing choices.

If the enemy of thought emanates from the killing rhetoric of nationalism, especially of the Romantic sort, then the move toward finding alternative ways of conceiving of dispersion beyond old pluralist models and a reactivation of the cosmopolitan argument seems like a useful tack to take. The rhetoric of cultural nationalism constantly leaks into vernacular arguments. One matter is certain: all academics who teach national literatures and languages have inherited the patriotic tones growing out of wars, and skirmishes over the ownership of territory continue to threaten the peace of the planet.

The cultural critique has focused on the ways in which modernity encounters the problems of homelands. Those who follow Benedict Anderson in seeing all nations as imagined communities subject to temporal and special invention make clear the political morass that such a relativist position seems to underwrite. I would be the last to contest the contingent character of any arguments for nation, hewing to a relativist position in the face of the terrible problems being faced by real people for whom the matter is one of life or death. I would like to encourage the convenient fiction that we ought to work toward an international rule of law, but such pious hopes do not assist those on the front line when they are asked to take up arms or leave the land. New technologies of community surveillance and control resist previous legal constructions of peacemaking and peacekeeping. Just as the idea of intellectual property rights is being rethought, so the way in which real property interests are protected and maintained needs rethinking as well, beyond legal ownership and physical occupation. In previous eras, be it remembered, Anon. owned the copyright to most artistic productions. But as the great copyrighter Anon. has found, dispersal works nicely with the concept of cultural properties. Now our fellow professionals are positioned to advertise ourselves as cultural conservators, trumpeting ethnic difference in the positive terms of choice-making and in the cause of preservation of the various species of *homo habilis*. We do this in the terms once used to promote social progress. By such a presentational strategy, we can place ourselves in the middle of a cultural production apparatus that serves both us and the people we choose to present, as well as maintaining such ideals as diversity, authenticity, and respect, and, most important, having and making friends across the great divide.

Giving a name and a set of dramatic frames to forced population movements is certainly legitimate. But let us be transparent about whatever motives and strategies are being called out. We observers have prospered by capitalizing on our abilities to recognize cultural differences and to use these observations in the service of demystification. We shouldn't delude ourselves into thinking there is innate virtue in calling a spade a spade. Getting at the real truth is also a rhetorical ploy, which should be examined as rigorously as the claims of those making the false claims. All moral claims carry buried motives. Sometimes those who make them assume a superiority that acts as a *cordon sanitaire*. The consequences are not nice or neat but often deadly, these days, when put forward by those who have all the answers in a holy book.

Whether in a ghetto or a camp outside the border, the children of the exiles are reminded of their heritage of victimization. But in the cases where the movement has been voluntary, an act of cosmopolitan liberation, what can be said of those who carry on the name of the tribe? Ethnic pride movements usually call on the sympathies of others by reminding them of the adversities they have been dealt. The pride of the group represented as ethnically different often resides in the different cultural practices carried into the present out of enslavement, imprisonment, or banishment. The motive is greater than simply a shaming move directed at the children of the oppressors. From its inception as a plea, in a representative democracy, it turns into a demand for remembrance's sake. Reparations are arranged, but this puts a price on the bodies of dead people and tints with shame those being bought off in this way. In fact, there is no end to this payment, for neither the guilt nor the shame will be erased. It is not blackmail, but the payments and the future relationships between the two "sides," if that is what they are, is subject to continual reminder, especially if it is attached to an annual reenactment of the expulsion. Whenever I hear "never forget" or "always remember," I look for a hidey hole. For this kind of remembrance has a tendency to become cancerous. There is no possibility of relief from this sharing of guilt and shame, only a continuing resentment from both sides.

I worry about complicity on our own part as we act as ethnographers of difference and as representatives of a proposed middle way. It is important to act as a cultural conservator, for human diversity seems threatened and with it, we know not what will be lost. Those concerned with the natural environment and the death of species can tell us a good deal about the consequences for the gene pool and all that, but is that an argument from similarity, or from the need to feel guilty? One way or another, it seems important to understand the way in which this cul-de-sac was engineered.

By studying and representing cultural difference from a position of neutrality, what are we asking of our audiences of the future? We must take a lesson from the past; there is no retreat from that. But what baggage are we carrying with us on this family vacation? Not only are we conservators of the old ways and, by extension, of human variety, but we have admitted to profiting from the very peoples we have chosen to bring out of the cave, the forest hideaway, the mountain retreat. It seems useful for us to ask the *cui bono* questions for our own good, then. I am not embarrassed by the depth of our sympathies as we represent these others in public presentations, for it seems useless to deny them opportunities for making their own choices. But there is little virtue for us to be derived from this enterprise. It calls for appropriate humility.

These revealed traditions of the group, maintained in the face of adversity and even growing out of it, are always subject to being replayed without their originating energies. Often enough, the display will be carried out by the children of those who we presume were the beneficiaries of the enslavement or banishment proceedings. Should we therefore become judges of who has the most compelling case?

Localisms and Cosmopolitanisms

We are faced with—and implicated in—the workings of a globalizing economy that will continue to build on stylistic differences. Wherever cultural styles can be exposed as a spectacular performance, it will be done by those in the business of producing shows. Am I calling for a simple recognition of our own system of practices, without making any kind of reparation? I just can't figure out what is to be repaired, or what kind of specie could be used to make payments.

Perhaps cosmopolitanism is the only possible outcome, and that might not be so bad. It does void the diasporas and the other forced marches of their own sense of history, which would be a loss for all of humanity. But we continue to dislocate ourselves from the past, and cosmopolitanism might be the only possible response short of self-immolation. Certainly, in principle we don't want our sins to be our children's inheritance. We must use our own experiences and those we read and hear about as a way of understanding our present condition. Maybe critical awareness will provide a bandage for these wounds. Surely the growth of our self-awareness is the only way out of this dilemma, unless we invent a new drug that will allow us to go beyond forgetting.

Just such a pill seems to be developing in the broadening of this notion of many diasporas. If, by calling ourselves diasporics, we license groups to display themselves in a positive way, and thus celebrate again a sense of community forged out of this experience in common, so much the better. All of life will be festivalized, carnivalized, made into a spectacular show. As servers say, "Enjoy." Then we can be mirrors of ourselves and our ancestors without paying any consequences other than facing our own decline.

Diasporic groups have been encouraged to use their history and cultural distinctiveness as resource in an economy which feasts upon stylistic differences. Community itself, historically an outgrowth of exclusion and residential containment, becomes a crop to be harvested by those who know how to make their history public and maintain their cultural practices in opposition to the hegemony of the host nations. Every people, then, becomes equally different, subject to being displayed in the same milieux as a constituent part of a plural polity. Each group in dispersal now uses that history to obtain equities in the present, but at the expense of exoticizing themselves and their immediate ancestors.

As globalization gathers momentum, many polities come under pressures caused by the constant flow of the "work force" from one nation to another.

All such movement is tied to the twin problems of residency rules and the perceived need of workers or their host nations to regularize the citizenship question. Fluctuations in labor markets affect these movements, especially as low-end jobs are created without an indigenous work force to fill them. Technological advances now permit the out-sourcing of information service jobs across national boundaries. Trained workers in one area of the world no longer have to relocate in order to fill computer- or telephonic-related positions. For many entrepreneurs, work can be transferred to the domicile, returning the work force from the office or store to the room at home in which the computer is housed.

Of prime interest for those concerned with the expressive economies of various communities, this situation of high mobility has sped the dispersion and recreation of new ethnic groups. Problems of citizenship and work permits affect how visible the newcomers will be in their new homes, especially in democratic polities that seek cultural equity among and between their diverse populations. Plural polities, which, in the past have created inter-ethnic rivalries for jobs and housing, now are encouraged to be openly ethnic in their dress and celebrations, adding to the display resources and perhaps the tourist economy. Municipal festivals emerge as ways of advertising the benefits of a culturally pluralistic polity. Each community may serve its own foods, perform as an ethnic side-show to the major civic celebrations, and find another way of becoming part of the economies of that locale. In the past, migrants were severely controlled by being slotted into a niche in the local economy, most openly in restaurants offering ethnic cuisine.

Under current conditions, with the imposition of cosmopolitan values, those from different parts of the world not only live in propinquity to one another, establishing neighborhoods on which they put their stamp, but are encouraged to exoticize themselves for civic celebrations. Parades, which in the past tended to exclude or marginalize such ethnic enclaves, now regularly encourage the formation of ethnic organizations to represent themselves in festive encounters. All are affected to some degree by the problems and prospects of cultural, as well as economic, exchanges; diverse styles and traditions rub shoulders, often at strange meeting places. Those nations which are involved in expanding markets become increasingly aware of the cultural consequences of population movements as workers gravitate to places where they may better their lives. Of course, the states of the United States, especially in the Midwest, were founded precisely because they provided gathering places for fugitives from poverty and social exclusion. Similar conditions are now being experienced in other countries engaged in manufacturing, not only in the West, but the Middle East, Indonesia, Malaysia, and Singapore, to name a few.

But other narratives of movement and victimization remain hidden to the view of folklorists: stories collected in combat zones, refugee encamp-

Bibliography

Abrahams, Roger D. 1966. Patterns of Structure and Role Relationship in the Child Ballads in the United States. *Journal of American Folklore* 79: 448–62.

———. 1967. The Shaping of Folklore Traditions in the British West Indies. *Journal of Inter-American Studies* 9: 456–80.

———. 1968a. Introductory Remarks to a Rhetorical Theory of Folklore. *Journal of American Folklore* 81: 143–58.

———. 1968b. Public Drama and Common Values in Three Caribbean Islands. *Trans-Action* 5 (8) (July–August): 62–71. Reprinted as Patterns of Performance in the British West Indies, in *Afro-American Anthropology: Contemporary Perspectives*, ed. Norman E. Whitten, Jr., and John F. Szwed, 163–79. New York: Free Press, 1970.

———. 1968c. A Rhetoric of Everyday Life: Traditional Conversational Genres. *Southern Folklore Quarterly* 32: 44–59.

———. 1969. The Complex Relations of Simple Forms. *Genre* 2 (2): 104–28. Revised and reprinted in *Folklore Genres*, ed. Dan Ben-Amos, 193–214. Austin: University of Texas Press, 1976.

———. 1970. *Positively Black*. Englewood Cliffs, N.J.: Prentice-Hall.

———. 1972. Proverbs and Proverbial Expressions; Folk Drama. In *Folklore and Folklife*, ed. Richard M. Dorson, 117–28, 351–62. Chicago: University of Chicago Press.

———. 1976. *Talking Black*. Rowley, Mass.: Newbury House.

———. 1977a. The Most Embarrassing Things That Ever Happened: Conversational Stories in a Theory of Enactment. *Folklore Forum* 10 (3): 9–15.

———. 1977b. Toward an Enactment-Centered Theory of Folklore. In *The Frontiers of Folklore*, ed. William R. Bascom, 79–120. Washington, D.C.: American Anthropological Association.

———. 1980. Folklore. In *Harvard Encyclopedia of American Ethnicity*, ed. Ann Orlov and Stephen Thernstrom, 370–70. Cambridge, Mass.: Harvard University Press.

———. 1981a. Doing Folklore Texas-Style. Introduction to *"And Other Neighborly Names": Social Process and Cultural Image in Texas Folklore*, ed. Richard Bauman and Roger D. Abrahams, 1–7. Austin: University of Texas Press.

———. 1981b. Shouting Match at the Border: The Folklore of Display Events. Afterword to *"And Other Neighborly Names": Social Process and Cultural Image in Texas Folklore*, ed. Bauman and Abrahams, 303–21.

———. 1982. The Language of Festivals. In *Celebration: A World of Art and Ritual*, ed. Victor W. Turner, 161–77. Washington, D.C.: Smithsonian Institution Press.

———. 1983. *The Man-of-Words in the West Indies*. Baltimore: Johns Hopkins University Press.

———. 1986. Ordinary and Extraordinary Experiences. In *The Anthropology of Experience*, ed. Victor W. Turner and Edward Bruner, 45–72. Urbana: University of Illinois Press.

———. 1987. An American Vocabulary of Celebrations. In *Time out of Time: Essays on the Festival*, ed. Alessandro Falassi, 173–83. Albuquerque: University of New Mexico Press.

———. 1988a. Antick Dispositions and the Perilous Politics of Culture: Costume and Culture in Jacobean England and America. In *Modern Dress: Costuming the European Social Body, 17th–20th Centuries*, ed. Regina Bendix and Dorothy Noyes. Special issue, *Journal of American Folklore* 111: 115–32.

———. 1988b. The Discovery of Marketplace Culture. *Intellectual History Newsletter* 10: 23–32.

———. 1988c. Rough Sincerities: William Wells Newell and the Discovery of Folklore in Late-19th Century America. In *Folk Roots, New Roots: Folklore in American Life*, ed. Jane S. Becker and Barbara Franco, 19–60. Lexington, Mass.: Museum of Our National Heritage.

———. 1988d. The West Indian Tea Meeting: An Essay in Creolization. In *Old Roots in New Lands: Historical and Anthropological Perspectives on Black Experiences in the Americas*, ed. Ann M. Pescatello, 173–209. Westport, Conn.: Greenwood Press.

———. 1992a. The Past in the Presence: An Overview of Folklorists in the Late Twentieth Century. In *Folklore Processed: In Honour of Lauri Honko*, ed. Reimund Kvideland, 32–51. Helsinki: Finnish Academy of Sciences and Letters.

———. 1992b. *Singing the Master: The Emergence of Afro-American Culture in the Plantation South*. New York: Pantheon Books.

———. 1993a. After New Perspectives: Folklore Study in the Late Twentieth Century. In *Theorizing Folklore: Toward New Perspectives on the Politics of Culture*, ed. Amy Shuman and Charles L. Briggs. Special issue, *Western Folklore* 52: 379–400.

———. 1993b. Phantoms of Romantic Nationalism in Folkloristics. *Journal of American Folklore* 106: 3–37.

———. 1998a. Custom and Cultural Invention in Jacobean England and America. *Journal of American Folklore* 11: 115–32.

———. 1998b. History and Folklore: Luck-Visits, House Attacks, and Playing Indian in Early America. In *History And . . . : Histories Within the Human Sciences*, ed. Michael S. Roth and Ralph Cohen, 268–95. Charlottesville: University of Virginia Press.

———. 2001. Afro-Caribbean Culture and the South: Music with Movement. In *The South and the Caribbean: Essays and Commentaries*, ed. Douglas Sullivan-González and Charles Reagan Wilson, 97–115. With commentary by Kenneth Bilby, 115–25. Jackson: University Press of Mississippi.

———. 2002. Introduction II: A Folklore Perspective. In *Riot and Revelry in Early America*, ed. William Pencak, Matthew Dennis, and Simon P. Newman, 21–37. University Park: Pennsylvania State University Press.

———. 2003. Notes on the Songs and the Recording Experience. In *The Alan Lomax Caribbean Collection*. Rounder Records.

Abrahams, Roger D., and Richard Bauman. 1978. Ranges of Festival Behavior. In *The Reversible World: Symbolic Inversion in Art and Society*, ed. Barbara A. Babcock, 193–208. Ithaca, N.Y.: Cornell University Press.

Abrahams, Roger D., and Alan Dundes. 1972. Riddles. In *Folklore and Folklife*, ed. Richard M. Dorson, 129–44. Chicago: University of Chicago Press.

Abrahams, Roger D., and John Szwed. 1977. After the Myth: Studying Afro-American Cultural Patterns in the Plantation Literature. In *African Folklore in the New World*, ed. Daniel C. Crowley. Austin: University of Texas Press.

———, eds. 1983. *After Africa: Extracts from British Travel Accounts and Journals of the 17th, 18th, and 19th Centuries Concerning the Slaves, Their Manners and Customs in the British West Indies*. New Haven, Conn.: Yale University Press.

Agnew, Jean-Christophe. 1986. *Worlds Apart: The Market and the Theater in Anglo-American Thought, 1550–1750.* Cambridge: Cambridge University Press.

Albert, Ethel M. 1964. "Rhetoric," "Logic" and "Poetics" in Burundi: Culture Patterning of Speech Behavior. *American Anthropologist* 66 (6), Part 2: 35–54. Reprinted as Culture Patterning of Speech Behavior in Burundi. In *Directions in Sociolinguistics,* ed. John J. Gumperz and Dell Hymes. New York: Holt, Rinehart, & Winston, 1972.

Amman, Jost, and Hans Sachs. 1568. *The Book of Trades.* Reprint New York: Dover, 1973.

American Folklore Society (AFS), Philadelphia chapter. 1890. Hints for the Study of Folklore in Philadelphia and Vicinity. *Journal of American Folklore* 3: 78–80.

Anderson, Benedict. 1983. *Imagined Communities: Reflections on the Origin and Spread of Nationalism.* London: Verso.

Appadurai, Arjun. 1990. Disjuncture and Difference in the Global Cultural Economy. *Public Culture* 2 (2):1–23. Reprinted in *Colonial Discourse and Post-Colonial Theory,* ed. Patrick Williams and Laura Chrisman, 324–339. New York: Columbia University Press, 1994; and in *Global Culture: Nationalism, Globalization and Modernity,* ed. Mike Featherstone, 356–82. London: Sage Publications, 1995.

Arewa, E. Ojo, and Alan Dundes. 1964. Proverbs and the Ethnography of Speaking Folklore. *American Anthropologist* 66 (6), Part 2: 70–85.

Arnett, D. W. 1957. Proverbial Lore and Word-Play of the Fulani. *Africa* 27: 379–96.

Austin, J. L. 1962. *How to Do Things with Words.* Cambridge, Mass.: Harvard University Press.

Baer, Florence E. 1980. Sources and Analogues of the Uncle Remus Tales. Folklore Fellow Communications, 228. Helsinki, Finland: Academia Scientiarum Fennica.

Bakhtin, Mikhail M. 1984 [1965]. Introduction. *Rabelais and His World.* Trans. Hélène Iswolsky. Bloomington: Indiana University Press.

———. 1981 [1975]. *The Dialogic Imagination.* Trans. Caryl Emerson and Michael Holquist. Austin: University of Texas Press.

Baron, Robert, and Ana Cara, eds. 2003. *Creolization.* Special Issue, *Journal of American Folklore* 116.

Barth, Frederick, ed. 1969. *Ethnic Groups and Boundaries: The Social Organization of Culture Difference.* Boston: Little, Brown.

Bascom, William R. 1954. Four Functions of Folklore. *Journal of American Folklore* 67: 333–49.

———, ed. 1977. *The Frontiers of Folklore.* Washington, D.C.: American Anthropological Association.

Bateson, Gregory. 1958 [1936]. *Naven.* 2nd ed. Stanford, Calif.: Stanford University Press.

———. 1972. A Theory of Play and Fantasy. In *Steps to an Ecology of the Mind,* 177–93. New York: Ballantine Books.

Bauman, Richard. 1971. Differential Identity and the Social Base of Folklore. *Journal of American Folklore* 84: 31–41. Reprinted in *Toward New Perspectives in Folklore,* ed. Américo Paredes and Richard Bauman, 31–41. Austin: University of Texas Press, 1972.

Bauman, Richard, and Roger D. Abrahams, eds. 1981. *"And Other Neighborly Names": Social Process and Cultural Image in Texas Folklore.* Austin: University of Texas Press.

Bauman, Richard, Roger D. Abrahams, Gary H. Gossen, and Barbara A. Babcock. 1977. *Verbal Art as Performance.* Rowley, Mass.: Newbury House. Reprint Prospect Heights, Ill.: Waveland Press, 1984.

Bausinger, Hermann. 1990 [1972]. *Folk Culture in a World of Technology.* Trans. Elke Dettmer. Bloomington: Indiana University Press.

———. 1992. Change of Paradigms? Comments on the Crisis of Ethnicity. In *Folklore Processed: In Honour of Lauri Honko,* ed. Reimund Kvideland, 73–77. Studia Fennica Folkloristica. Helsinki: Finnish Academy of Sciences and Letters.

Ben-Amos, Dan. 1971. Toward a Definition of Folklore in Context. *Journal of American Folklore* 84: 3–15. Reprinted in *Toward New Perspectives in Folklore,* ed. Américo Paredes and Richard Bauman, 3–15. Austin: University of Texas Press, 1972.

———, ed. 1976. *Folklore Genres.* Austin: University of Texas Press.

———. 1984. The Seven Strands of Tradition: Varieties in Its Meanings in American Folklore Studies. *Journal of Folklore Research* 21 (2–3): 97–131.

Ben-Amos, Dan, and Kenneth S. Goldstein, eds. 1975. *Folklore: Performance and Communication.* The Hague: Mouton.

Bendix, Regina. 1997. *In Search of Authenticity: The Formation of Folklore Studies.* Madison: University of Wisconsin Press.

Berlin, Ira. 1996. From Creole to African: Atlantic Creoles and the Origins of African-American Society in Mainland North America. *William and Mary Quarterly* 3rd ser. 53: 251–88.

Bernstein, Basil. 1964. Elaborated and Restricted Codes: Their Social Origins and Some Consequences. *American Anthropologist* 66 (6), Part 2: 55–69.

Bhabha, Homi K. 1993. *The Location of Culture.* London: Routledge.

Bianco, Carla. 1974. *The Two Rosetos.* Bloomington: Indiana University Press.

Blacking, John. 1961. The Social Value of Venda Riddles. *African Studies* 20: 1–32.

Bloom, Harold. 1984. Mr. America. *New York Review of Books,* 22 November, 19–24.

Boas, Franz. 1906. The Outlook for the American Negro. In *The Shaping of American Anthropology, 1883–1911: A Franz Boas Reader,* ed. George W. Stocking, Jr., 310–16. New York: Basic Books, 1974.

———. 1907. William Wells Newell: Memorial Meeting at First Church, Cambridge, Mass., March 10. *Journal of American Folklore* 20: 61–66.

———. 1938. An Anthropologist's Credo. *The Nation* 147 (6): 201–4.

Bolland, O. Nigel. 1992. Creolization and Creole Societies: A Cultural Nationalist View of Caribbean Social History. In *Intellectuals in the Twentieth-Century Caribbean,* ed. Alistair Hennessy, vol. 1, 50–79. London: Macmillan Caribbean.

Boyarin, Daniel, and Jonathan Boyarin. 1993. Diaspora: Generational Ground of Jewish Identity. *Critical Inquiry* 19 (4): 693–725.

Brathwaite, Edward Kamau. 1971. *The Development of Creole Society in Jamaica, 1770–1820.* Oxford: Clarendon Press.

———. 1984. *History of the Voice: The Development of Nation Language in Anglophonic Caribbean Poetry.* London: New Beacon Books.

Braudel, Fernand. 1982. *The Wheels of Commerce.* Vol. 2 of *Civilization and Capitalism: 15th–18th Century.* Berkeley: University of California Press.

Breck, Samuel. 1877. *Recollections of Samuel Breck, with passages from his notebooks (1771–1863),* ed. H. E. Scudder. Philadelphia: Porter and Coates.

Briggs, Charles L. 1988. *Competence in Performance: The Creativity of Tradition in Mexicano Verbal Art.* Philadelphia: University of Pennsylvania Press.

Brunvand, Jan Harold. 1968. *The Study of American Folklore.* New York: Norton.

———. 1981. *The Vanishing Hitchhiker: American Urban Legends and Their Meanings.* New York: Norton.

Burke, Kenneth. 1931. *Counter-Statement.* Berkeley: University of California Press, 1968.

———.. 1941. *The Philosophy of Literary Form: Studies in Symbolic Action.* New York: Vintage, 1961.

———.. 1945. *A Grammar of Motives*. Berkeley: University of California Press.

———.. 1950. *A Rhetoric of Motives*. Berkeley: University of California Press.

———.. 1966. *Language as Symbolic Action: Essays on Life, Literature, and Method*. Berkeley: University of California Press.

Burton, Richard E. B. 1997. *Afro-Creole: Power, Opposition, and Play in the Caribbean*. Ithaca: Cornell University Press.

Caillois, Roger. 1979 [1961]. *Man, Play, and Games*. Trans. Meyer Barash. New York: Schocken Books.

Canclini, Néstor Garcia. 1995. *Hybrid Cultures: Strategies for Entering and Leaving Modernity*. Trans. Christopher L. Chiappari and Silvia L. López. Minneapolis: University of Minnesota Press.

Cantwell, Robert. 1993. *Ethnomimesis: Folklife and the Representation of Culture*. Chapel Hill: University of North Carolina Press.

Cassidy, Frederick Gomes, ed. 1985. *Dictionary of American Regional English*. Vol. 1. Cambridge, Mass.: Harvard University Press.

Chamberlain, J. Edward. 1993. *Come Back to Me My Language*. Champaign: University of Illinois Press.

Clark, Katerina, and Michael Holquist. 1984. *Mikhail Bakhtin*. Cambridge, Mass.: Harvard University Press.

Clarke, Kenneth, and Mary Clarke. 1965. *A Concise Dictionary of Folklore*. Bowling Green, Ky.: Popular Press.

Clifford, James. 1994. Diasporas. *Cultural Anthropology* 9 (3): 339–44.

———. 1997. *Routes: Travel and Translation in the Late Twentieth Century*. Cambridge, Mass.: Harvard University Press.

Clifford, James, and George Marcus, eds. 1986. *Writing Culture: The Poetics and Politics of Ethnography*. Berkeley: University of California Press.

Cohen, Abner. 1971. Cultural Strategies of Trading Diasporas. In *The Development of Indigenous Trade and Markets in West Africa*, ed. Claude Meillassoux, 268–82. London: Oxford University Press.

Cohen, Robin. 1997. *Global Diasporas: An Introduction*. London: Routledge/Taylor & Frances.

Condé, Maryse. 1995. Cherchez nos Verites. In *Penser la creolite*, ed. Maryse Condé and Madeleine Cottenet-Hage. Paris: Karthala.

Crowley, Daniel J. 1966. *I Could Tell Old Story Good*. Berkeley: University of California Press.

———, ed. 1977. *African Folklore in the New World*. Austin: University of Texas Press.

Crumley, James. 1978. *The Last Good Kiss: A Novel*. New York: Vintage Contemporaries.

Csikszentmihalyi, Mihalyi. 1975. *Beyond Boredom and Anxiety*. San Francisco: Jossey-Bass.

Curtin, Philip D. 1984. *Cross-Cultural Trade in World History*. Cambridge: Cambridge University Press.

Danielson, Larry, ed. 1977. *Studies in Folklore and Ethnicity*. Special issue, *Western Folklore* 36 (1).

Daston, Lorraine, and Katherine Park. 1998. *Wonders and the Order of Nature: 1150–1750*. London: Zone Books.

Davis, Susan G. 1986. *Parades and Power: Street Theatre in Nineteenth-Century Philadelphia*. Philadelphia: Temple University Press.

Dayan, Joan. 1995. *Haiti, History, and the Gods*. Berkeley: University of California Press.

Dégh, Linda. 1956. Processes of Legend Formation. In *Proceedings of the IV Interna-*

tional Congress for Folk-Narrative Research in Athens, ed. Georgios A. Mega. Athens.

———. 1957. Some Questions of the Social Function of Storytelling. *Acta Ethnographica* 6: 91–143.

———.. 1968–1969. Survival and Revival of European Folk Cultures in America. *Ethnologia Europaea* 2–3: 97–108.

———.. 1969. *Folktales and Society: Story-Telling in a Hungarian Peasant Community*. Bloomington: Indiana University Press. Originally published as *Märchen, Erzähler und Erzählegemeinschaft*. Berlin, 1962.

———.. 1989. Two Old-World Narratives in Urban Settings. In *Kontakte und Greenzen: Probleme der Volks-, Kultur-, und Sozialforschung. Festschrift für Gerhard Heilfurth*, ed. H. F. Foltin, 71–86. Göttingen: Schwartz.

Devonish, H. 1986. *Language and Liberation: Creole Language Politics in the Caribbean*. London: Karia Press.

Dewey, John. 1925. *Experience and Nature*. Chicago: Open Court Publishing Co.

———. 1934. *Art as Experience*. New York: Capricorn Books.

Didion, Joan. 1979. *The White Album*. New York: Dutton.

Donoghue, Denis. 1976. *The Sovereign Ghost*. Berkeley: University of California Press.

Dorson, Richard M. 1952. *Bloodstoppers and Bearwalkers: Folk Traditions of the Upper Michigan Peninsula*. Cambridge, Mass.: Harvard University Press.

———. 1968. *The British Folklorists: A History*. Chicago: University of Chicago Press.

———. 1971. *American Folklore and the Historian*. Chicago: University of Chicago Press.

———. 1972a. Africa and the Folklorist. In *African Folklore*, ed. Richard M. Dorson. Garden City, N.Y.: Anchor Books.

———, ed. 1972b. *Folklore and Folklife*. Chicago: University of Chicago Press.

———, ed. 1979. *Folklore in the Modern World*. The Hague: Mouton.

Dundes, Alan. 1962. From Etic to Emic Units in the Study of Folktales. *Journal of American Folklore* 74: 142–45.

———. 1964. Texture, Text, and Context. *Southern Folklore Quarterly* 28: 251–65.

———, ed. 1965. *The Study of Folklore*. Englewood Cliffs, N.J.: Prentice-Hall.

———. 1975. On the Structure of the Proverb. *Proverbium* 15: 961–73.

———. 1976. African and Afro-American Tales. *Research in African Literature* 7: 181–89.

———. 1983. Defining Identity through Folklore. In *Identity Personal and Socio-Cultural*, ed. Anita Jacobson-Widding, 235–61. Uppsala: Uppsala Studies in Cultural Anthropology 5.

Ehn, Billy, Barbro Klein, Owe Rönstrom, and Annick Sjögren. 1990. *The Organization of Diversity in Sweden*. Stockholm: Swedish Institute of Immigration and Museum.

Emerson, Ralph Waldo. 1903–1904. *The Complete Works of Ralph Waldo Emerson*, ed. Edward W. Emerson. Boston: Houghton Mifflin.

Eriksen, Thomas Hylland. 2002 [1993]. *Ethnicity and Nationalism: Anthropological Perspectives*. Expanded edition. London: Pluto Press.

Erikson, Erik H. 1950. *Childhood and Society*. New York: Norton.

Feintuch, Bert, ed. 1995. *Common Ground: Keywords for the Study of Expressive Culture*. Special issue, *Journal of American Folklore* 108. Revised as *Eight Words for the Study of Expressive Culture*, ed. Bert Feintuch. Champaign: University of Illinois Press, 2003.

Feld, Steven. 1982. *Sound and Sentiment: Birds, Weeping, Poetics, and Song in Kaluli Expression*. Philadelphia: University of Pennsylvania Press. 2nd ed. 1990.

Ferguson, Charles. 1959. Diaglossia. *Word* 15: 325–40.

Fife, Austin E. 1964. Christian Swarm Chorus from the Ninth to the Nineteenth Centuries. *Journal of American Folklore* 77: 154–59.

Finnegan, Ruth H., comp. 1967. *Limba Stories and Story-Telling*. Oxford: Oxford University Press.

Fock, Niels. 1965. Personal communication. University of Copenhagen.

Frazier, E. Franklin. 1939. *The Negro Family in the United States*. Chicago: University of Chicago Press.

Freud, Sigmund. 1905. *Jokes and Their Relation to the Unconscious*. Vol. 8, *Standard Edition of the Complete Works of Sigmund Freud*. Trans. James Strachey. London: Hogart Press, 1960.

Friedman, Lawrence J. 1999. *Identity's Architect: A Biography of Erik H. Erikson*. New York: Prentice-Hall.

Fry, Gladys-Marie. 1975. *Night Riders in Black Folk History*. Chapel Hill: University of North Carolina Press, 1991.

Frye, Northrop. 1957. *Anatomy of Criticism: Four Essays*. Princeton, N.J.: Princeton University Press.

Furnivall, J. S. 1948. *Colonial Policy and Practice; A Comparative Study of Burma and Netherlands India*. Issued in cooperation with the International Secretariat, Institute of Pacific Relations. Cambridge: Cambridge University Press.

Gadamer, Hans-Georg. 1989. *Truth and Method*. 2nd rev. ed. Trans. Joel Weinsheimer and Donald G. Marshall. New York: Crossroad.

Gardner, Howard. 1999. The Enigma of Erik Erikson. *New York Review of Books*, June 24, 51–56.

Geertz, Clifford. 1971. Deep Play: Notes on the Balinese Cockfight. *Daedalus* (Winter): 1–38. Also in *The Interpretation of Cultures*, 412–53.

———. 1973. *The Interpretation of Cultures*. New York: Basic Books.

———. 1976. From the Natives' Point of View: On the Nature of Anthropological Understanding. In *Meaning in Anthropology*, ed. Keith H. Basso and Henry A. Selby, 221–38. Albuquerque: University of New Mexico Press.

———. 1977. Centers, Kings and Charisma: Reflections on the Symbolics of Power. In Raymond Aron et al., *Culture and Its Creators: Essays in Honor of Edward Shils*, 150–71. Chicago: University of Chicago Press.

———. 1980. Blurred Genres: The Refiguration of Social Thought. *American Scholar* 49 (2): 165–79.

———. 1982. The Way We Think Now: Toward an Ethnography of Modern Thought. *Bulletin, American Academy of Arts and Sciences* 35 (5): 14–34.

———. 1983. *Local Knowledge: Further Essays in Interpretive Anthropology*. New York: Basic Books.

———. 1986. Epilogue: Making Experiences, Authoring Selves. In *The Anthropology of Experience*, ed. Victor W. Turner and Edward M. Bruner, 253–75. Urbana: University of Illinois Press.

Georges, Robert. 1962. Matiasma: Living Folk Belief. *Midwest Folklore* 12: 69–74.

———. 1964. *Greek-American Folk Beliefs and Narratives*. New York: Arno Press, 1980.

Gilroy, Paul. 1987. Diaspora, Utopia, and the Critique of Capitalism. In *"There Ain't No Black in the Union Jack": The Cultural Politics of Race and Nation*, 153–222. London: Routledge.

———. 1992a. Diaspora Cultures. In *Modernity and Its Futures*, ed. Stuart Hall, David Held, and Tony McGrew. London: Polity Press.

———. 1992b. *The Black Atlantic: Modernity and Double Consciousness*. Cambridge, Mass.: Harvard University Press.

———. 1995. Roots and Routes: Black Identity as an Outernational Project. In *Racial and Ethnic Identity: Psychological Development and Creative Expression*, ed. Herbert W. Harris, Howard C. Blue, and Ezra E. H. Griffith, 15–30. London: Routledge.

———. 1996. British Cultural Studies and the Pitfalls of Identity. In *British Black Cultural Studies: A Reader*, ed. Houston A. Baker, Jr., Manthia Diawara, and Ruth A. Lindeborg, 223–39. Chicago: University of Chicago Press.

Gizelis, Gregory. 1972. *Narrative Rhetorical Devices of Persuasion in the Greek Community of Philadelphia*. Athens, 1976; New York: Arno Press, 1980.

Glassie, Henry. 1982. *Passing the Time in Ballymenone*. Philadelphia: University of Pennsylvania Press.

Glazer, Nathan, and Daniel P. Moynihan. 1970 [1963]. *Beyond the Melting Pot: The Negroes, Puerto Ricans, Jews, Italians, and Irish of New York City*. 2nd rev. ed. Cambridge, Mass.: Joint Center for Urban Studies, Harvard University Press and MIT Press.

Gleason, Philip. 1983. Identifying Identity: A Semantic History. *Journal of American History* 69: 910–31.

———. 1992. *Speaking of Diversity: Language and Ethnicity in Twentieth-Century America*. Baltimore: Johns Hopkins University Press.

Goffman, Erving. 1963. *Behavior in Public Places: Notes on the Social Organization of Gatherings*. Glencoe, Ill.: Free Press.

———. 1967. *Interaction Ritual: Essays on Face-to-Face Behavior*. Garden City, N.Y.: Doubleday Anchor.

———. 1974. *Forms of Talk*. Philadelphia: University of Pennsylvania Press.

Gordon, Milton M. 1964. *Assimilation in American Life: The Role of Race, Religion, and National Origins*. New York: Oxford University Press.

Grossberg, Larry, Cary Nelson, and Paula Treichler, eds. 1992. *Cultural Studies*. London: Routledge.

Gundaker, Grey. 1998. *Signs of Diaspora/Diaspora of Signs: Literacies, Creolization, and Vernacular Practice in African America*. Oxford: Oxford University Press.

Gumperz, John H., and Dell H. Hymes, eds. 1972. *The Ethnography of Communication*. Special issue, *American Anthropologist*, 66 (6), Part 2.

Hall, Stuart. 1993. Cultural Identity and Diaspora. In *Colonial Discourse and Post–Colonial Theory*, ed. Patrick Williams and Laura Chrisman, 392–403. Hemel Hempstead: Harvester Wheatsheaf; New York: Columbia University Press.

Handelman, Don. 1977. Play and Ritual: Complementary Frames of Metacommunication. In *It's a Funny Thing, Humour*, ed. Antony J. Chapman and Hugh C. Foot, 185–92. London and New York: Pergamon Press.

Handler, Richard. 1988. *Nationalism and the Politics of Culture in Quebec*. Madison: University of Wisconsin Press.

Handlin, Oscar. 1951. *The Uprooted: The Epic Story of the Great Migrations That Made the American People*. Boston: Little, Brown.

Hannerz, Ulf. 1987. The World in Creolization. *Africa* 57: 546–59.

———. 1992. *Cultural Complexity: Studies in the Social Organization of Meaning*. New York: Columbia University Press.

Hansen, Brooks. 1995. *The Chess Garden*. New York: Farrar, Straus & Geroux.

Hansen, Marcus Lee. 1940. *The Immigrant in American History*. New York: Harper & Row.

Heiberg, Marianne. 1989. *The Making of the Basque Nation*. Cambridge: Cambridge University Press.

Herberg, Will. 1955. *Protestant, Catholic, Jew*. Chicago: University of Chicago Press.

Herskovits, Melville J. 1927. When Is a Jew a Jew? *Modern Quarterly* 4: 109–17.

———. 1941. *The Myth of the Negro Past*. Boston: Beacon Press, 1958.

Herskovits, Melville J., and Frances S. Herskovits. 1958. *Dahomean Narrative: A Cross-Cultural Analysis*. Evanston, Ill.: Northwestern University Press.

Hill, Donald R. 1993. *Calypso Callaloo: Early Carnival Music in Trinidad*. Gainesville: University Presses of Florida.

Hobsbawm, Eric. 1959. *Primitive Rebels: Studies in Archaic Forms of Social Movement in the 19th and 20th Centuries*. New York: Norton.

———. 1992. Introduction: Inventing Traditions. In *The Invention of Tradition*, ed. Eric Hobsbawm and Terence Ranger. Cambridge: Cambridge University Press.

Hollinger, David A. 1995. *Postethnic America: Beyond Multiculturalism*. New York: Basic Books.

Hufford, Mary, ed. 1994. *Conserving Culture: A New Discourse on Heritage*. Urbana: University of Illinois Press.

Hugill, Stan. 1967. *Sailortown*. New York: E.P. Dutton.

Huizinga, Johan. 1938. *Homo Ludens: A Study of the Play-Element in Culture*. Trans. R. F. C. Hull. Boston: Beacon Press, 1955.

Hurston, Zora Neale. 1963 [1935]. *Mules and Men*. Bloomington: Indiana University Press.

———. 1984 [1942]. *Dust Tracks on a Road: An Autobiography*. Ed. Robert E. Hemenway. 2nd ed. Urbana: University of Illinois Press.

Hymes, Dell H., ed. 1971. *Pidginization and Creolization of Language: Proceedings of a Conference held at the University of the West Indies, Mona, Jamaica, 1968*. Cambridge: Cambridge University Press.

———, ed. 1972. *Reinventing Anthropology*. New York: Pantheon.

———. 1974. *Foundations in Sociolinguistics: An Ethnographic Approach*. Philadelphia: University of Pennsylvania Press.

———. 1975a. Breakthrough into Performance. In *Folklore: Performance and Communication*, ed. Dan Ben-Amos and Kenneth S. Goldstein, 11–74. The Hague: Mouton.

———. 1975b. Folklore's Nature and the Sun's Myth. *Journal of American Folklore* 88: 346–69.

James, William. 1970 [1903]. *The Meaning of Truth*. Ann Arbor: University of Michigan Press.

———. 1967. *The Writings of William James—A Comprehensive Edition*, ed. John McDermott. New York: Random House.

Jansen, William Hugh. 1959. The Esoteric-Exoteric Factor in Folklore. *Fabula: Journal of Folktale Studies* 2: 205–11. Reprinted in *The Study of Folklore*, ed. Alan Dundes, 43–51. Englewood Cliffs, N.J.: Prentice-Hall, 1965.

Jenkins, Richard P. 1997. *Rethinking Ethnicity: Arguments and Explorations*. London: Sage.

Jolles, André. 1929. *Einfache Formen*. Tübingen: Max Niemeyer, 1968.

Jordan, William Chester. 1993. *Women and Credit in Pre-Industrial and Developing Societies*. Philadelphia: University of Pennsylvania Press.

Kapchan, Deborah. 1996. *Gender on the Market: Moroccan Women and the Revoicing of Tradition*. Philadelphia: University of Pennsylvania Press.

Kapchan, Deborah A., and Pauline Turner Strong, eds. 1999. *Theorizing the Hybrid*. Special issue, *Journal of American Folklore* 112.

Kinser, Samuel. 1990. *Carnival, American Style: Mardi Gras in New Orleans and Mobile*. Chicago, University of Chicago Press.

Kirshenblatt-Gimblett, Barbara. 1972. Traditional Storytelling in the Toronto Jewish Community. Ph.D. dissertation, University of Michigan, Ann Arbor.

———. 1978. Culture Shock and Narrative Creativity. In *Folklore in the Modern World*, ed. Richard M. Dorson, 109–22. The Hague: Mouton, 1978.

———. 1986. Studying Immigrant and Ethnic Folklore. In *Handbook of American Folklore*, ed. Richard M. Dorson. Bloomington: Indiana University Press.

———. 1994. Spaces of Dispersal: Commentary on Clifford. *Cultural Anthropology* 9: 339–44.

———. 1995. Ordinary People, Everyday Life: Folk Culture in New York City. In *Urban Life: Readings in Urban Anthropology*, ed. George Gmelch and Walter Zenner. 3rd ed. Prospect Heights, Ill.: Waveland Press.

———. 1998. *Destination Culture: Tourism, Museums, and Heritage*. Berkeley: University of California Press.

Klepp, Susan E., and Roderick A. McDonald. 1997. "To detail the past": The Jamaica Journals of Maria Skinner Nugent (1801–1805) and Eliza Chadwick Roberts (1805). Unpublished ms.

Klymasz, Robert B. 1973. From Immigrant to Ethnic Folklore. *Journal of the Folklore Institute* 10: 133–37.

Köstlin, Konrad. 1997. The Passion for the Whole: Interpreted Modernity or Modernity as Interpretation. *Journal of American Folklore* 110: 261–66.

Kulikoff, Allan. 1992. *The Agrarian Origins of American Capitalism*. Charlottesville: University of Virginia Press.

Kupperman, Karen Ordahl. 1980. *Settling with the Indians: The Meeting of English and Indian Cultures in America, 1580–1640*. Totowa, N.J.: Rowan and Littlefield.

———. 1995. Introduction, *America in European Consciousness, 1493–1750*, ed. Kupperman, 1–31. Chapel Hill: University of North Carolina Press.

Kvideland, Reimund et al., ed. 1992. *Folklore Processed: In Honour of Lauri Honko*. Studia Fennica Folkloristica.. Helsinki: Finnish Academy of Sciences and Letters.

Labov, William, and Joshua Waletsky. 1967. Narrative Analysis: Oral Versions of Personal Experience. In *Essays in the Verbal and Visual Arts*, ed. June Helm, 12–44. Seattle: American Ethnological Society.

Leach, Maria, ed. 1949. *Standard Dictionary of Folklore, Mythology and Legend*. 2 vols. New York: Crown Publishers.

Lears, T. J. Jackson. 1981. *No Place of Grace: Antimodernism and the Transformation of American Culture, 1880–1920*. New York: Pantheon.

Levi, Albert William. 1977. Culture: A Guess at a Riddle. *Cultural Inquiry* 4.

Levine, Philippa. 1986. *The Amateur and the Professional: Antiquarians, Historians, and Archaeologists in Victorian England, 1838–1886*. Cambridge: Cambridge University Press.

Limon, Jose, and M. Jane Young. 1986. Frontiers, Settlements, and Developments in Folklore Study, 1972–1985. *Annual Review of Anthropology* 15: 437–60.

Lomax Hawes, Bess. 1968. *La Llorona* in Juvenile Hall. *Western Folklore* 27: 153–70.

Lutz, Catherine. 1982. The Domain of Emotion Words on Ifaluk. *American Ethnologist* 9: 113–28.

Malone, Jacqui. 1996. *Steppin' on the Blues: The Visible Rhythms of African American Dance*. Champaign: University of Illinois Press.

Marks, Morton. 1974. Uncovering Ritual Structures in Afro-American Music. In *Religious Movements in America*, ed. Irving I. Zaretsky and Mark P. Leone. Princeton, N.J.: Princeton University Press.

Massin. 1978. *Les cris de la ville: commerces ambulants et petits métiers de la rue*. Paris: Gallimard.

———. 1981. *Les célébrités de la rue*. Paris: Gallimard.

Matthias, Elizabeth, and Richard Raspa. 1985. *Italian Folktales in America: The Verbal Art of an Immigrant Woman*. Detroit: Wayne State University Press.

McDonald, Maryon. 1989. *"We Are Not French!": Language, Culture, and Identity in Brittany*. London: Routledge.

McDonald, Roderick, ed. 2001. *Between Slavery and Freedom: Special Magistrate John Anderson's Journal of St. Vincent During the Apprenticeship*. Philadelphia: University of Pennsylvania Press.

———. 1993. *The Economy and Material Culture of Slaves: Goods and Chattels on Sugar Plantations of Jamaica and Louisiana*. Baton Rouge: Louisiana State University Press.

McRobbie, Andrew. 1992. Post-Marxism and Cultural Studies: A Post-Script. In *Cultural Studies*, ed. Larry Grossberg, Cary Nelson, and Paula Treichler, 719–30. London: Routledge.

Mencken, H. L. 1919. *The American Language*. New York: Knopf.

Messenger, John. 1959. The Role of Proverbs in a Nigerian Judicial System. *Southwestern Journal of Anthropology* 15: 64–73.

Miller, Stephen Nachmonovitch. 1973. Ends, Means, and "Galumphing": Some Leitmotifs of Play. *American Anthropologist* 75: 87–98.

Minority Rights Group. 1990. *World Directory of Minorities*. Chicago: St. James Press.

Mintz, Sidney W. 1971. Men, Women and Trade. *Comparative Studies in Society and History* 13: 247–69.

———. 1974a. *Caribbean Transformations*. Chicago: Aldine.

———. 1974b. Les rôles économiques et la tradition culturelle. In *La femme de couleur en Amérique latine*, ed. Roger Bastide, 115–48. Paris: Éditions Anthropos.

———. 1994. Enduring Substances, Trying Theories: The Caribbean Region as *Oikoumene*. *Journal of the Royal Anthropological Institute* n.s. 2: 289–311.

Moore, A. W. 1891. *The Folklore of the Isle of Man*. London: privately printed.

Morris, Charles W. 1970. *The Pragmatic Movement in American Philosophy*. New York: George Braziller.

Mullaney, Steven. 1988. The Place of the Stage: License, Play, and Power in Renaissance England. Chicago: University of Chicago Press.

Myers, Fred. 1979. Emotions and the Self: A Theory of Personhood and Political Order and Pintupi Aborigines. *Ethos* 7: 343–70.

Newell, William Wells. 1883. *Games and Songs of American Children*. Boston: Harper and Bros.

———. 1888. On the Work of the American Folklore Society. *Journal of American Folklore* 1 (1).

Norbeck, Edward, ed. 1974. *The Anthropological Study of Human Play*. Special Issue, *Rice University Studies* 60 (November).

Noyes, Dorothy. 2003. *Fire in the Plaça: Catalan Festival Politics After Franco*. Philadelphia: University of Pennsylvania Press.

Ochs, Elinore, and Lisa Capps. 1996. Narrating the Self. *Annual Review of Anthropology* 25: 19–43.

Oliver, Paul. 1965. *Conversations with the Blues*. London: Heinemann; New York: Horizon.

Oring, Eliot. 1986. *Folk Groups and Folklore Genres*. Logan: Utah State University Press.

Paredes, Américo. 1959. *"With His Pistol in His Hand": A Border Ballad and Its Hero*. Austin: University of Texas Press.

———. 1961. On *Gringo, Greaser*, and Other Neighborly Names. In *Singers and Story-*

tellers, ed. Mody C. Boatright, Wilson M. Hudson, and Allen Maxwell, 285–90. Dallas: Southern Methodist University Press.

———. 1993. *Folklore and Culture on the Texas-Mexican Border*. Ed. Richard Bauman. Austin: University of Texas Press.

Paredes, Américo, and Richard Bauman, eds. 1972. *Toward New Perspectives in Folklore*. Austin: University of Texas Press.

Park, Robert E. 1950. *Race and Culture*. Chicago: University of Chicago Press.

Parry, Graham. 1996. *The Trophies of Time: English Antiquarians in the Seventeenth Century*. New York: Oxford University Press.

Petersen, William. 1980. Concepts of Ethnicity. In *The Harvard Encyclopedia of American Ethnicity*, ed. Stephen Thernstrom and Ann Orlov, 234–42. Cambridge, Mass.: Harvard University Press.

Peterson, William, Michael Novak, and Philip Gleason. 1980. *Concepts of Ethnicity*. Cambridge, Mass.: Harvard University Press.

Pratt, Mary Louise. 1992. *Imperial Eyes: Travel Writing and Transculturation*. London: Routledge.

Price, Richard, ed. 1973. *Maroon Societies: Rebel Slave Communities in the Americas*. 3rd ed. Baltimore: Johns Hopkins University Press, 1996.

———. 1983. *First Time: The Historical Vision of an Afro-American People*. Baltimore: Johns Hopkins University Press.

Price, Richard, and Sally Price. 1994. *On the Mall*. Bloomington: Indiana University Press.

———. 1997. Shadowboxing in the Mangrove. *Cultural Anthropology* 12: 3–36.

Raab, Max L., producer and director. 2001. *Strut!* Philadelphia: SidMax Productions.

Ranger, Terence. 1992. The Invention of Tradition in Colonial Africa. In *The Invention of Tradition*, ed. Eric Hobsbawm and Terence Ranger. Cambridge: Cambridge University Press.

Roberts, John W. 1999. ". . . hidden right out in the open": The Field of Folklore and the Problem of Invisibility. *Journal of American Folklore* 112: 119–40.

Rodgers, Daniel J. 1978. *The Work Ethic in Industrial America, 1850–1920*. Chicago: University of Chicago Press.

Rohlehr, Gordon. 1990. *Calypso and Society in Pre-Independence Trinidad*. Port of Spain: privately printed.

Rorty, Richard. 1989. *Contingency, Irony, and Solidarity*. Cambridge: Cambridge University Press.

Rorty, Richard. 1998. *Achieving Our Country: Leftist Thought in Twentieth-Century America*. Cambridge, Mass.: Harvard University Press.

Rose, Dan. 1982. Occasions and Forms of Anthropological Experience. In *A Crack in the Mirror: Reflective Perspectives in Anthropology*, ed. Jay Ruby, 218–30. Philadelphia: University of Pennsylvania Press.

———. 1987. *Black American Street Life: South Philadelphia 1969–1971*. Philadelphia: University of Pennsylvania Press.

Safran, William. 1991. Diasporas in Modern Societies: Myths of Homeland and Return. *Diaspora* 1 (1): 83–99.

Safran, William, and Ramon Maiz, eds. 2002. *Identity and Territorial Autonomy in Plural Societies*. New York: Frank Cass.

Sahlins, Marshall. 1972. *Stone Age Economics*. Chicago: University of Chicago Press.

St. George, Robert Blair. 1998. *Conversing by Signs: Poetics of Implication in Colonial New England Culture*. Chapel Hill: University of North Carolina Press.

Sapir, Edward. 1921. *Language: An Introduction to the Study of Speech*. New York: Harcourt, Brace.

Scher, Philip W. 2003. *Carnival and the Formation of a Caribbean Transnation.* Gainesville: University Presses of Florida.

Schorr, Daniel. 1977. *Clearing the Air: A Life in Journalism.* Boston: Houghton Mifflin.

Schutz, Alfred. 1970. *Alfred Schutz on Phenomenology and Social Relations: Selected Writings.* Ed. Helmut R. Wagner. Chicago and Evanston: Northwestern University Press.

Scott, James. 1990. *Domination and the Arts of Resistance: Hidden Transcripts.* New Haven, Conn.: Yale University Press.

Sears, John F. 1998. *Sacred Places: American Tourist Attractions in the Nineteenth Century.* Amherst: University of Massachusetts Press.

Shuman, Amy. 1986. *Storytelling Rights: The Uses of Oral and Written Texts by Urban Adolescents.* Cambridge: Cambridge University Press.

Shuman, Amy, and Charles Briggs, eds. 1993. *Theorizing Folklore: Toward New Perspectives on the Politics of Culture.* Special issue, *Western Folklore* 52: 2–4.

Simmel, Georg. 1955. *Conflict and the Web of Group Affiliations.* Trans. Kurt H. Wolf and Reinhard Bendix. Glencoe, Ill.: Free Press, 1964.

Simmonds, Lorne. 1987. Slave Higglering in Jamaica, 1780–1834. *Jamaica Journal* 20: 31–38.

Slyomovics, Susan. 1998. *The Object of Memory: Arab and Jew Narrate the Palestinian Village.* Philadelphia: University of Pennsylvania Press.

Smith, M. G. 1965. *The Plural Society in the British West Indies.* Los Angeles: University of California Press.

Smith, Robert J. 1975. *The Art of the Festival, as Exemplified by the Fiesta to the Patroness of Otuzco, La Virgen de la Puerta.* University of Kansas Publications in Anthropology 6. Lawrence: University of Kansas Department of Anthropology.

Stagl, Justin, 1995. *A History of Curiosity: Foundations of Anthropological Knowledge.* London: Routledge.

Stahl, S. Dolby. 1989. *Literary Folkloristics and the Personal Narrative.* Bloomington: Indiana University Press.

Stallybrass, Peter, and Allon White. 1986. *The Politics and Poetics of Transgression.* Ithaca, N.Y.: Cornell University Press.

Stern, Stephen. 1977. Ethnic Folklore and the Folklore of Ethnicity. *Western Folklore* 36: 7–32.

Stewart, Susan. 1984. *On Longing: Narratives of the Miniature, the Gigantic, the Souvenir, the Collection.* Durham, N.C.: Duke University Press, 1993.

———. 1991. *Crimes of Writing: Problems in the Containment of Representation.* New York: Oxford University Press.

Stuempfle, Stephen. 1995. *The Steelband Movement: The Forging of a National Art in Trinidad and Tobago.* Philadelphia: University of Pennsylvania Press.

Sutton-Smith, Brian. 1998. *The Ambiguity of Play.* Cambridge, Mass.: Harvard University Press.

Swann, Marjorie. 2001. *Curiosities and Texts: The Culture of Collecting in Early Modern England.* Philadelphia: University of Pennsylvania Press.

Taylor, Charles. 2004. *Modern Social Imaginaries.* Durham, N.C.: Duke University Press.

Toelken, Barre. 1979. *The Dynamics of Folklore.* Boston: Houghton Mifflin.

Tokofsky, Peter, ed. 1999. *Studies of Carnival in Memory of Daniel J. Crowley.* Special issue, *Western Folklore* 58 (3–4).

Trouillot, Michel-Rolph. 1992. The Caribbean Region: An Open Frontier in Anthropological Theory. *Annual Review of Anthropology* 21: 19–42.

Turner, Victor W. 1969. *The Ritual Process: Structure and Anti-Structure*. Chicago: Aldine Publishing.

———. 1974a. *Dramas, Fields, and Metaphors: Symbolic Action in Human Society*. Ithaca, N.Y.: Cornell University Press.

———. 1974b. Liminal to Liminoid, in Play, Flow, and Ritual. In *The Anthropological Study of Human Play*, ed. Edward Norbeck. Special Issue, *Rice University Studies* 60 (Nov.): 53–92.

———. 1977. Variations on the Theme of Liminality. In *Secular Ritual*, ed. S. Moore and B. Myerhoff, 26–52. Assen: Van Gorcum.

———. 1982. *From Ritual to Theater: The Human Seriousness of Play*. New York: Performing Arts Journal Press.

Turner, Victor W., and Edward M. Bruner, eds. 1986. *The Anthropology of Experience*. Urbana: University of Illinois Press.

Wainwright, Nicholas B., ed. 1978–1979. The Diary of Samuel Breck, 1814–1835, 1838. *Pennsylvania Magazine of History and Biography* 102 (1978): 469–508; 103 (1979): 85–113, 222–51, 356–82.

Ward, Ned. 1700. A Trip to Jamaica: With a True Character of the People and the Island. London: J. How. Reprinted in *Five Travel Scripts Commonly Attributed to Edward Ward*, 1–16. New York: Published for the Facsimile Text Society by Columbia University Press, 1933.

Williams, Raymond. 1975. *Keywords: A Vocabulary of Culture and Society*. London: Fontana.

Williams, Raymond. 1979. *Politics and Letters*. London: New Left Books.

Young, Alfred F., ed. 1976. *The American Revolution*. De Kalb: Northern Illinois University Press.

———. 1991. English Plebian Culture and Eighteenth-Century American Radicalism. In *The Origins of Anglo-American Radicalism*, ed. Margaret C. Jacob and James R. Jacob, 185–212. Atlantic Highlands, N.J.: Humanities Press/ Prometheus Books.

Young, Katherine Galloway. 1987. *Talewords and Storyrealms: The Phenomenology of Narrative*. Dordrecht: Martinus Nijhoff.

Zelizer, Barbie. 1992. *Covering the Body: The Kennedy Assassination, the Media, and the Shaping of Collective Memory*. Chicago: University of Chicago Press.

Zinik, Zinovy. 2004. Dublin Dragomans: The Pleasures and Pains of Literary Emigration. *Times Literary Supplement*, June 25.

Žližek, Slavoj. 1997. Multiculturalism, or the Cultural Logic of Multinational Capitalism. *New Left Review* 1/225 (Sept.–Oct.): 28–51.

———. 1999. You May! *London Review of Books* 21 (6), March 18, 3–6.

Index

Achieving Our Country (Rorty), 209
Adams, Henry, 112
AFS. *See* American Folklore Society
Alger, Horatio, 245
The Ambiguity of Play (Sutton-Smith), 96
American Folklore Society (AFS), 21, 143, 251–52; charter, 182
Americanization, stages of, 183
amity, moments of, 160–61
Anderson, Benedict, 253–54, 256
animals, as metaphors, 182
anxiety, proverbs and superstitions as naming, 41
Appadurai, Arjun, 214
Arewa, E. Ojo, 39
Arnold, Matthew, 15
art, artists, 125, 166; genres, 86–87. *See also* verbal art
auctions, 171–72
audience, 27–28
Austin, J. L., 95
authenticity, 143

Bakhtin, Mikhail, 149, 220, 224
Bateson, Gregory, 52, 97, 108, 201
Bauman, Richard, 190
behavior: interaction and, 85; recording/ archiving/analyzing, 10; in special zones, 147; taunts as regulators, 48
Bendix, Regina, 205
Berger, Peter, 122–23
Beyond the Melting Pot (Glazer), 177
Bianco, Carla, 188
Big Time, 122
Blacking, John, 34–35
blessings, 45
Boas, Franz, 215
boasts, 47
boundaries: community, 130; interactions across, 8; marketplace, 132–33; in oral literature, 190–91. *See also* zones
Braudel, Fernand, 133–34
Breck, Samuel, 159
Briggs, Charles, 40
Brunvand, Jan Harold, 56, 74–75

Burke, Kenneth, 1, 4, 9; contextualist viewpoint 26; on performed words' forcefulness, 24–25; on situations versus strategies, 25

Cable, George Washington, 252
Caillois, Roger, 106
Cantwell, Robert, 144
capitalism, 213
celebrations, 149; birthdays, 151; commodified, 4; creole, 228–29; cross-cultural exchange in, 170; of difference, 195; discussion of past, 153; and inclusive community, 11–12; nationhood, 150; opposition to, 150; power of, 229; reenacting feast at conclusion of strife, 161; and rule violation, 146–47; scripted performance, 8; social relations of common life, 4; vocabulary, 156. *See also* festive gatherings
charms, 46–47
Civil Rights Movement, 142
Clark, Petula, 107–8
Clemens, Samuel, 252
Clifford, James, 139
Cohen, Robin, 255
Coles, Robert, 201
combat zones, 142–44
common culture, poetics/politics of, 4–8
community: achieving, 28; Blacking on, 35; celebrations as reaffirmation of inclusive, 11–12; conversational forms, 49–50; and crowds, 150; culture/aesthetic patterns, 37–38; esoteric demonstration, 49; folk, 168; organic, 148; phenomena establishing, 50–51; proverbs in, 42; reconstituted through reconsecrating boundaries, 130; rhetoric, 8–12; ritual, 146; Simmel, 50; social cohesion, 9; social status, 130
competition, 95, 110
conflict: in expressive folklore, 28; in genres, 61–62, 66; scenes of, 89
contact zones: encounters in, 145; negotiations in, 144–47; Pratt on, 139; purity and, 145–46; resistance to authorities, 140; truth telling claims, 145; variety of people and, 144–45
conversation: ethnicity and, 181–82; jokes in, 93; in performance, 87

Acknowledgments

This book, like my whole life as a folklorist, engages a range of disciplines from literary criticism to cultural anthropology and explores expressive cultures in a set of places that spans the Atlantic and the Caribbean. Throughout my academic career, I have enjoyed the collegiality of scholars across the social sciences and humanities who generously shared their questions, insights, and fieldwork experiences with me.

Had I world enough and space, I would give wreaths to all those who generously allowed me to enter into their lives and communities while I as working in the field: in the Southern Mountains of Virginia and North Carolina; in the South Philadelphia neighborhood I called "Camingerly"; in East Texas; and in the once-British West Indies, on Nevis, St. Vincent, and Tobago. People unselfconsciously let me in on their ways of talking, of being well or ill behaved, of singing, dancing, performing, and celebrating. They answered so many stupid questions in the midst of their celebrations that, when replaying my tape-recordings, I am constantly amazed by how much I relied on them for exegesis. The big lesson I learned from these neighbors and friends is reflected on every page of this book: that I must never underestimate either the intelligence or the eloquence of those who feel entrusted with the old forms of play and display. They laughed at my misapprehensions and kindly set me on the right track toward understanding the other strokes of other folks. Many more people participated in immediate, material ways, helping me carry the paraphernalia required for doing fieldwork, tape-record and transcribe interviews, and check back with my informants.

Texts do not live without performances and celebrations—a lesson I learned early, when I moved from undergraduate studies in literature to graduate studies in folklore. Fieldwork enabled me to realize that performers and celebrants are, when asked, highly capable of explaining themselves and of translating their presentations into literate formulations. Indeed, most people, even in cultures that are described as oral/aural, are literate in a great many codes and varieties of language. Having found that the oldest traditional songs, dramas, and music might be collected in living color and stereo sound, I learned that these orts and shards of the past were important beyond the major holidays when folks came together; folklore enriched their lives throughout the year. Performances are rehearsed, replayed, discussed critically, and objectified without alienation taking place. Washing dishes or chopping wood offers a wonderful opportunity to get into such discussions. I found contentment enough just sitting, listening, and watching performances under the cover of participant observer. I could not distinguish the texts from the social situations in which I found them, the lives of the performers, and their audiences' interpretations of the songs, stories, games, or dances.

On the academic side of my life in folklore, the ideas of Kenneth Burke have had a profound influence on my both thinking and my feeling about cultural embodiments in literature and society. I encountered his books on literary criticism, *The Philosophy of Literary Form* (1941) and *Counter-Statement* (1931) in graduate school. As a student of literary and folklore texts as lived experiences, I was delighted to discover a truly interdisciplinary thinker who encouraged linking text and context as social practices. I found Burke's style of thought especially congenial for its contrariness and its grasp of the dialectics of rhetorical interaction. When I met Burke in 1961, however, I discovered that he looked askance at the ways in which I was appropriating his approach for my address to the traditional folklore genres, in part because in his own youth he had rebelled against academia. Moreover, he was not the least interested in the close observation of people in the field on which folklore is based. The willingness of junior scholars to run with his ideas and conceptual schema was not enough; he insisted that students buy his entire system of social and literary analysis, using terms of art that came from his reading of Aristotle and other Greeks. I tried to follow his agenda, reading *A Grammar of Motives* (1945) and *A Rhetoric of Motives* (1950) while writing about data collected in the field. But I was unwilling to use his awkward terms of art—the four "master tropes" of "metaphor, metonymy, synecdoche, and irony"— rather than the vernacular. We got around this problem when we were talking face to face by trading personal stories concerning how we had arrived at our sociopolitical outlook. Burke's stories were rich, ranging from his days in Greenwich Village with William Carlos Williams and Malcolm Cowley to his intellectual engagement with Marxism and his Popular Front sympathies during the 1930s. We went on exchanging stories and reflections on the politics of rhetorical criticism for the next decade or more. *Language as Symbolic Action* (1966), which collects Burke's later work on literary criticism, was less important to me than our conversations, and by then I was carrying his ideas in directions he would not have authorized. Readers who are acquainted with Burke will see the influence of his ideas on every page of this book.

As the study of expressive culture developed within academia and drew together scholars from various disciplines, I was privileged to enter into public debates about the lived experience of cultural forms and practices with some of the best minds and most persuasive characters in a developing drama over concepts of expression, performance, and celebration. Many of these framed activities drifted into my consciousness through conversations with colleagues and friends who were interested in related topics: Brian Sutton-Smith, Vic and

Edie Turner, Barbara Myerhoff, Alessandro Falassi, Erving Goffman, Dan Ben-Amos, Barbara Kirshenblatt-Gimblett, Joel and Dena Sherzer, Svatya Jacobson, and Mike Holquist. Dell and Ginnie Hymes not only heard me through on a number of these topics, but Dell sent me a good many of his fabled ten-page, single-spaced letters. Special thanks are due to those who have been long-term friends in spite of coauthoring publications with me: Alan Dundes, Dick Bauman, John Szwed, Susan Kalčik, and Dorry Noyes.

I enjoyed wonderful support and collegial conversations at each of the institutions where I have taught. At the University of Texas, I had a joint appointment in English and Anthropology and was affiliated with the Center for the Study of Intercultural Folklore and Oral History and served as the inaugural director of the research institute that later became the Center for African and Afro-American Studies. My boundary-crossing friends there included Américo Paredes, David DeLaura, Joe Moldenhauer, Rick Adams, Ed Steinhart, Annette Weiner, Joe Malof, Ernie Kaulbach, Roger Renwick, John Vlach, Bill Stott, Marsha Herndon, Bev Stoeltje, Robbie Davis, Meg Brady, Marilyn White, John McDowell, Ginger Farrar, Jose Limon, Frank Proschan, Nick Spitzer, and the great blues seekers, Robert Baron and Bob Cochran. While visiting at Scripps and Pitzer in California, I met several colleagues who have stayed in touch: Don Brenneis, Ron McCauley, Dan and Helen Horowitz, Michael Roth, and Ralph Ross.

During my twenty years at the University of Pennsylvania, I have enjoyed good fellowship and discussions with Kenny Goldstein, Dan Ben-Amos, Bob St. George, Margaret Mills, Regina Bendix, Jay Dautcher, Mike Zuckerman, Larry Silver, Phyllis Rackin, Carroll Smith-Rosenberg, Steve Feierman, Dan Rose, Lee Haring, Charles Briggs, Kwesi Yankah, Janet Theophano, and David Azzolina. David Azzolina is not only a bibliographer but a master of the new technologies and a constant source of help. Both Regina and Lee read several versions of these chapters and made suggestions that assisted greatly in the revisions. The graduate students with whom I was privileged to work—Dorry Noyes, Deborah Kapchan, Peter Tokofsky, Emily Sokolov, Anna Beresin, David Samper, Bev Butcher, Leslie Kaplan, Glenn Hinson, Doug DeNatale, Phil Scher, the late Hayley Thomas, Charlie McCormick, Frank Korom, and Tom Dubois—challenged me to be clearer and more nuanced in my thinking and were so persistent that these arguments bear the stamp of our deep discussions. Steve Winnick, Raquel Romberg, and Tom Green are especially well-remembered contrarians.

Many of the papers and arguments that formed the germ of this book were originally presented at various venues, professional and otherwise. Some were delivered as lectures when I was a Phi Beta Kappa scholar; others were tested on European audiences at the summer school of the Folklore Fellows in Turku, Finland, and later, when I was the guest of the Nordic Institute, at ten campuses across the Baltic region. Throughout the years, colleagues at other institutions, especially Henry Glassie, Lee Haring, John Roberts, Barbie Zelizer, and Bengt Holbek, allowed me to try some of these arguments out on them. Dick Dorson saw the novelty in these ideas, but mistook them for something altogether new. Although Alan Dundes remains convinced that this is not the right way for folklorists to go, he always treats my work as if it were worth the attention of himself and his very best students. I spent a lot of time trying to understand the Parisian theoreticians (I almost wrote morticians), but never got on the same wavelength in spite of careful tutelage from many otherwise sane friends.

Dr. Dr. Herb Adler may have saved my life, and he tells a good joke once in a while, too. My goodwife, Janet Anderson, heard many of these chapters *in ovo* and then read them in draft. She led me away from many infelicities, always insisting that there was a larger audience I wasn't taking into account. Janet believed in this book for many, many years. But the book would never have come into being had not my friend and editor Peter Agree said, after reading of couple of the chapters in earlier formulations, "I think there's a book here." With friends like that. . . . Grey Osterud has assisted in the editing. She warmed to the argument and brought her deeply erudite and politically informed perspectives to the work, finished some of my least well put sentences, responded to many more additions than I thought I could get away with, posed questions about key points in my arguments, maintained good humor and spirit throughout, and, and in the end, provided many of the most poetic of the chapter titles and section headings. I hesitate to mention her, as she is a genie and magician and, we like to think, a secret agent, and no one wants her cover broken. At Penn Press, in addition to Peter Agree, Barbie Zelizer discussed these chapters with me; Eric Halpern, sachem and general savant, remained a stalwart interested party throughout the process; and the gracious Ellie Goldberg provided invaluable assistance with the technicalities.

The project that became this book was initially conceived as a comprehensive survey of the folklore genres, starting with the simplest forms and moving toward public, elaborately ritualized celebrations. The work as completed here is both less and more ambitious, offering not a catalogue of texts in context but a series of forays into the field and a systematic approach by which vernacular practices may be understood as clues to culture. It draws on fifteen or so articles written over many years on folklore forms and practices, most of which were buried in conference proceedings, *festschriften*, and anthologies. These chapters bear remote resemblances to the papers and essays with which this project originated, but I give the details of their publication here.

Chapter One was developed from my essay, "Introductory Remarks to a Rhetorical Theory of Folklore," *Journal of American Folklore* 81 (1968): 143–58. Chapter Two draws on my article, "A Rhetoric of Everyday Life: Traditional

Conversational Genres," *Southern Folklore Quarterly* 32 (1968): 44–59. Both chapters pay homage to the work of Kenneth Burke, but I have not attempted to review all the scholarly responses to Burke's ideas since the late 1960s.

An early draft of Chapter Three was published in the journal *Genre* in a special double issue edited by Dan Ben-Amos, "The Complex Relations of Simple Forms," *Genre* 2 (1969): 104–28, and reprinted in revised form in *Folklore Genres*, ed. Dan Ben-Amos (Austin: University of Texas Press, 1976). The chapter also draws on a whole set of pieces comparing the simple forms of folklore. These include entries on "Proverbs and Proverbial Expressions," "Riddles" (with Alan Dundes), and "Folk Drama," in *Folklore and Folklife: An Introduction*, ed. Richard M. Dorson (Chicago: University of Chicago Press, 1972): 117–28, 129–44, 351–62; "The Literary Study of the Riddle," *Texas Studies in Literature and Language* 14 (1972): 177–99; "On Proverb Collecting and Proverb Collections," *Proverbium* 8 (1967): 181–85; "The Literary Use of Proverbs" (with Barbara Babcock), *Journal of American Folklore* 90 (1976): 414–29; "The Language of Festivals," in *Celebration: A World of Art and Ritual*, ed. Victor W. Turner (Washington, D.C.: Smithsonian Institution Press, 1982), 161–77; "Open and Closed Forms in Moral Tales," in *Studies in Aggadah and Jewish Folklore*, ed. Issachar Ben-Ami and Joseph Dan (Jerusalem: Magnes Press/ Hebrew University, 1983), 19–33; and "Play in the Face of Death: Transgression and Inversion in a West Indian Wake," in *The Many Faces of Play*, ed. Kendall Blanchard (Champaign, Ill.: Human Kinetics Press, 1986), 29–45.

Chapter Four draws on several slim essays: "Our Native Notions of Story," *New York Folklore* 11 (1985), 37–47 and "The Most Embarrassing Things that Ever Happened: Conversational Stories in a Theory of Enactment," *Folklore Forum* 10 (3) (Winter 1977): 9–15. Chapter Five began as "In and Out of Performance" in *Folklore and Oral Communication*, a special issue of *Narodna Umjetnost* (Belgrade, Yugoslavia, 1981): 69–78, and "Toward an Enactment-Centered Theory of Folklore," in *The Frontiers of Folklore*, ed. William R. Bascom (Washington, D.C.: American Anthropological Association, 1977), 79–120. Chapter Six borrows from "Play and Games," *Motif* 2 (June 1982): 5–7, as well as "Play," in *Proceedings of the Centennial of the Folklore Society*, ed. Venetia Newall (London: Folklore Society, 1981), 119–22. Chapter Seven draws upon some of the prose and ideas presented in "Ordinary and Extraordinary Experiences," in *The Anthropology of Experience*, ed. Victor W. Turner and Edward Bruner (Urbana: University of Illinois Press, 1986), 45–72, and "Pragmatism and the Folklore of Experience," *Western Folklore* 44 (1985): 324–32, although I have made major modifications in the argument here.

The next three chapters, although written especially for this book, include work I initially presented as conference papers. Chapter Eight began with papers presented in Turku, Finland, and the American Folklore Society in 1999. Chapter Nine draws on "An American Vocabulary of Celebrations" in *Time Out of Time*, ed. Alessandro Falassi (Albuquerque: University of New

Mexico Press, 1987), 173–83; "History and Folklore: Luck-Visits, House Attacks, and Playing Indian in Early America," in *History And . . . , ed. Michael Roth and Ralph Cohen, (Charlottesville: University of Virginia Press, 1998),* 268–95; *and "Introduction II: A Folklore Perspective," in Riot and Revelry in Early America,* ed. William Pencak, Matthew Dennis, and Simon P. Newman (University Park: Pennsylvania State University Press, 2002), 21–37. Chapter Ten develops arguments that originated in a paper Richard Bauman and I presented at a special session on carnivalization at the annual meeting of the American Anthropological Association, which was published in part as "Ranges of Festival Behavior" (with Richard Bauman), in *The Reversible World,* ed. Barbara A. Babcock (Ithaca, N.Y.: Cornell University Press, 1978), 193–208. It also incorporates material from "Shouting Match at the Border: The Folklore of Display Events," in *And Other Neighborly Names,* ed. Richard Bauman and Roger D. Abrahams (Austin: University of Texas Press, 1981), 303–21.

The last four essays were written expressly for this book. The germ of Chapter Eleven came from my entry, "Folklore," in the *Harvard Encyclopedia of American Ethnicity,* ed. Ann Orlov and Stephen Thernstrom (Cambridge, Mass.: Harvard University Press, 1980), 370–79. It also includes passages from "Equal Opportunity Eating," in *Foodways in the United States: The Matrix of Ethnic and Regional Identity,* ed. Linda Keller Brown and Kay Mussell (Nashville: University of Tennessee Press, 1984), 19–36; "Folklore and Cultural Pluralism" (with Susan Kalčik), in *Folklore in the Modern World,* ed. Richard M. Dorson (The Hague: Mouton, 1979), 223–35; and "Stereotyping and Beyond" (with Geneva Gay), in *Language and Cultural Diversity in American Education,* ed. Roger D. Abrahams and Rudolph C. Troike (Englewood Cliffs, N.J.: Prentice-Hall, 1972), 200–208. Chapter Twelve began in another form as "Identity," in *Common Ground: Keywords for the Study of Expressive Culture,* ed. Burt Feintuch, special issue, *Journal of American Folklore* 108 (1995), and was revised for *Eight Words for the Study of Expressive Culture,* ed. Bert Feintuch (Urbana: University of Illinois Press, 2003). Chapter Thirteen took off from a paper presented to the American Folklore Society Meetings and published as " 'The Dunghill of the Universe': Creolization in the Greater Caribbean," *Creolization,* a special issue of the *Journal of American Folklore,* ed. Robert Baron and Ana Cara, 116 (2003). Chapter Fourteen draws on my contribution to the festschrift for Barbro Klein, "Narratives of Location and Dislocation," in *Folklore, Heritage Politics and Ethnic Diversity,* ed. Pertti Johani Antonnen (Botkyrka, Sweden: Multicultural Center, 2000), 15–20.